# Transitions to Democracy

Lisa Anderson, Editor

COLUMBIA UNIVERSITY PRESS     NEW YORK

COLUMBIA UNIVERSITY PRESS
*Publishers Since 1893*
New York Chichester, West Sussex
Copyright © 1999 Columbia University Press
All rights reserved
Library of Congress Cataloging-in-Publication Data

Transitions to democracy / Lisa Anderson, editor.
    p.   cm.
   Includes bibliographical references.
   ISBN 0-231-11590-3 (cloth : alk. paper).—ISBN 0-231-11591-1
(pbk.)
   1. Democracy.   2. Democratization.   I. Anderson, Lisa.
JC423.T6637 1999
321.8—dc21                                     99-19925
                                               CIP

The following articles were originally published in *Comparative Politics* and are
   reprinted by kind permission of The City University of New York

Chapter 2, "Transitions to Democracy: Toward a Dynamic Model," by Dankwart
   A. Rustow, originally appeared in *Comparative Politics*, vol. 2, no. 2 (April
   1970), pp. 337–63.
The following articles originally appeared in *Comparative Politics*, vol. 29, no. 3
   (April 1997). Their original page numbers are given below.
Chapter 4, "The Political Economy of Democratic Transitions," by Stephan
   Haggard and Robert R. Kaufman, pp. 263–84.
Chapter 5, "Adding Collective Actors to Collective Outcomes: Labor and Recent
   Democratization in South America and Southern Europe," by Ruth Berins
   Collier and James Mahoney, pp. 285–304.
Chapter 6, "Myths of Moderation: Confrontation and Conflict During
   Democratic Transitions," by Nancy Bermeo, pp. 305–22.
Chapter 8, "The Paradoxes of Contemporary Democracy: Formal, Participatory,
   and Social Dimensions," by Evelyne Huber, Dietrich Rueschemeyer, and John
   D. Stephens, pp. 323–42.
Chapter 9, "Modes of Transition and Democratization: South America and
   Eastern Europe in Comparative Perspective," by Gerardo L. Munck and Carol
   Skalnik Leff, pp. 243–62.
Chapter 11, "Democratization in Africa After 1989: Comparative and Theoretical
   Perspectives," by Richard Joseph, pp. 363–82.
Chapter 12, "Fortuitous Byproducts," by John Waterbury, pp. 383–402.

Casebound editions of Columbia University Press books are printed on permanent
and durable acid-free paper.

Printed in the United States of America
c 10 9 8 7 6 5 4 3 2 1
p 10 9 8 7 6 5 4 3 2 1

# Transitions to Democracy

914-788-0813

843-6336

# Contents

# Contributors

Lisa Anderson is Professor of Political Science and Dean of the School of International and Public Affairs at Columbia University.

Irving Leonard Markovitz is Professor of Political Science at Queens College and the Graduate Center, City University of New York.

Stephan Haggard is Professor in the Graduate School of International Relations and Pacific Studies, University of California, San Diego.

Robert R. Kaufman is Professor of Political Science at Rutgers University.

Ruth Berins Collier is Professor of Political Science at the University of California, Berkeley.

James Mahoney is a doctoral candidate in political science at the University of California, Berkeley.

Nancy Bermeo is Associate Professor of Politics at Princeton University.

Ezra Suleiman is IBM Professor of International Studies and Director of the Committee for European Studies at Princeton University.

Evelyne Huber is Moorehead Alumni Professor of Political Science and Director of the Institute for Latin American Studies at the University of North Carolina, Chapel Hill.

Dietrich Rueschmeyer is Asa Messer Professor of Sociology at Brown University and Director of the Center for the Comparative Study of Development.

John D. Stephens is Professor of Political Science and Sociology at the University of North Carolina, Chapel Hill.

Gerardo L. Munck is Assistant Professor of Political Science at the University of Illinois.

**Carol Skalnik Leff** is Assistant Professor of Political Science at the University of Illinois.

**Šumit Ganguly** is Professor of Political Science at Hunter College and the Graduate Center, City University of New York.

**Richard Joseph** is Asa G. Candler Professor of Political Science at Emory University.

**John Waterbury** is Professor of Politics and President of the American University in Beirut.

# Acknowledgments

Obviously, this book would not exist were it not for Dan Rustow. Not only was he the author of the article around which the volume is organized, but for the editor and many of the contributors he was a wise and generous teacher and colleague. It is to be hoped that this book will introduce a new generation of political scientists and policy makers to his work.

Less obvious but also crucial to the production of this book were two remarkable professionals: Larry Peterson, the managing editor of *Comparative Politics*, whose command of English prose style and encyclopedic knowledge of the foibles of political scientists as writers, reviewers, and editors would be legendary were he not so insistently modest, and Leslie Bialler, editor at Columbia University Press, whose meticulous concern for detail is surpassed only by his wry sense of humor.

Many of the authors express their gratitude to those who contributed to the improvement of their essays in the individual chapter notes. The editor has several personal acknowledgements. Harpreet Mahajan, Director of Information Technology at the School of International and Public Affairs of Columbia University, made the translation from printed page to electronic version and back again look simple. Jo Leondopoulos, Executive Assistant to the Dean at the School of International and Public Affairs, makes the editor's life look simple. Sam Rauch and Isaac Rauch make the editor's life fun.

# 1 Introduction

*Lisa Anderson*

In 1970 few American comparative political scientists were preoccupied by democracy and democratization. Issues of development and dependency, political order and revolution seemed far more compelling. In the issue of *Comparative Politics* in which Dankwart A. Rustow's article, "Transitions to Democracy: Toward a Dynamic Model," originally appeared, other contributors addressed problems that were at least as significant at the time: Marxism in Africa, the military in politics, interest groups in the Soviet Union. These problems were important, but as the political predicaments that prompted their examination were superseded by other policy puzzles, the urgency of their analytical and theoretical contribution diminished as well.

Yet good social scientists are sometimes inspired to ask questions and explore issues that reflect not the policy considerations of the moment but instead the more eternal and universal dilemmas that constitute ordinary social and political life. Often these explorations fail to excite the readers of their day, preoccupied as they are with headlines and crises. Only later does the prescience of these remarkable exercises slowly become apparent as analysts, theorists, students, and teachers refer repeatedly to "the early article" that shaped their thinking.

"Transitions to Democracy" is one of these inspired exercises. While the cases cited very much reflect its time, Rustow's analytical perspective is far from dated. Indeed, though written well before the Spanish and Portuguese democratic transitions of the mid 1970s inaugurated the wave of regime changes that provide virtually all of the cases treated in this volume, "Transitions to Democracy" usually strikes readers today as almost clairvoyant, uncannily anticipating the debates about democratization that characterized the succeeding three decades.

To illustrate and celebrate Rustow's remarkable shrewdness, the editors of the journal *Comparative Politics* (of which Rustow himself was editor-in-chief from 1979 to 1995) assembled a special issue of articles written as comments on and extensions of his original insights. The articles in that issue, which was published in April 1997, are reprinted here, along with Rustow's original essay. In addition, three members of the editorial committee of *Comparative Politics*, who are prohibited by journal policy from publishing in *Comparative Politics* during their tenure on the committee, have contributed chapters written expressly for this book.

## "Transitions to Democracy": The Era and the Argument

Rustow began his discussion in "Transitions to Democracy" with the very simple and acute observation that much of the literature then available on the causes and conditions of democracy and democratization conflated the two. It assumed that the conditions that were required for the initiation of democratization were also dictated for the maintenance of established democracies. This assumption, as he pointed out, was mistaken: "the factors that keep a democracy stable may not be the ones that brought it into existence; explanations of democracy must distinguish between function and genesis." Thus did he open the conceptual space for considering democratic transitions independently from democracy.

This analytical maneuver permitted Rustow to develop a perspective that accentuated a dynamic process of change rather than stability, allowed ample room for violent conflict and struggle as well as civil competition, and underscored the importance of choices made by identifiable political actors in crafting democratic institutions. Although Rustow never denied the significance of structural and cultural conditions to the maintenance and stability of existing democratic regimes, he was more interested in identifying the factors that brought such regimes into existence in the first place. These factors he found to be a more varied mix of economic and cultural predispositions with contingent developments and individual choices.

The implicit optimism of this emphasis on choice seemed almost reckless in the early 1970s. At that time transitions to democracy were relatively rare; far more common—and certainly far more feared—were transitions from unstable democracies to authoritarian military regimes or, still worse, revolutionary totalitarian systems. The few contemporary cases of democratization were subsumed in the larger universe of "regime change," and in explaining the majority of the outcomes, most analysts were uncomfortable finding redeeming virtue in violence or attributing the collapse of democracy to voluntary choices made by strategic elites. The temptation already posed by the emphasis on democratic stability to adopt structural or cultural explanations was exacerbated by the reluctance of most American political scientists to attribute intention to those who rejected democracy.

However, by the end of the 1970s events in southern Europe and Latin America gave rise to a new sense of hopefulness, and with that hopefulness came a new openness to analysis which deemphasized constraints and highlighted the possibility of choice. Rustow's framework became more plausible and attractive.

His rejection of the "preconditions" then widely associated with democracies—for example, relatively high literacy rates and levels of per capita income and widespread adherence to liberal or democratic values—permitted analysts and activists alike to consider the prospects for democracy in many countries that had little likelihood of meeting these "preconditions" in the foreseeable future.

Because he thought the structural and cultural contexts of "pre-democratic" situations were enormously varied, Rustow identified only one "background condition" as common to all democratic transitions: national unity. Citizens' adherence to a common political community distinguished battles that could produce compromise over political institutions from civil war. Otherwise, as he put it, "the model deliberately leaves open the possibility of democracies (properly so called) in premodern, prenationalist times and at low levels of economic development."

Understandably, many analysts of the developing world were heartened by this sense of possibility. In their rush to encourage and support nascent democratic transitions, some overestimated Rustow's appraisal of political elites' realm of maneuver; Rustow himself recognized that, while the social structural conditions for democratic transitions are varied, they are not insignificant. In the period he called the "preparatory phase," he postulated that major battles must precede the compromise represented by democratic institutions and argued that "the protagonists must represent well-entrenched social forces." Their struggles will be profound and prolonged; typically, therefore, they are fought over deeply important structural or cultural issues: class, ethnic, religious conflicts.

Ultimately, if the democratic transition is to go forward, Rustow argued, these struggles must end in stalemates, creating the context in which angry and exhausted elites ultimately decide that their interests are better served in the compromise represented by democracy than in continued battle. However, the struggles and their structural foundations do not necessarily dictate or determine the content of these interests: "while the choice of democracy does not arise until the background and preparatory conditions are in hand, it is a genuine choice and does not flow automatically from those two conditions." Rustow shifted both the level and style of analysis in response to the particular exigencies of what he called the "decision phase," a period in which determining structural and cultural factors are less important than the choices, perceptions, preferences, and bargaining skills of individuals among the political elite.

During the late 1970s and 1980s, analysts and activists seized upon this perspective. Some were influenced by Rustow; many arrived at a similar perspective independently. As active participants, policy advisers, or merely academic promoters of democratization, the scholars swept up in the excitement of the new waves of democratization, first rippling out from southern Europe and Latin America, then dramatically bursting forth in eastern Europe, were better served by analytical perspectives that gave a prominent role to enthusiasts like themselves and emphasized choices, preferences, and bargains rather than constraints, interests, and class struggles.

The early euphoria of these democratic experiments gave way relatively quickly in both reality and in scholarly commentary to attention to the more mundane demands of what Rustow called the "habituation phase." The consolidation of democracy requires not only that the elites retain their commitment to and confidence in democratic procedures but also that "the population at large will become firmly fitted into the new structure." To assess this process, Rustow and many other commentators resumed their earlier focus on the constraints of structural factors: the collective interests and identities associated with existing economic positions and cultural communities would profoundly influence the integration of the general population into the new democracy. Indeed, for Rustow, the effectiveness of the new democratic institutions and procedures in conciliating and accommodating contending forces not only among elites but also in the broader society would ultimately define the strength and resilience of the democracy itself.

## "Transitions to Democracy": Responses and Refinements

The articles in this volume represent much of the current state of the large and growing literature on democratization in American political science. They both illustrate the remarkable reach of Rustow's essay across the decades and reveal some of its limits. Several of the contributors, for example, question the desirability of analytically divorcing structure from agency. The changing importance of individual actors and their collective constituencies in each of the phases Rustow distinguishes in the democratic transition was often echoed in far more caricatured forms by subsequent theorists of democratization. While Rustow's argument as a whole gives ample weight to both the structural conditions that prompt democratic initiatives and the role of individual actors in seizing opportunities, each of the phases taken separately exaggerates the importance of either structure or agency. This framework may therefore be limited in predicting specific institutional choices, despite empirical evidence of discernible patterns in the relationship between the strength of certain social groups and their elites and the choice of specific institutional arrangements.

Irving Leonard Markovitz returns to the roots of the United States' transition to democracy in the eighteenth century to illustrate how interests and institutions are linked through the actions of elites. He examines the work of the authors of the Federalist Papers, elites who constituted knowledgeable and interested actors in their society, as they fashioned constraints which would both serve their purposes — personal and class — and reach across centuries to bind their successors. In a literature in which long historical perspectives are ordinarily associated with structural analysis, Markovitz captures the signal importance of the individual, of fits of pique and strokes of genius, as well as the strategic interactions that produced the U.S. Constitution. Markovitz also suggests that in the eagerness of such elites to build a new polity, even Rustow's background condition — national unity — may have been a deliberate construct, designed rather than reflected by the framers of democratic institutions.

Stephan Haggard and Robert Kaufman draw on more contemporary cases to argue that much of the literature on democratization has failed to recognize, much less specify, the links between the elites who craft the democratic bargains and the followers who make them elites in the first place. However strategic and self-interested they may be, elites are not socially disembodied; virtually by definition they represent and draw upon collective groups, whether interest groups, mass organizations, social movements, classes, or ethnic and religious communities. Hence the status of such groups will influence the resources—the "bargaining chips"—of the elites as they enter negotiations and consequently the shape of the resulting institutions. Economic crises that weaken the bureaucratic and social bases of the incumbent elites undermine their bargaining position and, Haggard and Kaufman argue, produce an outcome of less restrictive democratic institutions and procedures.

In a similar vein, Ruth Berins Collier and James Mahoney argue that the struggles of collective actors are significant not only in a Rustovian preparatory stage but in the decision phase itself. In many of the southern European and Latin American cases of democratic transition, labor protest began during the early stages of political struggle and continued through the period of elite bargaining. Continuing protest, they suggest, not only ensured that negotiations did not stall but also permitted representatives of labor to participate in shaping far more inclusive outcomes.

Nancy Bermeo also explores the role of popular collective actors through examination of labor organizations, and she concurs with Collier and Mahoney in taking issue with the very widespread proposition that, as she puts it, "too much popular mobilization and too much pressure from below can spoil the chances for democracy." In contrast to Collier and Mahoney, however, Bermeo concludes that the significance of radical popular protest is determined not by its role in producing or pressuring elites at the negotiating table but by elite calculations of the strength of the protesters. She suggests that in a number of transitions, including Portugal and Spain, popular protest raised the cost of the status quo but also, equally importantly, meant that [elites'] estimates of the popular forces could be excluded from participation in the emerging democratic institutions.

As each of these essays suggests, the structural economic and cultural conditions in which elites operate, from economic crises to popular protests, may not determine but do clearly shape their calculations and strategic preferences during the decision phase, as they bargain over the adoption of

democratic institutions and procedures. Rustow's preliminary distinction between the levels of analysis appropriate to the different phases of a democratic transition merited critical refinement.

Other factors Rustow identified as contributing to the consolidation of
democracy in his habituation phase, as well as the periodization or configuration of the phases he proposed, have also been critically reexamined by
subsequent theorists. Evelyne Huber, Dietrich Rueschemeyer, and John
Stephens stress structural factors in their treatment of the conditions that
contribute to consolidating formal or liberal democracy, and they point out
that these same factors appear to inhibit extension of liberal democracy to
more participatory or social democratic institutional arrangements. Huber,
Rueschemeyer, and Stephens are prepared to specify with considerably more
precision than Rustow the nature of the struggle that produces the impetus
to democratization in the first place. For them, democracy is intimately
linked to capitalist development because capitalism undermines the power
of landholders and strengthens popular classes; this balance produces the
impetus toward democracy. The link between democratization and capitalist
development is the key to their understanding of the outcomes of the transition, including their insistence on the importance of international power
configurations.

Rustow's omission of international pressures was self-conscious and tactical. He viewed his essay as "a first attempt at a general theory" and therefore
chose to simplify his task by neglecting such foreign influences as defeat in
war and the contagion of democratic ideas. Yet, even more clearly now than
when Rustow was writing, international influences are crucial. As Huber,
Rueschemeyer, and Stephens argue, the globalization of the international
capitalist economy and the accompanying enthusiasm for liberal economic
arrangements and political institutions over the last several decades have had
a profound impact in both promoting the spread of liberal democracy and
weakening national commitments to social democracy.

Gerardo Munck and Carol Skalnik Leff are also concerned with identifying factors that contribute to the consolidation of democracy, but they
emphasize the role of elites and elite choices and look at the nature of the
transition itself. Rustow warned repeatedly against assuming that transitions,
once begun, inevitably produce consolidated democracies of any kind, ob-
serving that "a decision in favor of democracy . . . may be proposed and
rejected." To inquire about the circumstances that promote or inhibit decisions in favor of democracy, Munck and Leff systematically distinguish

between transitions from authoritarian regimes and transitions to democracy and examine factors internal to the transition itself—Rustow's decision phase—that may lead to the rejection or adoption and consolidation of democratic institutions.

Munck and Leff point to specific characteristics of the identities and strategies of the actors seeking and opposing change that shape institutions and influence the likelihood of their consolidation, particularly whether or not they are incumbents. They echo Bermeo's emphasis on the importance of the elite's strategic thinking and willingness to pursue confrontation or accommodation, but in marked contrast to conclusions reached by several other contributors, they take a sanguine view of the roles of the incumbents, hypothesizing that reforms from below produce more restrictive democratic institutions than transitions which more fully incorporate the incumbent elite and that dramatic breaks from the past create legacies of confusion and distrust that inhibit consolidation of new democracies.

Rustow's openness to a variety of paths to democracy and its consolidation is reflected in the variety of roles our contributors assign to incumbents, their social bases, and their interests and preferences. Šumit Ganguly illustrates the cumulative importance of each of the phases Rustow proposes in his examination of India, echoing Markovitz's emphasis on the role elites may play in constructing even the national unity Rustow deemed a necessary precondition. Ganguly warns, however, that sustaining one factor that Rustow neglected—the autonomy and capacity of the state—may be a key challenge to consolidation of Indian democracy over the long run.

Ezra Suleiman's examination of the relationship between the state and democratic consolidation in East Central Europe is the most explicit discussion in this book of the complex relationship between state formation, or reformation, and transitions to democracy. In East Central Europe, democratization has been associated with efforts to shrink the state bureaucracies of the Communist era; Suleiman concludes that advocates of democracy may find themselves in paradoxical circumstances, dismantling in the name of democratization the very administrative instruments they will need to implement their political reform.

The analytical consequences of Rustow's willingness to entertain the possibility that democracy might take root in what appears to be infertile terrain are reflected in the last two chapters. As Richard Joseph observes, more than half the fifty-odd states of Africa undertook liberal political reforms of some sort after 1989. Not only did it appear quite unexpectedly that democratic institutions might flourish·among poor, illiterate, diseased, and war-ravaged populations, but also, perhaps more plausibly, international influences played an increasingly important role in providing the impetus, rationale, and sometimes material support for democratic initiatives.

As Joseph points out, international pressure was certainly crucial to the developments in Africa, but the democracy being constructed in many of the ostensibly reformist regimes in sub-Saharan Africa was more virtual than real. This distinction is not the same as the widespread contrast, drawn here by Huber, Rueschemeyer, and Stephens, between formal or liberal democracy and more participatory, egalitarian, or social variants. Joseph's virtual democracy is not even liberal; it is designed to give the appearance of democratic government without conceding any significant measure of open debate or accountability. In the aftermath of the collapse of Communism predatory rulers in Africa, always acutely sensitive to the preferences of their international political and economic patrons, acted quickly to satisfy international desires for gestures toward more liberal and democratic regimes. In far more instances than most observers initially understood, these institutional concessions were little more than Potemkin villages, facades behind which authoritarian rulers continued to extract resources from both domestic groups and international patrons without significant oversight or accountability. Joseph is not optimistic that the transitions that produced these virtual democracies will proceed much further; indeed, he implies that many citizens of Africa will adopt and become habituated to, not genuine democratic values, but the distrust and cynicism behind these institutional facades.

Can individual or collective actors within these societies nonetheless seize such institutions and "realize" democracy? After all, as Rustow pointed out, for many who agreed to democratic compromises "democracy was not the original or primary aim." John Waterbury suggests, in the spirit of Rustow's argument, that we should consider the possibility that democracy may be an unintended consequence of far different and often far less benign processes than we customarily associate with the transition to democracy. Indeed, Waterbury is prepared to consider far more varied paths and pressures than Rustow himself, arguing that even Rustow's insistence upon national unity is too restrictive. He concedes, however, that some of his propositions smack of "heroic optimism." Many of the cases he considers are examples of struggles that can only charitably be construed even as part of a "preparatory phase."

The contributions to this volume illustrate much of the range of analytical and policy debate about democratization at the end of the twentieth century. Some of their differences reflect the effect of varied time horizons: those who treat the transition as a decades, even centuries, long process ordinarily emphasize the importance of macrosociological factors such as class structure and favor approaches associated with class analysis and political economy. Theorists who concentrate their focus on the weeks and days during which old regimes collapse and new ones are constructed usually see a more detailed picture of strategic interactions, through the lens of methodological individualism and strategic choices.

In style and level of analysis, these perspectives have often proven difficult to reconcile. Rustow himself sought to capture both by shifting analytical perspective as he moved from one phase to another in his historical narrative. Markovitz and Haggard and Kaufman attempt to resolve the tension by associating individuals and their choices with economic and ideological resources. Collier and Mahoney and Bermeo find a middle ground in collective actors.

Still another approach to this tension appears in the essays that examine cases in which state formation is at issue. Suleiman's warning that democratization should not imply dismantling the state upon which the new regime will rest, Joseph's examination of often ruthless state-building disguised as democratization, and Waterbury's brave effort to tease democratic by-products from struggles probably better understood as violent episodes of state construction all suggest the desirability of examining the contours and trajectory of state formation for analysis of democratization. Waterbury himself points to the importance of what Huber, Rueschemeyer, and Stephens call "the structure of the state and state-society relations." Indeed, a number of contributors question not only Rustow's emphasis on the necessity of national unity but also his neglect of the state.

In the decades after "Transitions to Democracy" was published, political scientists rediscovered the significance of the state both as an arena of contestation and as an instrument by which ruling elites exercise their power. The legacy of the oscillating emphasis on structure and agency that Rustow's essay reflected meant, however, that his failure to address the role of the state was only recently recognized, much less rectified, by students of democratic transitions.

Between the constraints imposed by societal interests and class struggles and the opportunities presented by individual choices and elite bargains are the political institutions that link the structures to the agents, knitting them together in complex ways. These institutions, particularly those of the state, represent both cause and effect, both the legacies of historical battles and the molds of contemporary disputes and bargains of democratic politics.

Rustow's almost promiscuous rejection of the "preconditions" then associated with democracy liberated analysts and policy advocates from the confines of functional analysis and Western historical models but, like a ship that has slipped its mooring, the study of democratic transitions seems to have been set adrift, as analysts cast about for any plausible association, any reasonable correlation, in predicting the initiation or explaining the consolidation of democratic transitions. Yet it is neither plausible nor reasonable to expect that elites whose societies have little semblance of the bureaucratic capacity, military power, or international recognition we associate with statehood in the contemporary world would be able to initiate and sustain a democratic transition.

The capacity of the state to extract adequate resources and implement public policy, and the ability of social groups to resist arbitrary and capricious government and to demand acknowledgment and enforcement of the rule of law would seem to constitute important conditions for both the adoption and the consolidation of democratic regimes. For example, variations in historical patterns of state formation between coercive and capital-intensive paths and in their reliance on internal or international dynamics may well create cultural and social structural predispositions toward certain types of political regime. As several contributors imply, further work needs to be done on the role of the character of the state—from the patterns of insertion of individual states into the international state system to their varied capacities for domestic extraction and maintenance of law and order—in shaping regimes and the prospects for democratic transitions.

Rustow's intuition that national unity is a necessary if not sufficient condition may have laid the accent on the wrong element of the then common formulation, "nation-state," but in pointing to some kind of institutional or ideological connection within society as a condition for democratic reform, he correctly excluded many polities that did not exhibit that common ground.

Although the ancients may have enjoyed democratic politics without modern bureaucracy, in our post-Westphalian world the trappings of statehood as understood by the international community of the time—whether the 1770s or the 1990s—are very likely necessary to democratic politics. They are the arenas in which democratic contestation takes place and the instruments over which classes, parties, and individuals contest. It is not by chance that many of the earliest theorists of liberal democracy, from Karl Marx to John Stuart Mill and Max Weber, were also preoccupied with comprehending the structures and institutions of the state.


## "Transitions to Democracy": Science and Politics

As this book so clearly illustrates, the scholarly and policy debates about democracy and democratization have only grown broader, more urgent, and more lively since the publication of Rustow's "Transitions to Democracy." This growing energy and enthusiasm are very different from the atmosphere in which Rustow wrote. As he himself observed in notes he composed more than twenty-five years after his article first appeared, the essay was written

> in the middle of the Cold War that pitted democracies against Soviet-style Communism in a worldwide struggle . . . and there was much concern to know how democracy could take hold in . . . countries only recently released from colonial rule. Above all, political scientists and sociologists at the time were concerned to transform their fields of study into precise sciences based on quantitative economic data or surveys of attitudes and opinions. Thus much of the scholarly writing on democracy at the time tried to establish correlations between democracy and quantifiable economic and social factors. . . . Too often the tacit assumption was that democracy could exist only within conditions of economic prosperity or social consensus.

Today, as political scientists, policy analysts, and citizens, we are released from the fevered controversies of the Cold War and are far more sophisticated about the uses of quantitative data. As importantly, we also are much more willing to commit ourselves normatively to democracy than in the late 1960s, when many social scientists cultivated a studied value neutrality and many political activists disdained and distrusted the trappings of liberal political democracy. The enormous opportunities of the post-Cold War world for the promotion of democratic government in parts of the world once thought hopelessly lost to authoritarian and totalitarian regimes enliven the debates and stimulate efforts to promote the more open, responsive, and accountable government we associate with democracy.

Rustow recognized the intellectual challenges posed by both the changed global environment and the academic scholarship that blossomed since publication of "Transitions to Democracy." In his notes, he anticipated many of the arguments its contributors would make.

It certainly remains true that domestic factors provide the crucial setting for the emergence of democracy and that democratization is a political rather than an economic or psychological process. Nevertheless, a quarter century later, I would emphasize the interaction between economic and political factors and also the importance of international relations in making "the world safer for democracy," as Woodrow Wilson put it.

Rustow noted that "democracy needs a well-established state (law and order)" and worried about the prospect of "institutional calcification," though less in developing contexts than in established democracies.

As Rustow himself was the first to acknowledge, "Transitions to Democracy" was not the last word on the subject. However, as the opening gambit in what has become a significant field of study, it is remarkably robust. It is a testament to Rustow's acuity as well as to our enduring concern to understand and promote democratic transitions that in posing our questions, framing our debates, and outlining our hypotheses, we so frequently and consistently turn to "that early article."

# 2 Transitions to Democracy: Toward a Dynamic Model

*Dankwart A. Rustow*

## I

What conditions make democracy possible and what conditions make it thrive? Thinkers from Locke to Tocqueville and A. D. Lindsay have given many answers. Democracy, we are told, is rooted in man's innate capacity for self-government or in the Christian ethical or the Teutonic legal tradition. Its birthplace was the field at Putney where Cromwell's angry young privates debated their officers or the more sedate House at Westminster, or the rock at Plymouth, or the forest cantons above Lake Lucerne, or the fevered brain of Jean Jacques Rousseau. Its natural champions are sturdy yeomen, or industrious merchants, or a prosperous middle class. It must be combined with strong local government, with a two party system, with a vigorous tradition of civil rights, or with a multitude of private associations.

Recent writings of American sociologists and political scientists favor three types of explanation. One of these, proposed by Seymour Martin Lipset, Philips Cutright, and others, connects stable democracy with certain economic and social background conditions, such as high per capita income, widespread literacy, and prevalent urban residence. A second type of explanation dwells on the need for certain beliefs or psychological attitudes among the citizens. A long line of authors from Walter Bagehot to Ernest Barker has stressed the need for consensus as the basis of democracy - either in the form of a common belief in certain fundamentals or of procedural consensus on the rules of the game, which Barker calls "the Agreement to Differ." Among civic attitudes required for the successful working of a democratic system. Daniel Lerner has proposed a capacity for empathy and a willingness to participate. To Gabriel Almond and Sidney Verba, on the other hand, the ideal "civic culture" of a democracy suggests not only such participant but also other traditional or parochial attitudes.[1]

A third type of explanation looks at certain features of social and political structure. In contrast to the prevailing consensus theory, authors such as Carl J. Friedrich, E. E. Schattschneider, Bernard Crick, Ralf Dahrendorf, and Arend Lijphart have insisted that conflict and reconciliation are essential to democracy.[2] Starting with a similar assumption, David B. Truman has attributed the vitality of American institutions to the citizens' "multiple membership in potential groups"—a relationship which Lipset has called one of "crosscutting politically relevant associations."[3] Robert A. Dahl and Herbert McClosky, among others, have argued that democratic stability requires a commitment to democratic values or rules, not among the electorate at large but among the professional politicians—each of these presumably linked to the other through effective ties of political organization.[4] Harry Eckstein, finally, has proposed a rather subtle theory of "congruence": to make democracy stable, the structures of authority throughout society, such as family, church, business, and trade unions, must prove the more democratic the more directly they impinge on processes of government.[5]

Some of these hypotheses are compatible with each other, though they may also be held independently—for example, those about prosperity, literacy, and consensus. Others—such as those about consensus and conflict—are contradictory unless carefully restricted or reconciled. Precisely such a synthesis has been the import of a large body of writing. Dahl, for instance, has proposed that in polyarchy (or "minorities rule," the closest real-life approximation to democracy) the policies of successive governments tend to fall within a broad range of majority consensus.[6] Indeed, after an intense preoccupation with consensus in the World War II years, it is now widely accepted that democracy is indeed a process of "accommodation" involving a combination of "division and cohesion" and of "conflict and consent"—to quote the key terms from a number of recent book titles.[7]

The scholarly debate thus continues, and answers diverge. Yet there are two notable points of agreement. Nearly all the authors ask the same sort of question and support their answers with the same sort of evidence. The question is not how a democratic system comes into existence. Rather it is how a democracy, assumed to be already in existence, can best preserve or enhance its health and stability. The evidence adduced generally consists of contemporary information, whether in the form of comparative statistics, interviews, surveys, or other types of data. This remains true even of authors who spend considerable time discussing the historical background of the phenomena that concern them—Almond and Verba of the civic culture, Eckstein of congruence among Norwegian social structures, and Dahl of the ruling minorities of New Haven and of oppositions in Western countries.[8] Their key propositions are couched in the present tense.

There may be a third feature of similarity underlying the current American literature of democracy. All scientific inquiry starts with the conscious or unconscious perception of a puzzle.[9] What has puzzled the more influential authors evidently has been the contrast between the relatively smooth functioning of democracy in the English-speaking and Scandinavian countries and the recurrent crises and final collapse of democracy in the French Third and Fourth Republics and in the Weimar Republic of Germany.

This curiosity is of course wholly legitimate. The growing literature and the increasingly subtle theorizing on the bases of democracy indicate how fruitful it has been. The initial curiosity leads logically enough to the functional, as opposed to the genetic, question. And that question, in turn, is most readily answered by an examination of contemporary data about functioning democracies—perhaps with badly functioning democracies and nondemocracies thrown in for contrast. The functional curiosity also comes naturally to scholars of a country that took its crucial steps toward democracy as far back as the days of Thomas Jefferson and Andrew Jackson. It accords, moreover, with some of the characteristic trends in American social science in the last generation or two—with the interest in systematic equilibria, in quantitative correlations, and in survey data engendered by the researcher's own questions. Above all, it accords with a deep-seated prejudice against causality. As Herbert A. Simon has strikingly put it, " . . . we are wary, in the social sciences, of asymmetrical relations. They remind us of pre-Humeian and pre-Newtonian notions of causality. By whip and sword we have been converted to the doctrine that there is no causation, only functional interrelation, and that functional relations are perfectly symmetrical. We may even have taken over, as a very persuasive analogy, the proposition 'for every action, there is an equal and opposite reaction.' "[10]

Students of developing regions, such as the Middle East, Southern Asia, tropical Africa, or Latin America, naturally enough have a somewhat different curiosity about democracy. The contrast that is likely to puzzle them is that between mature democracies, such as the United States, Britain, or Sweden today, and countries that are struggling on the verge of democracy, such as Ceylon, Lebanon, Turkey, Peru, or Venezuela. This will lead them to the genetic question of how a democracy comes into being in the first place.[11] The question is (or at least was, until the Russian invasion of Czechoslovakia in 1968) of almost equal interest in Eastern Europe The genesis of democracy, thus, has not only considerable intrinsic interest for most of the world; it has greater pragmatic relevance than further panegyrics about the virtues of Anglo-American democracy or laments over the fatal illnesses of democracy in Weimar or in several of the French Republics.

In the following sections of this article I should like to examine some of the methodological problems involved in the shift from functional to genetic inquiry and then proceed to outline one possible model of the transition to democracy.

## II

What changes in concept or method does the shift from functional to genetic inquiry imply? The simplest answer would be, "None at all." The temptation is to make the functional theories do double duty as genetic theories, to extend the perspective of Westminster and Washington versus Weimar and Paris to Ankara, Caracas, and Bucharest as well. If conditions such as consensus or prosperity will help to preserve a functioning democracy, it may be argued, surely they will be all the more needful to bring it into existence.

Alas, the simple equation of function and genesis is a little too simple, and the argument a fortiori is, in fact, rather weak.[12] The equation certainly does not seem to hold for most other types of political regimes. Military dictatorships, for instance, typically originate in secret plotting and armed revolt but perpetuate themselves by massive publicity and by alliances with civilian supporters. Charismatic leaders, according to Max Weber, establish their claim to legitimacy by performing seeming miracles but preserve it through routinization. A hereditary monarchy rests most securely on the subjects' unquestioning acceptance of immemorial tradition; it evidently cannot be erected on such a principle. Communist regimes have been installed by revolutionary elites or through foreign conquest but consolidated through the growth of domestic mass parties and their bureaucracies. From physics and chemistry, too, the distinction between the energy required to initiate and to sustain a given reaction is familiar. These arguments from analogy of course are just as inconclusive as the supposedly a fortiori one. Still, they shift the burden of proof to those who assert that the circumstances which sustain a mature democracy also favor its birth.

The best known attempts to apply a single world-wide perspective to democracy, whether nascent or mature, are the statistical correlations compiled by Lipset and by Cutright.[13] But Lipset's article well illustrates the difficulty of applying the functional perspective to the genetic question. Strictly interpreted, his data bear only on function. His statistical findings all take the form of correlations at a given single point in time. In the 1950s his "stable democracies" generally had substantially higher per capita incomes and literacy rates than did his "unstable democracies," or his unstable and stable authoritarianism. Now, correlation evidently is not the same as causation—it provides at best a clue to some sort of causal connection without indicating its direction. Lipset's data leave it entirely open, for example, whether affluent and literate citizens make the better democrats; whether democracies provide superior schools and a more bracing climate for economic growth; whether there is some sort of reciprocal connection so that a given increase in affluence or literacy and in democracy will produce a corresponding increment in the other; or whether there is some further set of factors, such as the industrial economy perhaps, that causes both democracy and affluence and literacy. A corresponding objection can be urged against the findings of Almond, Verba, and others that are based mainly on contemporary opinion or attitude surveys. Only further investigation could show whether such attitudes as "civic culture," an eagerness to participate, a consensus on fundamentals, or an agreement on procedures are cause or effect of democracy, or both, or neither.

Lipset's title is true to his functional concern. He is careful to speak of "Some Social Requisites," not prerequisites, "of Democracy," and thus to acknowledge the difference between correlation and cause. But the subtlety has escaped many readers who unthinkingly translate "requisites" into "preconditions."[14] The text of the article, moreover, encourages the same substitution, for it repeatedly slips from the language of correlation into the language of causality. Significantly, on all those occasions economic and social conditions become the independent, and democracy the dependent, variable.

A genetic theory will have to be explicit about distinguishing correlate from cause. This does not commit us to any old-fashioned or simple-minded view of causality, whereby every effect has but one cause and every cause but one effect. It does not preclude the "probabilistic" view recently argued by Almond and, indeed, espoused by every social statistician since Emile Durkheim and before.[15] It does not rule out somewhat more sophisticated causal concepts such as Gunnar Myrdal's spiral, Karl W. Deutsch's quorum of prerequisites, Hayward R. Alker's nonlinear correlations, or the notion of a threshold which Deane Neubauer recently applied to Lipset's and Cutright's propositions.[16] Above all, a concern for causality is compatible with — indeed is indispensable to — a sceptical view that attributes human events to a mixture of law and chance. Such semideterminism is tantamount to an admission that the social scientist will never know enough to furnish a complete explanation, that he is at least as unlikely as the natural scientist to rival Laplace's Demon. Nor do scholars who would theorize about the genesis of democracy need to concur in all their epistemology and metaphysics. But to be geneticists at all they do have to inquire into causes. Only by such inquiry, I would add, can the social scientist accomplish his proper task of exploring the margins of human choice and of clarifying the consequences of the choices in that margin.[17]

It probably is no simple confusion between correlate and cause that leads Lipset's readers astray, and, on occasion, the author as well. Rather it seems to be a tacit assumption that social and economic conditions are somehow more basic, and that we must look for the significant relations in this deeper layer rather than in the "superstructure" of political epiphenomena. Our current emphasis in political science on economic and social factors is a most necessary corrective to the sterile legalism of an earlier generation. But, as Lipset (together with Bendix) has himself warned in another context, it can easily "explain away the very facts of political life."[18] We have been in danger of throwing away the political baby with the institutional bathwater.

Note that this widespread American economicism goes considerably beyond Marx and Engels, who saw the state as created by military conquest, economic regimes defined by their legal relations of property, and changes from one to the next brought about through political revolution. If they proclaimed themselves materialists or talked like economic determinists, it was mainly in protest against the wilder flights of Hegelian "idealism."

Any genetic theory of democracy would do well to assume a two-way flow of causality, or some form of circular interaction, between polities on the one hand and economic and social conditions on the other. Wherever social or economic background conditions enter the theory, it must seek to specify the mechanisms, presumably in part political, by which these penetrate to the democratic foreground. The political scientist, moreover, is entitled to his rights within the general division of labor and may wish to concentrate on some of the political factors without denying the significance of the social or economic ones. With Truman, Dahl, and others, I would tend to see the patterns of conflict and of recurrent or changing alignments as one of the central features of any political system. With Apter, I would consider choice as one of the central concerns of the political process.[19]

What goes for economics and sociology goes for psychology as well. Here, too, the relationship with politics is one of interaction and interdependence, so that political phenomena may have psychological consequences as well as vice versa. In explaining the origins of democracy we need not assume — as does much of the current survey research literature — that beliefs unilaterally influence actions. Rather, we may recognize with Leon Festinger and other social psychologists of the "cognitive dissonance" school that there are reciprocal influences between beliefs and actions.[20] Many of the current theories about democracy seem to imply that to promote democracy you must first foster democrats — perhaps by preachment, propaganda, education, or perhaps as an automatic byproduct of growing prosperity. Instead, we should allow for the possibility that circumstances may force, trick, lure, or cajole nondemocrats into democratic behavior and that their beliefs may adjust in due course by some process of rationalization or adaptation.

To seek causal explanations, as I insisted earlier, does not imply simple-mindedness. Specifically, we need not assume that the transition to democracy is a world-wide uniform process, that it always involves the same social classes, the same types of political issues, or even the same methods of solution. On the contrary, it may be well to assume with Harry Eckstein that a wide variety of social conflicts and of political contents can be combined with democracy.[21] This is, of course, in line with the general recognition that democracy is a matter primarily of procedure rather than of substance. It also implies that, as among various countries that have made the transition, there may be many roads to democracy.

Nor does a model of transition need to maintain that democratic evolution is a steady process that is homogeneous over time. Such a notion of temporal continuity and presumably of linear correlation seems to lurk behind much of the literature of the Lipset-Cutright genre. Temporal discontinuity, on the contrary, is implicit in the basic distinction drawn earlier in this article between the functional and genetic questions. The same discontinuity may be carried into the genetic scheme itself. For instance, it may be useful to single out certain circumstances as background factors and to proceed step-by-step to other factors that may become crucial in the preparation, decision, and consolidation phases of the process.

Even in the same country and during the same phase of the process, political attitudes are not likely to be spread evenly through the population. Dahl, McClosky, and others have found that in mature democracies there are marked differences in the attitudes of professional politicians and of common citizens.[22] Nor can we take it for granted that the politicians will all share the same attitudes. In so far as democracy is based on conflict, it may take two attitudes to make a quarrel. All these differences are likely, moreover, to be compounded during the formative period when part of the quarrel must *ex hypothesi* be between democrats and nondemocrats. Finally, a dynamic model of the transition must allow for the possibility that different groups—e.g., now the citizens and now the rulers, now the forces in favor of change and now those eager to preserve the past—may furnish the crucial impulse toward democracy.

## III

The methodological argument I have been advancing may be condensed into a number of succinct propositions.

1. The factors that keep a democracy stable may not be the ones that brought it into existence: explanations of democracy must distinguish between function and genesis.
2. Correlation is not the same as causation: a genetic theory must concentrate on the latter.
3. Not all causal links run from social and economic to political factors.
4. Not all causal links run from beliefs and attitudes to actions.
5. The genesis of democracy need not be geographically uniform: there may be many roads to democracy.
6. The genesis of democracy need not be temporally uniform: different factors may become crucial during successive phases.

7.  The genesis of democracy need not be socially uniform: even in the same place and time the attitudes that promote it may not be the same for politicians and for common citizens.

My refrain, like Sportin' Life's, has been, "It ain't necessarily so." Each proposition pleads for the lifting of some conventional restriction, for the dropping of some simplifying assumption made in the previous literature, for the introduction of complicating, diversifying factors. If the argument were to conclude on this sceptical note, it would set the researcher completely adrift and make the task of constructing a theory of democratic genesis well-nigh unmanageable.

Fortunately, the genetic perspective requires or makes possible a number of new restrictions that more than compensate for the loss of the seven others. We may continue the listing of summary propositions before elaborating this second part of the methodological argument.

8.  Empirical data in support of a genetic theory must cover, for any given country, a time period from just before until just after the advent of democracy.
9.  To examine the logic of transformation within political systems, we may leave aside countries where a major impetus came from abroad.
10. A model or ideal type of the transition may be derived from a close examination of two or three empirical cases and tested by application to the rest.

That diachronic data, covering more than a single point in time, are essential to any genetic theory should be obvious. Such a theory, moreover, must be based on cases where the process is substantially complete. Although control data on nondemocracies and on abortive and incipient cases may become important at a later stage of theorizing, it is more convenient to start out by studying a phenomenon where it actually has come into existence. The "advent" of democracy must not, of course, be understood as occurring in a single year. Since the emergence of new social groups and the formation of new habits are involved, one generation is probably the minimum period of transition. In countries that had no earlier models to emulate, the transition is likely to have come even more slowly. In Britain, for example, it may be argued that it began before 1640 and was not accomplished until 1918. For an initial set of hypotheses, however, it may be best to turn to countries where the process occurred relatively rapidly.

The study of democratic transitions will take the political scientist deeper into history than he has commonly been willing to go. This implies many changes in method, beginning with suitable substitutions for survey data and for interviews. Even reliable statistics are harder to come by early in any democratic experiment. The United States Constitution (Article 1, Section 2) reminds us that our decennial census was introduced at that very time so that we might begin to govern ourselves by an accurate count of noses.

Whatever the difficulties in the vastly increased use of historical data by social scientists, at least three arguments can be made in extenuation and encouragement. Man did not become a political animal in 1960 or in 1945, as much of our recent literature pretends to suppose. History, to paraphrase Georges Clemenceau, is far too important a topic to be left just to historians. And recently scholars in comparative politics have turned with increasing zest to historical themes. The list includes Almond, Leonard Binder, Dahl, Samuel P. Huntington, Lipset, Robert E. Ward, and Myron Weiner—not to speak of those like Friedrich and Deutsch to whom a political-historical perspective was natural to start with.[23]

The next restriction—the omission early in the inquiry of cases where the major impulse to democratization came from the outside—is in accord with the conventional division of labor between the subfields of comparative politics and international relations. There are topics such as the theory of modernization where that division should be transcended from the start.[24] In tracing the origins of democracy, too, both perspectives may be applied at once, as witness the suggestive work of Louis Hartz, the masterly synthesis by Robert Palmer, and the current research by Robert Ward on Japanese-American interaction in the shaping of the 1947 constitution.[25] But for a first attempt at a general theory it may be preferable to stick to countries where the transition occurred mainly within a single system.

To speak of "major impulses from outside" or transitions "mainly within the system," acknowledges that foreign influences are almost always present. Throughout history, warfare has been a major democratizing force, because it has made necessary the marshalling of additional human resources.[26] Democratic ideas, moreover, have proved infectious whether in the days of Rousseau or of John F. Kennedy. And the violent overthrow of one oligarchy (e.g., France in 1830, Germany in 1918) has often frightened another into peaceful surrender (e.g., Britain in 1832, Sweden in 1918). From such ever present international influences we may distinguish situations where people arriving from abroad took an active part in the internal political process of democratization. A theory of democratic origins, that is to say, should leave aside at the beginning those countries where military occupation played a major role (postwar Germany and Japan), where democratic institutions or attitudes were brought along by immigrants (Australia and New Zealand), or where in these and other ways immigration played a major role (Canada, the United States, and Israel).

The preference expressed earlier for relatively rapid instances of transition and the omission of immigrant countries amount to a very serious restriction, for they leave out of account, at this first stage of theorizing, all the English-speaking democracies. The reasons, however, seem cogent. Indeed, it may well be that American social scientists have added to their difficulties in understanding transitions to democracy by paying undue attention to Britain and the United States, which for the reasons just suggested prove to be among the hardest instances to analyze in genetic terms. The total of eight provisional exclusions still leaves (among extant democracies) about twenty-three cases on which to base a comparative analysis, thirteen of which are in Europe: Austria, Belgium, Ceylon, Chile, Colombia, Costa Rica, Denmark, Finland, France, Iceland, Ireland, India, Italy, Lebanon, Luxembourg, Netherlands, Norway, Philippines, Sweden, Switzerland, Turkey, Uruguay, Venezuela.[27]

Among these twenty-odd democracies, the last methodological proposition urges an even narrower selection at this preliminary stage of theorizing. What is here involved is a choice between three research strategies: inclusion of all relevant cases, concentration on a single country, or some intermediate course.

Completeness is of course desirable, and all the more so where the "universe" consists of no more than twenty or thirty cases. But the more nearly complete the coverage, the shallower it will have to be. The number of possible variables is so enormous (economic conditions, social cleavages, political alignments, psychological attitudes) that they could be handled only by means of the kind of simplifying assumptions that we rejected earlier on logical grounds. A test, no matter how complete, of a fallacious set of propositions would hardly yield convincing results.

The country monograph would avoid this danger. Nor does it deliberately have to be antitheoretical or "merely descriptive." Any country study nevertheless sacrifices the advantages of comparison, the social scientist's nearest substitute for a laboratory. No such study can tell us which strands in a tangle of empirical factors represent the development of democracy and which the national idiosyncrasies of Monographistan.

The middle course avoids the twin dangers of inconclusive scholasticism and of fact-grubbing. Instead, it can offer a more balanced and hence more fruitful blend of theory and empiricism. The many possible variables that can affect the origins of democracy and the even more complex relations among them can best be sorted out by looking at their total configuration in a limited number of cases—perhaps no more than two or three at the start. What will emerge from this exercise is a model, or as Weber used to call it, an "ideal type," of the transition from oligarchy to democracy. Being an ideal type, it deliberately highlights certain features of empirical reality and deliberately distorts, simplifies, or omits others. Like any such construct, it must be judged initially by its internal coherence and plausibility but ultimately by its fruitfulness in suggesting hypotheses applicable to a wide variety of other empirical cases.[28] It is at this further stage of testing that the demand for completeness comes once again into its own.

The model I should like to sketch in the next few pages is based in large part on my studies of Sweden, a Western country that made the transition to democracy in the period from 1890 to 1920, and of Turkey, a Westernizing country where that process began about 1945 and is still underway. The choice of these two is accidental—except in terms of an autobiographical account for which this is not the occasion. I am now in the early stages of a study that will seek to refine the same set of hypotheses in the light of materials from a slightly larger and less arbitrary selection of countries.

## IV

### A. Background Condition

The model starts with a single background condition—national unity. This implies nothing mysterious about *Blut und Boden* or daily pledges of allegiance, about personal identity in the psychoanalyst's sense, or about a grand political purpose pursued by the citizenry as a whole. It simply means that the vast majority of citizens in a democracy-to-be must have no doubt or mental reservations as to which political community they belong to. This excludes situations of latent secession, as in the late Habsburg and Ottoman Empires or in many African states today, and, conversely, situations of serious aspirations for merger as in many Arab states. Democracy is a system of rule by temporary majorities. In order that rulers and policies may freely change, the boundaries must endure, the composition of the citizenry be continuous. As Ivor Jennings phrased it tersely, "the people cannot decide until somebody decides who are the people."[29]

National unity is listed as a background condition in the sense that it must precede all the other phases of democratization but that otherwise its timing is irrelevant. It may have been achieved in prehistoric times, as in Japan or Sweden; or it may have preceded the other phases by centuries, as in France, or by decades, as in Turkey. Nor does it matter by what means national unity has been established. The geographic situation may be such that no serious alternative has ever arisen—Japan once again being the best example. Or a sense of nationality may be the product of a sudden intensification of social communication in a new idiom developed for the purpose. On the other hand, it may be the legacy of some dynastic or administrative process of unification. The various hypotheses proposed by Deutsch clearly become relevant here.[30]

I have argued elsewhere that in an age of modernization men are unlikely to feel a preponderant sense of loyalty except to a political community large enough to achieve some considerable degree of modernity in its social and economic life.[31] This sort of hypothesis must be examined as part of a theory of nationhood, not of one of democratic development. What matters in the present context is only the result.

I hesitate to call this result a consensus, for at least two reasons. First, national unity, as Deutsch argues, is the product less of shared attitudes and opinions than of responsiveness and complementarity. Second, "consensus" connotes consciously held opinion and deliberate agreement. The background condition, however, is best fulfilled when national unity is accepted unthinkingly, is silently taken for granted. Any vocal consensus about national unity, in fact, should make us wary. Most of the rhetoric of nationalism has poured from the lips of people who felt least secure in their sense of national identity—Germans and Italians in the past century and Arabs and Africans in the present, never Englishmen, Swedes, or Japanese.

To single out national unity as the sole background condition implies that no minimal level of economic development or social differentiation is necessary as a prerequisite to democracy. These social and economic factors enter the model only indirectly as one of several alternative bases for national unify or for entrenched conflict (see B below). Those social and economic indicators that authors are fond of citing as "background conditions" seem somewhat implausible at any rate. There are always nondemocracies that rank suspiciously high, such as Kuwait, Nazi Germany, Cuba, or Congo-Kinshasa. Conversely, the United States in 1820, France in 1870, and Sweden in 1890 would have been sure to fail one or another of the proposed tests of urbanization or per capita income—not to speak of newspaper copies in circulation, or doctors, movies, and telephones available to each one thousand inhabitants.

The model thus deliberately leaves open the possibility of democracies (properly so called) in premodern, prenationalist times and at low levels of economic development. To find a meaningful definition of democracy that would cover modern parliamentary systems along with medieval forest cantons, ancient city states (the ones where slavery and metics were absent), and some of the pre-Colombian Indians may prove difficult. It is not a task that forms part of the present project; still, I should not like to foreclose the attempt.

## B. Preparatory Phase

I hypothesize that, against this single background condition, the dynamic process of democratization itself is set off by a prolonged and inconclusive political struggle. To give it those qualities, the protagonists must represent well-entrenched forces (typically social classes), and the issues must have profound meaning to them. Such a struggle is likely to begin as the result of the emergence of a new elite that arouses a depressed and previously leaderless social group into concerted action. Yet the particular social composition of the contending forces, both leaders and followers, and the specific nature of the issues will vary widely from one country to the next and in the same country from period to period.

In Sweden at the turn of the century, it was a struggle first of farmers and then of an urban lower-middle and working class against a conservative alliance of bureaucrats, large landowners, and industrialists; and the issues were tariffs, taxation, military service, and suffrage. In Turkey in the last twenty years it has mainly been a contest of countryside versus city, more precisely of large and middling-size farmers (supported by most of the peasant electorate) against the heirs of the Kemalist bureaucratic-military establishment; the central issue has been industrialization versus agricultural development. In both these examples, economic factors have been of prime importance, yet the direction of causality has varied. In Sweden, it was a period of intense economic development that created new political tensions; at one crucial point, rising wages enabled the Stockholm workers to overcome the existing tax barrier for the franchise. In Turkey, conversely, the demand for rural development was the consequence, not the cause, of beginning democratization.[32]

There may be situations where economic factors have played a much lesser role. In India and in the Philippines the prolonged contest between nationalist forces and an imperial bureaucracy over the issue of self-government may have served the same preparatory function as did class conflict elsewhere. In Lebanon the continuing struggle is mainly between denominational groups and the stakes are mainly government offices. Although political struggles of this sort naturally have their economic dimensions, only a doctrinaire economic determinist would derive colonialism or religious divisions from solely economic causes.

James Bryce found in his classic comparative study that, "One road only has in the past led into democracy, viz., the wish to be rid of tangible evils."[33] Democracy was not the original or primary aim; it was sought as a means to some other end or it came as a fortuitous byproduct of the struggle. But, since the tangible evils that befall human societies are legion, Bryce's single road dissolves into many separate paths. No two existing democracies have gone through a struggle between the very same forces over the same issues and with the same institutional outcome. Hence, it seems unlikely that any future democracy will follow in the precise footsteps of any of its predecessors. As Albert Hirschman has warned in his discussion of economic development, the search for ever more numerous preconditions or prerequisites may end up by proving conclusively that development always will be impossible—and always has been.[34]

More positively, Hirschman and other economists have argued that a country can best launch into a phase of growth not by slavishly imitating the example of nations already industrialized, but rather by making the most of its particular natural and human resources and by fitting these accurately into the international division of labor.[35] Similarly, a country is likely to attain democracy not by copying the constitutional laws or parliamentary practices of some previous democracy, but rather by honestly facing up to its particular conflicts and by devising or adapting effective procedures for their accommodation.

The serious and prolonged nature of the struggle is likely to force the protagonists to rally around two banners. Hence polarization, rather than pluralism, is the hallmark of this preparatory phase. Yet there are limitations implicit in the requirement of national unity—which, of course, must not only preexist but also continue. If the division is on sharply regional lines, secession rather than democracy is likely to result. Even among contestants geographically interspersed there must be some sense of community or some even balance of forces that makes wholesale expulsion or genocide impossible. The Turks are beginning to develop a set of democratic practices among themselves, but fifty years ago they did not deal democratically with Armenians or Greeks. Crosscutting cleavages have their place in this preparatory phase as a possible means of strengthening or preserving that sense of community.

Dahl notes wistfully that "one perennial problem of opposition is that there is either too much or too little."[36] The first two elements of the model between them will ensure that there is the right amount. But struggle and national unity cannot simply be averaged out, since they cannot be measured along the same scale. Strong doses of both must be combined, just as it may be possible to combine sharp polarization with crosscutting cleavages. Furthermore, as Mary Parker Follett, Lewis A. Coser, and others have insisted, certain types of conflict in themselves constitute creative processes of integration.[37] What infant democracy requires is not a lukewarm struggle but a hot family feud.

This delicate combination implies, of course, that many things can go wrong during the preparatory phase. The fight may go on and on till the protagonists weary and the issues fade away without the emergence of any democratic solution along the way. Or one group may find a way of crushing the opponents after all. In these and other ways an apparent evolution toward democracy may be deflected, and at no time more easily than during the preparatory phase.

## C. Decision Phase

Robert Dahl has written that, "Legal party opposition . . . is a recent and unplanned invention."[38] This accords with Bryce's emphasis on the redress of specific grievances as democracy's vehicle and with the assumption here that the transition to democracy is a complex process stretching over many decades. But it does not rule out suffrage or freedom of opposition as conscious goals in the preparatory struggle. Nor does it suggest that a country ever becomes a democracy in a fit of absentmindedness. On the contrary, what concludes the preparatory phase is a deliberate decision on the part of political leaders to accept the existence of diversity in unity and, to that end, to institutionalize some crucial aspect of democratic procedure. Such was the decision in 1907, which I have called the "Great Compromise" of Swedish politics, to adopt universal suffrage combined with proportional representation.[39] Instead of a single decision there may be several. In Britain, as is well-known, the principle of limited government was laid down in the compromise of 1688, cabinet government evolved in the eighteenth century, and suffrage reform was launched as late as 1832. Even in Sweden, the dramatic change of 1907 was followed by the further suffrage reform of 1918 which also confirmed the principle of cabinet government.

Whether democracy is purchased wholesale as in Sweden in 1907 or on the installment plan as in Britain, it is acquired by a process of conscious decision at least on the part of the top political leadership. Politicians are specialists in power, and a fundamental power shift such as that from oligarchy to democracy will not escape their notice.

Decision means choice, and while the choice of democracy does not arise until the background and preparatory conditions are in hand, it is a genuine choice and does not flow automatically from those two conditions. The history of Lebanon illustrates the possibilities of benevolent autocracy or of foreign rule as alternative solutions to entrenched struggles within a political community.[40] And of course a decision in favor of democracy, or some crucial ingredient of it, may be proposed and rejected—thus leading to a continuation of the preparatory phase or to some sort of abortive outcome.

The decision in favor of democracy results from the interplay of a number of forces. Since precise terms must be negotiated and heavy risks with regard to the future taken, a small circle of leaders is likely to play a disproportionate role. Among the negotiating groups and their leaders may be the protagonists of the preparatory struggle. Other participants may include groups that split off from one or the other side or new arrivals on the political stage. In Sweden these new and intermediate groups played a crucial role. Conservatives and Radicals (led by industrialists on one side and intellectuals on the other) had sharpened and crystallized the issues throughout the 1890s. Then came a period of stalemate when discipline in all the recently formed parliamentary parties broke down—a sort of randomization process in which many compromises, combinations, and permutations were devised and explored. The formula that carried the day in 1907 included crucial contributions from a moderately conservative bishop and a moderately liberal farmer, neither of whom played a very prominent role in politics before or after this decision phase.

Just as there can be different types of sponsors and different contents of the decision, so the motives from which it is proposed and accepted will vary from case to case. The forces of conservatism may yield from fear that continued resistance may lose them even more ground in the end. (Such thoughts were on the minds of British Whigs in 1832 and of Swedish conservatives in 1907.) Or they may belatedly wish to live up to principles long proclaimed; such was the Turkish transition to a multiparty system announced by President Inonu in 1945. The radicals may accept the compromise as a first installment, confident that time is on their side and that future installments are bound to follow. Both conservatives and radicals may feel exhausted from a long struggle or fearful of a civil war. This consideration is likely to loom large if they have been through such a war in recent memory. As Barrington Moore has aptly proposed, the English civil war was a crucial "contribution of early violence to later gradualism."[41] In short, democracy, like any collective human action, is likely to stem from a large variety of mixed motives.

The decision phase may well be considered an act of deliberate, explicit consensus. But, once again, this somewhat nebulous term should be carefully considered and perhaps replaced with less ambiguous synonyms. First of all, as Bryce suggests, the democratic content of the decision may be incidental to other substantive issues. Second, in so far as it is a genuine compromise it will seem second-best to all major parties involved—it certainly will not represent any agreement on fundamentals. Third, even on procedures there are likely to be continuing differences of preference. Universal suffrage with proportional representation, the content of the Swedish compromise of 1907, was about equally distasteful to the conservatives (who would rather have continued the old plutocratic voting system) and to the liberals and socialists (who wanted majority rule undiluted by proportional representation). What matters at the decision stage is not what values the leaders hold dear in the abstract, but what concrete steps they are willing to take. Fourth, the agreement worked out by the leaders is far from universal. It must be transmitted to the professional politicians and to the citizenry at large. These are two aspects of the final, or habituation, phase of the model.


## D. Habituation Phase

A distasteful decision, once made, is likely to seem more palatable as one is forced to live with it. Everyday experience can supply concrete illustrations of this probability for each of us. Festinger's theory of "cognitive dissonance" supplies a technical explanation and experimental support.[42] Democracy, moreover, is by definition a competitive process, and this competition gives an edge to those who can rationalize their commitment to it, and an even greater edge to those who sincerely believe in it. The transformation of the Swedish Conservative Party from 1918 to 1936 vividly illustrates the point. After two decades those leaders who had grudgingly put up with democracy or pragmatically accepted it retired or died and were replaced by others who sincerely believed in it. Similarly, in Turkey there is a remarkable change from the leadership of Ismet Inonu, who promoted democracy out of a sense of duty, and Adnan Menderes, who saw in it an unprecedented vehicle for his ambition, to younger leaders in each of their parties who understand democracy more fully and embrace it more wholeheartedly. In short, the very process of democracy institutes a double process of Darwinian selectivity in favor of convinced democrats: one among parties in general elections and the other among politicians vying for leadership within these parties.

But politics consists not only of competition for office. It is, above all, a process for resolving conflicts within human groups—whether these arise from the clash of interests or from uncertainty about the future. A new political regime is a novel prescription for taking joint chances on the unknown. With its basic practice of multilateral debate, democracy in particular involves a process of trial and error, a joint learning experience. The first grand compromise that establishes democracy, if it proves at all viable, is in itself a proof of the efficacy of the principle of conciliation and accommodation. The first success, therefore, may encourage contending political forces and their leaders to submit other major questions to resolution by democratic procedures.

In Sweden, for instance, there had been a general political stalemate in the last third of the nineteenth century over the prime issues of the day—the taxation and conscription systems inherited from the sixteenth century. But in the two decades after 1918, when democracy was fully adopted by the Swedes, a whole host of thorny questions was wittingly or unwittingly resolved. The Social Democrats surrendered their earlier pacifism, anticlericalism, and republicanism, as well as the demand for nationalization of industry (although they found it hard to admit this last point). The conservatives, once staunchly nationalist, endorsed Swedish participation in international organizations. Above all, conservatives and liberals fully accepted government intervention in the economy and the social welfare state.

Of course, the spiral that in Sweden went upward to greater and greater successes for the democratic process may also go downward. A conspicuous failure to resolve some urgent political question will damage the prospects of democracy; if such a failure comes early in the habituation phase, it may prove fatal.

Surveying the evolution of political debate and conflict in the Western democracies over the last century, it is striking to observe the difference between social and economic issues, which democracies handled with comparative ease, and issues of community, which have proved far more troublesome.[43] With the advantage of a century's hindsight, it is easy to see that Marx's estimate was wrong at crucial points. In nationality he saw a cloak for bourgeois class interests. He denounced religion as the opiate of the masses. In economics, by contrast, he foresaw very real and increasingly bitter struggles that would end by bringing bourgeois democracy crashing down. But in fact democracy has proved most effective in resolving political questions where the major divisions have been social and economic, as in Britain, Australia, New Zealand, and the Scandinavian countries. It has been the fight among religious, national, and racial groups, instead, that has proved most tenacious and has caused recurrent bitterness, as in Belgium, Holland, Canada, and the United States.

The reasons are not hard to find. On the socioeconomic front Marxism itself became a sufficient force in Europe to serve to some extent as a self-disconfirming prophecy. But beyond this there is a fundamental difference in the nature of the issues. On matters of economic policy and social expenditures you can always split the difference. In an expanding economy, you can even have it both ways: the contest for higher wages, profits, consumer savings, and social welfare payments can be turned into a positive-sum game. But there is no middle position between Flemish and French as official languages, or between Calvinism, Catholicism, and secularism as principles of education. The best you can get here is an "inclusive compromise"[44]: a log-rolling deal whereby some government offices speak French and some Flemish, or some children are taught according to Aquinas, some, Calvin, and some, Voltaire. Such a solution may partly depoliticize the question. Yet it also entrenches the differences instead of removing them, and accordingly it may convert political conflict into a form of trench warfare.

The difficulty that democracy finds in resolving issues of community emphasizes the importance of national unity as the background condition of the democratization process. The hardest struggles in a democracy are those against the birth defects of the political community.

The transition to democracy, it was suggested earlier, may require some common attitudes and some distinct attitudes on the part of the politician and of the common citizen. The distinction is already apparent during the decision phase when the leaders search for compromise while their followers wearily uphold the banners of the old struggle. It becomes even more readily apparent during the habituation phase, when three sorts of process are at work. First, both politicians and citizens learn from the successful resolution of some issues to place their faith in the new rules and to apply them to new issues. Their trust will grow more quickly if, in the early decades of the new regime, a wide variety of political tendencies can participate in the conduct of affairs, either by joining various coalitions or by taking turns as government and opposition. Second, as we just saw, experience with democratic techniques and competitive recruitment will confirm the politicians in their democratic practices and beliefs. Third, the population at large will become firmly fitted into the new structure by the forging of effective links of party organization that connect the politicians in the capital with the mass electorate throughout the country.

These party organizations may be a direct continuation of those that were active during the preparatory, or conflict, phase of democratization, and a suffrage extension at the time of the democratic "decision" may now have given them a free field. It is possible, on the other hand, that no parties with a broad popular base emerged during the conflict phase and that the suffrage extension was very limited. Even under such conditions of partial democratization of the political structure, a competitive dynamic that completes the process may have been set off. The parliamentary parties will seek support from constituency organizations to insure a steady supply of members for their group in future parliaments. Now this and now that political group may see a chance to steal a march on its opponents by enlarging the electorate or by removing other obstacles to majority control. This, roughly, would seem to have been the nature of British developments between 1832 and 1918. Complete democratization, of course, is the only logical stopping point for such a dynamic.

## V

The model here presented makes three broad assertions. First, it says that certain ingredients are indispensable to the genesis of democracy. For one thing, there must be a sense of national unity. For another, there must be entrenched and serious conflict. For a third, there must be a conscious adoption of democratic rules. And, finally, both politicians and electorate must be habituated to these rules.

Secondly, the model asserts that these ingredients must be assembled one at a time. Each task has its own logic and each has its natural protagonists—a network of administrators or a group of nationalist literati for the task of unification, a mass movement of the lower class, perhaps led by upper class dissidents, for the task of preparatory struggle, a small circle of political leaders skilled at negotiation and compromise for the formulation of democratic rules, and a variety of organization men and their organizations for the task of habituation. The model thus abandons the quest for "functional requisites" of democracy; for such a quest heaps all these tasks together and thus makes the total job of democratization quite unmanageable. The argument here is analogous to that which has been made by Hirschman and others against the theory of balanced economic growth. These economists do not deny that the transition from a primitive subsistence economy to a mature industrial society involves changes on all fronts—in working skills, in capital formation, in the distribution system, in consumption habits, in the monetary system, and so forth. But they insist that any country that attempted all these tasks at once would in practice find itself totally paralysed—that the stablest balance is that of stagnation. Hence the economic developer's problem, in their view, becomes one of finding backward and forward "linkages," that is, of devising a manageable sequence of tasks.

Thirdly, the model does suggest one such sequence from national unity as background, through struggle, compromise, and habituation, to democracy. The cogency of this sequence is brought home by a deviant development in Turkey in the years after 1945. The Turkish commitment to democracy was made in the absence of prior overt conflict between major social groups or their leading elites. In 1950 there was the first change of government as the result of a new electoral majority, but in the next decade there was a drift back into authoritarian practices on the part of this newly elected party, and in 1960–1961 the democratic experiment was interrupted by a military coup. These developments are not unconnected: Turkey paid the price in 1960 for having received its first democratic regime as a free gift from the hands of a dictator. But after 1961 there was a further evolution in the more appropriate sequence. The crisis of 1960–1961 had made social and political conflict for more acceptable, and a full range of social and economic issues was debated for the first time. The conflict that shaped up was between the military on one side and the spokesmen of the agrarian majority on the other—and the compromise between these two allowed the resumption of the democratic experiment on a more secure basis by 1965.

In the interests of parsimony, the basic ingredients of the model have been kept to four, and the social circumstances or psychological motivations that may furnish each of them have been left wide open. Specifically, the model rejects what are sometimes proposed as preconditions of democracy, c.g., high levels of economic and social development or a prior consensus either on fundamentals or on the rules. Economic growth may be one of the circumstances that produces the tensions essential to the preparatory or conflict phase—but there are other circumstances that might also serve. Mass education and social welfare services are more likely to be the result of democratization.

Consensus on fundamentals is an implausible precondition. A people who were not in conflict about some rather fundamental matters would have little need to devise democracy's elaborate rules for conflict resolution. And the acceptance of those rules is logically a part of the transition process rather than its prerequisite. The present model transfers various aspects of consensus from the quiescent state of preconditions to that of active elements in the process. I here follow the lead of Bernard Crick, who has strikingly written:

> . . . It is often thought that for this "master science" (i.e., democratic politics) to function, there must already be in existence some shared idea of a "common good," some "consensus" or consensus juris. But

this common good is itself the process of practical reconciliation of the interests of the various . . . aggregates, or groups which compose a state; it is not some external and intangible spiritual adhesive. . . . Diverse groups hold together, firstly, because they have a common interest in sheer survival, and, secondly, because they practice politics—not because they agree about "fundamentals," or some such concept too vague, too personal, or too divine ever to do the job of politics for it. The moral consensus of a free state is not something mysteriously prior to or above politics: it is the activity (the civilizing activity) of politics itself.[45]

The basis of democracy is not maximum consensus. It is the tenuous middle ground between imposed uniformity (such as would lead to some sort of tyranny) and implacable hostility (of a kind that would disrupt the community in civil war or secession). In the process of genesis of democracy, an element of what might be termed consensus enters at three points at least. There must be a prior sense of community, preferably a sense of community quietly taken for granted that is above mere opinion and mere agreement. There must be a conscious adoption of democratic rules, but they must not be so much believed in as applied, first perhaps from necessity and gradually from habit. The very operation of these rules will enlarge the area of consensus step-by-step as democracy moves down its crowded agenda.

But new issues will always emerge and new conflicts threaten the newly won agreements. The characteristic procedures of democracy include campaign oratory, the election of candidates, parliamentary divisions, votes of confidence and of censure—a host of devices, in short, for expressing conflict and thereby resolving it. The essence of democracy is the habit of dissension and conciliation over ever-changing issues and amidst ever-changing alignments. Totalitarian rulers must enforce unanimity on fundamentals and on procedures before they can get down to other business. By contrast, democracy is that form of government that derives its just powers from the dissent of up to one half of the governed.

NOTES

This article was presented at the annual meeting of the American Political Science Association, New York City, September 1969. The author is grateful for financial support at various stages of his researches into democracy from the John

Simon Guggenheim Foundation, the Ford Foundation, and the National Science Foundation. He jealously claims the full blame for his errors, foibles and follies as revealed in this essay.

1.  Ernest Barker, *Reflections on Government* (Oxford, 1942). p. 63; Daniel Lerner et al. *The Passing of Traditional Society* (Glencoe, 1958). pp 49ff, 60ff. Gabriel Almond and Sidney Verba, *The Civic Culture* (Princeton, 1963).

2.  Carl J. Friedrich, *The New Belief in the Common Man* (Boston, 1942). E. E. Schattschneider, *The Semi-Sovereign People* (New York, 1960); Bernard Crick, *In Defence of Politics*, rev. ed. (Penguin Books, 1964); Ralf Dahrendorf, *Class and Class Conflict in Industrial Society* (Stanford, 1959); Arend Lijphart, *The Politics of Accommodation* (Berkeley and Los Angeles, 1968).

3.  David B. Truman, *The Governmental Process* (New York, 1951), p. 514. S. M. Lipset, *Political Man* (New York, 1960), pp. 88ff. Already, A. Lawrence Lowell had spoken of the need for a party alignment where "the line at division is vertical," cutting across the horizontal division of classes. *Government and Parties in Continental Europe* (Boston, 1896), vol. 2, pp. 65ff.

4.  Robert A. Dahl, *Who Governs?* (New Haven, 1961); Herbert McClosky, "Consensus and Ideology in American Politics," *American Political Science Review*, LVIII (June 1964); James W. Prothro and Charles M. Grigg, "Fundamental Principles of Democracy: Bases of Agreement and Disagreement," *Journal of Politics*, XXII (May 1960).

5.  Harry Eckstein, *The Theory of Stable Democracy* (Princeton, 1961) and *Division and Cohesion in a Democracy* (Princeton, 1965).

6.  Robert A. Dahl, *A Preface to Democratic Theory* (Chicago, 1956).

7.  Lijphart, Eckstein; Dahl, *Pluralist Democracy in the United States: Conflict and Consent* (Chicago, 1967).

8.  Almond and Verba; Eckstein; Dahl, *Who Governs?* and ed. *Political Oppositions in Western Democracies* (New Haven, 1966).

9.  See Thomas Kuhn, *The Structure of Scientific Revolutions* (Chicago, 1962).

10. Herbert A. Simon, *Models of Man Social and Rational* (New York, 1957) p. 65.

11. For a general discussion of the question of democracy in the context of recent modernizing countries, see Rustow, *A World of Nations: Problems of Political Modernization* (Washington, 1967), Ch. 7, which states some of the present argument in summary form.

12. " . . . a political form may persist under conditions normally adverse to the *emergence* of that form" (Lipset, p. 46).

13. Seymour Martin Lipset, "Some Social Requisites of Democracy: Economic Development and Political Legitimacy," *American Political Science Review*. LIII (March 1959); idem, *Political Man*; Philips Cutright. "National Political Development: Measurement and Analysis," *American Sociological Review*, XXVIII (April 1963).

14. Rupert Emerson, *From Empire to Nation* (Cambridge, 1960), p. 278, para-
    phrases Lipset to this effect. M. Rejai, in his useful anthology and commentary,
    *Democracy: The Contemporary Theories* (New York, 1967), includes an excerpt
    from the article under the heading, "Socioeconomic Preconditions" (pp. 242–
    247).

15. Gabriel A. Almond and James S. Coleman, eds. *The Politics of Developing
    Areas* (Princeton, 1960), Introduction.

16. Gunnar Myrdal, *An American Dilemma* (New York, 1944), Appendix; Hayward
    R. Alker, Jr., "The Long Road to International Relations Theory: Problems of
    Statistical Non-Additivity," *World Politics* XVIII (July 1966); Deane Neubauer,
    "Some Conditions of Democracy," *American Political Science Review* LXI (De-
    cember 1967).

17. This statement of the function of the social scientist is taken from Rustow A
    *World of Nations*, p. 17; the next two paragraphs paraphrase ibid., pp. 142ff.

18. Reinhard Bendix and Seymour Martin Lipset, "Political Sociology," *Current
    Sociology*, VI, No. 2 (1957), p. 85.

19. David E. Apter, *The Politics of Modernization* (Chicago, 1965).

20. Leon Festinger, *A Theory of Cognitive Dissonance* (Stanford, 1957).

21. Eckstein, *Division and Cohesion*, pp. 183–85.

22. Dahl, *Who Governs?*; McClosky; Prothro and Grigg.

23. Almond, current study on nineteenth-century Britain; Leonard Binder, ed.
    *Politics in Lebanon* (New York, 1966); Dahl, see nn. 4, 7, and 8; Karl W.
    Deutsch, *Nationalism and Social Communication* (New York, 1953) and
    Deutsch et al., *Political Community and the North Atlantic Area* (Princeton,
    1957: Carl J. Friedrich, *Constitutional Government and Democracy* (Boston,
    1950): Samuel P. Huntington, "Political Modernization: America vs. Europe."
    *World Politics*, XVIII (April 19661; S. M. Lipset, *The First New Nation* (New
    York, 1963), and Lipset and Stein Rokkan, eds. *Party Systems and Voter Align-
    ments* (New York, 1967); Robert E. Ward and D. A. Rustow, eds. *Political
    Modernization in Japan and Turkey* (Princeton, 1964); Myron Weiner, current
    study on nineteenth-century social history of the Balkans.

24. In this combination lies the strength of Cyril E. Black's *Dynamics of Modern-
    ization* (New York, 1966) compared to most of the other literature on the
    subject.

25. Louis Hartz et al., *The Founding of New Societies* (New York, 1964); R. R.
    Palmer, *The Age of Democratic Revolution*, 2 vols. (Princeton, 1959–64).

26. See, e.g., Bertrand de Jouvenel, *On Power* (New York, 1948).

27. This list, together with the eight omissions noted (Australia, Canada, Germany,
    Israel, Japan, New Zealand, United Kingdom, United States), corresponds to
    the one I gave in *A World of Nations*, pp. 290ff., with the following exceptions:
    Greece has been omitted because democracy was superseded by a military

coup in 1967; Mexico was omitted because, on second thought, I do not believe that it meets the criterion of a government based on "three or more consecutive, popular, and competitive elections"—the problems of course being the severe de facto restrictions on competition; Turkey and Venezuela have been added because they now have begun to meet the criterion.

28. For a recent, lucid restatement of the rationale for such models or ideal types, see T. H. Bottomore, *Elites and Societies* (New York, 1965), p. 32.

29. W. Ivor Jennings, *The Approach to Self-Government* (Cambridge, 1956), p. 56

30. Deutsch *Nationalism and Social Communication*; Deutsch et al., *Political Community and the North Atlantic Area.*

31. Rustow, A *World of Nations*, pp. 30ff. and *International Encyclopedia of the Social Sciences*, s.v. "Nation."

32. For developments in Sweden see Rustow, *The Politics of Compromise: A Study of Parties and Cabinet Government in Sweden* (Princeton, 1955), Chs.1–3. and Douglas A. Verney, *Parliamentary Reform in Sweden, 1866–1921* (Oxford, 1957). On Turkey see Ward and Rustow and the following essays by Rustow: "Politics and Islam in Turkey," in R. N. Frye, ed. *Islam and the West* (The Hague, 1957), pp. 69–107; "Turkey: The Tradition of Modernity," In Lucian W. Pye and Verba, eds. *Political Culture and Political Development* (Princeton, 1965), pp. 171–198; "The Development of Parties in Turkey," in Joseph LaPalombara and Myron Weiner, eds. *Political Parties and Political Development* (Princeton, 1966), pp. 107–133; and "Politics and Development Policy," in F. C. Shorter, ed. *Four Studies in the Economic Development of Turkey* (London, 1967), pp. 5–31.

33. James Bryce, *Modern Democracies* (London, 1921), vol. 2, p. 602.

34. Albert O. Hirschman, *Journeys Toward Progress* (New York, 1963), pp. 6ff.

35. Ibid., and Hirschman, *The Strategy of Economic Development* (New Haven, 1958) and Hirschman, "Obstacles to Development: A Classification and a Quasi-Vanishing Act," *Economic Development and Cultural Change*, XllI (July 1965), 385–393.

36. Dahl et al., *Political Opposition in Western Democracies*, p. 397.

37. Mary Parker Follett, *The New State* (New York, 1918), and *Creative Experience* (New York, 1924); Lewis A. Coser, *The Function of Social Conflict* (Glencoe, 1956), p. 121 and passim. A widespread contrary position has recently been restated by Edward Shils, who writes in reference to Lebanon: "Civility will not be strengthened by crisis. It can only grow slowly and in a calm atmosphere. The growth of civility is a necessary condition for Lebanon's development . . . into a genuinely democratic system" (in Binder et al., *Politics in Lebanon*, p. 10). I find it hard to think of situations where there have been any notable advances in either civility or democracy except as the result of crisis.

38. Dahl et al., *Political Oppositions in Western Democracies*, p. xi.

39.  Rustow, *The Politics of Compromise*, p. 69.
40.  Binder, ed. *Politics in Lebanon*.
41.  Barrington Moore, Jr., *Social Origins of Dictatorship and Democracy* (Boston, 1966). p. 3
42.  Festinger, *A Theory of Cognitive Dissonance*.
43.  The contrast emerges implicitly from the country studies in Dahl, ed. *Political Opposition in Western Democracies*.
44.  Rustow, *Politics of Compromise*, p. 231.
45.  Crick, *In Defence of Politics*, p. 24.

# 3 Constitutions, The Federalist Papers, and the Transition to Democracy

*Irving Leonard Markovitz*

In reconsidering his essay, "Transitions to Democracy," two decades later, Dankwart Rustow offered the modest assessment that "my article has been widely quoted in the growing political science literature; yet, rereading it in the light of current events, it is obvious that the model needs to be modified and expanded."[1] Rustow went on to declare that in his earlier model of transitions he had concentrated on countries that had well established political institutions such as Britain and Sweden. Now, he would pay more attention to, among other things, "the constitutional provisions which make for parliamentary, presidential, or mixed systems."[2]

Constitution-making is among the most important of emerging nations' legislative concerns. The disintegration of the Soviet Union and the withdrawal of military regimes from active involvement in the forefront of politics in Asia, Africa, and Latin America have all added to the flood of constitutional instruments. Lawyers, politicians, and political scientists have hailed the present moment as the new era of constitution-writing. Constitution writers in large numbers ply their trade in the new republics of Central and Eastern Europe. From Poland to South Africa to Canada artful composers strive to revise contentious constitutional amendments. They write mightily and they write long: 150 pages for South Africa's constitution, 200 pages for Brazil, more than 500 for India.[3]

New regimes and democratic governments produce so many constitutions because so many "basic laws" do not last; constitutions too frequently

fall into the category of periodical literature. The United States Constitution—only ten pages long—is anomalous not only in its brevity, but in its
longevity; it is now the oldest written constitution in the world.

Rather than ask "Why has the American Constitution endured?" in this
essay I am concerned with Rustow's questions of how constitutional forms
can ease and smooth the transition to democracy. I discuss how some of the
founders of the American system went about thinking of what they wanted
to do which was, not to draw a few lines on parchment, but to intertwine
state and society. My analysis of how the Federalist authors went about constructing a new government brings me into some conflict with Rustow's
concept of the transition to democracy, especially his insistence on the prerequisite of a single background condition, national unity. Since Rustow's
original model required only this one prerequisite of national unity, it might
appear ungenerous to take issue with so limited a stipulation. This would
be particularly the case when Rustow explains: "It simply means that the
vast majority of citizens in a democracy-to-be must have no doubt or mental
reservations as to which political community they belong to."[4] Rustow,
however, goes on to say that "This excludes situations of latent secession, as
in the late Habsburg and Ottoman Empires or in many African states
today."[5]

I will argue that these states should not be automatically excluded on the
basis of what is an arbitrary criterion. The experience of the United States
as well as that of modern African states would tell us that the achievement
of unity is not a once and for all thing, but a process over time. Rustow
rightly rejects those theorists who insist on preconditions of democracy, e.g.,
high levels of economic development, and also those who insist on a prior
consensus either on fundamentals or on the rules of the game. As he put it,
"consensus on fundamentals is an implausible precondition. A people who
were not in conflict about some rather fundamental matters would have
little need to devise democracy's elaborate rules for conflict resolution."[6] But
the same is true for the background condition of national unity. Creation of
national identity is an ever changing process that requires a period of a
testing of the waters by those who are still not confident in their newly
emerging sense of national commitment.

Rustow is certainly correct when he says: "new issues will always emerge
and new conflicts threaten the newly won agreements. The characteristic
procedures of democracy include campaign oratory, the election of candidates, parliamentary divisions, votes of confidence and of censure—a host

of devices, in short, for expressing conflict and thereby resolving it."[7] So too are constitutions, devices *par excellence* for the resolution of old and ever new conflicts. They are as much snares as process, or—more to our point— snares in their processes.

## The Limits of Constitutions as Guarantors of Stability and Democracy

In offering the following reflections on constitutions as trap and process, I would like to begin by lowering expectations about what constitutions can accomplish in the transition to democracy. Social scientists as far apart ideologically and politically as Barrington Moore and Samuel Huntington, for example, agree that social forces far stronger than parchment provide the matrix in which constitutions will or will not be effective. In his *The Third Wave: Democratization in the Late Twentieth Century*, Huntington quotes Moore's most succinct formulation: "No bourgeoisie, no democracy."[8] To be realistic in our discussion of constitutions, we must always take into account the historical context and the social and economic realities. A constitution by itself, no matter how ingeniously designed, no matter how universally admired, will neither create democracy nor limit authoritarian rule.

Constitutions and the institutions they envision *are* important. But they will not create miracles. To be effective, constitutions must relate organically to a society's realities; they must accommodate, even as they guide a country's basic interests. The most successful constitutions will intertwine civil society and the state in ways that are most helpful to "the permanent and aggregate interests of the community."[9]

Rustow argued that, in the "preparatory phase,"

> . . . against this single background condition [national unity], the dynamic process of democratization itself is set off by a prolonged and inconclusive political struggle. To give it those qualities, the protagonists must represent well entrenched forces (typically social classes), and the issues must have profound meaning to them.[10]

This complicates matters somewhat. Clearly other "ingredients are indispensable to the genesis of democracy" besides a sense of national unity: "For another, there must be entrenched and serious conflict. For a third there must be a conscious adoption of democratic rules. And, finally, both politicians and electorate must be habituated to these rules."[11] The question becomes how the constitution and the society interrelate.

## Transitions From Authoritarian Rule, and Problems of Democratic Consolidation

In analyzing democratic transitions in recent years, social scientists have distinguished between problems of "transitions from authoritarian rule"[12] and problems of "democratic consolidation."[13] The first transition focuses on what undermines an authoritarian regime and will bring it down. The second transition focuses on "the broader and more complicated process associated with the institutionalization of a new and democratic set of rules for political life."[14] We distinguish between the two periods to understand the most important moments through which states evolve in democratic transitions, and to better understand *why* transitions start.

After much debate, political scientists have reached an apparent broad consensus that conflicts within the authoritarian coalitions are the primary reason for the advent of a transition, which is then advanced through a "series of bargains" between state and opposition elites.[15] Scientific typologies are constructed around distinctions among different types of transitions—transitions through transaction, transitions through reform, transitions through regime defeat, transition through rupture, and transition through extrication.[16] Gerardo Munck has argued, however, that only a detailed knowledge of intra-elite, establishment elite-opposition elite, and elite-mass interaction in specific countries will provide the basis for understanding what actually happened in those instances.

Moreover, we cannot assume that "transitional democracies," that is transitional *from* authoritarian regimes, will automatically, naturally, or inevitably become "consolidated democracies." What is necessary is the institutionalization of a "new regime type," and what the pluralists have called "a new set of rules for the political game."[17] How can a new state consolidate a democratic system at least to the extent that the major actors in a society become willing to accept the rules, to work within the new system for the advancement of their interests?

We still do not know enough about the circumstances under which political actors have the power to break free of supposedly deterministic forces to create their own society. We do, however, know that "institutional settings" are crucial elements in this process. What I would like to do, therefore, in the rest of this essay is to explore some of those elements that went into a constitution that seems to have been, by the measurement at least of time, effective.

## Background

The *Federalist Papers* consisted of a series of 85 essays written between 1787 and 1788 by James Madison, Alexander Hamilton, and John Jay. The essays appeared as paid advertisements in the newspapers of New York, sandwiched between advertisements for alcohol and tobacco. Their purpose was to convince the limited electorate of New York to vote for the new Constitution.

The Federalists considered the government under the first American Constitution, the Articles of Confederation, to be a failure. Adopted by the Continental Congress on November 15, 1777 and ratified in 1781, the Articles provided for a loose federal union, or as Article 3 put it, "A league of friendship for common defense." The government lacked a national executive; preserved most of the sovereignty and autonomy of each state; and had no power over individuals, either to tax or to raise an army. It could only request contributions from the states. The Federalists offered a far different alternative.[18]

Among the basic propositions found in the Federalist papers are the following: (1) Never trust those who tell you that "the people" should rule; (2) Since everybody will declare that "Democracy is a government of, by, and for the people," don't trust anyone; (3) Never believe "great men"; once in power they will, if left to their own devices, become corrupt; (4) Never believe anybody; human nature is inherently selfish and untrustworthy; (5) Society consists of multiple interests—all out for themselves; (6) Nevertheless—despite propositions 1 to 5—through what at the end of the eighteenth century was known as the new "science of politics," the Federalists were convinced, and sought to convince the public, that they could create a government so strong that it could guarantee stability, but so controlled that it would not threaten liberty.

## Keys to the New Constitutional Arrangements

Why did they think they would succeed? What did they think was the key to the new arrangement?

There were, in fact, three keys: (1) the Federalists brought civil society into the state, but did so in a calculated manner; (2) they gave an indirect answer to the question of what was the permanent and lasting good of the community, and that answer was that there was no defined substantive good, but that there was a process and a machinery, and *that* was what mattered; (3) although they never used the word "capitalism" (a word not even invented until the end of the nineteenth century), they assumed that most individuals' primary activities would take place outside the realm of the state. They envisaged, in other words, a strong state; but strong because it could be lean and mean, strong in limited areas for well-defined purposes.

They also counted on the patience of the people. They offered an implicit wager that if they could involve the factions of society in the process, if they could make that process important, then the process would be valued in itself. Their constitutionalism created a political culture of patience and forbearance.

This was not necessarily "good," which is why I present this inquiry as an analysis, not advocacy. I part company with those pluralists who have discussed the Constitution merely as a mechanism for the resolution of disputes among conflicting interest groups, or only as process not linked to substantive interests.[19] Among the substantive interests that the Federalists incorporated into the body of the Constitution, and that already had considerable protection in the laws of the states, as well as in the English common law, were: (1) the integrity, that is, the preservation of the power, of the state governments; (2) a limited franchise that made political participation, voting and office-holding difficult; and (3) the protection of property. None of these interests were made the subject of absolute injunctions or prohibitions. Everything could be changed. However, the Federalist linked *their* interests to the processes that *they* laid out in ways that still affect policy in contemporary politics. (That it is still difficult for a modern president to pass a coherent program was illustrated, for example, before the elections of 1994 when a minority of Republicans in the Senate used the filibuster to prevent the passage of President Clinton's health care and economic recovery programs.)

The problems that the Federalists faced differed, obviously, from those that face Ethiopia, Eritrea, and other developing countries today: those enormous issues of nationalities, of autonomous cultures, of the need for immediate universal franchise, of the necessity of rapid economic development. And yet, there is a family resemblance. The American colonies at the time were poor. Europeans, the British in particular, considered the Americans to be backward, and living conditions to be primitive. The Americans, they said, did not have a civilization, and certainly not one that they could call their own. (In 1954, Max Lerner offered a course at Brandeis University called "America as a Civilization." When he published a book with the same title, critics hailed his courage in acclaiming the existence of a unique *American* civilization.) The system of government proposed by the Federalists then offered few programs and little immediate gratification. It lowered expectations about what government would offer in the short term. However, despite the obvious materialist and other gender, religious and racial biases of the Federalists, their system did offer something of possibly more importance: hope and a promise about the future.

## Direct Action for the Dominant Class

For the elite and for the dominant bourgeoisie, the government *did* offer immediate programs. Under Alexander Hamilton as Secretary of the Treasury, the first American administration's action agenda included the assumption of all debt obligations of the previous government; a national bank; a mint; a standard currency; protective tariffs for infant industries; a unified currency; subsidies for business. This program met a real need in responding to the aspirations of a politically organized and militant, self-conscious and aware class.

For the mass of the farmers and town workers, for the slaves and women, for those without property and education, for those who did not know what or how to ask, the constitution offered an opening. The constitution offered a legal path for political participation for those of still dawning self-consciousness. The Federalists feared anarchy more than anything else, even foreign invasion. At least two of the "founding fathers," Gouverneur Morris and Alexander Hamilton, had their houses attacked by the "mob"; others had their carriages stoned; their lives threatened; their "honor" called into question. They feared the "people." And so they created channels to contain discontent. They wanted to keep "the people" off the streets, and they did this by getting them into the voting booths.[20] However, by opening the door of electoral participation, they created a new definition of equality, and they established a new standard of fairness.

"Equality" would be determined by who had the right to participate in the electoral system. The system as it then existed was obviously unequal and the procedures were blatantly unfair. This was true for both office-holders and candidates for office, and for electors. Whole categories of voters— slaves, women, the unpropertied and uneducated—were automatically excluded. The fight became one to "equalize" procedures and electoral opportunities. As Harvey Mansfield put it, this democracy forced society to substitute an indirect question for a direct one.[21] The question became, not "What has government done for us?"; but "Has the government provided fair procedures? Have the means for the selection of the government been proper?" If so, then the people can have no complaint because their rights have been safeguarded. So long as they have had the opportunity to have "input into the system," moreover, the responsibility for the outcomes is "on their heads." They had their chance. If the properly chosen representatives create policies not of their liking, it is the fault of the people. And the remedy is also at hand: at the next election, the people can choose other representatives. They have the ability to turn out of office "the rascals," and to pursue their interest with other persons. "Equality" of social condition could be sought by the people if that is their wish, and they have the opportunity to do so. But if they are frustrated in this pursuit, they have only themselves, not their government, to blame.

Built into this system, then, is also a time perspective that looks "to the long run," to repeated and to future efforts. Those with thwarted aspirations will have their day. What they must do is go back to the "grass roots" and organize. But the discontented must organize not to overthrow the government or to change the basic institutions of the state. They must organize to win the next, and the next, and the next of many elections. This is how to create a culture of the long view and of vast horizons.

Voting studies by contemporary political scientists have confirmed what the Federalist authors intuitively knew: most people, most of the time, simply want to mind their own business; they want to be left alone. All that most people, most of the time, ask of government is the hope of improvement, sometime, not always *now*, and even more surprising, not even always for themselves. If they can be reasonably assured that the life-chances of their children will be better, the majority of people, most of the time, will tolerate great abuse from the social order.[22] The best way to create this faith, this long-range perspective, this culture of hope and optimism, is to bring the people into the system, to interrelate government and society.

How was all of this to be done? What is the evidence from the *Federalist Papers* for these propositions?[23]

## Appeals to the People and National Unity

Publius appealed to the people and alleged national unity, but feared the one and knew that the other did not exist. Rather than assume the existence of national unity as a "background factor" or a prerequisite for their new democracy, as Rustow's thesis would warrant, they were confident that their new system would manufacture what did not in fact exist.

In Federalist Paper No.1,[24] Alexander Hamilton begins by addressing the people of the state of New York to tell them that they are called upon to deliberate on a new Constitution for the United States, and that "nothing less than the existence of the Union, the safety and welfare of the parts of which it is composed, the fate of an empire in many respects the most interesting in the world," are at stake.[25] Even in the first paragraph of the first paper, however, Hamilton equivocates and qualifies his appeal to the people, when he says: "It has been *frequently remarked* that it *seems* to have been reserved to the people of this country, *by their conduct and example*, to decide the important question, whether societies of men are really capable or not of establishing good government from reflection and choice, or whether they are forever destined to depend for their political constitutions on accident or force."[26]

John Jay also begins with flattery of the "people" in Federalist Paper 2, especially in his declaration of national unity. He surely stretched the truth when he expressed his pleasure that Providence has given "this one con-nected country to one united people—a people descended from the same

ancestors, speaking the same language, professing the same religion, at-
tached to the same principles of government, very similar in their manners
and customs . . . ."[27] Nothing could have been further from the truth, even
if one takes into account the flush of enthusiasm that came from the rebels'
victory in their struggle with Great Britain (and forget for the moment the
quarter of the population that fled to Canada, Great Britain, or abroad, and
the probable majority which did not share Publius's perspectives). Well-
founded fear of domestic insurrection, as the Whiskey rebellion of Western
Pennsylvania and Shays's rebellion of Western Massachusetts demonstrated,
drove the early American political establishment in their constitutional la-
bors. They knew that they did not have national unity in any profound sense.
They sought to create it through their constitutional endeavors.

In the second paper, John Jay declares that "the people of America" are
called upon to decide one of the most important questions that ever engaged
their attention. He then immediately demands that since "Nothing is more
certain than the indispensable necessity of government," "the people must
cede to it some of their natural rights . . . "[28] In Federalist 3, Jay lays out the
need for a strong central government because of the danger to the preservation of peace and tranquility ostensibly from "foreign arms and influence,
as from dangers of the *like kind* (Jay's emphasis) arising from domestic
causes."[29] Under guise of worrying about foreign invasions, Jay clearly laid
out what for him and his fellows was the much greater danger, one stemming
from a lack of national unity. What Jay worried about, in his words and in
his emphasis, was a *"disunited* America."[30] He worried about "direct and
unlax violence" and about unjust wars: "Such violences are more frequently
occasioned by the passions and interests of a part than of a whole, of one or
two States than of the Union."[31]

Providing for "the safety" of the people is the first great objective of government. While external aggression would be a natural fear for those who
had just fought for their independence from Great Britain, by Federalist 3,
clearly the danger to "peace and tranquility" "arising from *domestic* causes"
is the great concern of the Federalists.[32] Hamilton forthrightly declares: "A
firm Union will be of the utmost moment to the peace and liberty of the
States as *a barrier against domestic faction and insurrection.*"[33]

While constantly alleging that "the people are the only legitimate fountain of power"[34], the Federalists' fear of the people was so great that all of
Federalist 49 is devoted to explaining why nobody in his or her right mind
would trust the people, or think of continuously appealing to their judgment.

There were "insuperable objections against the proposed recurrence to the people." Among those objections were that: "The reason of man, like man himself, is timid and cautious when left alone, and acquires firmness and confidence in proportion to the number with which it is associated." They didn't trust the "public," (a word of then recent appearance) because they feared its "passion." They warned: "The danger of disturbing the public tranquility by interesting too strongly the public passions is a still more serious objection against a frequent reference of constitutional questions to the decision of the whole society."[35]

## The Majority as a Faction

The Federalist authors, however, did not merely fear the "people" as a great beast. They feared government by the majority. James Madison begins that most famous of the Federalist Papers, No. 10, by arguing that: "Among the numerous advantages promised by a well constructed Union, none deserves to be more accurately developed than its tendency to break and control the violence of faction."[36] The Federalists *fulminate* against the "violence" of faction. The factions that really worry them are those consisting of the majority of the people. Madison defines faction in this way:

"By a faction I understand a number of citizens whether amounting to *a majority* or minority of the whole who are unified and actuated by some common impulse of passion, or of interest, adverse to the rights of other citizens, or to the permanent and aggregate interests of the community."[37]

In the same paper Madison states that "our governments are too unstable, that the public good is disregarded in the conflict of rival parties, and that measures are too often decided, not according to the rules of justice and the rights of the minor party, but by *the superior force of an interested and overbearing majority*."[38]

So what did they propose to do about it?

## The Nature of Man

The Federalists' beliefs about basic human nature complicated their task. They were challenged by those who maintained that because Americans were one people (as they had themselves proclaimed), they had no motive in fighting each other and therefore no need of a strong central government. Hamilton replied:

> A man must be far gone in Utopian speculations who can seriously doubt that if these states should either be wholly disunited, or only united in partial confederacies, the subdivisions into which they might be thrown would have frequent and violent contests with each other. To presume a want of motives for such contests as an argument against their existence would be to forget that men are ambitious, vindictive, and rapacious.[39]

If the ordinary run of mankind could not be trusted, perhaps the rare, extraordinary individual, the "great man" merited confidence. After all, most Americans admired General George Washington. His most ardent followers had demanded that instead of an elected president, a grateful citizenry should crown him emperor. These partisans of Washington had gone so far as to proscribe the proper ceremony, including the stipulation of a robe of ermine.[40]

This was an age that admired the Classical Period of Greece of the fifth century B.C. The "beau ideal" of the framers was the Athenian statesman. They considered, therefore, the greatest man of all time to be Pericles, lawgiver and leader of Athens at the height of the polis' power.

## What Does Hamilton Tell us About Pericles?

"The celebrated Pericles,"

in compliance with the resentment of a prostitute, at the expense of much of the blood and treasure of his countrymen, attacked, vanquished and destroyed the city of the Samnians. The same man, stimulated by private pique against. . . . another nation of Greece, or to avoid a prosecution in which he was threatened as an accomplice in a supposed theft of statuary . . . or to get rid of the accusations prepared to be brought against him for dissipating the funds of the state in the purchase of popularity, or from a combination of all these causes, was the primitive author of that famous and fatal war, distinguished in the Grecian annals by the name of the Peloponnesian war; which, after various vicissitudes, intermissions, and renewals, terminated in the ruin of the Athenian commonwealth.[41]

If you can't trust Pericles, who can you trust? The answer is clear: no one. Especially to govern. As Madison observes, "in framing a government which is to be administered by men over men, the great difficulty lies in this: you must first enable the government to control the governed; and in the next place oblige it to control itself."[42]

## The New Science of Politics

How was this to be done? The Federalists harbored no doubt of their ability to create a stable, lasting, and even just government. They did not share Gramsci's dictum, "Pessimism of the intellect; optimism of the will." They radiated an optimism of both will and intellect.

Children of the Enlightenment, they were heirs of the French *Philosophes*. Voltaire, Diderot, and later Montesquieu adapted the perspectives of naturalists like Galileo and Isaac Newton who had, from the beginning of the seventeenth century, laid the foundations of modern science. These "Newtonian" scientists considered that the world could be steadily observed; that these observations could be reduced to a few knowable laws; and that these laws, when properly understood, could be used in ways that could manipulate nature; and that this manipulation would result in tremendous new levels of productivity.[43] That meant that humankind had a future of unlimited potentiality.

Mankind had only to reexamine all institutions, and to see them as they were, that is, without the prejudices of faith, or of interest, or of self-love. Their tool, taken from the scientists—and the Age made no distinction between physical and social science—was "Reason," written with a capital "R." The *philosophes*, adapting the Christian model, substituted for the belief that all persons had a spark of the divine in them, the faith that every person had within themselves the capacity to Reason, and to arrive at universally reasonable conclusions.

This is what Hamilton reflected in Federalist No. 9: "The science of politics, however, like most other sciences, has received great improvement. The efficacy of various principles is now well understood, which were either not known at all, or imperfectly known to the ancients."[44]

## No Paper Constitution; Not Merely Checks and Balances

After two World Wars, Freud, and the Atomic Bomb, we may well wonder at the naive optimism of the Founders. On at least one point, however, we may still take them seriously: on their insistence that they did not want to produce a paper, or as they put it, a "parchment" constitution. They were aware from their own study of constitutions that this was a possibility, and they determined to guard against it.

Now how did they propose to do this? In the way that we usually read the *Federalist Papers*, the answer is clear: through a system of checks and balances, a division of powers, and what turned out to be an independent judiciary. In Federalist No. 9, where they declare that they know new scientific principles, they begin with, as their examples:

> The regular distribution of power into distinct departments; the introduction of legislative balances and checks; the institution of courts composed of judges holding their offices during good behavior; the representation of the people in the legislature by deputies of their own election: these are wholly new discoveries, or have made their principle progress toward perfection in modern times.[45]

They also go on to explicitly acknowledge their intellectual debts for these ideas, especially to Montesquieu. Something, however, is missing. They say of these institutional arrangements: "They are means, and powerful means, by which the excellencies of republican government may be retained and its imperfections lessened or avoided."[46] And by saying these are "means," they imply that there are other means, and other considerations that may be *more* important. Indeed, they add one more element:

> To this catalogue of circumstances that tend to the amelioration of popular systems of civil government, I shall venture, however novel it may appear to some, to add one more, on a principle which has been

made the foundation of an objection to the new Constitution; I mean the Enlargement of the Orbit within which such systems are to revolve.[47]

Now what did they mean by this phrase "ENLARGEMENT OF THE ORBIT," which Hamilton set off by capital letters, something almost never done in the Papers, and which he introduced with apparent modesty but with the warning that this *was* something important, "*however novel it may appear to some.*"

Checks and balances and separation of powers were insufficient unless they organically grew, not merely out of *political* interests, but out of *social* and *economic* interest as well. Those who have not read Montesquieu carefully, Hamilton warns us, "seem not to have been apprised of the sentiments of that great man expressed *in another part of his work* (obviously the part that most of us would not have read where the truth of his message really is to be found), nor to have adverted to the consequences of the principle to which they subscribe with such ready acquiescence."[48] If you accept Montesquieu's principles we, and the country, will suffer terrible consequences.

Now this is not the "appreciation" of Montesquieu that we had expected from the Federalists. However, there is no mistake. Hamilton accuses him of having made distinctions "more subtle than accurate"[49] that have merely resulted in "the novel refinements of an erroneous theory."[50] But more than this, to accept the ideas of Montesquieu is to risk catastrophe. Hamilton lashes out at one who is supposed to be his compatriot in ideas with bitterness. Hamilton says of Montesquieu:

> If we therefore take his ideas on this point as the criterion of truth, we shall be driven to the alternative either of taking refuge at once in the arms of monarchy, or of splitting ourselves into an infinity of little, jealous, clashing, tumultuous commonwealths, the wretched nurseries of unceasing discord and the miserable objects of universal pity or contempt.[51]

What was the "point" that so concerned Hamilton? Montesquieu had erred, not so much in suggesting that "a confederacy" might sometimes be an acceptable form of government, as in recommending "a small extent for republics," that is, a small state, "far short of the limits of almost every one of these States." To be certain that the point be well comprehended, Hamilton went on: "Neither Virginia, Massachusetts, Pennsylvania, New York, North Carolina, nor Georgia can by any means be compared with the models from which he reasoned and to which the terms of his description apply."[52]

We cannot understand Hamilton's vehemence in rejecting Montesquieu's recommendation for small states as an ideal—an apparently reasonable suggestion—without reading Paper No. 9 in conjunction with Paper No. 10. Paper No. 10 appears to drop the subject of its predecessor and is written by Madison. It says nothing more about Montesquieu, and is about factions, but it is an example of how all the Federalist authors agreed on fundamentals.[53]

Madison unhesitatingly continues Hamilton's key theme: a large state is essential for liberty. Why? Because of the many factions it contains. Factions cannot be eliminated; only their effects can be controlled. By whom? Only by other factions. This was an essential key to the genius of the Federalists' system. They turned what appeared to be an insurmountable barrier to good and limited government into the foundation of democracy's survival and existence. They said, "let faction combat faction." But there had to be a lot of factions in existence in society for this to happen. Otherwise, if a majority steadily fought a minority, the majority would prevail.[54]

In insisting that checks and balances had to exist in society, the Federalists went beyond Montesquieu whom, they argued, could not have properly understood that formal legal and institutional arrangements require a societal basis; otherwise he would not have recommended small states where homogeneity would make restraints on power more difficult.

## Bringing Society Into the State

The Federalists went beyond Montesquieu in another way, a way that is of particular relevance for those who talk about "civil society" today, and for those in modern Africa and other emerging societies who want a limited state that will leave private associations alone. The Federalists' message was: one could not trust the state to keep its hands off anything. The state must be made to curb itself. They could accomplish this only by bringing society itself into the state. Diverse elements in society must be properly seated in the state, that is, they must properly institutionalize those necessary factions.[55]

The identity of factions, their nature and composition, would vary over time. Reasonable persons could also differ over conceptions in the detail of the prescribed institutions. Drawing a line, however, or rather, *not* drawing a line between state and civil society was what really mattered. This is what was key. This is what Montesquieu did not understand. This is what those contemporary thinkers who see civil society apart from the state, or who hope or pray that the state will tolerate or leave alone civil society, do not understand. *The constitution lays down a process that results in the incorporation of factions into the institutionalized offices of the state.*

Madison explicitly links together state and civil society in one of the rare passages where he uses the term "civil society" when he tells us that: "Stability in government is essential to national character and to the advantages annexed to it, as well as to that repose and confidence in the minds of the people, which are among the chief blessings of civil society."[56] Stability, however, will not be achieved in a small society. In Federalist No. 10, Madison implicitly addresses Montesquieu when he says:

> . . . a small number of citizens, who assemble and administer the government in person, can admit of no cure for the mischief of faction. A common passion or interest will, in almost every case, be felt by a majority of the whole; a communication and concert results from the form of government itself; and there is nothing to check the inducements to sacrifice the weaker party or an obnoxious individual. Hence it is that such democracies have ever been spectacles of turbulence and contention; have ever been found incompatible with personal security or the rights of property; and have in general been as short in their lives as they have been violent in their deaths.[57]

What is to be done is clear: "Extend the sphere and you take in a greater variety of parties and interests; you make it less probable that a majority of the whole will have a common motive to invade the rights of other citizens; or if such a common motive exists, it will be more difficult for all who feel it to discover their own strength and to act in unison with each other."[58]

## Practical Difficulties in Creating A Constitution

The difficulties of constructing a self-limiting government are many. There are matters of expert knowledge; and there are matters of delicate balance and of judgment where reasonable persons can differ. "On comparing these vital ingredients with the vital principles of liberty," Madison tells us, in determining the length of the terms of officials, for example, and weighing the demands of stability with the need for keeping officials dependent, "we must perceive at once the difficulty of mingling them together in their due proportions." Madison goes on to say that: "Not less arduous must have been the task of marking the proper line of partition between the authority of the general and that of the State governments."[59] And constitution makers must also face matters of judgment and fact that require special empirical investigation when it comes to deciding on the exact division and separation of powers:

> When we pass from the works of nature, in which all the delineations are perfectly accurate and appear to be otherwise only from the imperfections of the eye which surveys them, to the institutions of man, in which the obscurity arises as well from the object itself as from the organ by which it is contemplated, we must perceive the necessity of moderating still further our expectations and hopes from the efforts of human sagacity. Experience has instructed us that no skill in the science of government has yet been able to discriminate and define, with sufficient certainty, its three great provinces—the legislative, executive, and judiciary; or even the privileges and powers of the different legislative branches. Questions daily occur in the course of practice which prove the obscurity which reigns in these subjects, and which puzzle the greatest adepts in political science.[60]

The work of the political scientists, Madison is telling us is difficult—but, not impossible. What they have is a method, and basic principles. If properly applied, this new "science of politics" can be effective, not just in the new American states, but anywhere, presumably including Ethiopia and Eritrea.

We know, for example, that: "The accumulation of all powers, legislative, executive, and judiciary, in the same hands, whether of one, a few, or many, and whether hereditary, self-appointed, or elective, may justly be pronounced the very definition of tyranny."[61] But we also know, and we must never forget, that legal scribbling is not the real world, and so: " . . . a mere demarcation on parchment of the constitutional limits of the several departments is not a sufficient guard against those encroachments which lead to a tyrannical concentration of all the powers of government in the same hands."[62]

So how and what will make this system work in the real world? Madison puts the question this way:

> To what expedient then, shall we finally resort, for maintaining in practice the necessary partition of power among the several departments as laid down in the Constitution? The only answer that can be given is that as all these exterior provisions are found to be inadequate the defect must be supplied, by so contriving the interior structure of the government as that its several constituent parts may, by their mutual relations, be the means of keeping each other in their proper places.[63]

A number of institutional practices and provisions can help keep "the several constituent parts" in "their proper places." Among these, " . . . it is evident that each department should have a will of its own; and consequently should be so constituted that the members of each should have as little agency as possible in the appointment of the members of the others."

The greatest safeguard of liberty, however, was to link together the office, the man and the social interest in a system where every office, person and social interest was pitted against every other; where the battles of society were brought into the halls of government, as well as into the smoke-filled rooms of politics. As Madison put it, "But the great security against a gradual concentration of the several powers in the same department consists in giving to those who administer each department the necessary constitutional means and personal motives to resist encroachments of the others."[64] Only one method could succeed in this fundamental endeavor. "Ambition must be made to counteract ambition. The interest of the man must be connected with the constitutional rights of the place."

To think, and to plan in this way, he admitted, was not very nice. Realistically, however, there was nothing else that one could do:

> It may be a reflection on human nature that such devices should be necessary to control the abuses of government. But what is government itself but the greatest of all reflections on human nature? If men were angels, no government would be necessary. If angels were to govern men, neither external nor internal controls on government would be

necessary. In framing a government which is to be administered by men over men, the great difficulty lies in this: you must first enable the government to control the governed; and in the next place oblige it to control itself.

The defects of human nature, therefore, *can* be remedied by constitutional arrangements:

> This policy of supplying, by opposite and rival interests, the defect of better motives, might be traced through the whole system of human affairs, private as well as public. We see it particularly displayed in all the subordinate distributions of power, where the constant aim is to divide and arrange the several offices in such a manner as that each may be a check on the other—that the private interest of every individual may be a sentinel over the public rights. These inventions of prudence cannot be less requisite in the distribution of the supreme powers of the State.[65]

Again, however, they warn that institutional restraints will carry and protect the union only to a limited degree. They can only work if they are properly anchored in society.

## "To Guard One Part of Society Against the Injustices of the Other Part"

Madison advises that: "It is of great importance in a republic not only to guard the society against the oppression of its rulers, but to guard one part of the society against the injustice of the other part." For Madison, society is a complex entity made up of many conflicting interests: "Different interests necessarily exist in different classes of citizens." Again, the biggest problem is the majority: "If a majority be united by a common interest, the rights of the minority will be insecure." Madison then expands upon the remedy:

> There are but two methods of providing against this evil: the one by creating a will in the community independent of the majority—that is, of the society itself; the other by comprehending in the society so

many separate descriptions of citizens as will render an unjust combination of a majority of the whole very improbable, if not impractible.

The first method has the danger that the dominant authority might act
arbitrarily. The second method is that of the federal republic of the United
States: "Whilst all authority in it will be derived from and dependent on the
society, the society itself will be broken into so many parts, interests and
classes of citizens, that the rights of individuals, or of the minority, will be
in little danger from interested combinations of the majority."[66] The "permanent and aggregate good of the community" is both ascertained through,
and constituted by, the process as well as the outcome of government.

## Justice Is the End of Civil Society

Madison has one argument left. And this is a surprise from one who has
all along maintained that selfishness and vindictiveness characterizes the
action of man. He appeals to "justice":

> Justice is the end of government. It is the end of civil society. It ever
> has been and ever will be pursued until it be obtained, or until liberty
> be lost in the pursuit. In a society under the forms of which the stronger
> faction can readily unite and oppress the weaker, anarchy may as truly
> be said to reign as in a state of nature, where the weaker individual is
> not secured against the violence of the stronger; and as, in the latter
> state, even the stronger individuals are prompted, by the uncertainty
> of their condition, to submit to a government which may protect the
> weak as well as themselves; so, in the former state, will the more pow-
> erful factions or parties be gradually induced, by a like motive, to wish
> for a government which will protect all parties, the weaker as well as
> the more powerful.[67]

Madison's plea is also a warning: it is a claim for higher principle—the
quest for justice. It is a declaration that protecting the weak, that apparently
altruistic actions, can also be self-protecting. And it is a testament that where
the weak are not made secure in a rightful pursuit, the strong will not be
secure either, and all will be threatened by the specter of a Hobbesian state

of nature. Thomas Hobbes did not have to look into his imagination to find "a state of nature" where the life of man was " solitary, poor, brutish, nasty, and short." Hobbes wrote of the horrors of early seventeenth century England decimated by the civil wars.

Is it too much to hope that the wars of genocide, of rape camps, of ethnic cleansing in Bosnia, and of the fratricide in Somalia might not have taught African and other intellectuals—those in power, and we who speak of constitutions—that we must seek to create secure places for all cultural and ethnic interests?

## Failures of the Federalists and of the Constitutional System

To speak of justice in contemporary academic and political circles is not modish. But those who would hold the American Constitution and the American system as a model for the emulation of others, must recognize certain lasting deficiencies of that system.

Without providing a full scale critique, one must at least point out that in one of the richest countries of the world children still go to bed hungry, thousands of the homeless beg in the streets, people of color lead lives below the national standard, the middle-class fears for its old-age, even the affluent worry about the affordability of medical care, and the top four percent of Americans earn as much in wages and salaries as the bottom fifty-one percent.[68] We must count substantial portions of whole generations as part of the social costs of "indirect" government.

These lesser and lessened Americans are not the result of "mistakes," accidents, or irrationalities. The "system" has produced these results. The Constitution guarantees only participation in process, and not concrete socially beneficial results; the structure is founded on limited interests; the political culture that encourages the deprived to think in terms of timespans that cannot meet their real needs.

Today, every international agency, every bank and lending agency, every government and transnational corporation, as well as most academic experts, urges governments of "emerging nations" to "restructure" and to cut back or eliminate every social program.

As the Federalists would say, "there is much truth in this advice." We should, however, remember that to postpone aiding those in need, for "the long run" is to sacrifice for some "higher purpose" that which may never be. Once communism called for sacrifice in the name of future generations. How ironic, and how equally believable, when capitalism demands the same.

## Conclusion

In creating a new democracy, the Federalists claimed that they sought justice as the end of the state and of civil society. They did not view the state and civil society as standing apart, or as in dangerous balance. Rather they envisaged, and they encouraged the intertwining of states and factions, of rapacious man and of balancing offices. They designed a system of government that made it difficult for "the people" to get anything done, that specially protected and furthered the interests of property. But they instituted a mechanism for participation that promoted a long view, that trapped the impatient, and that built hope in the future. These constitutional values were not directed to the issues of the elimination of abject poverty and extreme inequality except very indirectly.

This is my understanding of the transition to democracy laid down by the founding fathers and the American Constitution, and it was a mixed blessing.

Dankwart Rustow warned in his "Transitions to Democracy" that " . . . a country is likely to attain democracy not by copying the constitutional laws or parliamentary practices of some previous democracy, but rather by honestly facing up to its particular conflicts and by devising or adapting effective procedures for their accommodation."[69] For the "people" in Publius' sense, in the United States as well as in emerging nations, that still sounds like not only good analysis but excellent advice.

### NOTES

I wish to express my appreciation to John Bowman, Alem Habtu, Joseph S. Murphy, Larry Peterson, Solomon Resnik, Burton Zwiebach and Ruth Markovitz. They encouraged an earlier form of this effort, saved me from error, and contributed special insight. They also stopped their own work to accommodate my schedule.

An earlier version of this paper, "Constitutions, Civil Society, and the Federalist Papers" was presented to the symposium "On the Making of the New Ethiopian Constitution," sponsored by the Inter-African Group, Addis Ababa, Ethiopia, May

17–19, 1993. Another variation, focusing on "checks and balances" was given to the meeting on "Constitution and Constitution-making," sponsored by the Constitutional Commission of Eritrea, Asmara, Eritrea, January 7–11, 1995. I wish to thank the organizers of those conferences and especially Abdul Mohammad in Ethiopia, and Bereket Habte Selassie and Amare Tekle in Eritrea, for the opportunity to participate.

1. "Democracy In The Late Twentieth Century: Historic Perspectives on a Global Revolution," Unpublished paper presented to CUNY Political Science Conference, March 9, 1990, p. 5.

2. Ibid. Page 18.

3. See for example, Anthony DePalma, "Constitutions Are the New Writers' Market," *New York Times*, November 30, 1997. See also as examples of the vast current literature of this genre, *inter alia*, the following collections: Arend Lijphart and Carlos H. Waisman, eds., *Institutional Design in New Democracies* (Boulder: Westview Press, 1996); Mary Ellen Fischer, ed., *Establishing Democracies* (Boulder: Westview Press, 1996); Karol Edward Soltan and Stephen L. Elkin, eds., *The Constitution of Good Societies* (University Park: Pennsylvania State University Press, 1996); and Abdo I. Baaklini and Helen Desfosses, eds., *Designs for Democratic Stability: Studies in Viable Constitutionalism* (Armonk, N.Y.: M.E. Sharpe).

4. "Transitions to Democracy: Toward a Dynamic Model," *Comparative Politics* 2, no. 2 (April 1970) p. 350.

5. Rustow goes on to say: "National unity is listed as a background condition in the sense that it must precede all the other phases of democratization but that otherwise its timing is irrelevant. It may have been achieved in prehistoric times, as in Japan or Sweden; or it may have preceded the other phases by centuries, as in France, or by decades, as in Turkey." p. 351. One way or another, the unity must be there.

6. Ibid., p. 362.

7. Ibid., p. 363.

8. Samuel P. Huntington, *The Third Wave: Democratization in the Late Twentieth Century* (Norman: University of Oklahoma Press, 1991), p. 37. Cf. Barrington Moore, *Social Origins of Dictatorship and Democracy: Lord and Peasant in the Making of the Modern World* (Boston: Beacon Press, 1966). Neither Moore nor Huntington tells us what type of bourgeoisie, or how much of a bourgeoisie, is necessary for democracy to take root. For an exploration of these contentions see Irving Leonard Markovitz, *Power and Class in Africa* (Englewood Cliffs: Prentice-Hall, 1977); and especially the introduction, pp. 3–21, in *Studies in Power and Class in Africa* (New York: Oxford University Press), 1987.

9. Alexander Hamilton, James Madison and John Jay, *The Federalist Papers* (New York: New American Library, 1961), No. 10, p. 78.

10.  Rustow, p. 352.

11.  Ibid, p. 361.

12.  G. O'Donnell, P. Schmitter and L. Whitehead, eds., *Transitions from Authoritarian Rule: Prospects for Democracy* (Baltimore: The Johns Hopkins University Press), 4 vols.

13.  Scott Mainwaring, Guillermo O'Donnell and J. Samuel Valenzuela, eds., *Issues in Democratic Consolidation: The New South American Democracies in Comparative Perspective* (South Bend, Ind.: University of Notre Dame Press, 1992).

14.  Gerardo L. Munck, *Comparative Politics* 26 (April 1994), pp. 355–375. Cf. Adam Przeworski, *Democracy and the Market: Political and Economic Reforms in Eastern Europe and Latin America* (New York: Cambridge University Press, 1991).

15.  However, see further Huntington, *The Third Wave*, who offers an eclectic array of underlying causative factors for the transitions to democracy that range from issues of legitimacy to changing social structures to foreign interventions to demonstration effects of the experiences of other countries to changing religious doctrines. But Huntington also focuses on different types of elite interactions when it comes to understanding the advance of the transition. See especially Chapter 2.

16.  "Transition through transaction" and "transition through reform" are really different terms used by different social scientists to describe the same type of process of negotiated reform; "transition through rupture" and "transition through regime defeat" are also roughly equivalent terms used by different authors in the literature; "transition through extrication" is when the rulers of an authoritarian regime continue to hold enough power so that they can negotiate their retreat from power. Cf. Munck, "Democratic Transitions in Comparative Perspective," p. 359.

Still another regime transition modality is typified by a departing authoritarian elite which holds enough power to determine not merely their retreat from office, but policies and structures, and values of their "democratic" successors. We could, unfortunately call this "transition through perpetuation." Cf. J. Patrice McSherry, *Incomplete Transition: Military Power and Democracy in Argentina* (New York: St. Martin's Press, 1997), who does not use the term, but who shows how the military can maintain power through affecting basic organs of the state and society.

17.  Cf., e. g. Arthur Bentley, *The Process of Government* (Chicago: University of Chicago Press, 1908); and David Truman, *The Governmental Process* (New York: Knopf, 1951).

18.  Yet, a forceful opinion has maintained that the government under the Articles effectively served popular ends. Who needed a "strong" government? "Strong"

in terms of what? To put down debtors marching on banks, or small farmers protesting their mortgage foreclosures? When exactly this situation arose in Massachusetts, and the State government could not raise the funds for an army to put down Daniel Shays's rebellion in 1786–87, the propertied classes panicked. Cf. Herbert J. Storing, *What the Anti-Federalists Were For: The Political Thought of the Opponents of the Constitution* (Chicago: University of Chicago Press, 1981). This is the first volume, published separately, of Storing's mammoth, seven-volume, *The Complete Anti-Federalist*, published by the University of Chicago Press in 1977. For the argument of this paper, see especially Storing's second chapter, "The Small Republic," pp. 15–23. Cf. Merrill Jensen, *The Articles of Confederation* (Madison: University of Wisconsin Press, 1940).

Over the years, scholars have debated the extent to which the constitution was the result of economic interests of the dominant establishment. See, e. g., Charles Beard's classic case for *An Economic Interpretation of The Constitution* (New York: Macmillan, 1913; and Forrest McDonald's impressive refutation, *We, The People* (Chicago: University of Chicago Press, 1958).

19. See for example Seymour Martin Lipset, *Political Man* (Garden City: Doubleday, 1960); and *The First New Nation*. Cf. Robert Dahl, *Preface to Democratic Theory* (Chicago: University of Chicago Press, 1956).

20. But they did not *rush* to get the people onto the electoral rolls. Back in 1940, John Herman Randall,Jr. made the point very nicely when he said: "Benjamin Franklin, for example, believed that 'as to those who have no landed property then allowing them to vote for legislators is an impropriety'; and Hamilton thought that those who possessed no property could not rightly be regarded as having any will of their own. In not one of the new state constitutions was the vote granted to as much as half the adult male population. Office-holders were required to possess a considerable property in land: in Massachusetts the governor had to possess a freehold valued at £1000, in Maryland at £5000, and in South Carolina at £10,000.," *The Making of the Modern Mind* (Boston: Houghton Mifflin, p. 347).

When Alexander Hamilton returned to the private practice of the law in 1795, he exemplified the new alliance forged between legal and commercial interests. In one of his first new cases, Hamilton won the gigantic damage judgment of $120,000. Morton J. Horwitz, *The Transformation of American Law, 1780–1860* (Cambridge: Harvard University Press, 1977, p. 141).

21. Cf. Harvey C. Mansfield, "Hobbes and the Science of Indirect Government," *American Political Science Review* 65 (1) (1971), pp. 97–110.

22. Cf. Kay Lehman Schlozman and Sidney Verba, *Insult to Injury: Unemployment, Class, and Political Response* (Cambridge: Harvard University Press, 1979).

23. For a much more sanguine interpretation of the constitution and of the driving

forces behind the Federalists, see the 1993 Pulitzer Prize winning *The Radicalism of the American Revolution* by Gordon S. Wood (New York: Knopf, 1992). Wood denies that Madison and the Federalists were modern-day pluralists. Rather, he maintains—in direct conflict with the thesis of this paper—that: "They still clung to the republican ideal of an autonomous public authority that was different from the many interests of the society." And they were able to do so because they believed that the men holding office in the new national government would more apt to be "disinterested gentry who were supported by proprietary wealth and not involved in the interest mongering of the marketplace."p. 253.

The image that Wood conveys of America as a "prosperous, scrambling, enterprising society" consisting almost entirely of a "middle class" is jarring, not only because it downplays the existence and the condition of slaves, but also because of its failure to give significant weight to all of those class divisions in city, farm and the regions. See for example the essays in Alfred F. Young, ed., *The American Revolution: Explorations in the History of American Radicalism* (DeKalb: Northern University Press, 1976), especially the essays by Edward Countryman on "Northern Land Rioters," pp. 37–70; Rhys Isaac, "Popular Culture and the Revolution in Virginia," pp. 125–158; Dirk Hoerder, "Boston Leaders and Boston Crowds, 1765–1776," pp. 233–272; and Joan Hoff Wilson, "Women and the American Revolution," pp. 383–446.

24. Federalist 1, p. 33.
25. Ibid., p. 33.
26. Ibid., p. 33. Emphasis added.
27. Federalist 2, p. 38.
28. Federalist 2, p. 37.
29. Federalist 2, p. 42.
30. Federalist 2, p. 42.
31. Federalist 2, p. 44.
32. Federalist 3, p. 42.
33. Federalist 9, p. 71. Emphasis added. Hamilton goes on to say: "It is impossible to read the history of the petty republics of Greece and Italy without feeling sensations of horror and disgust at the distractions with which they were continuously agitated, and at the rapid succession of revolutions by which they were kept in a state of perpetual vibration between the extremes of tyranny and anarchy." p. 71.
34. Federalist 49, p. 313.
35. Federalist 49, p. 315.
36. Federalist 10, p. 77.
37. Federalist 10, p. 78.
38. Federalist 10, p. 77.

39. Federalist 6, p. 54.
40. Cf. Henry Steele Commager, *Majority Rule and Minority Rights* (New York: Oxford University Press, 1943).
41. Federalist 6, p. 55.
42. Federalist 51, p. 323.
43. See for example, W. W. Rostow, *The Stages of Economic Growth: A Non-Communist Manifesto* (New York: Cambridge University Press, 1960); Nathan Rosenberg and L. E. Birdzell, Jr., *How the West Grew Rich: The Economic Transformation of the Industrial World* (New York: Basic Books, 1986); Joel Mokyr, *The Lever of Riches: Technological Creativity and Economic Progress* (New York: Oxford University Press, 1990); Alfred W. Crosby, *The Measure of Reality: Quantification and Western Society, 1250–1600* (New York: Cambridge University Press, 1997).
44. Federalist 9, p. 72.
45. Federalist 9, p. 72.
46. Federalist 9, p. 73.
47. Federalist 9, p. 73.
48. Federalist 9, p. 73.
49. Federalist 9, p. 75.
50. Federalist 9, p. 76.
51. Federalist 9, p. 73.
52. Federalist 9, p. 73.
53. For a fascinating discussion of the "split personality" of Publius, and an effort to find a foreshadowing of the deep rupture that would reveal itself between Alexander Hamilton and James Madison see Stanley Elkins and Eric McKitrick, *The Age of Federalism: The Early American Republic, 1788–1800* (New York: Oxford University Press, 1993), pp. 103–105. Of main concern for this essay, Hamilton was clearly more ready to use force, if all else failed, to maintain national unity than Madison or Jay.
54. This was the vision of another student of the American system, and of the Federalist Papers, Alexis de Tocqueville. Despite his fulsome praise of their understanding of politics, de Tocqueville fundamentally disagreed with the faith of the Federalist authors in the ability of factions to check the rise of tyranny. His sense of terror stemming from "the inexorable spread of equality" made the tyranny of the majority, and then of one man, virtually unstoppable. Alexis de Tocqueville, *Democracy in America*, Vol. I (New York: Vintage).
55. In Federalist 10, Madison says: "The regulation of these various and interfering interests forms the principal task of modern legislation and *involves the spirit of party and faction in the necessary and ordinary operations of government.*" p. 79. Emphasis added.
56. Federalist 37, p. 226. Madison adopts, but subtly changes the Lockean use of

the term "civil society." Madison, like Locke, views civil society and the state as two separate entities, the dominant view by the middle of the eighteenth century. However, unlike Locke, who develops the theme of civil society and the state as *different* entities, the Federalists are preoccupied with their inter-relationships. This is a different theme than that of the mid-nineteenth century where, in Hegel, for example, the new theme is the state *against* civil society. The Federalists are particularly occupied with using the new "science of politics" to encourage and develop the intertwining of state and civil society. Cf. John Keane, ed., *Civil Society and the State* (London: Verso, 1988); Ellen Meikins Wood, "The Uses and Abuses of 'Civil Society,' " pp. 60–84, in Ralph Miliband, ed., *The Socialist Register, 1990* (New York: Monthly Review Press, 1991); and Irving Leonard Markovitz, "Uncivil Society: Capitalism and the State in Africa," in Nelson Kasfir, ed., *Civil Society and Democracy in Africa: Critical Perspectives* (London: Frank Cass, 1998), pp. 21–53.

57.  Federalist 10, p. 81.
58.  Federalist 10, p. 83.
59.  Federalist 37, p. 227.
60.  Federalist 37, p. 228.
61.  Federalist 47, p. 301. Here again is an instance where poor Montesquieu did not "get it." Madison declares: "From these facts, by which Montesquieu was guided, it may clearly be inferred that in saying 'There can be no liberty where the legislative and executive powers are united in the same person, or body of magistrates,' or, 'if the power of judging be not separated from the legislative and executive powers,' he did not mean that these departments ought to have no *partial agency* in, or no *control* over, the acts of each other. His meaning, as his own words import, and still more conclusively as illustrated by the ex-ample in his eye, can amount to no more than his, that where the *whole* power of one department is exercised by the same hands which possess the *whole* power of another department, the fundamental principles of a free constitution are subverted." Ibid, p. 302.
62.  Federalist 48, p. 313.
63.  Federalist 51, p. 320.
64.  Federalist 51, p. 321.
65.  Federalist 51, p. 322. Federalism, as provided by the Constitution, provides a particularly effective institutional check on power: "In the compound republic of America, the power surrendered by the people is first divided between two distinct governments, and then the portion allotted to each subdivided among distinct and separate departments. Hence a double security arises to the rights of the people. The different governments will control each other, at the same time that each will be controlled by itself" (Federalist 51, p. 323).
66.  Federalist 51, p. 324.

67. Federalist 51, pp. 324–25.
68. For statistics on income distribution, see, e. g., Donald L. Barlett and James B. Steele, *America What Went Wrong* (Kansas City: Andrews and McMeel, 1992), p. xi and passim.
69. Rustow, p. 354.

# 4 The Political Economy of Democratic Transitions

*Stephan Haggard and Robert R. Kaufman*

Dankwart A. Rustow's article on transitions to democracy has served as a reference point in current debates about democratization. Almost half of it was devoted to the rejection of "functional" approaches that focused on democracy's economic, sociopolitical, and psychological prerequisites. Given the prevalence of such explanations in 1970, Rustow's accent on agency, process, and bargaining broke new ground.[1]

However, the emphasis on process has come to exercise a disproportionate influence on the theoretical analysis of regime change, going far beyond what Rustow himself intended.[2] Though bargaining lies at the core of most contemporary models of regime change, they are typically weak in specifying the resources that contending parties bring to the negotiation and even the institutional stakes of the negotiation itself. Since these models are disconnected from underlying economic conditions and social forces, they miss important determinants of bargaining power as well as substantive concerns that drive parties to seek or oppose democratization in the first place.

Our approach to the political economy of democratic transitions, in contrast, stresses the effect of short-term economic conditions on the bargaining power and interests of incumbents and oppositions. Drawing on the experience of ten middle-income Latin American and Asian countries, it traces the impact of economic crises on the terms of transition and nature of new political alignments.

## Theories of Regime Change Since Rustow

The timing of Rustow's article was inauspicious. Published in 1970, "Transitions to Democracy" appeared just as the number of bureaucratic-authoritarian regimes in Latin America was cresting and as the authoritarian nature of politics in postcolonial Africa and Southeast Asia and the Middle East was becoming abundantly clear. Students of the Third World were preoccupied, not with democratization, but with the emergence of new types of authoritarian rule.

One interpretation of authoritarian rule derived from sociological and Marxist traditions and highlighted conflicts over capital accumulation and distribution. Its centerpiece was Guillermo O'Donnell's *Modernization and Bureaucratic Authoritarianism.*[3] O'Donnell's model was frequently summarized in terms of the relationship he posited between industrial deepening and the propensity to authoritarian rule. In fact, his analysis was far richer; it drew on a range of social conflicts and political strains that arise in the course of rapid economic transformation. Nonetheless, the broad causal thrust of O'Donnell's argument was clear: economic change generated social conflict, political polarization, and incentives for both militaries and key social groups to abandon democracy.

Meanwhile, Juan Linz and Alfred Stepan constructed an alternative approach from comparative studies of the breakdown of democracy in Europe and Latin America.[4] Their project, particularly Arturo Valenzuela's penetrating study of the Chilean coup of 1973, questioned the centrality of economic factors in democratic breakdowns.[5] Rather, electoral institutions and the strategies of politicians either amplified or muted tendencies toward polarization. Even when "structural strains" were implicated in authoritarian transitions, polarization was "generally a reflection of a failure of democratic leadership."[6]

The collapse of authoritarian rule in southern Europe and Latin America that began in the 1970s revived interest in regime transitions. A striking feature of the literature on this "third wave" of democratization has been the prominence of theories that mirror Rustow's emphasis on strategic interaction and negotiation.[7]

The most important contribution in this vein was O'Donnell and Schmitter's essay on "Tentative Conclusions about Uncertain Democracies" in the multivolume comparative project, *Transitions from Authoritarian Rule.*[8] For

O'Donnell and Schmitter, economic interests and political institutions important in the analysis of stable regimes were less relevant during democratic transitions. In the tradition of Rustow, Linz, and Stepan, they highlighted contingent choice, "the high degree of indeterminacy embedded in situations where unexpected events (*fortuna*), insufficient information, hurried and audacious choices, confusion about motives and interests, plasticity and even indefinition of political identities, as well as the talents of specific individuals (*virtù*) are frequently decisive in determining outcomes."[9]

If O'Donnell and Schmitter were sometimes extreme in embracing indeterminacy, they were not alone in placing strategic interaction at the heart of the transition process. Adam Przeworski used the distinction between hardliners and softliners to develop a game-theoretic model of authoritarian withdrawals.[10] Donald Share and Scott Mainwaring offered a "transactional" approach that drew on Linz's distinction between *reformas*, controlled by incumbent leaders, and ruptures, where oppositions are in command.[11] Huntington structured his discussion of transition paths similarly around the relative power of government and oppositions.[12] Giuseppe Di Palma characterized democratization as the "crafting" of alliances in the transition process.[13] Michael Burton, Richard Gunther, and John Higley attributed democratic consolidation to "elite settlements" and "elite convergence."[14]

To be sure, some scholars placed greater emphasis on structural and institutional constraints.[15] In an influential critique Terry Karl argued that the notion of contingent choice "has the danger of descending into excessive voluntarism if it is not explicitly placed within a framework of structural historical constraints."[16] Yet she built her own scheme around a typology of transition paths that rested ultimately on the possibilities of elite pact-making.

The specifics of these approaches differ in important respects, yet they converge on a number of points that can be traced directly to Rustow. First, the key actors in the transition process are political elites, whether in the government or opposition, not interest groups, mass organizations, social movements, or classes. Second, actors are typically defined in terms of their orientation toward regime change (hardliners-softliners, moderates-extremists) rather than by interests rooted in economic structures and conditions or institutional roles. Third, actors behave strategically; their actions are influenced by expectations concerning the behavior of allies and rivals. Finally, democratization is the outcome of explicit or implicit negotiation; new institutions are "bargains among self-interested politicians."[17]

The ascent of this line of thinking and the turn away from structuralism constitutes an interesting puzzle in the sociology of knowledge. They partly reflect broader theoretical trends in political science. Structural analyses emphasizing class conflict, dependency, and economic development often took a functionalist form and did not provide the microfoundations that were increasingly emphasized in the discipline. The transactional approach, by contrast, lent itself to game-theoretic treatment, exemplified in the simple yet compelling models of Adam Przeworski's *Democracy and the Market*.

The emphasis on bargaining also reflected political objectives. A focus on strategy allowed political science to address powerful actors in democratizing countries, to identify ways they might influence the process, and above all to avoid the pessimistic and self-fulfilling prophecies derived from relatively immutable economic and social constraints on democratic rule.

It is now impossible to formulate a theory of democratic transitions that does not explicitly address the strategic interactions between and within the government and opposition. However, the ascent of elite bargaining approaches has not been without costs. First, such theories require a clear specification of the preferences and capabilities of the players and delineation of the agenda over which they are negotiating. However, many models take the relative power, preferences, and agenda of the actors as given, as in Linz's distinction between *reforma* and *ruptura*, Huntington's "transformation," "transplacement," and "replacement," and Karl's "elite ascendant" and "mass ascendant" transitions. They fail to address the factors that shape actors' preferences and capabilities in the first place and the conditions under which they might change over time. The opportunity to link the strategic behavior of actors to underlying situational imperatives is foregone.

Second, some analyses use the relative power of the actors largely as an organizing device in describing how the negotiation of the transition process unfolds.[18] But the weight placed on transitional processes can be justified only if they provide some insight into the nature of the political bargain struck. O'Donnell and Schmitter make such a claim, for example, when they argue that explicit negotiations and pacts "enhance the probability that the process will lead to a viable political democracy," with the crucial corollary that a *ruptura pactada* will necessarily be economically and socially conservative.[19]

However, if all transitions imply an element of strategic interaction and negotiation, then the distinction between negotiated and nonnegotiated and between pacted and nonpacted transitions seems difficult to sustain. Strategic interaction occurs even in the most extreme cases of regime collapse. Totally defeated in war, the Japanese were nonetheless able to argue successfully for the retention of the emperor and subtly to sabotage some of the American occupiers' designs. The key issue concerns, not the presence of a negotiation process, but rather the resources contending parties bring to bear in influencing the terms of the transition and the stability of the outcome in the face of subsequent challenges.

Third, strategic approaches to transitions pay relatively little attention to economic variables and interests. This lacuna partly resulted from timing. Conclusions about the weak causal significance of economic factors were reached prior to the crises of the 1980s, well before the economic fallout of the debt crisis could be fully evaluated.[20]

Our approach to democratization draws on strategic analysis but focuses on the effects of economic conditions on the preferences, resources, and strategies of key political actors in the transition "game." We acknowledge at the outset that many factors contributed to the dramatic political transformations of the 1980s and 1990s: international diplomatic pressures stemming from the end of the Cold War, the "contagion effect" of transitions in neighboring countries, and structural changes associated with long-term economic development. Moreover, there is no simple relationship between economic crisis and regime change. Although the withdrawal of authoritarian rulers coincided with severe economic crises in a number of Latin American and eastern European countries, in other important instances authoritarian rulers survived crises or withdrew under favorable economic circumstances.

We do not, therefore, offer an economic theory of democratization. Rather, we focus on how economic conditions influence the timing and terms of democratic transitions and posttransition political alignments. We distinguish between transitions that occur in conjunction with economic crises and those that occur when economic performance is strong. Economic crises undermine the "authoritarian bargains" forged between rulers and key sociopolitical constituents and expose rulers to defection from within the business sector and protest "from below." The resulting isolation of incumbent authoritarian leaders tends to fragment the ruling elite further and reduce its capacity to negotiate favorable terms of exit. Posttransition democratic politics in these settings is characterized by low political barriers to entry and tendencies to political fragmentation.

Where authoritarian governments avoid or overcome crisis, rulers are likely to maintain backing from powerful segments of civil society even as they exit office. This support allows them to impose an institutional framework that not only maintains their prerogatives, but also favors their political allies' chances and restricts their opponents' freedom of maneuver.

## Political Responses to Economic Crises

The economic crises of the 1970s and 1980s had two defining characteristics. First, aggregate economic performance, as measured by declining growth and accelerating inflation, deteriorated. Not all groups lose during crises, and some may gain. However, the distributional politics of winners and losers is poorly understood. For incumbents, deteriorating economic performance cuts across social strata and affects a wide swath of society. Second, crises were not self-correcting. Temporary shocks may have triggered them, but existing policy approaches could not be sustained without continued economic deterioration. Crises thus raised the challenge of policy reform and the political costs it entailed.

Though crises are neither necessary nor sufficient to account for authoritarian withdrawal, poor economic performance reduces the bargaining power of authoritarian incumbents and increases the strength of oppositions. To understand why, we must consider the political interests, strategies, and capabilities of three sets of actors: private-sector business groups, middle-class and "popular sector" organizations, and the elites who control the state and the main instruments of coercion.

Deteriorating economic performance disrupts the political bargains rulers typically forge with segments of the private sector. The specific bases of business support depend, of course, on the structure of the economy and the political project of the government. Authoritarian regimes have rested on a wide variety of coalitional foundations, from agro-export elites to import-substituting industrialists and export-oriented manufacturing firms. But in all mixed economies the cooperation of some segments of the business elite is crucial for the stability of authoritarian rule.

The initial reactions of the private sector to economic decline typically focus on changes in specific policies or government personnel. But if private-sector actors lose confidence in the ability of the government to manage crises effectively, they can quickly recalculate the costs associated with democratization. They are particularly likely to do so when there are opportunities to ally with moderate oppositions.[21]

The defection of private sector groups substantially weakens the power of authoritarian incumbents. Not only can business groups play a direct organizational and financial role within the opposition, but the loss of confidence confronts the government with bleak prospects for future investment and growth.

Middle- and lower-income groups, by contrast, are more vulnerable to repression. Their primary political asset is the mobilization of protest: strikes, street demonstrations, and at times electoral campaigns. Strategically, these actions seek to render the polity ungovernable and to so raise the cost of coercion that authoritarian rulers are forced to make concessions.

Protest actions are frequently directed at political objectives, but it would be misleading to interpret their origins and popularity as purely political. Such movements often originate in reaction to economic grievances: unemployment; inflation in the prices of staples, fuel, and transportation; declining real wages. Crisis conditions provide oppositions with new opportunities to draw adherents by linking economic circumstances to the exclusionary nature of the political order.

Most crucial to the survival of authoritarian regimes is the continuing loyalty of the political-military elite itself: the heads of the armed forces, strategic segments of the state apparatus, and the individuals who control the machinery of the ruling party. The proximate cause for the exit of authoritarian regimes can almost always be found in splits within this elite.[22]

Divisions between "hardliners" and "softliners" are not necessarily linked directly to differences over economic policy. Yet even where economic crises are not the source of factional conflicts within the authoritarian elite, they are likely to exacerbate them. Economic downturns affect the loyalty of the political-military elite by reducing the ability of the government to deliver material benefits. Like any other component of the public sector, military establishments are threatened by adjustment measures, particularly budget cuts. The defection of private sector groups and the widening of popular sector protest also increase divisions over the costs and benefits of coercion, making the maintenance of a united authoritarian front problematic.

In noncrisis circumstances, incumbent authoritarian leaders tend to enjoy greater leverage. Some segments of business usually provide key support to military intervention; they are much less likely to be disaffected with the political status quo when economic performance is good. Good performance does not rule out purely political protest; the surge of middle class demonstrations in Korea in 1987 provides an example. Authoritarian regimes may fissure even in periods of robust economic performance. Nonetheless, other things being equal, authoritarian leaderships will enjoy wider support, less protest, and fewer internal divisions when economic performance is strong.

To explore these arguments empirically, we compare ten transitions from military rule. The six crisis transitions include Argentina (1983), Bolivia (1980), Uruguay (1985), the Philippines (1986), Brazil (1985), and Peru (1980). In Argentina, Bolivia, Uruguay, and the Philippines, regime transitions occurred during deep recessions; the Latin American countries also suffered from high inflation. Although the Brazilian and Peruvian transitions occurred during brief economic upswings, both countries had experienced extraordinarily severe shocks only a few years earlier. They continued to face severe inflation and a long agenda of unresolved adjustment challenges.

The four noncrisis transitions were Chile (1990), Korea (1986), Thailand (1983), and Turkey (1983). Authoritarian governments withdrew under a variety of international and domestic political pressures, but each transition occurred against the backdrop of successful economic reform, high rates of growth, and relative macroeconomic stability. These conditions help account for variations in the terms of the transition and the political alignments that emerged under new democratic regimes. The differences are summarized in table 4.1.

## The Consequences of Crisis I: The Terms of Transition

By the terms of transition, we refer to both the formal constitutional rules and the informal understandings that govern political contestation in the new democratic system. These terms include military prerogatives, rights of participation in political life, and the design of representative and decision-making institutions. They were not definitely settled at the time of transition in any of the cases we examined. Nevertheless, the terms of the transition exerted a powerful influence on subsequent political developments.

Differences between the crisis and noncrisis cases are evident in both the processes through which constitutional orders evolved and their substance. In three of the noncrisis transitions—Chile, Turkey, and Thailand—transitions occurred under constitutions written by the outgoing authoritarian government. Although incoming oppositions succeeded in negotiating some amendments, these constitutions provided the framework within which new

TABLE 4.1 The Political Economy of Democratic Transitions

|  | Crisis Transitions | Noncrisis Transitions |
|---|---|---|
| *Political challenges to authoritarian rule* | *Political demands overlap with:*<br>• Defection of business elites<br>• Economically motivated mass protest<br>• Divisions within government over resource distribution | • Primary political demands for liberalization |
| *Process of constitutional reform* | • Strong opposition influence | • Dominated by authoritarian incumbents |
| *Jurisdiction of elected officials* | • Elimination of authoritarian enclaves<br>• Reduced military prerogatives | • Significant authoritarian enclaves<br>• Substantial military prerogatives |
| *Barriers to political entry* | • Few limits on participation<br>• Permissive voter and party registration laws | • Conflicting limits on some political groups<br>• Restrictive voter and party registration laws |
| *Political cleavages and alignments* | • Weak constituent parties<br>• Fragmented and/or polarized party systems | • Strong constituent parties<br>• Centrist party systems |

democratic governments operated. In Korea, Chun Doo Hwan's government was forced to make substantial concessions to opposition demands after the mass protests of spring and summer 1987. Nonetheless, the constitution was written prior to the military's exit and reflected the military government's preferences in important ways.

In the crisis transitions, opposition forces wielded much greater influence. Their influence was particularly strong where authoritarian rule collapsed relatively swiftly, in the Philippines and Argentina; opposition politicians made institutional choices with little input from the outgoing government and returned to constitutions that predated authoritarian rule. In Bolivia, groups linked to the authoritarian order participated to a greater extent but yielded the presidency to a representative of the most militant opposition. In Uruguay, deteriorating economic conditions and mounting protest forced

the government to abandon constitutional demands that would have per-
petuated the influence of the military and its supporters within the traditional parties.

Authoritarian leaders and their allies had greater influence over the transition in Peru and Brazil, but opposition politicians still played a larger role
than in the noncrisis cases. In Peru, a new constitution was written while
the military remained in power, but it was drafted by a constitutional assembly dominated by opposition parties. In Brazil, the military maintained many
of its prerogatives in the 1988 constitution, but the congress that drafted the
constitution was elected a year after the transfer of authority to civilians.

The relative strength of authoritarian and opposition forces in the negotiation process influenced institutional design. Outgoing rulers typically had
two central objectives. First, they sought to preserve the military's organizational autonomy and to perpetuate their substantive policy agenda. The
principal means of accomplishing this objective were to create decision-
making enclaves, particularly with respect to the military establishment itself,
that were insulated from democratic oversight and control. Second, they
sought to impose limits on the opposition. Specific outcomes varied across
the cases, but with consistent differences between the crisis and noncrisis
transitions.

### Military Prerogatives and Decision-Making Enclaves

Outgoing rulers were most successful in creating "authoritarian enclaves"
in the noncrisis transitions. Thailand's incremental and ambiguous transition stands out in this respect. With respect to both budget and internal
organization, the military remained a power unto itself and, notwithstanding
the expansion of electoral politics, continued to be the dominant force
within the political system. Political power was exercised both formally,
through legally prescribed arrangements, and extraconstitutionally. The
1978 constitution provided for an appointed senate which initially exercised
veto power over decisions of the elected lower chamber. Thailand was also
the only noncrisis case where political authorities faced attempted coup.
Democracy was even reversed briefly in the early 1990s.[23]

In Latin America, the contrast between Chile and the other transitions
is especially sharp. In Chile, Pinochet remained at the helm of the armed

forces following the transition, and he and his appointees sat on the national security council.[24] Military budgets were sustained through a guaranteed share of revenues from copper exports. Such arrangements went well beyond the prerogatives maintained by the armed forces in Brazil, the most influential military establishment among the crisis transitions. Even more significant were the enclaves created within the broader political system. Before leaving office, Pinochet appointed supreme court justices, mayors, regional governors, and one-fifth of the new senate. These appointments provided the military's conservative allies with the power to block or delay the policies of the incoming democratic government.

The institutional arrangements imposed by the Turkish military paralleled those in Chile.[25] In 1983 it exercised a veto power over which parties could contest the transitional election and sought to maintain influence through control of the presidency and national security council. Though these restrictions did not go unchallenged, civilian oversight of the military was distinctively limited. Martial law remained in place in the southeast of the country, where the government became embroiled in an escalating conflict with Kurdish separatists.

In Korea, the scale of social protest against the regime was greater, and the position of the military correspondingly weaker, than in Thailand, Chile, and Turkey.[26] However, Roh Tae-woo was himself a military man and posed no threat to the institutional interests of the armed forces. Roh maintained the internal autonomy of the army and continued the security establishment's long history of domestic surveillance and intervention in politics.

In the crisis cases, economic difficulties and loss of support prevented outgoing rulers from preserving either military prerogatives or other means of political influence. The Argentine military, decisively defeated in the Malvinas/Falklands conflict, poses the starkest contrast with the noncrisis cases.[27] It could not avoid prosecution for human rights abuses and faced sharp reductions in financing and organizational autonomy. In Uruguay, Bolivia, and Peru, militaries also emerged in a weakened position, though in better circumstances than in Argentina.

Among the crisis transitions, the Brazilian and Philippine militaries stood at the opposite end of the spectrum from Argentina and were closest to the noncrisis cases in terms of political influence and prerogatives. In the Philippines, the new democratic government rapidly purged high-ranking Marcos cronies in the military. However, one faction of the army provided crucial support for the democratic transition. The military thus exercised considerable influence within the new democratic government.

The Brazilian military retained the most extensive institutional prerogatives of any military among the crisis transitions.[28] As in most of the other
crisis cases, however, it left office constrained by deep internal divisions and
a substantial decline in support among both politicians and the general
public. Compared to Chile, its influence on the new constitutional order
was far more limited.[29]

### Restrictions on Participation

The extent to which organized interests excluded under the authoritarian
order, particularly unions and political parties of the left, regained legal and
political opportunities to participate in politics also differed. In the noncrisis
cases, mechanisms of exclusion ranged from bans on political activity and
outright repression to more subtle manipulation of electoral laws. These
restraints were much less evident in the crisis cases.

Exclusionary mechanisms were most visible in Turkey. The government
used legal restrictions on Islamic fundamentalism and on criticism of its
Kurdish policies to intimidate and arrest journalists and politicians. The
main labor confederation remained banned after the transition in 1983, and
as late as 1986 the government indicted union activists for seeking to achieve
"the domination of one social class over another." The military also prohibited linkages between parties and interest groups and banned a number of
organizations outright.[30] High electoral thresholds limited the electoral prospects of smaller left parties.

In Korea, despite the explosion of labor and left militancy in 1987–88,
unions remained legally barred from participating in rallies and demonstrations, and their formal right to strike was severely constrained.[31] Bans on the
organizing role of leftist groups also remained in place. During the late 1980s
such provisions provided the legal basis for the government to limit debate
over crucial issues such as reunification and workers' rights.

In Chile, opposition politicians succeeded in lifting outright bans on the
participation of left parties and union activity. But these gains were possible
in part because the left agreed to abandon its historic antipathy to market-
oriented policies and to accept the leadership of the centrist Christian Democratic party in the anti-Pinochet coalition. Moreover, electoral laws pro-
mulgated under the old regime limited the opposition's gains. The
establishment of two-member congressional districts under a d'Hondt allo-

cation rule almost guaranteed that conservative parties would secure at least one seat in many districts.

Among the noncrisis cases, Thailand went furthest in eliminating substantial legal barriers to the formation of interest groups and the registration of political parties. But the preservation of nondemocratic enclaves and the continuing political power of the military reduced the real influence of the parties and the elected parliament more than in the other transitions.

In the crisis cases, the elimination of restrictions on labor and political groups was much more complete. Restrictive labor legislation remained on the books in some cases, but in contrast to Korea and Turkey unions rapidly regained the right to organize, strike, and press their political demands. In Bolivia, the union confederation functioned virtually as a cogovernment during the first five years of democratic rule, although it eventually suffered a harsh crackdown during the hyperinflation of 1985.

Differences between the two sets of cases could also be found in the design of voter and party registration laws. In general, authoritarian elites sought to limit the opportunities of small, ideologically defined parties by forcing them into broader party coalitions, as they did in Chile, Korea, and Turkey. In the crisis cases, opposition politicians pressed successfully for rules enabling them to respond to the pent-up demands of constituencies that had been systematically excluded under the old order. Changes generally involved lowering the voting age, easing registration procedures, and lifting restraints on party registration. In Bolivia, for example, extremely low thresholds for party registration led during the late 1970s to the appearance of some seventy new parties.[32] Comparable patterns are visible in the other crisis cases.

## The Consequences of Crises II: Political Cleavages and Alignments

Explaining political cleavages by reference to short-term economic conditions is more risky. Party systems and patterns of interest organization did not emerge *de novo* in response to economic crisis, and not all political alignments can be explained simply as the result of the new constitutional frameworks and electoral rules. In Latin America, most transitions were really redemocratizations. Consequently, the organization and behavior of political parties and interest groups reflected historical legacies to some extent.

Nonetheless, economic conditions combined with the institutional rules established at the time of the transition influenced the relative strength of contending political forces. In the crisis cases, economic distress and low barriers to political entry encouraged parties and interest groups on the left or with antimarket ideological orientations. Party systems were both more polarized and more fragmented. In the noncrisis cases, these centrifugal pressures were more likely to be contained, not only by restrictions imposed by outgoing military rulers, but also by the relative strength of political forces on the right.

One indicator of the balance of political power in the new democracies is the extent of support for "continuist" parties. Though these parties did not typically back the continuation of military rule, they supported the policy project of the *ancien régime*. In the noncrisis cases, such parties fared surprisingly well. In Korea, Roh Tae-woo garnered over a third of the vote in the 1986 presidential elections, and his party fared almost as well in the legislative elections. Moreover, the leader of one of the main opposition parities, Kim Jong-pil, was closely identified with Park Chung-hee, Chun Doo Hwan's authoritarian predecessor. In Chile's 1989 presidential race, candidates of the right garnered almost 45 percent of the vote, and the combined vote for rightist congressional candidates was more than double that obtained in 1973![33]

In Turkey and Thailand, outgoing rulers maintained more direct control over party competition, and it is thus more difficult to gauge the underlying electoral strength of continuist parties. Nevertheless, their strength initially appeared substantial in both countries. In Turkey, the military's preferred candidate was defeated, but the victor, Turgut Özal, had been the military's economic czar during the first two years of authoritarian rule. In Thailand, all the main parties maintained links to military factions. Those with the most explicit links to the restrictive political agenda of the military, the *Chart Thai* and the *Prakchacorn Thai* parties, received over a third of the popular vote in the 1983 parliamentary elections.

Candidates who campaigned on the achievements of the old regime fared worse in the crisis cases. As incumbent, Marcos garnered a surprising share of the popular vote in the Philippines' presidential election of 1986, but by the 1987 elections for the lower house no organized political force openly represented continuity with the Marcos era. In Uruguay's 1984 presidential election the candidate identified most closely with the military regime won less than 10 percent of the vote. In Argentina and Peru, right-wing political parties identified with the military's economic project gained only a handful of votes.

Continuist parties were larger in Bolivia and Brazil, but still weaker than in the noncrisis countries. In Bolivia, the ex-dictator Hugo Banzer eventually emerged as a major contender for the presidency, but in part because his party was not associated with the military factions that ruled so disastrously in the early 1980s. He gained less than 20 percent of the vote in the 1979 and 1980 elections and finished third behind candidates of the left and center.

In Brazil, where the president was chosen by an electoral college in 1985, surveys indicate that Paulo Maluf, the promilitary candidate, was supported by only 10 percent of the public. In the 1986 congressional election the conservative Liberal Front (PFL) won a respectable 24 percent of congressional seats, and the opposition PMDB itself incorporated many candidates and politicians who had formerly supported the military government. But they survived in large part because they joined the opposition. The loyalist faction (the PDS) won only about 7 percent of the vote, and even the combined PFL-PDS total was generally lower than support for continuist parties in the noncrisis cases.

The political isolation of continuist political forces in the crisis cases was mirrored in the relative strength of left and populist parties. In Bolivia, Peru, Brazil, and Uruguay, parties with socialist or Marxist ideologies reemerged as important political forces. In new congresses elected in Peru and Uruguay, the share of seats held by the socialist coalition in the legislature ranged from 14 to about 30 percent, well above the totals of their conservative competitors. In Bolivia, the left coalition backing Hernan Siles was the largest political force in the early 1980s. In Brazil, the left's electoral share was smaller, but two leftist politicians, Leonel Brizola and Luíz Inacio Lula da Silva, seriously contended the presidency.

The strength of antimarket parties in the crisis cases is still more impressive if we include nonsocialist populist or "movement" parties such as the Peronists in Argentina and the Apristas in Peru. The Peronists and Apristas had moved toward the right in terms of their relationship to other political forces, but each continued to make statist and distributive appeals that were sharply antithetical to market-oriented reforms.

In a number of crisis cases, the relative strength of the left was coupled with a fragmentation of the party system. At the onset of the democratic

period in Peru, Brazil, and Bolivia, there were between three and five effective parties,[34] but the data on the number of effective parties tend to under-
state the actual degree of fragmentation. The left coalitions in both Bolivia
and Peru were deeply divided internally, and a bitter internal power struggle
rent APRA in Peru following the death of its founder, Haya de la Torre, in
1980. In Brazil, parties were weakened internally by the federalist constitution and open list PR system, which reinforced the power of local bosses
and state governors at the expense of national party leaders. Thus, although
the opposition PMDB won a congressional majority in 1986, it began to
splinter rapidly in subsequent years.

Finally, although deeply rooted support for the Radicals and Peronists
appeared to create a durable two-party structure in Argentina, both parties
remained divided internally, and small provincial parties held the balance
of power in the legislature. These alignments created serious problems for
Alfonsín's administration, although over time both major parties moved toward the center with reference to economic reform issues.[35] Similar patterns
of internal party fragmentation and weak party discipline were visible in the
Philippines as well.

In the noncrisis cases, the left was weaker, the programmatic stance of
the opposition much more restrained, and the extent of electoral polarization
correspondingly limited. Chile provides the most dramatic instance. During
the early 1970s the historic antagonisms between the Marxist left and other
parties produced one of the most polarized party systems in the world.[36] By
the late 1980s, however, most of the left accepted market reforms and formed
part of a coalition headed by centrist Christian Democrats. During the 1990s
previously strong centrifugal pulls gave way to competition between this
moderate center-left bloc and the conservative right.

In Korea and Turkey, there were also significant constraints on electoral
polarization. Korea experienced bitter industrial conflicts and extensive mobilization by radical students following the transition, but party forces converged on the center-right. Closest to a left party in the 1987 and 1988
elections was Kim Dae Jung's Peace and Democracy Party (PDP), which
gained about 25 percent of the presidential vote. But to count Kim Dae
Jung's party as "leftist" is questionable, in part because its appeal was as much
regional as ideological, in part because its program was surprisingly conservative. Kim Young Sam's opposition had even shallower ideological roots,
and in 1990 he entered a grand conservative coalition with the ruling party.

Distributive and religious conflicts escalated in Turkey during the late

1980s as restraints on political contestation eased. However, in the early years of the transition constitutional restrictions and support for Özal constrained tendencies toward fragmentation and polarization. When bans on the left eased in the mid 1980s, two moderate social democratic parties, Ecevit's Social Democratic Party and the Social Democratic Populist Party, reentered the political fray. But their total vote share still lay well below support for ANAP and other conservative parties. Electoral thresholds and the disproportional nature of the modified PR system limited their parliamentary gains. In the municipal elections of 1989 and the general election of 1991 the biggest winners were the conservative opponents of ANAP, the True Path and Republican parties. ANAP finally fell to a coalition that included both the center-left SHP and the more conservative, rural-based True Path Party. The possibility of serious political polarization reemerged only in the mid 1990s with the strengthening of Islamicist parties.

Thailand stands out as the most fractionalized of the systems reviewed here. Despite a new electoral law in 1981 aimed at raising the threshold of representation, the number of effective parties in the 1983 legislature (5.7) was very high. But the apparently fragmented system masked a single dominant coalition composed of three major parties. None of the contenders could be considered leftist, Marxist, or populist.[37]

These cross-national differences in the terms of transition and the initial alignment of political forces were not immutable. In Argentina, the Philippines, Bolivia, and Uruguay, steps taken by new democratic governments to dismantle military prerogatives led to dangerous military backlashes, underlining the limits on the power of new democratic governments. Conversely, in all four noncrisis cases nondemocratic enclaves and unreformed military establishments provided continuing targets for political protest. Over time, the power of these authoritarian enclaves weakened, and restrictions on political participation fell. However, while political and institutional circumstances changed over time, they remained significant in the politics of the transition.

## Consequences of Crisis III: The Political Economy of New Democracies and "Consolidation"

The elite bargaining highlighted by Rustow is an element in all transitions. We have sought to place strategic interactions in their wider socioeconomic context. This context has important implications for the policy dilemmas, political institutions, and alignments of new democratic governments and the longer-term prospects for stability and "consolidation." We reject the argument that social interests and relations determine the prospects for democracy.[38] However, the opportunities for political elites to mobilize support or opposition in new democracies will continue to depend on how economic policy and performance affect both the level and distribution of income across different social groups, and economic performance over time can affect preferences about democratic institutions, particular policies, and incumbents.

First and most obviously, the economic legacy of authoritarian rule determines the policy agenda of its democratic successors. New democratic governments that come to power in the wake of crises confront a difficult and politically unpleasant menu of economic policy choices, at the center of which stand macroeconomic stabilization and wider structural adjustment measures.[39] The transition to democracy may in some respects ease the task of reform. New democratic leaders can exploit honeymoons and trade political gains for short-run economic losses; several eastern European countries provide examples of these opportunities. However, the transition itself raises expectations that government will respond to new political constituencies. Moreover, policy reform is difficult precisely because economic problems are more acute and demands for short-term economic relief more widespread.

Economic evidence from middle-income developing countries provides broad support for these expectations. Under the first democratic administrations in the crisis cases, average fiscal deficits were almost twice the level of the pretransition period, whereas in the noncrisis cases deficits remained comparatively low. Not coincidentally, four of the crisis cases—Argentina, Bolivia, Brazil, and Peru—experienced hyperinflation during their first democratic governments. Although new democratic governments inherited adverse economic conditions, policy actions and stalemates after the transition typically contributed to further economic deterioration.[40]

In the noncrisis transitions, new democratic governments faced a different, but not necessarily less serious, agenda of policy reforms. Macroeconomic adjustments were less pressing, but even the most economically successful authoritarian governments left problems of income inequality, poverty, and political exclusion that could become explosive under democratic rule.

Among the noncrisis transitions, the political consequences of a large "social deficit" were especially severe in Turkey, where real wages fell dramatically over the 1980s. By the early 1990s organized labor once again became militant, social and religious tensions escalated, and the political system was gripped by a new economic crisis. But industrial relations were also a source of social conflict in Korea, as were income and regional disparities in Thailand. These problems were not intractable; Chile's center-left government made impressive headway in reducing poverty while maintaining macroeconomic stability. Even there, however, the continuing power of interests linked to the old regime placed limits on the extent to which the new democratic government could address the economic demands of previously excluded social groups.

Transition paths also affect the evolution of the political institutions through which economic demands and policy dilemmas are addressed. In the noncrisis cases, new democratic governments had to contend with the persistence of nondemocratic enclaves, the continuing autonomy of the military establishment, and close links between political and business elites, all of which raised questions about the full extent of democratization. Yet efforts to address these political legacies in an aggressive fashion risked unraveling the democratic bargain, inviting right wing reprisals, and replaying coup poker.

The crisis cases exhibited a different set of institutional dilemmas. Pressing economic circumstances encouraged executives to concentrate authority, even to the extent of ruling by decree. This pattern has been particularly evident where very high inflation requires complex stabilization packages. Centrifugal forces within the party system, partly a result of crisis itself, increased the difficulty of sustaining electoral or legislative support and strengthened the incentives for executives to govern autocratically.

The normative evaluation of such behavior is tricky. In profound economic crises, particularly those characterized by hyperinflation, democratic institutions may well be undermined by the failure to take swift and effective action. However, the risks associated with *decretismo* are equally grave. In the absence of institutionalized consultation with legislators and interest groups, decisionmakers are deprived of feedback that may be essential in correcting mistakes. Reforms are more exposed to popular backlash and rapid reversal. *Decretismo* in economic policymaking also reinforces the broader tendency toward plebiscitarian rule—what Guillermo O'Donnell has called "delegative democracy."[41]

The connection between the politics of new democratic governments and the long-term prospects for consolidation must be approached with extreme caution. Consolidation will be affected by political choices that modify the initial terms of the transition, as well as international and domestic developments beyond the control of political leaders. Because of the many causal factors that impinge on the stability of democratic rule, we are skeptical of the emphasis placed on characteristics of the transition, such as pact-making, for the prospects of stable democratic rule.

Nonetheless, political and economic developments during the first two or three democratic governments constitute the first links in a longer causal chain that connects the initial transition to the elusive "long run." If our theory of authoritarian withdrawals has merit, it should also be applicable to the stability of democratic regimes: consolidation should hinge to some extent on the capacity to implement sustainable growth-oriented policies. Economic expansion eases the tradeoffs associated with the organization of political support, in part by permitting compensation to negatively affected groups. More generally, growth can reduce the conflicts resulting from inequality or other social cleavages and can thus mute the tendency to political alienation, polarization, and destabilizing social violence.[42]

During the 1980s and 1990s these expectations would appear to be undermined by the survival of the vast majority of new democratic governments even where economic performance was poor. Their survival was attributable to a variety of factors, including the collapse of the Soviet Union and a corresponding decline in western willingness to back anticommunist authoritarian governments. In many countries, the recent memory of inept and/or repressive authoritarian rule also helped to keep elected governments in place in the face of substantial economic adversity.

However, it is important to distinguish between regimes that are held in place by international pressures and short-term political contingencies and those that rest on widespread support. Democratic governments enjoy advantages that authoritarian regimes lack; disaffected citizens can replace incumbents rather than challenge the regime itself. However, the prolonged failure of elected governments to address effectively challenges of growth and equity are likely to erode the depth and stability of support for democracy.

It is easy to sketch a stylized model of countries experiencing prolonged economic distress, in which constitutional institutions are drained of their democratic content even in the absence of formal regime change. Such a cycle would begin with developments already evident in Peru, Brazil, Russia, and other developing and formerly socialist countries: an increase in political cynicism and apathy, decline in effective political participation, and inability of the political system to generate stable, representative ruling coalitions. Next, crime, civil violence, and organized revolutionary or antirevolutionary ("death squad") activity contribute to a gradual erosion of the substance of democratic rule through intermittent repression of opposition groups, emergency measures, and declining integrity of legal guarantees. Finally, though still short of a formal transition to authoritarian rule, electoral institutions are rendered a facade. Elected officials become subject to the veto power of military elites or little more than fronts for them.

In some cases, such as Peru, this process eventually reversed democracy, and we cannot rule out the possibility of setbacks elsewhere. A general erosion of faith in the capacity of democratic governments to manage the economy would increase the appeal of authoritarian solutions, among not only elites but also mass publics. Leaders or parties with plebiscitarian or openly authoritarian ambitions could be elected. Economic decline might also reverse democratization more indirectly by fostering increased crime, strikes, riots, civil violence, and polarization between extreme left and right groups. The deterioration of social order and increasing social polarization provide the classic justification for military intervention. Where support for authoritarian rule is absent, the state could collapse entirely as an organization with a credible claim to a monopoly of force.

In short, economic policy and performance will condition the future of democracy as they did the transitions.

### NOTES

This article draws on Stephan Haggard and Robert Kaufman, *The Political Economy of Democratic Transitions* (Princeton: Princeton University Press, 1995), chs. 1, 4, 5, and 10. Our thanks to Richard Snyder for his comments on an earlier draft.

1. Dankwart A. Rustow, "Transitions to Democracy: Toward a Dynamic Model," *Comparative Politics* 2 (April 1970), pp. 337–63 [and reprinted in this volume].

2. Rustow did not reject the importance of social structural variables; indeed, he saw an increase in social polarization as a key antecedent to the emergence of democracy. Ibid., pp. 352–55.

3. Guillermo O'Donnell, *Modernization and Bureaucratic-Authoritarianism*, (Berkeley: Institute for International Studies, 1973), and the subtly different

"Reflections on the Patterns of Change in the Bureaucratic-Authoritarian Regimes in Latin America," *Latin American Research Review* 13 (1978), pp. 3–38. Also, David Collier, ed., *The New Authoritarianism in Latin America* (Princeton: Princeton University Press, 1979).

4.  Juan J. Linz and Alfred Stepan, eds., *The Breakdown of Democratic Regimes* (Baltimore: The Johns Hopkins University Press, 1978).

5.  Arturo Valenzuela, *The Breakdown of Democratic Regimes: Chile* (Baltimore: The Johns Hopkins University Press, 1978).

6.  Juan J. Linz, *The Breakdown of Democratic Regimes: Crisis, Breakdown, Reequilibration* (Baltimore: The Johns Hopkins University Press, 1978), p. ix.

7.  Samuel P. Huntington, *The Third Wave: Democratization in the Late Twentieth Century* (Norman: University of Oklahoma Press, 1991).

8.  Guillermo O'Donnell and Philippe C. Schmitter, "Tentative Conclusions about Uncertain Democracies," in Guillermo O'Donnell, Philippe C. Schmitter, and Laurence Whitehead, eds., *Transitions from Authoritarian Rule* (Baltimore: The Johns Hopkins University Press, 1986).

9.  Ibid.. p. 5.

10.  See Adam Przeworski, *Democracy and the Market: Political and Economic Reforms in Eastern Europe and Latin America* (New York: Cambridge University Press, 1991), ch. 2, and "Games of Transition," in Scott Mainwaring, Guillermo O'Donnell, and Samuel Valenzuela, eds., *Issues in Democratic Consolidation* (Notre Dame: University of Notre Dame Press, 1992).

11.  Donald Share and Scott Mainwaring, "Transitions through Transaction: Democratization in Brazil and Spain," in Wayne Selcher. ed., *Political Liberalization in Brazil: Dilemmas and Future Prospects* (Boulder: Westview Press, 1986).

12.  Huntington, *The Third Wave*, p. 107, ch. 3.

13.  Giuseppe Di Palma, *To Craft Democracies: An Essay on Democratic Transitions* (Berkeley: University of California Press. 1990).

14.  Michael G. Burton and John Higley, "Elite Settlements,' *American Sociological Review* 52 (1987), pp. 295–307; John Higley and Richard Gunther. eds., *Elites and Democratic Consolidation in Latin America and Southern Europe* (Cambridge: Cambridge University Press, 1992).

15.  See, for example, Dietrich Rueschemeyer, Evelyne Huber Stephens, and John D. Stephens, *Capitalist Development and Democracy* (Chicago: University of Chicago Press, 1992). On the impact of authoritarian institutions on democratization, see Karen Remmer, "Redemocratization and the Impact of Authoritarian Rule in Latin America," *Comparative Politics* 17 (April 1985).

16.  Terry Lynn Karl, "Dilemmas of Democratization in Latin America," *Comparative Politics* 23 (October 1990), pp. 1–22.

17.  Barbara Geddes, "New Democratic Institutions as Bargains Among Self-Inter-

ested Politicians," paper presented to the American Political Science Association meetings, Washington, D.C., 1990.

18. Huntington, for example, entitles chapter 3 "How: Processes of Democratization."

19. O'Donnell and Schmitter, "Tentative Conclusions," p. 39.

20. For example, the papers for O'Donnell, Schmitter, and Whitehead, eds., *Transitions from Authoritarian Rule*, were first presented in 1979–81 and updated only through 1984.

21. See Ernest Bartell and Leigh A. Payne, eds., *Business and Democracy in Latin America* (Pittsburgh: University of Pittsburgh Press, 1995); and Jeffry Frieden, *Debt, Development and Democracy: Modern Political Economy and Latin America* (Princeton: Princeton University Press, 1991).

22. O'Donnell and Schmitter, pp. 15–17; Przeworski, *Democracy and the Market*, pp. 51–94.

23. See, for example, Suchit Bungbankorn, *The Military in Thai Politics, 1981–86* (Singapore: Institute of Southeast Asian Studies, 1987); Chai-Anan Samudavanija and Sukhumbhand Paribatra, "Thailand: Liberalization Without Democracy," in James Morley, ed., *Driven by Growth: Political Change in the Asia-Pacific Region* (Armonk: M. E. Sharpe, 1993), pp. 128–34.

24. See David Pion-Berlin, "Crafting Allegiance: Civilian Control and the Armed Forces in Uruguay, Argentina, and Chile," unpublished ms.

25. See John H. McFadden, "Civil-Military Relations in the Third Turkish Republic," *Middle East Journal* 39 (Winter 1985), pp. 69–85; Henri J. Barkey, "Why Military Regimes Fail: the Perils of Transition," *Armed Forces and Society* 16 (Winter 1990), pp. 169–92.

26. See Chung-in Moon and Mun-Gu Kang, "Democratic Opening and Military Intervention in South Korea: Comparative Assessment and Implications," in James Cotton, ed., *Korean Politics in Transition* (New York: St. Martin's, forthcoming).

27. Alfred Stepan, *Rethinking Military Politics: Brazil and the Southern Cone* (Princeton: Princeton University Press, 1988), pp. 114–16.

28. Ibid., pp. 86–88.

29. See Bolivar Lamounier, "Brazil: Toward Parliamentarism?," in Juan J. Linz and Arturo Valenzuela, eds., *The Failure of Presidential Democracy: The Case of Latin America*, vol. 2 (Baltimore: The Johns Hopkins University Press, 1994), p. 205.

30. See Ergun Özbudun, "The Post-1980 Legal Framework for Interest Group Associations." in Metin Heper, ed., *Strong State and Economic Interest Groups: The Post-1980 Turkish Experience* (Berlin: Walter de Gruyter, 1991), pp. 41–54.

31. Asia Watch, *Retreat from Reform: Labor Rights and Freedom of Expression in South Korea* (New York: Asia Watch, 1989), pp. 7–26.

32. Eduardo A. Gamarra and James M. Malloy, "The Patrimonial Dynamics of Party Politics in Bolivia," in Scott Mainwaring and Timothy Scully, eds., *Building Democratic Institutions: Party Systems in Latin America* (Stanford: Stanford University Press, 1995), p. 412.

33. Timothy R. Scully, "Reconstituting Party Politics in Chile," in Scully and Mainwaring, eds., ibid., pp. 124–25.

34. See Markku Laakso and Rein Taagepera, "The Effective Number of Parties: A Measure with Application to Western Europe," *Comparative Political Studies* 12 (April 1979), pp. 3–27. For complete data, see Haggard and Kaufman, *The Political Economy of Democratic Transitions*, Table 4–3, pp. 140–47.

35. Ronald H. McDonald and J. Mark Ruhl, *Party Politics and Elections in Latin America* (Boulder. Westview Press, 1989), p. 161.

36. Valenzuela, *The Breakdown of Democracy*; Ruth Berins Collier and David Collier, *Shaping the Political Arena: Critical Junctures, the Labor Movement, and Regime Dynamics in Latin America* (Princeton: Princeton University Press, 1991).

37. Richard Doner and Anek Laothamatas, "The Political Economy of Adjustment in Thailand," in Stephan Haggard and Steven B. Webb, eds., *Voting for Reform: The Politics of Adjustment in New Democracies* (New York: Oxford University Press, 1994).

38. For political economy approaches to democratization, see Frieden, *Debt, Development, and Democracy*, and Rueschemeyer, Stephens, and Stephens, *Capitalist Development and Democracy*. Rueschemeyer, Stephens, and Stephens, pp. 12–39, provide a comprehensive review of the modernization literature on democratization. One issue we do not address is the role of ethnic homogeneity and heterogeneity in transition processes. See Donald Horowitz, *A Democratic South Africa? Constitutional Engineering in a Divided Society* (Berkeley: University of California Press, 1991).

39. See Stephan Haggard and Robert Kaufman, eds., *The Politics of Adjustment: International Constraints, Distributive Politics, and the State* (Princeton: Princeton University Press, 1992).

40. For further empirical detail, see Haggard and Kaufman, *The Political Economy of Democratic Transitions*, ch. 6.

41. Guillermo O'Donnell, "Delegative Democracy?," East-South Systems Transformation, University of Chicago, Working Paper No. 21; Luiz Carlos Bresser Pereira, José Maria Maravall, and Adam Przeworski, *Economic Reforms in New Democracies* (New York: Cambridge University Press, 1993), p. 208.

42. This supposition is implicit in quite contending theoretical approaches to social violence. For empirical tests and reviews, see William H. Flanigan and Edwin Fogelman, "Patterns of Political Violence in Comparative Historical Perspective," *Comparative Politics* 3 (October 1970), pp. 1–20; and Arthur A.

Goldsmith, "Does Political Stability Hinder Economic Development? Mancur Olson's Theory and the Third World," *Comparative Politics* 19 (July 1987), pp. 471–80. However, Olson argues that rapid growth can be destabilizing because it produces shifts in the relative position of different economic sectors and income groups. Mancur Olson, "Rapid Growth as a Destabilizing Force," *Journal of Economic History* 23 (December 1963), pp. 529–52.

# 5 Adding Collective Actors to Collective Outcomes: Labor and Recent Democratization in South America and Southern Europe

*Ruth Berins Collier and James Mahoney*

The study of late-twentieth-century democratic transitions has become a major topic in comparative politics, and one particular analytic framework, which gives primacy to elite strategic choice, has become virtually hegemonic.[1] Despite a number of critiques, this approach continues to shape scholarly understandings of the recent process of democratization. Yet a single framework cannot possibly embrace the whole panoply of issues raised by these transitions. An alternative line of analysis not easily accommodated within the dominant account is the role of collective actors. Contra the dominant paradigm, the present study explores the role of one particular collective actor, the organized labor movement, in recent democratic transitions in South America and southern Europe.

Focusing on collective action undertaken by unions and labor-affiliated parties, we argue that the labor movement often played an important role in recent transitions. Labor was not limited to an "indirect" role, in which protest around workplace demands was answered through cooptive inclusion in the electoral arena. Rather, the labor movement was one of the major actors in the political opposition, explicitly demanding a democratic regime. In some cases union-led protest for democracy contributed to a climate of ungovernability and delegitimation that led directly to a general destabilization of authoritarian regimes. Moreover, continual protest, rather than creating an authoritarian backlash, kept the transition moving forward. Finally, while the protest of other groups also put the regime on the defensive, labor-based organizations went further in two ways: they often won a place in the negotiations, and they expanded the scope of contestation in the successor regime.

The dominant paradigm has built upon the founding essay by O'Donnell and Schmitter, which emphasizes the role of leadership and elite interaction. While that essay suggests that "the greatest challenge to the transitional regime is likely to come from . . . the collective action of the working class," it also emphasizes the ephemeral nature of the "popular upsurge" and the subsequent "decline of the people."[2] Other comparative analyses and theoretical accounts, focusing more exclusively on elite interaction, have not picked up on this theme. This article argues that union-led protest was much more central to the democratization process than implied by an elite-centric perspective, which sees labor's role primarily as altering the strategic environment of elite negotiators and theoretically underrates the role of mass opposition, labor protest, and collective actors generally.

Three related points can be made about the overall perspective of this "transitions literature." First, it has emphasized leadership and crafting, thus signaling the importance of individual rather than collective actors. Second, it tends to define actors strategically (for example, hardliners and softliners) with respect to their position in the "transition game," thus sidelining questions about class-defined actors. Third, despite an emphasis on government-opposition negotiations, it has tended to be state-centric, thus subordinating social actors; scholars have tended to classify transitions either as initiated and to some degree controlled by incumbents or as resulting from regime collapse seen in terms of a state-centric image of implosions.[3] Therefore, the dominant framework is not very useful for present purposes because its basic theoretical assumptions and orienting concepts almost preclude the problematization of the labor movement and collective action in the first place.

Exploring five of the eleven recent South American and southern European transitions, those which have become particularly important points of reference in the literature, we elaborate two patterns of democratization that depart from the standard account (see table 5.1).

Both patterns suggest that the labor movement was more central to the politics of democratization than has been recognized and that its role often began earlier and continued to the end. The first pattern is the biggest departure in terms of the countries it groups together and the characterization of the transitions: in the pattern of destabilization/extrication, collective pro-

TABLE 5.1 Patterns of Democratization

|  | Destabilization/Extrication | Transition Game |
|---|---|---|
| *Authoritarian Incumbents* | No project; defensive exit | Limited democracy project; negotiated exit |
| *Labor Movement* | Destabilizes authoritarian regime; triggers transition | Derails incumbent project; advances transition |
| *Cases* | Spain 1977<br>Peru 1980<br>Argentina 1983 | Uruguay 1984<br>Brazil 1985 |

test, within which labor protest was prominent, destabilized and delegitimated the authoritarian regime. Authoritarian incumbents adopted no transition project prior to this destabilization, and, instead of elite negotiation, the transition is better characterized as forced retreat. In the second pattern, transition game, the incumbents adopted a legitimation project, but this project was derailed. Subsequently, collective protest, in which the labor movement had a prominent role, helped to reshape the transition and keep it moving forward. In both patterns, collective action secured the legalization of labor-affiliated parties, which otherwise might have fallen victim to elite negotiation.

The present analysis adopts a different temporal conceptualization from the prevailing framework, which starts with divisions in the state and ensuing rule changes. That conceptualization reinforces the emphasis on state and elite actors and effectively makes questions about the origins of state divisions exogenous. By contrast, this article explores the origins of these divisions. Furthermore, analyses within the dominant framework concentrate on the final stage of the transition. We see this stage as a closing end-game, necessarily dominated by elites establishing rules for the actual transfer of power and designing the institutions of new democracies. Our emphasis is again on an earlier period, on the decision of authoritarian actors to exit and on the effective ceding of control to opposition or elected authorities, even if the outgoing incumbents still attempt, sometimes successfully, to exert influence.

## Destabilization/ Extrication

In Peru, Argentina, and Spain, union-led protests were crucial in destabilizing authoritarianism and opening the way for democratization. Authoritarian incumbents had not formulated a reform project when labor took the
offensive in strikes and protests against the regime. Incumbents were unable
to ignore such opposition or formulate a response to these challenges. In
each case, the regime was destabilized, and incumbents made the decision
to relinquish power, clearly pursuing a defensive extrication in which the
goal was ultimately to step down and salvage whatever terms they could.
These terms varied. The Peruvian and particularly the Argentine military
incumbents came away with much less than the Spanish civilians, who were
able to transform themselves into democratic actors. In Peru, labor protest
propelled the regime into crisis, and following a successful general strike in
1977 the government moved quickly to announce elections for a constituent
assembly which assumed direction of the transition. In Argentina, the human rights movement helped galvanize opposition to authoritarianism. But
the issue of union power had divided the military from the beginning, and
labor protest was important in preventing the consolidation of the military
regime. With the failure of the Malvinas invasion, intended to forestall the
regime crisis, the government quickly called for the elections that marked
the regime transition. In Spain, labor protest produced a severe challenge
to the regime even before the death of Franco and undermined the initial
Francoist and post-Franco responses. Suárez then came to power and immediately built a consensus for a transition election. In all these cases, negotiations between the authoritarian government and the prodemocratic opposition parties continued after the extrication decision, and these
discussions included left and labor-affiliated parties.

### Peru

Unlike most cases, the authoritarian regime in Peru did not initially en-
gage in the systematic repression of labor.[4] Rather, during the government
of General Velasco (1968–1975) Peruvian authoritarianism had a distinctly
"populist" character in which labor organizing was strongly encouraged.
Nevertheless, by 1973 organized labor moved increasingly into opposition

*cooptation*

in conjunction with several factors—the onset of a severe economic down-turn, increasing attempts to replace the Communist-led union federation (CGTP) with a state-controlled one (CERP), and the grave illness of General Velasco. In that year strikes increased substantially (roughly double the average for the previous five years), creating a climate of instability and facilitating the fall of Velasco's government in August 1975.[5]

Under the subsequent government of Morales Bermúdez, state-labor relations quickly became antagonistic, and organized labor emerged as the major antiauthoritarian actor. The new administration moved sharply away from Velasco's populism, adopting antilabor policies and carrying out repression more characteristic of other authoritarian regimes. In the second half of 1976 the labor movement responded with a series of strikes, which symbolized a new posture of direct and confrontational opposition against the authoritarian regime.

The single most important event in triggering the transition of 1980 was the general strike of July 19, 1977 (the first since 1919 and the largest strike in Peru's history). This strike united nearly all trade union bodies and paralyzed industrial activity in Lima. In addition to workplace concerns, the strike demanded basic democratic freedoms. "The 1977 strike carried the unmistakable message that attempts by the military to slow or avoid a transfer of power to civilians would result in only greater turmoil that would further undermine the military's already weak credibility."[6] The general strike reflected labor's leadership of the antiauthoritarian opposition; other opposition groups generally mobilized later when they joined with unions to form a fractious coalition known as the "popular movement."

In the aftermath of the strike, members of the traditional political parties and economic elite argued that a return to democracy was necessary to restore political order and economic growth. Indeed, as a result of the strike "Morales Bermúdez was obligated to announce a timetable for the return to civilian rule."[7] In August 1977 the government lifted the state of emergency and announced constituent assembly elections for June 1978. Thus, the military decided to extricate itself and proceed with a transition. Until the assembly elections of June 1978, strikes and popular mobilization continued, including further general strikes in February, April, and May 1978.

During the final phase of transition, mobilization declined "because the assembly marked an important step in the military's road back to the barracks—the one aim which united the fragile coalition of groups which made up the 'popular movement.' "[8] Nevertheless, labor unions and labor-affiliated

parties continued to play a role. APRA, the party with historic ties to the
labor movement, won 35 percent of the vote to the constituent assembly.
More important, with the shift in partisan affiliation of the labor movement
that occurred during the military regime, the left won 33 percent. Further,
the constituent assembly solicited advice from many social groups, including
union leaders, and during this period the military government kept up con-
tacts with party leaders, especially APRA's but also including the left. In July
1979 all citizens over eighteen years of age were enfranchised, and elections
in May 1980 completed the transition.


## Argentina

While it is true that the democratic transition in Argentina in 1983 followed the regime's collapse after military defeat in the Falkland Islands/
Malvinas war, the standard characterization ignores the factors that brought
on the military expedition in the first place. The still-limited research on
this topic reveals two points at which labor may be interpreted as playing a
key role. First, labor protest contributed to the division in the military between hardliners and softliners which the invasion of the Malvinas was intended to overcome. Second, some analysts maintain that labor protest directly prompted the generals to carry out the Malvinas invasion. Either way,
evidence suggests that this military regime, like the one a decade earlier
(1966–1973), was destabilized by labor protest.[9]

The labor question had long been at the core of Argentine politics, and
it remained crucial throughout the period of military rule from 1976 to 1983.
The 1976 coup was itself partly a response to worker activism, and within a
month of coming to power the military government considered a new labor
law to deactivate the labor movement. Early military factionalism was closely
linked to divisions over how to handle the labor question. One faction favored a direct assault on unions, while another favored an older pattern of
state-labor relations in which labor moderation was bought with concessions
granting a still limited but more positive role for unions. Under the leadership of General Videla, the hardline faction emerged dominant within the
government and executed the harsh policies of political repression associated
with the "dirty war," a policy of economic liberalization that constituted an
attack on labor interests, and a labor law that has been described as com-
pleting the unprecedented onslaught against labor.[10]

Despite government repression, "defensive strikes" were mounted after the coup. While unions willing to cooperate with the military coalesced around the CNT, by early 1977 some unions formed the Commission of 25 to oppose the government and its project for a new labor law. In 1979 union opposition accelerated, starting with the first general strike under the military dictatorship. Centered primarily on wage policy, the strike did not yet constitute a pro-democratic movement. Soon after, however, in reaction to the new labor law, the labor movement united in the CUTA, which undertook overtly oppositional activities on multiple fronts. It announced a plan to fight the new law through "national plebiscites" in the workplace; it initiated contact with political parties, labor lawyers, and the ILO; and it developed its organization in regular labor groupings. Individual unions also stepped up their activity. Although the CUTA soon split, the oppositionist CGT "displayed growing boldness, worked to develop thicker organization networks through contact with various actors within society, and made direct calls for a change in labor policy and of the regime itself."[11] Thus, the unions took the lead in mobilizing opposition and attempting to coordinate other social sectors, at the same time that the political parties rejected the initiative and business groups were divided.

Open divisions within the ruling authoritarian regime emerged in this context of labor protest, accompanied by economic deterioration. With growing social instability, the succession to the presidency of the softliner General Viola in March 1981 became the focus for ideologically based antagonisms among top officers. The discontent of the navy was particularly pronounced since, in addition to having been cut out of "its turn" in the succession, it was identified with a hardline approach and opposed Viola, who favored a more pragmatic economic policy and more normalized relations with conciliatory unions.

Labor opposition contributed to Viola's inability to consolidate power. Initially divided over cooperation with Viola, the union movement reunited in an overtly oppositionist and prodemocratic stance when it became clear that Viola's promised conciliation would not be forthcoming. In July 1981, the CGT mounted another general strike, and under its leadership the opposition fostered a climate of instability and a sense "that civil society was getting out of control" so that opposition to Viola grew even within his own branch of the military.[12] On November 7, 1981, the CGT called another mass mobilization, and two days later Viola was forced to resign.

The removal of General Viola exposed deep divisions that compromised the military's institutional control of government. With the defeat of the softliners, the new president, General Galtieri, returned to a hardline authoritarian stance and launched the Malvinas invasion to placate the navy, which favored the venture.

According to the first argument, then "diverse views on how to deal with society produced internal divisions within the Armed Forces."[13] Labor's prodemocratic opposition prevented the military regime from consolidating power and led to its destabilization by reinforcing and intensifying splits within it, which the disastrous military adventure was intended to repair.

According to the second argument, labor protest directly prompted the decision of the generals to invade the Malvinas. As Ronaldo Munck put it, "the military adventure of the generals cannot be explained in purely 'military' terms. . . . It was the constant level of working-class resistance since 1976, which was moving from a defensive to an offensive phase by 1982, which alone explains [the] bizarre political gamble by the armed forces."[14]

Opposition and protest increased after the ouster of Viola. The CGT took steps to coordinate joint action with the parties, now organized in the *Multipartidaria*, and on March 30, 1982, along with human rights groups and political parties, it staged the largest demonstration since the 1976 coup. By this time "the CGT's massive demonstrations were threatening the stability of the government and appeared to have pushed the military rulers to take a desperate step . . . ."[15] Three days later, Argentina invaded the Malvinas islands. In this account, in order to shore up support in the face of the opposition's offensive, Galtieri activated plans for the invasion. By reviving a long-standing nationalist cause he hoped to rally the country behind the regime.[16]

In either interpretation, the invasion was a desperate move to preserve a regime already in deep trouble, and pressure from the CGT was, directly or at a step removed, a major source of the problem. The invasion was launched either to address splits within the military exacerbated by labor protest or to deal with the challenge of accelerating popular mobilization in opposition to the authoritarian regime in which the CGT played a central initiating and coordinating role.

The military gamble failed. Not only did Argentina lose the ensuing war against Britain, but the invasion failed to defuse labor protest. Though the labor movement supported the military campaign, it remained active in opposition to the regime throughout the war. By mid June 1982, with the loss of the war and ongoing massive mobilization, the discredited military quickly moved to extricate itself by installing a "caretaker" government and announcing that general elections would be held in October 1983.

The labor movement was an important player in the remaining phases of the transition. The interim government attempted to negotiate the military's extrication more extensively than is generally recognized, but three successive plans to shape the subsequent government were rejected by the *Multipartidaria*, in which the union movement was a prominent influence. Throughout, "the junta made a special effort to negotiate the transition with Peronist union leaders."[17] Though all these attempts came to naught, it is noteworthy that labor was the major interlocutor in these efforts. The victory of Raúl Alfonsín in the 1983 elections completed the transition.

## Spain

According to most authors, Spain is a prototypical case of democratization by elite negotiations.[18] The dominant interpretation of Spain sees the democratization process as beginning roughly with the death of Franco in November 1975 and points to adept elite leadership in the ensuing uncertain environment to explain successful democratization. Particularly important was the skill of regime moderates, most notably Adolfo Suárez, in pursuing democratic negotiations simultaneously with both the moderates from the "democratic opposition" and the continuistas of the Franco establishment. Further, by pursuing these negotiations and reforms incrementally, Suárez garnered support for this carefully crafted democratization.

This interpretation misses the crucial role played by labor.[19] First, by the early 1970s, even before the death of Franco, labor pressures for an end to authoritarian rule set off a deepening regime crisis. Second, dramatic labor protests undermined attempts to establish a system of "Francoism without Franco." Finally, once the regime was destabilized, elements of the labor movement helped define a more moderate opposition strategy that enabled Suárez to negotiate the final agreements leading up to the democratic elections of June 1977. As Maravall states:

> popular pressure "from below" played a crucial part in the transition, especially that coming from the workers' movement. It was a causal factor in the Francoist crisis, in the non-viability of any mere "liberalization" policy, in the willingness on the part of the "democratic

right" to negotiate the transition and carry through reform up to the point of breaking with Francoism, and in the initiative displayed by the Left up to the 1977 elections.[20]

The labor movement was in a unique position to open space within the authoritarian regime. In 1948 the Communist Party decided to use union elections to penetrate the official, corporative structure, eventually facilitating the emergence of the parallel, more oppositionist Workers' Commissions. In different but symbiotic ways, both the legal unions and illegal Commissions became important sites of opposition and channels for undermining authoritarianism. By the 1960s it was clear that the official unions were not functioning as integrative mechanisms; the Commissions mounted sustained working-class protest; and the per capita strike rate became one of the highest in Europe. Toward the end of the decade the labor movement's agenda increasingly turned from workplace demands to demands for broad political liberties. Its orientation also shifted toward mobilization aimed at toppling the regime; Communist Party and labor leaders began to discuss openly the possibility of a *ruptura democrática* (democratic rupture). With the failure of its labor project, the government was forced to choose between repression and democratic opening.

In part as a consequence of labor opposition, serious divisions emerged within the regime. Hardliners were initially dominant, and repression increased from 1967 to 1973. Franco decided to insure the future of authoritarianism through a Francoist monarchy with Juan Carlos as king. Yet repression was ineffectual in reducing social protest. During 1970 labor strikes rose to over 1,500,[21] nationalist terrorism also accelerated, and "the government had no political answer to this increasing level of conflict."[22] Softliners became increasingly vocal in pressing for a change of policy. In late 1972 and early 1973 Franco and his prime minister, Carrero Blanco, responded in speeches that suggested that some type of political opening would be forthcoming.

Sustained labor protest in 1973 helped keep the government on the defensive in search of a new formula for stability. After the assassination of Carrero Blanco in December 1973, Franco appointed a moderate, Carlos Arias Navarro, whose strategy was to establish a *dictablanda*, or softer dictatorship, but labor activism prevented its stabilization. Strikes increased dramatically under Arias to the largest number in Spanish history in 1974. The strike record was again broken in 1975. In reaction to this labor protest, the hardliners retrenched, favoring a severe crackdown and driving a deeper wedge in the regime. "When the news of Franco's illness broke . . . everything seemed to show that the regime was in crisis."[23] In the opening months of 1976 labor strikes and demonstrations once again reached unprecedented levels, but in the face of this offensive "the ministry remained impotent."[24] Labor protest thus undermined the strategy of limited liberalization pursued by Arias. When he resigned in July 1976, it had become clear that, "if a catastrophic clash between the irresistible force of the left and the immovable object of the right was to be avoided, it was essential that rapid progress be made to the introduction of democracy."[25]

By the time Suárez became prime minister, then, the labor movement had done much both to destabilize the authoritarian regime and to reject government attempts to respond in ways that fell short of democracy. It seemed clear that the government had to find some means of effecting a speedy transition. Suárez accomplished this task in about two months. He won the cabinet's approval of a transition project that committed the government to elections within a year. Within another two months, the project was approved by the *Cortes* (legislature).

These events are worth pondering. The task—and triumph—of Suárez, as many have emphasized, involved nothing less than convincing the *Cortes* to agree to its own replacement in a very short time. How was he successful? The key question is not whether Suárez was a skilled negotiator. Rather, can what he did be seen as an extrication? Did Suárez, in other words, negotiate an extrication, even though he did it very well, with ultimately positive implications for democratic consolidation? It is difficult to imagine that an entrenched *Cortes* would participate so quickly in its own demise without the high level of pressure of oppositional mobilization and regime crisis. Even analysts like Linz and Stepan, who emphasize the agency of Suárez, refer to the "fear of a vacuum of authority, of a sudden transfer of power to the then quite radical opposition forces," in prompting Suárez and the reformers to act.[26]

Beyond its role in provoking the transition, labor opposition also shaped the way it unfolded. Even before Suárez came to power, the democratic opposition, led by the Communist Party, affiliated trade unions, and the Socialist Party, recognized that it could not directly overthrow the government and abandoned the strategy of *ruptura democratica* in favor of *ruptura pactada* (negotiated rupture), which envisioned a provisional government and a constituent *Cortes* to determine the successor regime. The reform

project that Suárez proposed in October and that the *Cortes* passed in November 1976 paralleled this project by providing for the election of the
constituent assembly, but it rejected a provisional government. Once Suárez
engineered a consensus behind the transition project, the rest followed
quickly according to the adopted timetable. In June 1977 free elections were
held to choose the democratic *Cortes*, which wrote a constitution and provided the institutional structure of the new democracy.

Although in the final months of the transition labor and the left opposition lost power to the more moderate opposition, their role in bringing about
and shaping the transition should not be underestimated. They precipitated
the transition, and in many ways their *ruptura pactada* strategy gave the
transition its particular form. Indeed, discussions and negotiations took place
between the government and left parties, including the Communist Party,
which was legalized during the transition. The argument here is not that
labor single-handedly brought about the demise of authoritarianism or constructed the new democracy. Nor is it that labor was the most important of
an array of players (including industrialists, students, Basque and Catalan
nationalists, and the king). Nevertheless, labor exerted constant pressure on
the regime for about ten years, and this pressure continued during the years
of the transition itself. Despite the widely noted "moderation" of labor in
these years, Pérez-Díaz notes the "explosion" in the level of industrial conflict and collective action in 1976–79 and a rise in real wages at a rate almost
double the OECD average in 1973–79.[27] Certainly, Suárez used the legal
instruments of the Francoist system to bring about its liquidation and demonstrated impressive leadership skill in negotiating a broad consensus around
the transition. Yet to begin the story of Spanish democratization from this
point is to focus on the final step of a longer process and to miss the important role of labor. Labor protest destabilized the authoritarian regime,
made impossible a reform that stopped short of democratization, and thus
forced incumbents to undertake a rather speedy extrication.

## Transition Game

Two traits of the Uruguayan and Brazilian transitions more closely fit the
standard model. First, elite strategic games involved a protracted series of
moves and countermoves and formal and informal negotiations among military incumbents and party leaders. These strategic games arose in a particular
context in which from the very beginning the military sought legitimation

through a facade of civilian rule operating through chosen groups of politicians and a restricted electoral arena. These regimes thus embraced an
incumbent project which defined a game between government and leaders
of selected political parties, whether long-established (Uruguay) or newly
formed under government guidance (Brazil). Second, collective action by
labor organizations appeared relatively late in a larger process of civic acti-
vation and rejuvenation and followed the action of party leaders, who were
the first on the scene and figured centrally in the government's legitimation
project from the beginning.

Nevertheless, this account understates the role of mass popular opposition
in general and of labor protest in particular. Legitimation projects adopted
by both military governments were undermined by popular opposition expressed in the limited electoral arena. A 1980 plebiscite marked the first
failure of the government project of Uruguay, and opposition gains in the
1974 elections portended the failure of the government project in Brazil.
Henceforth both regimes were thrown on the defensive; incumbents contin-
ually scrambled to alter their project and change the rules of the political
game in the face of an opposition increasingly on the offensive. Given the
pattern and target of repression, the space for social movements, and particularly for the labor movement, opened later. Once it emerged, however,
labor activity was forceful in the final transition stage.

Furthermore, the activities of labor opposition undermined government
attempts to control and limit the party system, created room for the entry of
a political left, and were particularly important where formal (Uruguay) and
informal (Brazil) negotiations between government and major party leaders
could have led to an agreement to exclude left parties. Indeed, in both cases
the Communist party remained banned. Nevertheless, in Brazil labor protest
gave rise to a new socialist party based in the new union movement, and in
Uruguay the reconstitution of the labor movement and its protest activities
provided an outlet for the banned *Frente Amplio*, its participation in various
opposition fora, and finally its legalization and participation in the final
negotiations, thus allowing the stalled transition to proceed.

## Brazil

In Brazil, movement toward a democratic regime was initiated autono-
mously by the authoritarian incumbents, who came to power in a 1964
military coup.[28] At the onset the military sought legitimation through a con-

trolled two-party system operating in a very restricted electoral space. In 1974, after a more repressive interlude, military softliners regained the upper hand and during the presidency of General Geisel reinstituted a period of "decompression."

With decompression, leaders of the officially recognized opposition party found space for more autonomous action and made electoral gains in 1974 and again in 1976. With the failure to engineer a political opening that would favor the progovernment party and the rise of many groups in civil society calling for a democratic transition, the military closed congress and further manipulated the electoral law to reestablish some control.

At this point, in the late 1970s, the labor movement burst onto the political scene. The more limited process of liberalization was transformed into one of democratization, in which the party and electoral systems were opened. This process ultimately culminated in the (indirect) election of a civilian president in 1985. It is difficult to determine how decisive the activities of the labor movement were in these developments, given inroads already made by the opposition party and other social groups. Nevertheless, they fundamentally shaped the transition process.

Repressed following a 1968 strike, the labor movement developed a new form of resistance in the early 1970s. By 1978, especially in the multinational automobile plants, it crystallized in the new unionism, which "signaled the existence of massive, organized discontent with the regime, and . . . constituted powerful evidence that democratization was necessary to resolve the potential for social conflict."[29] The metalworkers' strike of 1978 spread to more than one-half million workers.[30] One of the largest strike waves in Brazilian history followed it in 1979, as over three million workers participated in more than one hundred strikes.[31]

This dramatic resurgence of the labor movement placed it at the forefront of a broad spectrum of social movements then emerging in opposition to the authoritarian regime. Though many of its actions began as worker demands, the protests quickly became more overtly political. Initially factory based, the movement led by labor spread in two complementary directions. The first went beyond the union sector to the larger working-class neighborhoods and communities, where labor protests won the active involvement and material support of church groups and the larger community. Second, the labor movement moved beyond narrower workers' issues to champion the demands and concerns of the lower classes more generally. Though many groups already expressed antiauthoritarian sentiment, the labor movement identified itself with a broad constituency and played an important role in building and leading a more unified, prodemocratic mass movement.[32] In addition, labor leaders became important national political figures who articulated broad political demands.

When the government, defensively scrambling to divide the Opposition, abandoned its two-party project, unions organized an avowedly socialist Workers' Party, further frustrating the government's attempt to exorcise the left. This party served as an "instrument of struggle for the conquest of political power" by embracing an overtly political strategy predicated on the attainment of a democratic regime.[33] Thus, labor leadership expanded from union-based activity not only to a broader social movement, but also to a political organization. By 1983 labor mobilization culminated in a strike of over three million workers, and the following year workers participated in a massive campaign for direct presidential elections. Though the campaign was not successful in its immediate goals, it helped deepen the succession crisis faced by the regime and force the government to allow an opposition victory when the electoral college chose the first civilian president in 1985.

Hence organized labor played an important role in the Brazilian transition. It provided more than the mass pressure used by traditional party leaders in pursuing their own strategies. Labor protest and mobilization were directly responsible for expanding political and electoral space to include a new force on the left and for securing the legality and participation of the union-based Brazilian Workers' Party.

## Uruguay

Uruguay's authoritarian regime did not originate in a definitive military coup but rather in a two-sided process in which democracy eroded and the military gradually increased its autonomy and took over as it conducted an "internal war" against urban guerrillas. The military-dominated regime thus continued to seek electoral legitimation and the collaboration of political parties. As in Brazil, the Uruguayan military committed itself to regularly scheduled elections and developed projects for a new regime. At the same time, the labor movement was an important prodemocratic actor in the transition process and figured prominently in the events leading up to the installation of a democratic regime in 1985.[34]

The "gradual coup" was completed by 1973, though the military initially continued to rule behind the civilian facade of the elected president and retained its commitment to holding the elections scheduled for 1976. As the elections approached, the military abandoned that commitment and devised a new plan for "limited redemocratization" under military control and created a civilian-military body charged with drafting a constitution, which would be submitted to a plebiscite in 1980.[35] When the plebiscite was held, voters defeated the constitution, throwing the government project off track. Once again relying on party collaboration, the military initiated conversations with the traditional parties and proposed a transition in 1985 according to a new constitution it would negotiate with the parties. To rehabilitate the parties, a new law, written in collaboration with party leaders, called for primary elections in 1982. The primaries dealt the military another defeat: instead of the intended purge of the parties in favor of the collaborating factions, factions less friendly to the government were victorious.

The following years have been analyzed in terms of the "coup poker" strategies of the parties, the alternating harder and softer lines of the government, and the moves and countermoves of an elite strategic game. With stops and starts, formal negotiations took place between the military and party leaders, culminating in the 1984 Naval Club Pact, signed by the participants, who in the end included the left parties except for the Communists. In accord with the agreements laid down in the pact, elections were held later that year, and a new democratic government took power in 1985.

This standard account misses an additional story from below in which the labor movement played an important part. That organized labor was an avid prodemocratic actor can be seen in its initial resistance. The day the military made the final move to assure its political control by closing the legislature in 1973, workers began a general strike against the dictatorship, thereby emerging as the only group to register its opposition publicly. For two weeks thousands of workers occupied factories, perpetrated acts of sabotage, and closed down the economy until the strike was broken. If the labor movement was not heard from in the following years, it was due to the ensuing repression in which unions were dismantled and many leaders were arrested or forced into exile.

Mass actors reemerged in connection with three developments. The first was the stunning defeat dealt the military in the 1980 plebiscite, not because of opposition parties, which hardly had an opportunity to mobilize, but because the electorate used the vote to reject the military's project. It has been suggested that, although unions were also severely repressed at the time, workers played an important clandestine role in mobilizing for the "no" victory.[36] Despite the appearance of "surrogates" for the exiled or imprisoned political leaders of the noncollaborating parties and factions, the plebiscite was clearly a case of mass action and victory from below.

Second, the outcome of the 1982 party primaries may have been significantly affected by union activity. A law of the previous year authorized unions at the enterprise level. Though the law was very restrictive, in a contested decision workers decided not to reject it but to use it both to organize openly and to gain some legal protection. From the outset, these enterprise unions had a democratic political program, so that the primaries took place in a period of increasing labor mobilization.

Third, and more definitively, the limited liberalization following the plebiscite created space for the opposition to mobilize. Along with the cooperativists, the union movement began to revive in 1982, first at the enterprise level and then at the national level when the Inter-Union Plenary of Workers (PIT) was formed. Linked with the grass roots, the PIT had a special capacity for mass mobilization. On May Day 1983 the PIT carried out the first major demonstration since 1973, attracting an estimated 100,000 to 200,000 people, and explicitly called for the immediate return of democratic liberties.[37] The May Day demonstration catapulted the PIT to the leadership of the social movement and, according to Caetano and Rilla, represented a qualitative change in the politics of transition.[38]

For the next year, collective actors, especially the PIT, set the pace and led the prodemocracy opposition. In the face of constant pressure from mass protest, the military was ultimately forced to retreat. In the beginning of 1983 the military attempted to write yet another new constitution, but by the end of the year important sectors of the military dropped the idea and began to focus instead on finding "the best exit."[39]

The general strike called by the PIT in January 1984 gave a decisive impetus to the military's retreat. Previously, it had responded to growing mobilization with increased repression. After the strike it lifted censorship and allowed the Communist leader of the left-wing *Frente Amplio* to return to the country. The strike also changed the relationship between the traditional parties and the social movement. Sanguinetti, the leader of the opposition faction of the Colorado Party, in effect apologized to the PIT for his party's opposition to the successful January strike and proposed a reorganization of the democratic opposition to coordinate the activities of the parties (including the left) and the PIT in a new *Multipartidaria*.

During the next months the *Multipartidaria* entered prenegotiations with the government, while it kept up the pressure by calling a series of symbolic one-day strikes. These strikes succeeded in pressuring the government to make concessions, including, at the end of July 1984, legalization of the *Frente Amplio* and its constituent parties, except for the Communist Party and the Tupamaros. Negotiations came to a rapid conclusion in the Naval Club Pact, signed in August, in which the military got very little (the most popular Blanco candidate as well as some Frentistas were excluded from running in the November transition elections). The PIT's protests were thus important not only in pushing the transition forward, but also in forming the *Multipartidaria* as a more inclusive democratic opposition that negotiated the end of authoritarianism.

## Conclusion

Although it would be wrong to treat labor organizations as the principal force behind democratization at the end of the twentieth century, the literature as a whole has erred in the other direction in portraying transitions as primarily an elite project, a conversation among gentlemen, with labor protest having relatively little consequence. It has done so even though case-study analyses by country experts have regularly pointed to the key role of collective action in general and labor protest in particular. Hence there is a disjuncture between the evidence presented in case-study material and the general interpretations offered in the literature on transitions.

Why have scholars who study transitions from a comparative theoretical perspective failed to recognize the importance of workers and other collective actors? Empirical oversight on the part of comparative theorists is not the reason. Our disagreement is not over the facts: we have relied on the same secondary literature as proponents of the dominant framework and, where relevant, have even used their own original research. Rather, we disagree over analytical framing. In necessarily privileging some facets of reality over others, frameworks can be useful in illuminating particular questions, but they should not be made hegemonic.

The original framework was appropriate in problematizing a leader-based strategy for achieving democratization. However, this framework does not travel well to other analytic concerns. When adopted more generally, it becomes a conceptualization of democratic transitions as fundamentally driven by and ultimately "about" intra-elite dynamics and politics within the state, while it ignores other important questions. Scholars working within the assumptions of the dominant framework lack the means to conceptualize the role of social opposition adequately, even when they clearly want to acknowledge its importance. Linz and Stepan, for example, acknowledge that Spanish political reform occurred in a "context of heightened societal pressure for, and expectations of, change" and that "popular pressure kept the transition going forward." Yet they resist situating the role of mass pressure and collective action theoretically on a level equal to elite negotiation and designate Spain "a 'regime initiated transition' although under the pressure of society."[40]

In sum, our analysis has supplemented the focus on elites with one on collective action by paying particular attention to the labor movement. In initial stages of democratization, labor mobilization in the pattern of destabilization/extrication contributed to divisions among authoritarian incumbents, who previously had no transitional project. During relatively early stages in the transitions game labor protest for democracy helped to derail the legitimation projects of incumbents.

In later stages of the transition labor mobilization had two effects. First, depending on the pattern, protest provoked or quickened the transition and kept it on track. These effects were the consequence of pressure exerted to the very end. Our case evidence thus calls into question the perspective that labor restraint during the final transition phase contributes to democracy by convincing elites that democracy can lead to social and political order, thereby facilitating elite negotiations.[41] In fact, unprecedented levels of labor mobilization occurred in Spain up through the elections of 1977; labor protest in Peru continued until the constituent assembly elections; the pressure of collective action, including labor protest, accelerated in Brazil in the final stage; and the labor movement in Uruguay continued to flex its muscles through a series of one-day strikes.

Second, mobilization and protest won labor-based parties a place among the negotiators and also in the successor regimes. The Peronists in Argentina, the Spanish Communist Party, the Peruvian left, and to some degree Uruguay's *Frente Amplio* all won such a place. Even in Brazil, where no negotiating role was attained, collective action underpinned the founding of the socialist Brazilian Workers' Party. The collective action of labor movements thus played a key democratic role not only in propelling a transition, but also in expanding political space and the scope of contestation in the new democratic regime.

NOTES

Ruth Berins Collier would like to acknowledge the support of the Center for Advanced Study in the Behavioral Sciences and the National Science Foundation (Grant No. SBR-9022192). The authors would also like to thank David Collier, Giuseppe Di Palma, Robert Fishman, Guillermo O'Donnell, Gabriela Ippolito-O'Donnell, and Philippe Schmitter for their comments.

1. The exemplar of this framework is Guillermo O'Donnell and Philippe C. Schmitter, *Transitions from Authoritarian Rule: Tentative Conclusions about Uncertain Democracies* (Baltimore: The Johns Hopkins University Press, 1986). See also James Malloy and Mitchell Seligson, eds., *Authoritarians and Democrats: Regime Transition in Latin America* (Pittsburgh: University of Pittsburgh Press, 1987); Enrique Baloyra, ed., *Comparing New Democracies: Transition and Consolidation in Mediterranean Europe and the Southern Cone* (Boulder: Westview, 1987); Giuseppe Di Palma, *To Craft Democracies: An Essay on Democratic Transitions* (Berkeley: University of California Press, 1990); John Higley and Richard Gunther, eds., *Elites and Democratic Consolidation in Latin American and Southern Europe* (Cambridge: Cambridge University Press, 1992).

2. O'Donnell and Schmitter, *Transitions*, pp. 52, 55.

3. On the elaboration of Linz's initial distinction between transition by *reforma* and transition by *ruptura*, see Juan Linz, "Some Comparative Thoughts on the Transition to Democracy in Portugal and Spain," in Jorge Braga de Macedo and Simon Serfaty, eds., *Portugal Since the Revolution: Economic and Political Perspectives* (Boulder: Westview, 1981); Donald Share and Scott Mainwaring, "Transitions through Transaction: Democratization in Brazil and Spain," in Wayne Selcher, ed., *Political Liberalization in Brazil: Dynamics, Dilemmas, and Future Prospects* (Boulder: Westview, 1986); Samuel Huntington, *The Third Wave: Democratization in the Late Twentieth Century* (Norman: University of Oklahoma Press, 1991); J. Samuel Valenzuela, "Democratic Consolidation in Post-Transitional Settings: Notion, Process, and Facilitating Conditions," in Scott Mainwaring, Guillermo O'Donnell, and J. Samuel Valenzuela, eds., *Issues in Democratic Consolidation* (Notre Dame: University of Notre Dame Press, 1992).

4. This analysis is based primarily on Nigel Haworth, "The Peruvian Working Class, 1968–1979," in David Booth and Bernardo Sorj, eds., *Military Reform-*

*ism and Social Classes: The Peruvian Experience, 1968–1980* (London: Macmillan, 1983); Julio Cotler, "Military Interventions and 'Transfer of Power to Civilians' in Peru," in Guillermo O'Donnell, Philippe Schmitter, and Laurence Whitehead, eds., *Transitions from Authoritarian Rule: Latin America* (Baltimore: The Johns Hopkins University Press, 1986); Nigel Haworth, "Political Transition and the Peruvian Labor Movement," in Edward Epstein, ed., *Labor Autonomy and the State in Latin America* (Boston: Unwin Hyman, 1989); Henry Pease García, *Los caminos del poder: Tres años de crisis en la escena política* (Lima: DESCO, 1979); Cynthia McClintock, "Peru: Precarious Regimes, Authoritarian and Democratic," in Larry Diamond, Juan Linz, and Seymour M. Lipset, eds., *Democracy in Developing Countries: Latin America* (Boulder: Lynne Rienner, 1989); Latin American Bureau, *Peru: Paths to Poverty* (London: Latin American Bureau, 1985); Henry Dietz, "Elites in an Unconsolidated Democracy: Peru During the 1980s," in Higley and Gunther, eds. *Elites and Democratic Consolidation*; Julio Cotler, *Democracia e integración nacional* (Lima: Instituto de Estudios Peruanos, 1980).

5. David Scott Palmer, *Peru: The Authoritarian Tradition* (New York: Praeger, 1980), p. 114.

6. Dietz, "Elites in an Unconsolidated Democracy," p. 241.

7. Latin American Bureau, p. 70.

8. Haworth, "The Peruvian Working Class," p. 76.

9. This analysis is based primarily on Gerardo Munck, "State Power and Labor Politics in the Context of Military Rule: Organized Labor, Peronism, and the Armed Forces in Argentina, 1976–1983," (Ph.D. diss., University of California, San Diego, 1990); Andres Fontana, *Fuerzas armadas, partidos politicos y transición a la democracia en Argentina* (Buenos Aires: Estudios CEDES, 1984); Ariel Colombo and V. Palermo, *Participación política y pluralism en la Argentina contemporánea* (Buenos Aires: Centro Editor de América Latina, 1985); Edward Epstein, "Labor Populism and Hegemonic Crisis in Argentina," in Epstein, ed.; Ronaldo Munck, *Argentina: From Anarchism to Peronism* (London: Zed Books, 1987); James McGuire, "Interim Government and Democratic Consolidation: Argentina in Comparative Perspective," in Yossi Shain and Juan Linz, eds., *Interim Governments and Transitions to Democracy* (Cambridge: Cambridge University Press, 1996).

10. G. Munck, "State Power and Labor Politics," pp. 268–84.

11. Ibid., pp. 305–6.

12. Ibid., pp. 318–19.

13. Ibid., p. 326.

14. R. Munck, *Argentina: From Anarchism to Peronism*, pp. 78, 79.

15. G. Munck, "State Power and Labor Politics," p. 327.

16. R. Munck, *Argentina: From Anarchism to Peronism*, p. 79.

17.  McGuire, "Interim Government and Democratic Consolidation," p. 189.

18.  See, for example, Huntington, *The Third Wave*, pp. 125–27; Share and Main-
     waring; Linz, "Some Comparative Thoughts"; Kenneth Medhurst, "Spain's
     Evolutionary Pathway from Dictatorship to Democracy," in Geoffrey Pridham,
     ed., *New Mediterranean Democracies: Regime Transition in Spain, Greece, and
     Portugal* (Totowa: Frank Cass, 1984); Di Palma, *To Craft Democracies*, pp. 6–
     8; Richard Gunther, "Spain: The Very Model of the Modern Elite Settlement,"
     in Higley and Gunther, eds.; Terry Lynn Karl and Philippe Schmitter, "Modes
     of Transition in Latin America, Southern and Eastern Europe," *International
     Social Science Journal*, 128 (May 1991); Juan Linz and Alfred Stepan, *Problems
     of Democratic Transition and Consolidation: Southern Europe, South America
     and Post-Communist Europe* (Baltimore: The Johns Hopkins University Press,
     1996).

19.  In addition to the sources in the previous note, this discussion is based primarily
     on José Maravall, *The Transition to Democracy in Spain* (London: Croom
     Helm, 1982); José Maravall, *Dictatorship and Dissent* (London: Tavistock,
     1978); Raymond Carr and Juan Pablo Fusi Aizpurua, *Spain: Dictatorship to
     Democracy* (London: George Allen & Unwin, 1979); Paul Preston, *The Tri-
     umph of Democracy in Spain* (London: Methuen, 1986); Robert Fishman,
     *Working-Class Organization and the Return of Democracy in Spain* (Ithaca:
     Cornell University Press, 1990); Victor Pérez-Díaz, *The Return of Civil Society:
     The Emergence of Democratic Spain* (Cambridge: Harvard University Press,
     1993); Joe Foweraker, "The Role of Labor Organizations in the Transition to
     Democracy in Spain," in Robert Clark and Michael Haltzel, eds., *Spain in the
     1980s: The Democratic Transition and a New International Role* (Cambridge:
     Ballinger, 1987); José Félix Tezanos, Ramón Cortarelo, and Andrés de Blas,
     eds., *La transición democrática española* (Madrid: Sistema, 1989).

20.  Maravall, *The Transition to Democracy*, p. 14.

21.  Maravall, *Dictatorship and Dissent*, p. 33.

22.  Car and Fusi, *Spain: Dictatorship to Democracy*, p. 192.

23.  Ibid., pp. 205–6.

24.  Ibid., p. 210.

25.  Preston, *The Triumph of Democracy in Spain*, p. 91.

26.  Linz and Stepan, *Problems of Democratic Transition*, p. 92.

27.  Pérez-Díaz, *the Return of Civil Society*, pp. 238–39, 242.

28.  This analysis is based primarily on Thomas Skidmore, *The Politics of Military
     Rule in Brazil, 1964–1985* (New York: Oxford University Press, 1988); Maria
     Helena Moreira Alves, *State and Opposition in Military Brazil* (Austin: Uni-
     versity of Texas Press, 1985); Gay Seidman, *Manufacturing Militance: Workers'
     Movements in Brazil and South Africa, 1970–1985* (Berkeley: University of
     California Press, 1994); Margaret Keck, *The Workers' Party and Democratiza-*

*tion in Brazil* (New Haven: Yale University Press. 1989); Maria Helena Moreira Alves, "Trade Unions in Brazil: A Search for Autonomy and Organization," in Epstein, ed. *Labor Autonomy and the State in Latin America.*

29.  Keck, *The Workers' Party*, p. 42.
30.  Alves, *State and Opposition*, pp. 194–97.
31.  Ibid., p. 199.
32.  Seidman, *Manufacturing Militance*, p. 197.
33.  Ibid., p. 169.
34.  This analysis is based primarily on Gerardo Caetano and José Rilla, *Breve historia de la dictadura (1973–1985)* (Montevideo: CLAEH/Ediciones de la Banda Oriental, 1991); Luis González, *Political Structures and Democracy in Uruguay* (Notre Dame: University of Notre Dame Press, 1991); Charles Gillespie. *Negotiating Democracy: Politicians and Generals in Uruguay* (Cambridge: Cambridge University Press, 1991); Juan Rial, *Partidos políticos, democracia y autoritarismo* (Montevideo: CESU/Ediciones de la Banda Oriental, 1984); Gerónimo De Sierra, *El Uruguay post-dictadura: Estado-política-actores* (Montevideo: Facultad de Ciencias Sociales, Universidad de la República, 1992): Martin Gargiulo, "The Uruguayan Labor Movement in the Post-Authoritarian Period," in Epstein, ed.; Jorge Chagas and Mario Tonarelli, *El sindicalismo Uruguayo bajo la dictadura, 1973–1984* (Montevideo: Ediciones del Nuevo Mundo, 1989).
35.  Rial, *Partidos politicos*, vol. I, pp. 73–74.
36.  De Sierra, *El Uruguay post-dictadura* p. 218.
37.  Ibid., p. 220; Gillespie, *Negotiating Democracy*, p. 131.
38.  Caetano and Rilla, *Breve historia de la dictadura*, p. 91.
39.  Ibid., p. 95.
40.  Linz and Stepan, *Problems of Democratic Transition*, p. 88 (emphasis added).
41.  In addition to O'Donnell and Schmitter, see especially J. Samuel Valenzuela, "Labor Movements in Transitions to Democracy: A Framework for Analysis," *Comparative Politics*, 21 (July 1989).

# 6 Myths of Moderation: Confrontation and Conflict During Democratic Transitions

*Nancy Bermeo*

In a 1970 essay that marked the beginning of a new wave of writing on democratization, Dankwart A. Rustow argued persuasively that democracy is the fruit of "choice" and "conscious decision" on the part of political elites.[1] This perception seems widely shared, for our current literature is full of tactical insights on how elites might be induced to choose democracy over alternative political systems. This essay focuses on the tactics of the transition period, defined as the time between the breakdown of the dictatorship and the conclusion of the first democratic national elections. It examines what I call the "moderation argument": that radical popular organizations threaten democratic transitions if they fail to moderate their demands and behavior as the moment of elite choice approaches. Implicit and explicit variations of the moderation argument are widely purveyed, and this essay assesses their merits in light of evidence from Iberia, Latin America, and Asia. It concludes by explaining when the moderation argument does and does not hold.

## Popular Mobilization in the Literature

The current literature on democratization accords much less attention to popular organizations than to political elites. Thus, the role of popular organizations in the transition process remains a subject of some confusion.

Many of the major theoretical works on democratization suggest that popular mobilization is important for regime change, but even this very simple proposition is not universally shared. Some scholars argue that a "popular upsurge during the transition is by no means a constant,"[2] while others argue that "social mobilization is undoubtedly indispensable."[3] Although most of the generalizations regarding the role of mass publics in the transition to democracy are neither widely shared nor very clearly specified, a few related propositions nevertheless emerge.

One proposition argues that too much popular mobilization and too much pressure from below can spoil the chances for democracy, what I have called the moderation argument. Though the conclusion that popular participation sometimes harms rather than enhances democratization is politically unpalatable, it is nevertheless widely drawn. For example, Terry Karl writes that "no stable political democracy has resulted from regime transitions in which mass actors have gained control even momentarily over traditional ruling classes."[4] Myron Weiner writes that pressures from left-wing parties are often least effective for democratization because they frequently provoke "only . . . increased authoritarianism,"[5] and Samuel Huntington argues that "democratic regimes that last have seldom, if ever, been instituted by mass popular action."[6] Daniel Levine concludes that the "obvious" lesson from experience is that "conservative transitions are more durable."[7] Even Rueschemeyer, Stephens, and Stephens, who argue that democracy is the outcome of working-class mobilization, assert that radical mass parties are more likely to "evoke strong defensive, anti-democratic reactions."[8]

Fear of the masses lies at the root of this cautionary argument. For some, this fear emerges from the conviction that the general citizenry may not have the values a sustainable democracy requires. For example, Juan Linz and Larry Diamond argue that in many Latin American states "the choice of democracy by political elites clearly preceded . . . the presence of democratic values among the general public."[9] In other cases the argument develops from an awareness that pivotal political groups harbor a fear of the masses themselves and often act upon it. Robert Kaufman argues that "the threat from below . . . is the lowest common denominator and the most important bond of cohesion within bureaucratic-authoritarian coalitions."[10] Kaufman's observation, like the others cited above, has clear tactical implications: if a transition is to be carried out successfully, the "threat from below" must somehow be moderated.

Of course, what constitutes "the threat from below" varies from one regime to another, just as "extremism" lies in the eyes of the beholder. In some cases, the most threatening pressures will come from students and other relatively well-educated urban groups. In other cases, the primary threat will come from armed opposition with a rural base, subnationalist groups, or organized labor. I use the term "popular organizations" to denote a varied set of nonelite but formally organized actors who are perceived as extremists by existing elites. Who these actors are sociologically needs to be contextually defined.

Discussions that focus on labor organizations are especially explicit on the need for moderation. Adam Przeworski argues that "complete docility and patience on the part of organized workers are needed for a democratic transformation to succeed" and reminds us that the "democratic system was solidified in Belgium, Sweden, France, and Great Britain only after organized workers were badly defeated in mass strikes and became docile as a result."[11] Samuel Valenzuela makes a similar point. He writes that labor mobilization may "act like a double edged sword and permit a reversal of the process of redemocratization" and cautions that waves of "strikes and demonstrations may lead to a protracted crisis [and] may lead employers to reconsider their commitment . . . to supporting the process of democratic change."[12]

Valenzuela speaks directly to the question of tactics. He argues that the "ideal mix" for democratization is "high labor mobilization at certain critical moments of the breakdown of authoritarian institutions," followed by "restraint when the political agenda shifts in favor of redemocratization."[13] This and the other readings of democratization suggest that citizen mobilization is effective, even essential, but that it is ultimately dangerous if it continues too long or with too much intensity.[14]

But how much is too much? Guillermo O'Donnell and Philippe Schmitter offer us some leads in their now classic study of uncertain transitions. They argue that increased activity is useful up to a point but that it will provoke a dictatorial reaction "if widespread violence recurs" or if it threatens "the vertical command structure of the armed forces, the territorial integrity of the nation-state, the country's position in international alliances, [or] . . . the property rights underlying the capitalist economy." If any of these extremes are reached, they write, "then even bland regime actors will conclude that the costs of toleration are greater than those of repression" and the movement for democracy will fail.[15]

This cautionary message corresponds with Robert Dahl's argument in

*Polyarchy*, and it is intrinsically appealing.[16] It makes sense to distinguish between the amount of opposition activity and its content. It also makes sense to argue that the likelihood of democracy decreases as the costs of toleration rise. But how are the costs of toleration calculated? To answer this question we must think systematically about popular mobilization and elite response in concrete cases of successful transition.

## The Realities of Transition Tactics in Portugal and Spain

Portugal and Spain provide good places to begin our inquiry. They were among the first transitions of the "third wave" and thus have had a special impact on our thinking about transitions in general. They are also useful because they are alleged to represent two radically different routes to democratic transition. Any commonalities we find in these contrasting cases are likely to be shared by a broad spectrum of others.

### Portugal

The Portuguese transition, beginning in April 1974, violated most of the cautionary parameters set out by the literature on democratization. The laboring classes were far from docile. Capitalist property rights were challenged successfully on a very broad scale. The country's position in international alliances was the subject of strenuous debate, and decolonization shattered the territorial integrity of the state. The vertical command structure of the armed forces was completely transformed. Nevertheless, democracy muddled through. Individual actors might have concluded that the costs of toleration were greater than those of repression, but no one succeeded in reversing the transition.

Because the details of the Portuguese transition are not well known, these points require some elaboration. The Portuguese working class took the world by surprise by leading the most massive seizures of property in Europe since the Russian Revolution. Workers occupied more than 23 percent of the nation's farmland in less than twelve months and took control of more than 940 industrial enterprises.[17] Two thousand houses were seized in the two weeks following the fall of the dictatorship, and in February 1975 2,500 apartments were occupied in Lisbon alone.[18]

Provisional governments legitimated property seizures through a variety of legal supports and eventually nationalized banks, insurance firms, and all basic industries.[19] The constitution, approved by the freely elected constitutional assembly of April 1975, promised a "classless society" and the "transformation of capitalist relations of production and accumulation."[20]

Just as property relations were being radically restructured, so were the territorial boundaries of the Portuguese state. The Salazar-Caetano dictatorship had gone to great lengths to convince mainland Portuguese that Portugal's colonies were an integral part of the Portuguese nation. (The colonies were officially called "the overseas provinces.") Yet the men who controlled the provisional governments after April 1974 granted independence to Guinea, Mozambique, Cape Verde, and São Tomé-Príncipe within a year of taking power and withdrew from Angola in November 1975. Millions of dollars of property were lost, and 800,000 refugees flooded onto the Portuguese mainland.[21]

The vertical command structure of the armed forces was radically transformed as part of the process of ending the colonial wars. The middle-ranking officers who toppled the dictatorship engineered the most extensive purges of any democratic state in the third wave, including those of eastern Europe. The first set of purges affected the ultras, who supported the old regime, while the second set embraced top-ranking centrists.[22] Even General António de Spínola, the head of the first provisional government, was forced from office in September 1974. A dramatic breakdown in discipline occurred in the lower ranks when radicalized enlisted men organized a movement for the democratization of the armed forces in September 1975.[23] The intense politicization of the military caused the rise and fall of six provisional governments.[24]

Although official pronouncements emphasized that Portugal would not change its status as a loyal member of NATO, western powers were extremely concerned about Portugal's loyalty to its old allies.[25] The chaos within the Portuguese military, the strong Communist presence in the cabinets of Portugal's provisional governments, and the occasional popular demonstrations against NATO led Henry Kissinger to advocate covert action against the Armed Forces Movement. How much covert action took place is still unclear, but we do know that other western powers were also fearful of Portugal's loyalty and that the nation was expelled from NATO's nuclear planning group.[26]

This brief review of the Portuguese case illustrates that democratic transitions can, indeed, survive radical pressures from below and that they can even survive radical provisional governments. But is Portugal simply an exception to the rule? A close look at other successful transitions suggests that the radical elements of civil society have a much more boisterous and enduring presence in the drama of democratization than we originally believed.


## Spain

Spain is particularly instructive in understanding the limits of the moderation argument because it is so often held up as the model of peaceful and "pacted" transition. Elite pacts were certainly key to the democratization of Spain, but these pacts were forged in a situation in which extremism and moderation existed simultaneously. The law that guaranteed free elections was passed by the Francoist Cortes in November 1976 and approved by a popular referendum in December of the same year. However, 1976 was also a year of widespread violence and unceasing mobilization. Scholars have placed so much emphasis on the comparatively peaceful nature of Spain's transition that it is easy to forget its violent elements.

In fact, violence was much more pervasive in Spain than in "revolutionary" Portugal. ETA (*Euskadi Ta Askatasuna*), the armed wing of the Basque separatist movement, provided a source of "widespread violence" throughout the transition period and threatened "the territorial integrity of the nation state." Yet the Cortes passed the Law of Political Reform just eighteen months after the declaration of a state of emergency in the Basque country and just thirteen months after five separatists were publicly executed following a season of terrorist activity and bombings. The majority of Basques did not support ETA violence but were radically opposed to the central authorities' treatment of separatists. As the year of democratization began, some two-thirds of the Basque population struck in protest against police repression, and on March 3 five workers were killed when police shot into a crowd of Basque nationalist protesters in Vitoria.[27] In early October, barely a month before the approval of the Law of Political Reform, ETA murdered the head of the provincial council. On December 11, 1976, GRAPO, another revolutionary organization, kidnapped the president of the council of state and the resident of the superior council of military justice.[28]

Violence did not decrease with the successful referendum on political reform in December 1976. In what became known as the Black Week, in January 1977, two students, five labor lawyers, and five police were gunned down in separate incidents on the streets of the capital.[29] Between the passage of the reform laws and the nation's first free elections, Spain experienced "a full-scale destabilization attempt from terrorists" of both the left and the right.[30] Although the attempt was unsuccessful, it was unleashed in full force and is of great importance for our conclusions about the necessity of moderation. Statistics show that violence did not decrease as the transition progressed. Kidnapping rose steadily through 1979, as did the number of people wounded in political violence. Political killings rose steadily through 1980.[31]

The Spanish working class never challenged property relations as their counterparts did in Portugal, but they exceeded their Portuguese neighbors in their level of strike mobilization. In 1976 alone, over 3.6 million Spanish workers participated in strikes affecting all major industrial centers and public services in Madrid and Barcelona. Worker mobilization continued well into the following year.[32]

The existence of what reactionary forces might have deemed extremism was not confined to trade union and separatist circles. Spain's Socialist party (PSOE) emerged from the dictatorship with a vocal radical faction. Although the party cultivated a moderate image in some settings to attract middle-class support, it also emitted strong signals which reactionaries could read as threatening to both "alliances" and "property rights." The party's position on international alliances was one of "active neutrality." It sought to dissociate Spain from its bilateral ties with the United States and from its former role in the Atlantic alliance.[33] Political actors who feared that democratization would threaten capitalist property relations could easily find justification in party documents. According to official party principles, formulated in December 1976, the Socialists aspired to "the possession of political power for the working class [and] the transformation of individual or corporate ownership of the instruments of labor into collective, social or common property."[34] As time passed, the radical elements in the PSOE were either transformed or overpowered, but at the time that the regime disassembled itself, there was no guarantee that this change would take place. Thus, even in Spain, the model of the controlled transition, "extremist" forces were far from absent.

These two very different transitions took place in the context of radical popular mobilization and perceived extremism, but it would be a mistake to dismiss the moderation hypothesis altogether. There are clearly cases in which extremism and mass mobilization provoked the installation of a more coercive dictatorial elite. The reversals of the liberalization in Chile in 1983 and of the milder liberalization in Argentina in 1981 illustrate that right-wing reactions are not mythical.[35] Yet these negative cases do not in themselves make an argument for moderation. Such an argument can be supported only by assembling a large number of cases in which democratic regimes actually replaced dictatorships and then showing that in each case popular mobilization rose, crested, and became moderate before the successful transition was completed. Portugal and Spain clearly did not follow this pattern. Is the moderation hypothesis better sustained by cases that came later in the third wave?

## Comparative Perspectives

Cross-national time series data for a phenomena as varied as "popular mobilization" are not available, but we can learn something from analyzing strike data, because organized labor is often thought to be a prime source of "immoderate" demands and destabilization.

Table 6.1 provides some suggestive evidence on the number of strikes in six states in which dictatorships gave way to formal democracies between 1977 and 1989.[36] These states vary in level of development, regime longevity, and political culture. Yet worker mobilization decreased substantially prior to democratization in only one case. Aside from Ecuador, where a left-wing military regime was ousted, worker mobilization either rose or was extremely high when the first democratic elections were held. If we consider the number of workers involved in these strikes, the pattern remains the same (see table 6.2).

This evidence does not show that workers become more moderate as successful transitions are being negotiated. It suggests, instead, that a successful transition to democracy does not require moderation on the part of the working class. If we look carefully at the details of the cases, we see that there is much more leeway for "extremist" pressures than the literature on democratization leads us to believe.

*Peru*

The transition from dictatorship in Peru in 1977–78 provides compelling evidence that formal democracies can be constructed amid violence and

**TABLE 6.1** Annual Strike Statistics: Number of Strikes/Year[a]

| Year[b] | Brazil | Chile | Ecuador | South Korea | Peru | Philippines |
|---|---|---|---|---|---|---|
| −5 | 534 | 38 | NA | 206 | 788 | 260 |
| −4 | 843 | 42 | 61 | 186 | 570 | 158 |
| −3 | 1,494 | 41 | 61 | 88 | 779 | 155 |
| −2 | 2,369 | 81 | 58 | 98 | 440 | 282 |
| −1 | 1,954 | 72 | 9 | 114 | 234 | 371 |
| First Free Elections | 4,189 | 101 | 7 | 265 | 364 | 581 |

[a]Excludes work stoppages involving less than 10 work days.
[b]Years correspond to the following calendar years: *Brazil* 1984–1989, first elections November 15, 1989; *Chile* 1984–1989, first elections December 14, 1989; *Ecuador* 1973–1978, first elections July 16, 1978; *South Korea* 1980–1985, first elections February 1985; *Peru* 1973–1978, first elections June 22, 1978; *Philippines* 1981– 1986, first elections February 7, 1986; *Spain* 1972–1977, first elections June 15, 1977.

Source: International Labour Office, "Yearbook of Labour Statistics."

high levels of popular mobilization. Peruvian democracy was destroyed by a presidential coup in 1992 and thus was not consolidated, but the transition which began in the late 1970s produced a regime which held together for approximately fourteen years. Peru's transition to democracy began on July 28, 1977, when Francisco Morales Bermúdez announced that the armed forces would hold free elections for a civilian constitutional assembly the following year. The announcement came less than ten days after "the entire nation was shut down by . . . the most massive [general strike] in the country's history."[37]

The promise of free elections did not curtail the growing wave of popular mobilization. On the contrary, in May 1978, less than one month before the scheduled elections, the military government declared a state of emergency after strike waves and bombings left twenty people dead and fifty injured in a single week.

The elections nevertheless took place on June 18, 1978, and showed a dramatic shift to the Marxist left. Marxist parties garnered 29 percent of the vote, far exceeding the 5 percent they had won in the past (and in spite of the fact that the government had arrested and deported many leftist leaders,

**TABLE 6.2** Annual Strike Statistics: Workers Involved

| Year[a] | Brazil | Chile | Ecuador | South Korea | Peru | Philippines |
|---|---|---|---|---|---|---|
| −5 | NA | 3,595 | NA | 48,970 | 416,250 | 98,585 |
| −4 | 5,431,000 | 8,532 | 5,948 | 34,586 | 362,740 | 53,824 |
| −3 | 7,146,000 | 3,900 | 11,913 | 8,967 | 617,120 | 33,638 |
| −2 | 8,304,000 | 9,900 | 7,016 | 11,100 | 258,100 | 65,306 |
| −1 | 7,136,000 | 5,600 | 802 | 16,400 | 1,315,400 | 111,260 |
| First Free Elections | 14,099,000 | 17,900 | 538 | 28,700 | 1,398,400 | 169,480 |

[a]Years correspond to those in Table 6.1.

Source: International Labour Office, "Yearbook of Labour Statistics."

shut down many politically oriented publications, and decreed that illiterates would not be allowed to vote).

The convening of the constitutional assembly also did not curtail the growing wave of popular mobilization. Teachers', health workers', and debilitating miners' strikes were timed deliberately to coincide with assembly debates. Ten provinces were placed under a state of emergency in August 1978 as the assembly was just beginning. In October the nation's cities were rocked by more rioting, but the assembly continued to meet.

Though *Sendero Luminoso* had no more than three hundred members when the military began to withdraw from power, it had already begun to shoot officials who tried to enter what was (even then) known as "*Senderista* territory."[38] In 1980, the year of the nation's first postdictatorial presidential election, *Sendero* launched 505 terrorist attacks.[39] *Sendero Luminoso* apparently did not play a central role in elite calculations at the time,[40] but the fact that the group was not taken seriously lends support to the argument that the mere existence of radical forces does not threaten the transition from authoritarianism to democracy.

## The Philippines

The transition from dictatorship in the Philippines shows how an electoral democracy can be constructed in a state with an even larger guerrilla presence. The "People's Power" movement that toppled the Marcos dictatorship was a coalition of moderate forces drawn from all classes of Philippine society. But the coalition was forged at a time when a decidedly nonmoderate group, the New People's Army (NPA), was expanding rapidly. The NPA was founded in 1968 as the armed wing of the Communist Party of the Philippines. From its inception, its ultimate goal has been the overthrow of the Philippine capitalist state. Its method, like that of *Sendero Luminoso*, is the armed mobilization of the rural poor.

The NPA did not waver in its commitment to armed struggle when the possibility of a peaceful ouster of Marcos presented itself. The Communist Party of the Philippines boycotted the February 1986 presidential elections, declaring that dictators could not be ousted through the polls and that in any case Corazon Aquino was not significantly different from Marcos.[41] The NPA had proved remarkably successful outside of any coalition of moderate groups and had few organizational incentives to change course. It grew tenfold after martial law was declared in 1972 and won the loyalty of 23,000 rebels by 1986.[42] Its fifty-odd guerrilla units penetrated 32 percent of the nation's *barangays*.[43] In 1985, just as the moderate movement for democracy was taking shape, the NPA launched 5,000 violent attacks.[44]

The NPA was clearly an "extremist" force when the Marcos regime entered its final crisis. It was also a relatively powerful force: U.S. intelligence experts believed that it could actually take armed control of the Philippine state by 1990.[45] Yet moderate, prodemocratic political actors succeeded in forging an electoral democracy. The existence of uncompromising forces in the opposition did not lead to the triumph of reaction.


## South Korea

The establishment of electoral democracy in South Korea offers a final illustration of successful democratization despite high levels of popular mobilization and widespread violence.

South Korea's construction of electoral democracy began on June 29, 1987, when Roh Tae Woo, the designated successor to Chun Doo Hwan, announced that he would accept the demands of the political opposition and allow direct popular elections for the presidency. Roh's action did not result from compromise and bargaining among political elites. On the contrary, it came as a complete surprise to the opposition and followed three weeks of serious rioting in which tens of thousands of students and middle class citizens "effectively broke government control" of important commercial areas.[46]

The opposition to the South Korean dictatorship was a highly heterogeneous group with important moderate elements, but opposition extremists remained unchecked throughout the months between Roh's announcement and the holding of elections. Within the universities, anti-American groups seeking to alter the nation's "position in international alliances" dominated the student movement. Underground study groups called *chiha* served as bases for vanguard demonstrations of 200 to 300 students that often involved the hurling of gasoline bombs.

Violence did not decrease with the approach of elections. As the draft of the new national constitution was being debated in August 1987, the dictatorial regime faced the most serious strikes in its history, along with massive rioting linked to the killing of a worker by a tear gas canister.[47] The presidential campaigns were marked by violence as well. In Kunsan, hundreds of rioters attacked Roh's campaign motorcade with bricks, bottles, and homemade bombs. His planned visit to Chonju was canceled because of further rioting and fears for the president's life. Most significant, perhaps, the extremists did not confine their attacks to the dictator himself.[48] Moderate opposition candidates were also physically attacked on several occasions by leftist groups, yet the transition to electoral democracy continued.[49]

## Rethinking Moderation

The examples reviewed above provide compelling evidence that high levels of popular mobilization do not inevitably sidetrack the transition from authoritarian to democratic rule. The more recent transition in South Africa suggests that we might find supportive evidence in other regions as well.[50] Moderation is not a prerequisite for the construction of democracy; the parameters of tolerable mobilization are broader than we originally anticipated. In many cases, democratization seems to have proceeded alongside weighty and even bloody popular challenges.

Why do members of the old dictatorial coalition give in to demands for democracy when immoderate forces elevate its risks? In the Portuguese case, we might argue that the old dictatorial coalition had no choice. But this argument would not apply to nonrevolutionary transitions, and in Portugal, as elsewhere, a new dictatorial coalition might have emerged during the transition period. Why do actors who might be harmed by extremism risk an expansion of liberties that may work to their disadvantage? The key to the puzzle lies in how risks are calculated. These actors do not calculate their risks in the manner we initially surmised.

Robert Dahl's seminal work, *Polyarchy*, has encouraged us to think that the likelihood of democratization increases as the cost of suppression rises and the cost of toleration declines. None of the empirical materials presented here contradict these general assumptions. Yet the comparative study of various transitions suggests that we should think more systematically about how elites calculate these costs.

The axiom related to the costs of suppression helps explain why we have found so many regimes that democratized despite extremism. The cost of suppression increases as the level of popular mobilization rises and the number of attacks on the dictatorship increases. Rustow argued that democratization requires "a hot family feud" and "a prolonged and inconclusive struggle."[5] If antiregime forces of any sort succeed in elevating the sense of struggle and raising the costs of suppression, they affect half the decision calculus and win half the battle.

Yet the battle can easily be lost if the costs of toleration remain too high. For the costs of toleration to seem bearable, pivotal elites must believe that they will not be ruined by reform. Dictatorial regimes will pay extremely high suppression costs if the costs of toleration leave them no other choice. The logic of this argument explains why calls for moderation emerge so frequently in the democratization literature.

However, we are wrong to think that the costs of toleration are a simple function of the presence or absence of extremism. Neither the presence nor the scope of extremist activities is as important an element in elite calculations as their estimates of what the effects of extremism will be. We can resolve the seemingly dramatic differences between the cautionary arguments in the literature and the many cases reviewed here if we recognize that elite projections about the effects of extremism can take at least three forms.

In a first, pivotal elites, defined as those who have the capacity to reverse the transition, project that extremism will have powerful and wholly pernicious effects. They predict that democratization will lead to the triumph of extremist groups and to the disastrous end of the pivotal elites themselves.

If this belief is widely shared, the likelihood of an antidemocratic reaction is extremely high. Democracy is therefore seen as intolerable and is rejected. The moderation argument cautions us against this scenario. As the 1989 mobilization in China illustrates, it is far from mythical.

But let us suppose that pivotal elites forecast that extremism will have other effects. They are convinced that extremists will not win the democratic game. Under these conditions, democracy may prove acceptable, and two more desirable scenarios emerge.

In the first, pivotal elites opt for democratization because they have been unable to control extremism themselves and are no longer willing to pay the high institutional costs of failing to provide political order. They forecast that democratic elections will be won by nonextremists and that ceding control to moderate actors in an electoral democracy is less risky than continuing with the status quo. Peru's transition from authoritarianism in 1977–78 provides an example of this scenario. In it, democracy is seen as a means of escape.

In the second, pivotal elites opt for democracy despite extremism because they predict that they will win the transition elections themselves. In this case, they see democracy as a formula for their own legitimation. This scenario has two variants. In the renovating variant, the pivotal elites are associated with the old dictatorship. They accede to electoral democracy because they believe it will provide them with a new formula for legitimating their rule. In the revolutionary variant, democracy becomes the legitimating formula for a new elite. Revolution has forced the old guard into political inactivity, and the pivotal elites are the military officers and civilian politicians who oppose both the threatening extremists and the previous dictatorship. Portugal provides a classic example of this revolutionary scenario. Spain provides an example of the renovating variant.[52]

The existence of extremist groups is not an insurmountable obstacle for democratic forces in either the escape or the legitimation scenarios. Extremism always raises the costs of governance. When the known costs of governance rise, the projected costs of democracy will seem relatively low if pivotal elites predict that nonextremist forces will take control of the new democratic regime. If pivotal elites can exclude certain groups from electoral competition, if they can shape electoral laws for their own purposes, and if radical forces sometimes refuse for their own reasons to participate in elections, these predictions may not be at all unreasonable. Table 6.3 provides a summary of the projected effects of extremism and the different scenarios these projections are likely to produce.

TABLE 6.3 Elite forecasts of the Effects of Extremism and the Resulting
Scenarios for Transitions to Democracy

| Scenario | If pivotal elites forecast . . . | they . . . | Because they see democracy as . . . | As happened in . . . |
|---|---|---|---|---|
| I | Extremist victory | will reject democracy | an intolerable threat | China, 1989 |
| II | Extremist defeat and moderate victory | may accept democracy | a means of escape | Peru, 1977 Greece, 1975 |
| III | Extremist defeat and their own victory | may accept democracy | a form of legitimation | Portugal, 1974 Spain, 1976 |

Real life cases may not fit squarely in a single scenario because the pivotal elites in many transitions are heterogeneous. There may be differences in how sectors of the pivotal elite view the effects of extremism and thus in how they calculate their own particular risks. Nevertheless, if we use these categories as a guide in thinking about elite calculations, we can understand better why particular transitions turned out as they did.

Portugal is clearly a case in which a new political elite used democracy as a legitimating formula for a new regime. The pivotal elites in Portugal were the moderate military officers, who constituted a majority in the military establishment, and the democratic but not radical civilian politicians who headed political parties and occupied various cabinet positions in the provisional governments. After a period of disorientation provoked by the surprise of the revolution itself, both groups became convinced that democratic processes would work against the extremist forces of the PCP and the ultra-left. Socialist Party leader Mario Soares was certain that extremists were "not even close to having the popular support" that they required to seize control of the transition. He was also convinced that "the armed forces-even the [radical] armed forces in Lisbon-would never agree to such a suicidal act."[53] He publicly stated that there was "very little possibility" of a Communist coup if for no other reason than that the Communists knew it would be immediately reversed.[54] Despite the highest levels of radical mobilization in Portuguese history, a broad spectrum of nonradical elites consistently advocated continued democratization. Elections were consistently purveyed as a solution to disorder because pivotal elites were convinced that they would gain legitimized control of the state if democracy proceeded.[55]

Spain provides us with an example of the legitimation scenario in its renovating rather than revolutionary variant. The most visible pivotal elites in the Spanish transition were King Juan Carlos and Adolfo Suárez. They were directly associated with the old regime and clearly needed a new formula for the legitimation of a renovated elite. Suárez explicitly referred to this legitimation function when he presented the Law for Political Reform in September 1976: free elections were the means through which "respectable political groups who had no popular mandate could become representative of the public."[56]

Suárez and Juan Carlos were able to take the risks of democratization despite extremism because they forecast that continued democratization would not lead to the triumph of radical forces. Elite discourse on the nature of the Spanish people had changed dramatically by the death of Franco.[57] On the eve of Suárez's reforms, ABC, one of Spain's most important conservative newspapers, was full of references to the moderate and centrist nature of the people of Spain. If the Spanish people were indeed "prepared for democracy" and "ready to use liberty responsibly," as these sources claimed, then democracy despite extremism was not so threatening.[58]

In both Spain and Portugal, pivotal elites were able to formulate their projections about the effects of extremism with highly credible information about popular preferences. In Portugal this information came from the elections for the constitutional assembly in April 1975. With a 91.7 percent turnout, these free elections were a key indicator of how the Portuguese people were grouped on the ideological spectrum. The Communist Party and the ultra-left attracted approximately one vote in five but were electorally overwhelmed by the Socialists and the centrist Popular Democrats, who together attracted over 64 percent of the vote.[59] Moderate civilian and military leaders recognized that, if they could ensure a fair series of elections, they would gain power, and extremism would be held in check. This prediction held true.

In Spain pivotal elites formulated their projections about the effects of extremism with two sorts of information. One came from the public opinion polls conducted before and after the transition to democracy began. These polls indicated that Spanish society was ideologically moderate, so moderate in fact that the PSOE would have to move toward the ideological center if it were ever to be elected. Communism, even in its Eurocommunist variant, attracted surprisingly little enthusiasm, and popular support for violence as a means of solving subnationalist questions was overwhelmingly rejected, even in the regions in which subnationalist sentiments were strongest. In Spain, where the legislature of the dictatorship literally voted itself out of office, this information on popular preferences was absolutely essential in calculating the risks.[60]

Voting results provided a second source of information for Spain's pivotal elites. The December 1976 referendum on political reform showed that 94 percent of the voters approved the transition to democracy and thus that the costs of reversing the transition might be very high. The June 1977 general elections confirmed the findings of the opinion polls. Neither the extreme right nor the extreme left won any parliamentary seats. The PCE attracted only 9 percent of the votes, and regionalist parties failed to attract the support of more than 7 percent of voters.[61] Centrists overwhelmingly dominated the Spanish electorate, and knowledge of this fact diminished the risks of continued democratization.

The puzzle of why two very different transitions could proceed despite extremist mobilization is thus resolved if we consider how pivotal elites perceived the effects of extremism. In both Portugal and Spain pivotal elites saw democracy as a solution to the problem of extremism rather than a problem in itself.

Scholars who have seen extremism as a barrier to democratization did not misread the drama of regime transition. They simply focused on only one of several scenarios. A broader array of cases shows that democracy can be created despite so-called "extremist" demands and despite high levels of mobilization in civil society. In many cases, a "hot family feud" may, indeed, provide the proper environment for the forging of a new democracy.

NOTES

1.  Dankwart A. Rustow, "Transitions to Democracy," *Comparative Politics* 2 (April 1970), pp. 337–63.
2.  Guillermo O'Donnell and Philippe Schmitter, "Tentative Conclusions about Uncertain Democracies," in Guillermo O'Donnell, Philippe Schmitter, and Laurence Whitehead, eds., *Transitions from Authoritarian Rule* (Baltimore: The Johns Hopkins University Press, 1986), p. 56.
3.  Manuel Antonio Garreton, "Popular Mobilization and the Military Regime in

Chile: The Complexities of the Invisible Transition," in Susan Eckstein, ed., *Power and Popular Protest: Latin American Social Movements* (Berkeley: University of California Press, 1989), p. 275.

4. Terry Lynn Karl, "Dilemmas of Democratization in Latin America," *Comparative Politics* 23 (October 1990), p. 8.

5. Myron Weiner, "Empirical Democratic Theory," in Myron Weiner and Ergun Özbudun, eds., *Competitive Elections in Developing Countries* (Durham: Duke University Press, 1987), p. 26.

6. Samuel Huntington, "Will More Countries Become Democratic?," *Political Science Quarterly* 99 (Summer 1984), p. 212.

7. Daniel Levine, "Paradigm Lost: Dependence to Democracy," *World Politics* 40 (April 1988), p. 392.

8. Dietrich Rueschemeyer, Evelyne Huber Stephens, and John D. Stephens, *Capitalist Development and Democracy* (Chicago: University of Chicago Press, 1992), pp. 271, 223. Their comparison is with moderate clientelistic parties.

9. Larry Diamond and Juan Linz, "Introduction," in Larry Diamond, Juan Linz, and Seymour M. Lipset, eds., *Democracy in Developing Countries*, Volume 4: Latin America (Boulder: Lynne Rienner, 1989), p. 12.

10. Robert Kaufman, "Liberalization and Democratization in South America: Perspectives from the 1970s," in O'Donnell, Schmitter, and Whitehead, eds., *Transitions from Authoritarian Rule*, p. 88.

11. Adam Przeworski, "Some Problems in the Study of the Transition to Democracy," in ibid., p. 63.

12. J. Samuel Valenzuela, "Labor Movements in Transitions to Democracy," *Comparative Politics* 21 (July 1989), p. 449.

13. Ibid., p. 450.

14. These same thoughts about the need for moderation affected the Brazilian opposition. Margaret E. Keck, *The Workers' Party and Democratization in Brazil* (New Haven: Yale University Press, 1992), p. 34.

15. O'Donnell and Schmitter, *Transitions from Authoritarian Rule*, p. 27.

16. Robert Dahl, *Polyarchy: Participation and Opposition* (New Haven: Yale University Press, 1971), p. 15.

17. Nancy Bermeo, *The Revolution within the Revolution* (Princeton: Princeton University Press, 1986), p. 5, and "Worker Management in Industry: Reconciling Representative Government and Industrial Democracy in a Polarized Society," in Lawrence S. Graham and Douglas L. Wheeler, eds., *In Search of Modern Portugal* (Madison: University of Wisconsin Press, 1983), pp. 183–84.

18. Charles Downs, "Residents' Commissions and Urban Struggles in Revolutionary Portugal," in ibid., pp. 151–63.

19. Since the banks owned most of the nation's newspapers, they were nationalized,

too. Maria Belmira Martins et al., *O Grupo Estado* (Lisbon: Ediçôes Jornal Expresso, 1979).

20.   Reinaldo Caldeira and Maria do Ceu Silva, *Constituiçâo Política da República Portuguesa* (Lisbon: Livraria Bertrand, 1976).

21.   Because the mainland population was just over 8 million, this influx was especially disruptive.

22.   Lawrence S. Graham, "The Military in Politics: The Politicization of the Portuguese Armed Forces," in Lawrence S. Graham and Harry M. Makler, eds., *Contemporary Portugal: The Revolution and Its Antecedents* (Austin: University of Texas Press, 1979), p. 237.

23.   John L. Hammond, *Building Popular Power* (New York: Monthly Review Press, 1988), pp. 233–35.

24.   The first, second, third, and sixth provisional governments were considered politically moderate. The fourth and fifth were radical.

25.   Nancy Bermeo, "Regime Change and Its Impact on Foreign Policy: The Portuguese Case," *Journal of Modern Greek Studies* 6 (May 1988), p. 13.

26.   Álvaro de Vasconçelos, "Conclusion," in Kenneth Maxwell, ed., *Portuguese Defense and Foreign Policy since Democratization* (New York: Camôes Center Special Report No. 3, Columbia University, 1991), p. 83.

27.   Donald Share, *The Making of Spanish Democracy* (New York: Praeger, 1986), p. 77.

28.   On the *Grupos de Resistencia Antifascista Primero de Octubre*, see Paul Preston, *The Triumph of Democracy in Spain* (London: Methuen, 1986), pp. 106–7.

29.   José Maria Maravall, *La Política de la Transición* (Madrid: Taurus, 1981), pp. 24–25.

30.   Share, p. 121.

31.   José Maria Maravall and Julian Santamaria, "Crisis del Franquismo, Transición Política y Consolidación de la Democracia en España," *Sistema* 68–69 (November 1985), p. 105.

32.   Nancy Bermeo, "Sacrifice, Sequence, and Strength in Successful Dual Transitions: Lessons from Spain," *Journal of Politics*, 56 (August 1994).

33.   Eusébio Mujal-León, "Foreign Policy of the Socialist Government," in Stanley Payne, ed., *The Politics of Democratic Spain* (Chicago: Council on Foreign Relations, 1986), p. 197. See also Fernando Morán, *España en Su Sítio* (Barcelona: Plaza and Janes, 1990).

34.   Felipe Gonzalez and Alfonso Guerra, *PSOE* (Bilbao: Ediciones Alba, 1977), pp. 23–24.

35.   In Chile in 1983 copperworkers led a cross-class alliance in school and store boycotts and *caceroleos* (intensive pot-bangings) against Pinochet's regime. The protests continued monthly until Pinochet declared a state of siege in Novem-

ber 1984. In Argentina a mild liberalization was sponsored by General Viola, then reversed by General Galtieri.

36. "Suggestive" because different methods in recording strikes cross-nationally make the accuracy and comparability of strike data problematic. Interesting here is the similar direction of historical trends.

37. Cynthia McClintock, "Peru: Precarious Regimes, Authoritarian and Democratic," in Diamond, Linz, and Lipset, eds., *Democracy in Developing Countries*, p. 351.

38. Cynthia McClintock, "Why Peasants Rebel: The Case of Sendero Luminoso," *World Politics* 37 (October 1984), pp. 52, 81.

39. Ibid., p. 51.

40. I owe this insight to Catherine Conaghan of Queens University.

41. Carolina Hernández, "Reconstituting the Political Order," in John Bresnan, ed., *Crisis in the Philippines: The Marcos Era and Beyond* (Princeton: Princeton University Press, 1986), p. 184.

42. Robert Manning, "The Philippines in Crisis," *Foreign Affairs* 63 (Winter 1984–1985), p. 392.

43. B. M. Villegas, "The Philippines in 1986: Democratic Reconstruction in the Post-Marcos Era," *Asian Survey* 27 (Fall 1987), p. 198.

44. David Rosenberg, "The Changing Structure of the Philippine Government from Marcos to Aquino," in Carl Lande, ed., *Rebuilding a Nation: Philippine Challenges and American Policy* (Washington, D.C.: Washington Institute Press, 1987), p. 304.

45. Manning, p. 404.

46. "DJP's No Tae-U Advocates Direct Election," *Seoul Hanguk Ilbo*, June 29, 1987, p. 1, in FBIS Daily Report-East Asia, 124, June 29, 1987.

47. "Daewoo Shipyard Worker Dies from Injuries" *Seoul YONHAP*, Aug. 22, 1981, in FBIS Daily Report-East Asia, 163, Aug. 24, 1987.

48. "No Tae-U's Election Rally in Chonju Aborted," Seoul Domestic Service (in Korean) Dec. 10, 1987, in FBIS Daily Report-East Asia, 237, Dec. 10, 1987.

49. Kim Young Sam was attacked with bottles and rocks during a campaign address in Kwangju. John McBeth, "South Korea to Curb Campaign Violence," *Far Eastern Economic Review*, Nov. 26, 1987, p. 10. Kim Dae Jung was attacked on December 6, 1987. South Korea actually experienced more radical group activity as democracy approached. Lo Shiu Hing, "Political Participation in Hong Kong, South Korea, and Taiwan," *Journal of Contemporary Asia*, 20 (1990), 245.

50. See Glenn Adler and Eddie Webster, "Challenging Transition Theory: The Labor Movement, Radical Reform and Transition to Democracy in South Africa," *Politics and Society*, 23 (March 1995), 75–106. In eastern Europe, Poland may be the only case in which the debate about the requirement for moder-

ation is relevant. The collapse of dictatorship was so rapid in the other East European cases that the nature of the tactical discussions was very different.

51. Rustow, p. 352.

52. The transition from authoritarianism in the Philippines began as a renovating version of the legitimation scenario. Faced with pressure from the NPLA but still confident that he could win national elections, Marcos used a United States television interview to announce surprise elections. He was surprised by his overwhelming defeat, but his intention was to use a popular mandate to renovate a severely troubled regime.

53. Mario Soares, *Entre Militantes: PS, Frontiera da Liberdade* (Lisbon: Portugal Socialista, 1979), p. 18; and "Aviso aos interessados," in *PS, Fronteira da Liberdade* (Lisbon: Portugal Socialista, 1979), p. 69.

54. Mario Soares, *Democratização e Descolonização* (Lisbon: Dom Quixote, 1975), p. 194, also 17, 156, 179, 190, 215, and 275.

55. Francisco Sa Carneiro, leader of the center-right PPD, shared Soares' faith in the outcome of a free poll. See his interviews and speeches in *Por uma Social-Democracia Portuguesa* (Lisbon: Dom Quixote, 1975), pp. 154, 176.

56. Adolfo Suárez Gonzalez, *Un Nuevo Horizonte para España: Discursos del Presidents del Gobierno 1976–1978* (Madrid: Colección Informe, 1978), p. 20.

57. For more evidence see Victor Pérez-Díaz, *The Return of Civil Society* (Cambridge, Mass.: Harvard University Press, 1993).

58. *ABC*, May 1975, p. 51; *ABC*, June 10, 1975. J. M. Areilza stated: "Between the Bunker and subversion there is an enormous segment of the Spanish population that is not inclined toward either of these formulas." *ABC*, Aug. 1, 1975, p. 109. Another editorial stated that "there is an enormous sector of society between *socialismo* and *integrismo*." *ABC*, Feb. 1976, p. 53. Not all of Spain's political elites shared this perspective. Within the Spanish military, there were clearly actors who were much less certain that extremism could be held in check. They tolerated democracy by default because of institutional links to the king and out of a sense of inevitability. This point shows how the Spanish transition had elements of other scenarios, too.

59. Thomas C. Bruneau, "Popular Support for Democracy in Postrevolutionary Portugal: Results from a Survey," in Graham and Wheeler, eds., *In Search of Modern Portugal*, pp. 21–42.

60. Paul Preston reports that the opinion polls "carried out by the government [before the law on political reform] convinced them that a center-right party not too tainted by Franco and backed by Suárez would have a healthy electoral future." Ironically, polls conducted by the Socialists and Communists concluded that the conservative AP was more popular than it actually proved to be. Preston, *The Triumph of Democracy in Spain*, p. 108.

61. Maravall and Santamaria, "*Crisis del Franquismo*," p. 96.

# 7  Bureaucracy and Democratic Consolidation: Lessons from Eastern Europe

## Ezra Suleiman

In much of the literature on transition to democracy, the state and its capacity to carry out basic functions do not assume an important role. Neither in the phase of transition to nor in the phase of consolidation of democracy does the state seem to have much to contribute.

This is a curious omission in view of the place that the state has come to occupy in the political analysis of different types of political systems. In addition to the "interplay of forces," what matters, as Dankwart Rustow noted, is what politicians actually do, the agreements which are reached, and how they are actually transmitted to the citizenry. Politics, in other words, co-exists with the capacity to realize objectives.[1]

The absence of state capacities in the analysis of democratic transitions is probably at least partially owing to the preeminent role that free market, anti-statist ideology has assumed the world over. What has been thought to be salutary for democratic societies has simply been transposed to societies that have recently emerged from authoritarianism and that are seeking to devise democratic procedures and build democratic institutions.

This chapter discusses the relationship between democracy and bureaucratic institutions. It follows the arguments set out by classical theorists maintaining that an intimate link, or dependence, exists between bureaucracy and democracy. Whereas the strong contemporary anti-statist ideology claims that bureaucracy is antithetical to democracy, the classical theorists claimed the opposite: no democracy can be truly anchored or consolidated unless the state has a reliable, competent bureaucratic organization at its disposal.


## Bureaucracy and Democracy

All modern states possess a trained, more or less professional civil service organized along hierarchical lines and operating, in Weber's terms, according to "calculable rules and without regard for persons."[2] As Weber put it: "The more perfectly the bureaucracy is 'dehumanized,' the more completely it succeeds in eliminating from official business love, hatred, and all purely personal, irrational, and emotional elements which escape calculation. This is the specific nature of bureaucracy and it is appraised as its special virtue."[3]

The antistatist fervor ascribes little virtue to bureaucracy. This institution is seen as being opposed to democracy, or as irrelevant or nefarious for a free society and an efficient economy. It is, in Ronald Reagan's famous words, not "part of the solution, but the problem." Although democratic and democratizing societies have sympathized with or embraced this ideological position, there exists no empirical evidence to support the view that amputation of the instrument of the state advances the cause of democracy or spurs economic development.

Weber maintained that bureaucracies are inevitable instruments in modern and modernizing societies, and that no state can function without an efficient bureaucratic instrument. Schumpeter went even further and identified bureaucracy as indispensable to democracy. He lists the existence of a professional bureaucracy as one of the five conditions necessary for a democratic order. Bureaucracy, he wrote, "is not an obstacle to democracy but an inevitable complement to it. Similarly, it is an inevitable complement to modern economic development."[4]

Schumpeter cautions, however, that "recognition of the inevitability of comprehensive bureaucratization does not solve the problems that arise out of it."[5] Nonetheless, there is no escaping the fact that no democratic society can preserve itself without a professional bureaucracy. "Democratic government in modern industrial society must be able to command, for all purposes the sphere of public activity to include . . . the service of a well-trained bureaucracy of good standing and tradition, endowed with a strong sense of duty and no less a strong *esprit de corps*."[6]

The charge that government is often unable to respond to society's needs and that it is run inefficiently has become a familiar one. Schumpeter argued that a well-trained bureaucracy "is the main answer to the argument about government by amateurs. Potentially, it is the only answer to the question so often heard in this country: democratic politics has proved itself unable to produce decent city government, how can we expect the nation to fare if everything . . . is to be handed over to it?"[7]

Ours is not the first epoch in which bureaucracies have been attacked for incompetence and for stifling freedom. It is possible—even desirable—to accept Schumpeter's and Weber's argument concerning the importance of an efficient bureaucracy for a democratic order without accepting Schumpeter's view that the bureaucracy "must be a power in its own right."[8] Nonetheless, bureaucracies have more often operated as forces of modernization than as obstacles to the process. Most of the literature on transitions leaves aside the organization of the state. Some of this literature takes the availability of adequate state structures as given. Transitions can go on for long periods, even if there is always the hope of repeating the "Spanish miracle."[9]

At the very least a consolidated democracy requires a state capable of carrying out its main functions (protection of citizens, collection of taxes, delivery of services) in an orderly, predictable, and legal manner. To do this, the state must have a capable instrument at its disposal. Juan Linz and Alfred Stepan are among the first scholars of transitions to democracy to point to the importance of a professional bureaucracy in the consolidation of a democracy. They consider a professional bureaucracy to be as critical to democratic consolidation as an independent civil society, an autonomous political society, and the rule of law. They observe that no matter how one views the state's role, a modern, professionalized bureaucracy is indispensable to democratic consolidation.

To protect the rights of its citizens, and to deliver some other basic services that citizens demand, the democratic government needs to be able to exercise effectively its claim to the monopoly of the legitimate use of force in the territory. Even if the state had no other function than this, it would have to tax compulsorily in order to pay for police, judges, and basic services. Modern democracy, therefore, needs the effective capacity to command, regulate, and extract. For this it needs a functioning state and a state bureaucracy considered usable by the new democratic governments.[10]

Linz and Stepan have essentially updated Schumpeter or, rather, made Schumpeter relevant to the process of democratic transition and consolidation. As this process has gotten underway and been in the making for several years in a number of societies in eastern Europe, the absence of a professional bureaucracy is becoming more evident.

The extent to which bureaucratic instruments of democratizing states need to resemble a strict Weberian model may be an open question. But that such instruments form part and parcel of a state's authority which is indispensable to the preservation of liberties is indisputable, even if not fully recognized.

A critical element in democratic consolidation is a bureaucracy that begins to operate in an impersonal manner, according to known rules and regulations, and in which the officials are able (or obliged) to separate their own political and personal interests from the offices they occupy. As Jacek Kochanowicz observes, "a bureaucracy plays not only a technical, but also a symbolic role. Like the flag, the national anthem, an army uniform, or a presidential mansion, it is a symbol through which the state—and the nation—is perceived. Citizens who have to deal with inefficient or corrupt officials will not respect the state, and the links tying the national community together will loosen." Kochanowicz goes on to observe that creating a new, more efficient, more autonomous bureaucracy "could be a way to strengthen the legitimacy of the state."[11]

State authority requires state capacities which assure state legitimacy. All this is merely a means to the protection of individual rights. As Stephen Holmes notes in a perceptive essay on the weakness of the Russian state,

> Today's Russia makes excruciatingly plain that liberal values are threatened just as thoroughly by state incapacity as by despotic power. Destatization is not the true solution, it is the problem. For without a well-functioning public power of a certain kind there will be no prevention of mutual harm, no personal security. . . . The rights inscribed in the 1977 Brezhnev Constitution went unprotected because of a repressive state apparatus. The rights ascribed in the 1993 Yeltsin Constitution go unenforced because the government lacks resources and purpose.[12]

The Russian example Holmes analyzes stresses the importance of endowing a democratizing state with capacities because "authority enhances freedom." As he puts it, "If the state is to have a monopoly of violence, the monopoly must be vested only in officials whom the public can hold accountable for its use. Liberalism demands that people without guns be able to tell people with guns what to do."[13]

A democratizing regime never starts with a new instrument. Much of what the new regime wants to rectify, propose, and reform depends on the instrument at its disposal, which, in all cases, is the state bureaucracy. That bureaucracy had previously operated under different guidelines, ethics, and ideology. To reach the top of the bureaucratic structure implied embracing a political doctrine and serving the single party that dominated society and political life.

Recruitment and promotion were linked more to loyalty to the party than to any technical expertise, which is, of course antithetical to the Weberian concept of bureaucracy. To be sure, political loyalty among top bureaucratic officials is important in almost all democratic societies. Indeed, today it threatens to compromise the independence and professionalism of the bureaucracies of France, Britain, Spain, and the United States. That there have been strong political influences on the most professional bureaucracies has long been recognized.[14] But in the case of the former single-party states of the Soviet Union and eastern Europe, professionalism was almost always secondary to recruitment based on party loyalty.

### Bureaucracies and New Regimes

What happens to the main instrument of governing when a regime is overthrown? Is the bureaucracy purged, or does the new regime govern with those who served the old order?

Many new regimes, whether democratic or authoritarian, have had to confront this familiar problem from the moment the old order was overthrown. It was Marx who called for smashing the bureaucracy—that instrument of the bourgeoisie—once the revolutionary force took power. Lenin subscribed to this view but had to wait several years before purging the Russian bureaucracy of the last vestiges of its bourgeois elements. His need for a state machine to carry out immediate reforms was greater than the need to purge this machine upon taking power.

To take a very different example, when Clement Attlee became prime minister of Britain's first postwar Labour government, he was repeatedly warned that he would be unable to govern with what was essentially a conservative bureaucracy long accustomed to serving conservative governments, a "representative bureaucracy," that represented not society but the ruling elite. Despite being urged to replace the higher civil servants, however, Attlee did not attempt a purge. And indeed he subsequently claimed to have received loyal service from the higher civil service.

In recent times different French governments have had to face the problem of bureaucratic loyalty. The Vichy regime saw a large segment of the bureaucracy adapt rapidly to the Pétanist regime, whereas the Liberation forces had to sanction some of those who had served Vichy. But even in the postwar years, there was no major purge of the bureaucracy. When the left-wing government came to power in France in 1981, after twenty-three years of uninterrupted right-wing rule, it planned to make massive personnel changes in the bureaucracy. After the initial tremors and some changes in personnel at the top of the bureaucratic pyramid, however, all major reforms that threatened the structure, personnel, and promotion process were abandoned.

Although all revolutionary governments plan to overthrow existing bureaucratic structures and replace an ostensibly hostile personnel with a new partisan elite, radical change rarely occurs and the pace of change is almost always slow. For the most part, the case of eastern Europe conforms far more to this pattern than to the pattern of China after the accession of the communist forces in 1949, when scores are settled rapidly, brutally, and without regard for immediate consequences.

Why then in the cases of more gradual and nonrevolutionary changes have plans to effect mass change been so quickly shelved? In large part, the answer is related to (1) the fear of creating further instability; (2) the need to reassure the society of certain continuities; and (3) the absence of a counterelite.

In an examination of regime change and its impact on the bureaucracy in France, Germany, and India, Graham Wilson observed that reality very quickly sets in for the new political leaders and "accommodation is reached."[15] As Wilson notes, either a bureaucracy can be an initiator and an implementer of policy, or it can be a mere implementer, as occurs under regimes that set clear policy directives. By and large, as Wilson observes, new rulers come to terms with the bureaucracy:

The French example suggests more clearly that counter elites may be forced today more than in the past to come to terms with bureaucracies. The increased scale and complexity of government has made it even less plausible than in the past to pull up a bureaucracy by the roots and plant a new one. The larger and more complex government is, the greater the attraction of maintaining its machinery intact, as in India.[16]


## Reform and Stability

In the wake of a revolutionary change of regimes (or governments, as in the case of the socialists coming to power in Spain in 1982 or the French Socialist Party taking the reigns of power in 1981), the new rulers face two, often contradictory tasks. First, they need to distinguish themselves immediately from their predecessors by taking radical steps to fulfill the longings of their supporters for reforms long sought and long promised while the party was in opposition. Second, they need to minimize the degree of instability so as to avoid discouraging those who run the key economic, social, and administrative institutions. Severe political instability also leads to capital flight—to an acute decrease in investments—and it ultimately creates a new set of problems that ends up requiring further drastic action on the part of the new government. New drastic actions in turn only serve to heighten the prevalent instability, as happened in France, in 1981–82, when "strong party pressure . . . compelled the government to continue its innovation campaign in the face of waning authorization and dwindling resources, thus producing increasingly disappointing and counterproductive results."[17]

In the case of eastern Europe, since there had not been any meaningful competitive elections prior to the collapse of the communist regimes, there were no clear reforms or mandates for reform that could serve as guides for the new governments. By any measure, however, the revolutionary change created what some analysts have seen as "policy windows," that is, an opportunity for major policy innovations.[18] What were the priorities set by the new governments?

On the whole, these priorities were determined in part by the rejection of the old order and in part by the international context in which the transition from communism to democracy took place. It hardly needs emphasizing that "successful dismantlement of the old order does not guarantee a democratic outcome."[19] Furthermore, it is not clear to students of transitions what it is that guarantees such an outcome.

The priorities of the new regimes in Poland, Hungary, and the Czech Republic have generally sought to dismantle the centralized state apparatus. Among the particular policies advocated have been privatization and decentralization. Consequently, the most important policy in the economic area has been the movement away from central planning and regulation toward market-oriented economies. In the administrative area, the most important policy has been, not the restructuring and revitalization of the central administration, but rather the devolution of power toward subnational units. These policies reflect a rejection of the old order characterized above all by centralized bureaucratic power that served neither democracy nor efficiency. As Lena Kolarska-Bobinska notes about Poland, there is an "absence of the any conception of the role [that] the state should play in social and economic life besides a very general call for the reduction of its role."[20] There is nonetheless a recognition that the state is responsible, in Leszek Bakerowitz's words, "for the construction of a new economic system."[21]

A reduction in the role of the state, the policy followed in the countries of central and eastern Europe for reasons already explained, has also had the consequence of not according the reform of the state the attention it deserves. As Peter Drucker observes, "downsizing" is not synonymous with reforming or "reinventing" government.

> By now it has become clear that a developed country can neither extend big government, as the (so-called) liberals want, nor abolish it and go back to nineteenth-century innocence, as the (so-called) conservatives want. The government we need will have to transcend both groups. The twentieth-century megastate is bankrupt, morally as well as financially. It has not delivered. But its successor cannot be "small government." There are far too many tasks, domestically and internationally. We need effective government—and that is what the voters in all developed countries are actually clamoring for.[22]

Effective government requires developing a competent bureaucratic apparatus, and the first step toward achieving this goal is recognizing the need to train professional public employees.

## Undoing the State: Privatization and Devolution

The reduction of state power, considered to be part and parcel of the democratic transition, is being accomplished through two measures: privatization of state enterprises and devolution of state power to local authorities. Both these trends are not unfamiliar to the countries of western Europe, where since the early 1980s the reaction to statism has led to the privatization of state industrial and financial enterprises[23] and to the decentralization of administrative authority.

The privatization of industrial enterprises has been the chief element of the economic reforms in eastern Europe. The extent and modalities of the privatization process have not been uniform across eastern Europe. But regardless of the methods adopted, it remains clear that the government of the former Soviet bloc have sought to end the command economy through the sale of state enterprises.[24]

Privatization did indeed remove from the payroll a substantial number of state employees and state organizations responsible for running sectors of the economy. But in every country a new structure had to be created to administer the privatization process. In the Czech and Slovak cases, the process fell to the Privatization Ministry, the Federal Finance Ministry, and the Federal and Republican Funds of National Property. In Poland, a Ministry of Ownership Transformation was created and was charged with selecting and overseeing the transfer of ownership. Hungary, which already possessed a less controlled economy prior to the overthrow of the Communist Party, did not create a Ministry of Privatization and was able to maintain a relatively decentralized privatization process that assigned responsibility for initiating the process to enterprise managers. There is, however, a State Property Agency (SPA), created in 1990, that oversees all privatization and that is headed by a minister without portfolio.[25] As in Western Europe, the process of privatization in eastern Europe also entailed either the creation of a new bureaucratic agency or supervision of existing agencies. It is also likely, as in some West European cases, that privatization will eliminate the agencies and personnel that ran the state enterprises, but will require setting up regulatory agencies. This is particularly likely with enterprises that remain largely monopolistic. In the case of the privatization of gas, water, and telecommunications in Great Britain, the government of Margaret Thatcher had to resort to the creation of additional regulatory agencies for these privatized firms.[26]

If the transition to democracy implies a reduced role for the state in the economy, even more does it imply a reduced role for the state in administration and policymaking. This has been an article of faith, such that reform of the state bureaucracy has largely been synonymous with its diminishing role. The state reduces its role by delegating greater functions to local units.

One study of the reforms of public administration in Hungary, confined almost entirely to the devolution of power, even went so far as to warn about what it calls the "artificial contrasting, . . . according to which the central state administration organs are bad ones, necessarily serving state interventions while the local and regional self-governing administrative organs are the title to the democratic public administration, consequently all scope of tasks and authority can be placed on them."[27]

In the Czech and Slovak Republics restructuring public administration has also largely meant altering the relationship between the center and the periphery. Thus, the Czech Republic abolished the level of region, the intermediate administrative level between the central administration and the district level, of which there had previously been seven. There were three such regions in Slovakia, and these too were abolished. There are now seventy-one districts in the Czech Republic and thirty-six in Slovakia. The only difference between the Czech and Slovak administrative structures is that the latter has a subdistrict level.[28] In Poland the reorganization of the administrative structure has resulted in the granting of greater autonomy to local governments. "The twofold subordination of local government under the Communist party bureaucracy and the directives of central government has been broken."[29] In fact, the local government law drastically restricts central authority over local authorities.

In Poland, Hungary, and the Czech and Slovak Republics, the reforms of the organization of the state apparatus have been largely concerned with altering the balance between the center and the periphery. The report by Hesse and Goetz concludes that "in sum . . . local governments and administration in Poland have gone through major upheavals during the past two years. The territorial organization of local governance has remained largely unchanged, but there have been far-reaching functional, political administrative and financial reforms which have begun to transform the role of the local level in the governance of Poland."[30] But it is not only administrative structures that are changed in the devolution of central powers and functions. Lurking in the background are some profoundly political repercussions that may threaten the very structure of a state initiating such reforms.

The devolution of state authority to local units may in particular contexts lead to the rise of strong regional sentiments, as has occurred in western and southern Europe. Hesse and Goetz observe that in the Czech Republic, "there have long been for [sic] the re-establishment of some form of regional government for the historical lands of Bohemia, Moravia, and Silesia. . . .

Should those regions be reconstituted, it is most probable that they will have the character of self-governing entities, i.e. they would not be part of state administration."[31]

The post-communist phase of the transition to democracy has been influenced by the ideology of the previous regime and by the global context within which transitions took place. The concordance of both led in a single direction: loosening the hold of the state on the economy and on the society. The first implied the policy of privatization; the second led to the devolution of power of the central administration. Both policies have received loud applause, though it is the policy of privatization that has received by far the greater attention. Only the modalities of the move to a market economy have been debated ("shock therapy" versus "gradualism"). To be sure, the regimes of 1989 in eastern Europe were not the same as those of the 1950s or the 1960s, which explains why the communists of the 1980s have been able to return to positions of authority in Poland, Hungary, Romania, and even in the Czech and Slovak Republics. As Przeworski noted:

> By the seventies, repression had subsided as the communist leadership became bourgeoisified, it could no longer muster the self-discipline required to crush all dissent. Party bureaucrats were no longer able to spend their nights at meetings, to wear working class uniforms, to march and shout slogans, to abstain from ostentatious consumption. What had developed was "goulash communism," "Kadarism," "Brezhnevism," an implicit social pact in which elites offered the prospect of material welfare in exchange for silence. And the tacit premise of this pact was that socialism was no longer a model of a new future, but an underdeveloped something else . . . We [did not understand] how feeble the communist system had become.[32]

Feeble though the communist system had become, it remained associated with the party-bureaucratic state. Its organization in the transition phase had to be associated with the "undoing" of a strong state apparatus. And yet, if the task facing central and eastern Europe is, as Janos Simon believes, nothing less than what Karl Polanyi called a "Great Transformation," then it does not necessarily follow that the "undoing" of the state's capacity is the ideal solution. Simon argues that the transition process in central and eastern Europe is essentially a more complicated one than it was in Latin America and southern Europe, because in the former set of countries it is the entire model of social reproduction that needs to be transformed. The task before these countries is "not only the democratization of an authoritarian political system (as was the case in other transitions), but also the carrying out of a thorough transformation of their economic and political systems."[33]

How is the "Great Transformation" to be carried out? What mechanisms are to be put into effect to ensure the delivery of services and the efficient execution of the extractive tasks that all states perform? How is the state to break with its habits of serving an ideology or a class or a political movement? How, in short, is the state to develop a stable, professional bureaucracy subject to the rule of law and capable of applying the law.

One of the most striking aspects of the transition process in central and eastern Europe is the absence of recognition, at least in the essential phase of the transition, that a professional bureaucracy is crucial to both the consolidation of the democratic process and the imperatives of economic development. As Frydman and Rapaczynski note, the transfer of state assets to the private sector does not obviate the need for a neutral state. Rather, it renders it all the more necessary. "Privatization," these authors observe,

> is a transfer of valuable resources from the control of some parties (state bureaucrats) to others, and one of the primary effects of this transfer is to enfranchise owners and make them more powerful, not merely in the economic, but also in the political sense. This in turn means that the new owners are as likely to make a political use of their new resources as they are to use them in a more conventional, economic fashion.[34]

What needs to be guarded against, in other words, are the "effects of the privatized resources that might create new and ever more successful forms of rent-seeking behavior."[35]

## Building a Professional Bureaucracy

"The habits of communist bureaucracy run counter to Weberian principles such as the rule of law, meritocracy, or professionalism,"[36] observes Jacek Kochanowicz. But what of the postcommunist regimes? Have they been more inclined to create a professional bureaucracy that transcends political loyalty?

The bureaucracy remains a critical institution because it is both a necessary institution in a democracy as well as the indispensable instrument of the state. Kochanowicz summarizes the role that the state needs to fulfill and the important functions that a state bureaucracy carries out. He observes that the market economy is just as much in need of a "strong state" as a nonmarket economy. The state is needed to set norms and regulations by which society can function. In effect, the state has a modernizing role to play.[37] Consequently, a "revitalized and reoriented state capacity is crucial to the success of both market-oriented reforms and consolidation of democracy."[38]

It is worth raising the question of what might have occurred in western Europe had the state not played the role of instigator, orienter, and planner in the years following World War II. The most accurate and best description of the economic policies undertaken by European governments in those years remains Andrew Shonfield's.[39] Shonfield showed that the spectacular economic results achieved in western Europe following the devastation of the war were due largely to the role assumed by the state and its bureaucracy. Through the combination of a market economy and "indicative planning," the economies of western Europe were able to achieve full employment and increased productivity.

The states were able to do this because (1) they assumed control of a key economic mechanism, the credit sector, through the Ministries of Finance and the Treasuries; and (2) they had at their disposal professional bureaucratic structures run by competent, well-trained officials. Both factors allowed for the orientation of investments that were expected to meet production targets.

The states in western Europe were expected to play a role in orienting investments. The French Planning Commission and the way in which the state ensured itself a cadre of highly qualified officials were soon being imitated in Italy, Great Britain, and Germany. The existence of a competent, even elitist bureaucracy was an indispensable complement to economic growth and to democracy, even if bureaucratic stability was often called upon to compensate for political instability.

The countries of central and eastern Europe cannot, of course, be expected to follow the path taken by their neighbors in western Europe. In the first place, the world in which they find themselves struggling to develop economically and to consolidate economic institutions is vastly different from the one that existed in 1945. It is a much more competitive one, and one in which the number of competitors has substantially increased.

Second, the ideological shift within the successful cases of economic growth today precludes an important role for the state. The term "indicative planning" implied a model that offered an alternative to uncontrolled market allocations and to Soviet planning, and gave an important role to the state. Today, such a model, or such a term, would be met with opprobrium. Not surprisingly, as Kochanowicz notes, of all the state functions, whether rectifying the environmental devastation caused by the communist regimes, or investing in human capital, or managing the national debt, "by far the most controversial concerns industrial policy—whether industries need a push from a development-promoting state in order to compete internationally."[40] Behind this controversy lies an ideological conflict that questions the role of the state, a conflict that had been absent in the countries of western Europe after the Second World War.

Third, the countries of eastern Europe have been left to their own devices to a far greater extent than were their Western neighbors in the postwar period. They have not benefited from a Marshall Plan. Nor did they have an immediate need to ensure the existence of a professional bureaucratic structure to administer such a plan. Besides, the international organizations that exist today to help East European societies develop their economies— IMF, the World Bank, the Bank for European Reconstruction and Development (BERD), the European Union—tend to dictate economic policies.

These are all powerful factors that explain to a very large extent the difficulties faced by East European societies in their quest for economic growth and democracy. What is surprising, however, is that these countries have not chosen to tackle problems that it is within their power to resolve. The development of a central bureaucratic structure that is built on Weberian principles and that is administered by professional officials requires no negotiations and compromises with international organizations. It would allow the state to avoid the pitfalls of privatization that lead to the excessive power of new "rent seekers," would reduce corruption in the decisionmaking process, and would ultimately strengthen the legitimacy of the state. Despite these immense advantages and possibilities, no state in central and eastern Europe has yet accorded priority to this task.

## Reforming State Bureaucracies

Reforming state bureaucracies in central and eastern Europe has not been high on the priority list of any country in the region. Yet, as is now sufficiently recognized, the capacity needed by these states is no less important in today's era of "rolling back" the state than it was in the past. In fact, it can be argued that between the decentralization of states and the global constraints to which eastern European countries are subject, state power is being eroded. But it is eroded further in the absence of a professionalized bureaucracy.

Bureaucratic reform has largely been limited, as we noted, to the devolution of power. Indeed, devolution and bureaucratic reform have become almost synonymous. Jan Kubik notes, for example, that "Poland carried out the most comprehensive administrative reform in east central Europe thus far. As a result local communities were burdened/blessed with a number of administrative prerogatives and responsibilities.[41] Such far-reaching reforms have been undertaken in Hungary and in the Czech and Slovak Republics. But Kubik recognizes that such ambitious reforms of politico-administrative units themselves come to have an impact on the state's capacities. "I would also argue," he says, "that decentralization which led to the decoupling of central and local fields, worked against substantivists' political ambitions."[42]

Altering the balance of power between center and periphery sidesteps the need for bureaucratic reform. The importance of such a reform is stated succinctly in the mission statement of the OECD's Sigma (Support for Improvement in Governance and Management of central and eastern European Countries):

> The governments of central and eastern European countries (CEECs) are in an unprecedented situation. They have to build up democratic systems of governance and transform to market-oriented economies simultaneously. But they must do this without experienced political/administrative elites, without mature structures to mediate and aggregate interests; and without appropriate social, legal, and constitutional frameworks.[43]

"The idea of public service as understood in developed countries is absent" in eastern Europe, states another recent OECD report. Public service is simply held in "low esteem." In addition, the developing private sector offers more pecuniary advantages, so that public service comes to be reserved for those unable to "make it" in the private sector. This is the case today in Hungary, Poland, Romania, and the Czech Republic. The OECD report goes on to note that the "concept of a professional and apolitical public service is slow in gaining acceptance around a region where for decades politics pervaded every decision throughout society, not just in the administrative realms."[44]

No serious attempt has been made thus far either to make wholesale changes in bureaucratic personnel or to prepare a new bureaucratic elite to manage the bureaucratic apparatus. It is rare, as we noted earlier, for a new regime to proceed to make wholesale changes in bureaucratic personnel. "In general," notes Graham Wilson, " in the modern state the arrival of a counter elite in power does not result in immediate radical changes in the bureaucracy. The counter elite may remove a significant minority of the bureaucracy, but the remainder stay on giving adequate if not enthusiastic service. The report of officials who have endangered their careers or lives by resisting a new regime is not very high."[45] But it is not merely the potential resistance of the bureaucrats of the *ancien régime* that is at stake. It is the willingness of the new regime to maintain those who served the old order. Why is this the case in eastern Europe?

First, the nonviolent nature of the revolutions in eastern Europe dictated that the settling of scores would be kept to a minimum. The refusal of the regimes to hold accountable the elite of the communist regimes extended to the bureaucracy.

Second, in none of the countries of eastern Europe was there a counter-elite ready to assume the reins of power. Those most responsible for fighting the former regime, the dissidents, were immensely influential in bringing down communism. But they were ill prepared to assume the reins of the state. Indeed, it is astonishing to see how little they count for in the new world they did so much to pave the way for. Timothy Garton Ash explains it this way:

> With remarkable speed, the intelligentsia has fragmented into separate professions, as in the West: journalists, publishers, academics, actors, not to mention those who have become officials, lawyers, diplomats. The milieus have faded, the "circles of friends" have dispersed or lost their special significance. Those who have remained in purely "intel-lectual" professions—above all, academics—have found themselves impoverished. Moreover, it is the businessmen and entrepreneurs who are the tone-setting heroes of this time. Thus, from having an abnormal importance before 1989, independent intellectuals have plum-meted to abnormal unimportance.[46]

The dissidents always had a natural ambivalence about holding power, in part, no doubt, because they could not embrace Weber's "ethic of responsibility" and in part because the "coffee shop" and "the circle of friends" are more conducive to awakening a public to a ruthless regime's abuses than to managing a society in which "technical" knowledge—law, economics, managerial skills—are prized.[47]

It has been argued that wholesale purges were unnecessary in countries such as Poland and Hungary, where the communist regime was in any case undergoing major changes. In these countries "an incremental replacement of elites had already taken place during the dying stages of the old regimes."[48] Klaus von Beyme distinguishes between the model of "regime collapse" and the "erosion of power" model. In the former, a gerontocracy that refused to renew itself by integrating younger party activists led to the collapse of the regime. This was the case in East Germany, Czechoslovakia, and Romania. In the latter case, as in Poland and Hungary, there was a gradual renewal of the communist elites in the 1980s, but even here mobility was restricted so that those below the top echelons of the bureaucracy had no qualms about switching sides when the communists were deposed.[49]

In no country in central and eastern Europe, with the exception of the GDR, were there wholesale changes in the bureaucratic personnel. Indeed, except at the top, the changes in bureaucratic structures and personnel have been kept to a minimum. Graham Wilson concludes the special number of the journal *Governance* devoted to this very issue thus: "We may look forward in years ahead to seeing whether the expectation that in modern states the need for bureaucracy outweighs distaste for the past behavior of bureaucrats, or whether drastic changes in bureaucratic personnel occur; so far, there have been few instances of radical personnel changes."[50] The political elite experienced a far greater renewal than did the bureaucratic elite, and this was the case in almost all the countries of the region. In Hungary, for example, over 95 percent of those in the 1990 legislature were first-time members. "Many of the new insiders were outsiders in the communist era, most of them were simply non-players."[51] The explanation for the relative stability of bureaucratic elites and the renewal of political elites is to be found in the availability of replacements.

Access to a political career is relatively simple in societies which suddenly experience an explosion of political parties. The number of parties competing in the elections of 1991 and 1992 varied from eleven in Albania to forty-five in Hungary, sixty-seven in Poland, and seventy-four in Romania.[52] No particular skills are called for, and what is required can be acquired on the job. The job is also relatively unconstraining. To be a bureaucrat is vastly different: it requires skills and a high tolerance for routine, anonymity, and subordination. While many were flocking to take up politics, few were seeking to join the bureaucracy.

In short, the regimes can scarcely afford to disturb the only structures that they can use as instruments. It is not at all certain that political leaders who topple regimes have the patience for the process of governing (although the cases of Walesa and Yeltsin may suggest the contrary). But in all cases, the new leaders must rely to a large extent on those who served the previous regime. Nonetheless the question raised by Kolarska-Bobinska remains valid: "can the old bureaucratic structures implement change in the social order to the extent necessary to bring about a system that is a result of negotiations among various interests and social forces?" She observes that "there has been no essential change in the personnel in the state administration at lower levels because of a lack of experts and professionals. How many persons, and in what posts, must be replaced if the bureaucracy is to be inspired with a new spirit?"[53]

## The Case of the GDR

In the countries that were governed by the Communist Party, many members of the old *nomenklatura* either began a conversion in the years preceding the demise of the communist regimes or adapted to the new regimes. But in all those countries, as in all postrevolutionary situations, there existed a political "elite vacuum."[54]

In most cases, this vacuum is filled with a combination of a degree of elite circulation and the old (transformed or co-opted) *nomenklatura*. This does not imply that the relatively kind treatment of the old elite does not pose political and moral problems, as the case of the Lustration Law in the Czech Republic shows. This law prohibits former high officials of the Communist Party from occupying positions of authority for a period of five years. The application of this law—whether to fire people currently holding office or to refuse to hire qualified people—is generally recognized as problematic.[55]

Vaclav Havel proclaimed that it was possible to reconcile politics and morality and that all one needed was "tact, the proper instincts, and good taste." In fact, he said that he had discovered "that good taste is more useful here than a degree in political science." No sooner had he uttered these words than "fate played a joke on me. It punished me for my self-assurance by exposing me to an immensely difficult dilemma." This dilemma was the Lustration Law, which many have considered a "morally flawed" law passed by a "democratically elected parliament."[56] Havel decided to sign the bill and then asked parliament to amend it.

Havel's dilemma was a moral one: the law did not sufficiently guarantee the civil rights of those who would be affected. But there was a practical side, one that was likely to render the law difficult to apply: the demand for competence, relative as this may be, meant in effect that the vacuum could not be filled by a readily available new elite.

The only case where the old elite was removed is found in the GDR, but this was also the only case where an alternative elite was immediately available. Moreover, as Klaus von Beyme notes, of "all the East European countries currently in transition, only East Germany does not need to change its political and economic systems simultaneously."[57] Nonetheless, East Germany, like the other East European states, did undergo a revolution, one that meant a new state and new institutions. During this process the economies and most public functions have to continue to operate, which is why no wholesale purges of bureaucracies take place. This was also the case in the early phase of the transition in the GDR.

The GDR entered an entirely different phase when reunification with the West occurred. It was not merely that reunification dissolved the GDR. It was that

> the reality of unification gave the decision-makers an additional and unique opportunity: elite transfer. This term refers to a wide and broad deployment of western public servants drawn from the Bonn government, from the western State (Lander) governments, from western municipalities and western specialized agencies and institutions to the new administrative structures of the eastern regimes.[58]

Koing shows in his study of replacement of the old East German *nomenklatura* that from the beginning of the unification process, civil servants from the West were being shuttled to Berlin by the hundreds to keep the administrative machine running. Subsequently, with the transfer of civil servants from the West to the East, what had been a temporary process became permanent. Consequently, as Koing concludes, "It can be safely said that West Germans are represented in all administrative branches and in all public service ranks."[59]

Following the reunification of Germany, the new rules that went into effect permitted the dismissal of officials for a large number of reasons (lack of qualifications, violation of human rights, cooperation with the Stasi, administrative reorganization). Thus, a former bureaucracy that was characterized by what Derlien has referred to as "politicized incompetence"[60] was in fact replaced.

Although several factors may explain the successful replacement of the East German elite, one stands out: the availability of alternative elites. This also explains why the political elites have experienced a greater degree of new entrants in all East European countries than have the bureaucratic elites. The existence of what Derlien call "the reservoir of new elites" and the concomitant "elite import"[61] distinguished the case of the GDR from the other countries that experienced a transition to democracy. Competence is always in short supply and the new political leaders have to confront the urgent task of reforming political institutions while keeping economic institutions running. If administrative incompetence or loyalty to a party-bureaucratic state is to be replaced by a competent bureaucracy based on the rule of law, then measures need to be taken to develop a system of recruitment and training of public officials. The posttransition period may be able to make do with the relics of the bureaucratic apparatus of the ancien regime, but what of the future? How will the needs of a democratic, industrial welfare state be administered? More pertinently, have the countries of central and eastern Europe been hesitant to link the consolidation of their democratic regimes with the creation of a professionalized bureaucratic structure?

The transition has given rise to considerable debate on constitutional issues, economic reform, and the relationship between center and periphery. Absent from these debates has been the creation of professionalized structure. There are both cultural and political reasons for this failure.

The cultural hurdles concern the fact that public service has never been accorded much importance. In fact, its longtime association with the Communist Party has made it an object of scorn. It was a politicized bureaucracy, substantially incompetent and known for its arbitrariness. That this remains the general attitude toward the bureaucratic apparatus may not be surprising. What is surprising, however, is that the political elite itself has been slow to recognize the importance of setting in motion a process of developing a bureaucratic structure that has a legal basis and that is characterized by professionalism. What Hesse and Goetz observe for the Czech and Slovak

Republics applies to the other countries of eastern Europe. These countries have not

> been able to formulate and implement policies which could be expected to result in major improvements in the personnel sector. The steps which have been taken have principally been directed at alleviating some of the most pressing short-term difficulties, but have failed to tackle more deep-seated structural problems. Moreover, there is little indication that in adopting measures concerning particular elements of personnel policy, sufficient thought has been given to their interlinkages. In other words, isolated steps, without reference to a more comprehensive reform design, have predominated.[62]

None of the countries of central and eastern Europe has developed a civil service statute akin to anything that exists in the Western democracies. The development of these statutes was long in coming, and while they may be questioned today in some western democracies, they remain important elements in an orderly process of recruitment that privileges competence over patronage. In the east European countries there is yet no civil service statute in effect. In fact there is no civil service that is recognized as such. Even "the idea of a public service as such does not have a basis in law."[63]

Civil service statutes in the west recognize a legal basis of employment for public servants that is separate from the labor laws that obtain in these societies. They regulate rights and duties, provide protection, and set salary scales for all public servants. There have been discussions and drafts of laws in eastern Europe that are moving toward the creation of a unified civil service. As of now, such a service does not exist. Each minister organizes his ministry according to his own wishes. Hiring is done by the individual ministry and party politics predominates in the process.

A professional bureaucracy requires competent civil servants and tomorrow's bureaucracies will be the result of the measures taken today to train higher civil servants. Efforts in this direction have not gone very far. "It is difficult," Writes Lazlo Keri, "to find a trace of an overall concept in the selection and appointment process of executives."[64] Even less is it possible to find a policy that facilitates the training of those who will run the state apparatus in the years to come. In Poland and Hungary schools exist for the training of middle-level civil servants, but neither carries much prestige or has made progress toward creating a cadre of high-ranking officials.

The OECD has sought to encourage the creation of an SES (senior

executive service) group within the bureaucracies of the East European
countries. While the American SES reform never materialized in the way
that the reformers intended, there are variants of the model (the German
model of *Beamtpolitische*, the ENA model in France). The logic behind the
creation of a senior civil service elite is that such a reform would strengthen
the bureaucracy, would professionalize it, and would increase the morale of
the entire structure because it would show those lower in the hierarchy that
the government now valued this institution. But this is unlikely to happen,
at least in the near future, because, as two OECD officials have noted,
politicians are not interested in issues that affect the bureaucracy, and neither is the public.[65]

The creation of a professional cadre of senior civil servants is considered
crucial for the efficient working of the government structure because the
task of coordination would be facilitated. There are few functions today that
can be totally carried out within a single ministry. The policymaking process
depends on the capacity of the governmental and bureaucratic machine to
coordinate both the making of policy and the implementation of policies.
This now represents a new challenge to the bureaucracies of the East European countries, and one for which they find themselves singularly
unprepared.

## Conclusion: Bureaucracy in the Transition Phase

The transition to democracy in central and eastern Europe is associated
with a departure from a repressive state whose chief instrument was a large,
politicized, and arbitrary bureaucratic apparatus. Not surprisingly, the transition process in all democratizing eastern European societies has been preoccupied with divesting the state of its all-embracing role in the economy
and in society.

While any transition to a democratic order need to concern itself with
creating political competition, establishing a new constitutional order, and
separating civil and political society, it remains the case that no society is
conceivable without a bureaucratic apparatus. Just as the nation-state is the
dominant form of territorial organization, so no state operates without the
instrument of a bureaucracy.

Democracy requires more than an apparatus. It calls for the development
of a competent, legally based, accountable, and professional bureaucratic

structure. Creating such an institution has evidently not been a central pre-occupation in central and eastern Europe. The new regimes are inevitably reacting against the critical instrument used by the old order. Paradoxically, the instrument of political power (the vast network of bureaucratic institutions) is the object of far more suspicion, mistrust, and derision in the post-communist era than was the locus of power (the party) during the reign of communism. In part this is because of the omnipresence of the bureaucracy, with its multiple police and security forces, in the daily lives of citizens. The reappearance of the party politicians also poses less of a threat than does the reappearance of bureaucrats because the former participate today in the political process without enjoying the monopoly they once possessed. Yet another factor helps drive the antistatist or antibureaucratic fervor of the democratizing societies: the global context within which the transition is taking place. This context, defined mostly by a reaction to statism and to state intervention in the economy, is also characterized by deregulation and privatization of state assets, even of services long provided by the state. Within this global context there is inevitably a considerable degree of emulation, or bandwagoning. Emulation, notes John Ikenberry,

> is an important process by which policies spread because states tend to have similar general goals. All states are interested in doing better rather than worse; they prefer economic and political success to any alternatives, and the experience of other states provide lessons and examples of how success might be achieved. The guiding rule is: copy what works.[66]

It has become evident by now that the study of postcommunism requires a new vocabulary and a new approach. At the same time, it invites us to reconsider classical principles which have been long entrenched in our liberal tradition. It shows, for example, that less state power does not always mean more freedom. On the contrary, a weak state might be a serious obstacle to the success of economic, political, and social reforms. Liberalization cannot succeed under conditions of state collapse or inefficient bureaucracy. As Stephen Holmes points out, the main problem of postcommunism seems to be the crisis of governance. Administratively weak states prove to be incapable of implementing reform. As Holmes and others have noted, post-communist studies should shift the agenda away from cultural traditions toward discovering the way in which eastern European countries are being governed. Liberal rights are difficult to implement without effective, administrative, and adjudicative authorities. That is why it is high time to reconsider the role of bureaucracy in the transition to democracy.

NOTES

1. Dankwart A. Rustow, "Transitions to Democracy: Toward a Dynamic Model," *Comparative Politics* 2, no. 2 (August 1970), pp. 356–357.
2. Max Weber, "Bureaucracy," in H. H. Gertz and C. Wright Mills, eds., *From Max Weber: Essays in Sociology* (New York: Oxford University Press, 1962), p. 215.
3. Ibid., p. 216.
4. Joseph Schumpeter, *Capitalism, Socialism, and Democracy*, 3rd edition (New York: Harper, 1949), p. 206.
5. Ibid.
6. Ibid. p. 293.
7. Ibid.
8. Ibid.
9. See Adam Przeworski, *Democracy and the Market: Political and Economic Reforms in Eastern Europe and Latin America* (New York: Cambridge University Press, 1991), p. 8. It is worth noting that Spain was endowed with a competent bureaucratic structure that was immediately usable by the post-Franco regime.
10. Juan Linz and Alfred Stepan, *Problems of Democratic Transition and Consolidation: Southern Europe, South America, and Eastern Europe* (Baltimore: Johns Hopkins University Press, 1996), p. 11. Jacek Kochanowicz, "Reforming Weak States and Deficient Bureaucracies," in Joan Nelson, ed., *Intricate Links: Democratization and Market Reforms in Latin America and Eastern Europe* (New Brunswick, N.J.: Transaction Publishers, 1994), p. 202.
11. Kochanowicz, "Reforming Weak States and Deficient Bureaucracies," p. 203.
12. Stephen Holmes, "What Russia Teaches Us Now: How Weak States Threaten Freedom," *The American Prospect* (July–August 1997), p. 32.
13. Ibid. p, 33.
14. See Ezra Suleiman, ed., *Bureaucrats and Policy-Making: A Comparative Perspective* (New York: Holmes & Meier, 1983).
15. Graham Wilson, "Counter Elites and Bureaucracies," *Governance* 6 (July 1993), p. 433.
16. Ibid., p. 434.
17. John Keeler, "Opening the Windows for Reform: Mandates, Crises, and Extraordinary Policy-Making," *Comparative Political Studies* 25 (January 1993), p. 66.

18. See John Kingdon, *Agendas, Alternatives, and Public Policies* (Boston: Little Brown, 1984).

19. Russel Bova, "Political Dynamics of the Post-Communist Transition: A Comparative Perspective," in Nancy Bermeo, ed., *Liberalization and Democratization: Change in the Soviet Union and Eastern Europe* (Baltimore: Johns Hopkins University Press, 1992), p. 118.

20. Lena Kolarska-Bobinska, "The Role of the State in the Transition Period," unpublished ms., p. 2.

21. Cited in Lena Kolarska-Bobinska, "The Role of the State: Contradictions in the Transition to Democracy," in Douglas Greenberg et al., *Constitutionalism and Democracy: Change in the Soviet Union and Eastern Europe* (Baltimore: Johns Hopkins University Press, 1992), p. 301.

22. Peter Drucker, "Really Reinventing Government," *Atlantic Monthly* (February 1995), p. 61.

23. See Ezra Suleiman and John Waterbury, eds., *The Political Economy of Public Sector Reform and Privatization* (Boulder, Colo.: Westview Press, 1990).

24. See R. Frydman et al., *The Privatization Process in Central Europe* (London: Central European University Press, 1993).

25. Ibid.

26. Jeremy J. Richardson, "Pratique des privatisations en Grand-Bretagne," in Vincent Wright *Les Privatisations en Europe: Programmes et problèmes* (Paris: Acte Sud, 1993)

27. *The Reform of Hungarian Public Administration* (Budapest: Hungarian Institute of Public Administration, 1991), p. 15. For further information on decentralization in Hungary, see *Public Administration in Hungary* (Budapest: Hungarian Institute of Public Administration, 1992).

28. See Joachim Jens Hesse and Klaus H. Goetz, "Public Sector Reform in Central and Eastern Europe: The Case of the Czech and Slovak Federal Republic," (Unpublished report, Oxford and Geneva, July 1992), pp. 31–32.

29. Joachim Jens Hesse and Klaus H. Goetz, "Public Sector Reform in Central and Eastern Europe: The Case of Poland" (Unpublished report, Oxford and Geneva, July 1992), p. 37.

30. Ibid., p. 39.

31. Hesse and Goetz (note 27), p. 33.

32. Adam Przeworski, "Eastern Europe: The Most Significant Event in Our Time?" cited in Hans-Ulrich Derlien and George J. "Eastern European Transitions: Elite, Bureaucracies, and the European Community," *Governance* 6 (July 1993), pp. 306–7.

33. Janos Simon, "Post-Paternalist Political Culture in Hungary: Relationship between Citizens and Politics During and After the Melancholic Revolution (1989–1991)," *Communist and Post-Communist Studies* 26 (June 1993), p. 227.

34. Roman Frydman and Andrej Rapaczynski, *Privatization in Eastern Europe: Is the State Withering Away?* (New York and Budapest: Central European University Press, 1994), p. 175.

35. Ibid., pp. 175–76.

36. Kochanowicz "Reforming Weak States and Deficient Bureaucracies," p. 219.

37. Ibid., pp. 197–203.

38. Joan M. Nelson, "How Market Reforms and Democratic Consolidation Affect Each Other," in Joan Nelson, ed., *Intricate Links: Democratization and Market Reforms in Latin America and Eastern Europe*, p. 78.

39. Andrew Shonfield, *Modern Capitalism: The Changing Balance of Public and Private Power* (London: Oxford University, 1965).

40. Kochanowicz, "Reforming Weak States and Deficient Bureaucracies," p. 199

41. Jan Kubik, "Post-Communist Transformation in East Central Europe: Dual (Political-Economic) or Quadruple (Political-Economic-Administrative-Cultural)? A Study of Cieszyn, Silesia, Poland (Manuscript, February 1994), pp. 10–11.

42. Ibid., 40.

43. OECD, SIGMA, "Mission Statement" (Paris), p. 2.

44. SIGMA, *Bureaucratic Barriers to Entry: Foreign Investment in Central and Eastern Europe* (Paris: OECD: GD 94, 124, 1994), pp. 16–17.

45. Wilson, Counterelites and Bureaucracies," p. 433.

46. Timothy Garton Ash, "Prague: Intellectuals, and Politicians," *New York Review of Books* (January 12, 1995), p. 40.

47. Ibid, for an interesting discussion of Vaclav Havel's relationship to power.

48. Klaus von Beyme, "Regime Transition and Recruitment in Eastern Europe," *Governance* 6 (July 1993), p. 411.

49. Ibid, p. 413.

50. Wilson, "Counterelites and Bureaucracies," p. 436.

51. Thomas F. Remington, ed., *Parliaments in Transition: The New Legislative Politics in the Former USSR and Eastern Europe* (Boulder, Colo.: Westview Press, 1994), p. 33.

52. *The Economist*, p. March 13, 1993.

53. Kolarska-Bobinska, "The Role of the State in the Transition Period," p. 309.

54. Derlien and Szablowski, "Eastern European Transitions: Elite, Bureaucracies, and the European Community," *Governance* 6 (July 1993), p. 311.

55. Nonetheless, the Romanian case shows that any delay in passing a law regulating the access to the files of the former secret police may not be favorable to the political and moral climate of the country.

56. Cited in Ash, "Prague: Intellectuals and Politicians," pp. 37–38

57. Von Beyme, "Regime Transition and Recruitment of Elites in Eastern Europe," p. 410.

58. Klaus Koing, "Bureaucratic Integration by Elite Transfer: The Case of the Former GDR," *Governance* 6 (July 1993), p. 389.
59. Ibid., p. 391.
60. Hans-Ulrich Derlien, "Matching Responsiveness and Expertise: Political and Administrative Elite in Germany," in Henry Mendras and Ezra Suleiman, eds., *Elites in Democratic Societies* (London: Francis Pinter, forthcoming). See the French version of Derlien's chapter in Ezra Suleiman and Henri Mendras, eds., *Le recruitement des élites en Europe* (Paris: La Decouverte, 1995).
61. Ibid.
62. Hesse and Goetz, "Public Sector Reform in central and eastern Europe," p. 42.
63. Ibid.
64. Lazlo Keri, "Decision-Making of the Government from the Point of View of Organizational Sociology," (unpublished manuscript), p. 89.
65. Jak Jabes and Staffan Synnerstrom, "La Reforme de l'administration publique dans les pays d'Europe centrale et orientale," *Revue Française d'Administration Publique*, no. 70 (April–June 1995), p. 275.
66. G. John Ikenberry, "The International Spread of Privatization Policies: Inducements, Learning, and 'Policy Bandwagoning'," in Ezra Suleiman and John Waterbury, eds., *The Political Economy of Public Sector Reform and Privatization* (Boulder, Colo.: Westview Press, 1990), p. 103.

# 8 The Paradoxes of Contemporary Democracy: Formal, Participatory, and Social Dimensions

*Evelyne Huber, Dietrich Rueschemeyer, and John D. Stephens*

We made this assertion when we introduced the results of a broad-based comparative historical investigation of the roots of democracy in capitalist development: "We care about formal democracy because it tends to be more than merely formal. It tends to be real to some extent. Giving the many a real voice in the formal collective decision-making of a country is the most promising basis for further progress in the distribution of power and other forms of substantive equality."[1]

We held that formal democracy was valuable in its own right, but we emphasized that it makes deepening toward more fully participatory democracy and progress toward increasing equality possible. And we argued, further, that the same social and historical conditions that promoted formal democracy—in particular, a shift in the class balance of power in civil society favoring subordinate classes—would also advance the cause of greater social and economic equality. Yet in the current historical conjuncture strides toward introducing and consolidating formal democracy in Latin America and eastern Europe appear to be combined with movements away from more fully participatory democracy and equality. We want to analyze this apparent anomaly in this essay.

We begin by defining formal, participatory, and social democracy. By formal democracy we mean a political system that combines four features: regular free and fair elections, universal suffrage, accountability of the state's administrative organs to the elected representatives, and effective guarantees for freedom of expression and association as well as protection against arbitrary state action. Indeed, the word democracy is commonly understood in this way when it is used with some conceptual care. Often, however, it is used more loosely. Current political discourse bestows the label frequently on any country that has held an election roughly free of fraud. Even if elections are held with some regularity, it is worthwhile to inquire whether opposition could be expressed and organized without fear and to what extent the state apparatus is in fact accountable to elected officials. If in the past limitations of the suffrage were the most common means to abridge democracy, today restricting the state's accountability and curtailing civil rights are the less easily visible tools of choice.[2]

Even if all four requirements are met, a country may still be far from equality in the process of making collective decisions. Formal democracy does not entail an equal distribution of political power. And—presumably related closely to differences in the distribution of actual political power—formally democratic countries will differ considerably in social policies that reduce social and economic inequality. We therefore introduce two additional dimensions: high levels of participation without systematic differences across social categories (for example, class, ethnicity, gender) and increasing equality in social and economic outcomes. We call a political system that meets the requirements in the first four plus the fifth dimension participatory democracy.[3] Social democracy denotes a political system that meets the requirements in all six dimensions.[4] Social democracy is thus akin to T. H. Marshall's concept of "social citizenship." Policies that effectively advance it will be called "social democratic" policies.[5]

Formal democracies fall far short of the ideals associated with this conception of social democracy. But to dismiss them as merely formal would be problematic and even politically and intellectually irresponsible. Certainly, protection of human rights and thus the elimination of fear of the military and police brutality are immensely important to all citizens in their daily lives. Even the formal share in political decisionmaking represented by voting in regular intervals has often brought real advantages to the many. And governmental accountability to elected representatives restrains abuses of power that are clearly detrimental to the interests of citizens at large. Above all, however, formal democracy opens the possibility of, and is a requisite for, advances toward participatory and social democracy.

Formal democracy can support advances toward social democracy where higher levels of political mobilization support reformist political movements and social democratic policies. Egalitarian social policies in turn enable more citizens to participate in the political process and thus contribute to the consolidation and deepening of democracy. Historical developments can demonstrate such a virtuous cycle.

Yet this virtuous cycle is not the only possibility. Formal democracy may remain formal. A disjunction between formal and social democracy was not a problem for nineteenth-century liberals. Indeed, they predicted and desired it, and many of today's neoliberals would take the same position.

Finally, a more detrimental but equally realistic possibility is a vicious cycle. Inegalitarian policies and the poverty they create engender such problems as marginalization and crime. Politically, they may lead to demobilization, the corrosion of judicial and civil rights, and a "delegative democracy" that sharply reduces the accountability of the government.[6] The possibility of a vicious cycle is particularly relevant for new and transitional democracies, where we often find considerable variation in the extent to which the criteria for formal democracy are met and where the foundations of democracy are particularly vulnerable.

In the following we will discuss determinants of formal, participatory, and social democracy in the current historical conjuncture, drawing primarily on developments in Latin American countries that have made transitions to democracy since the late 1970s. Before we turn to these current Latin American developments, however, we will first briefly restate the theoretical framework we developed and put to the test in our earlier comparative historical analysis of the conditions of formal democracy, then develop theoretical expectations about the conditions of participatory and social democracy based on the literature dealing with mature industrial democracies.[7]

## On the Conditions of Formal Democracy

Democracy, even formal democracy, is a matter of power and power sharing. This premise led us to focus on three clusters of power as shaping the conditions for democratization as well as for the maintenance of formal democracy. First, the balance of class power is the most important aspect of the balance of power in civil society. Second, the structure of the state and state-society relations shapes the balance of power between state and civil society and also influences the balance of power within society. Third, transnational structures of power are grounded in the international economy and the system of states; they modify the balance of power within society, affect state-society relations, and constrain political decisionmaking.

Shifts in the balance of power in society and particularly in the balance of power among social classes are the major explanation for the overall relationship between capitalist development and democracy. Capitalist development, we found, reduces the power of landlords and strengthens subordinate classes. The working and the middle classes, unlike other subordinate classes in history, gain an unprecedented capacity for self-organization due to such developments as urbanization, factory production and new forms of communication and transportation. And collective organization in associations, unions, and parties constitutes the major power resource of the many, who lack power based on property, coercion, social status, or cultural hegemony. These changes in the balance of class power link democracy to development, even though the particular outcomes vary across countries due to differences in the politics of mobilization and class alliances.

This finding negates other explanations of the link between capitalist development and democracy. This link is not due primarily to an expansion of the middle classes. Nor can it be explained by a structural correspondence between capitalism and democracy, by the thesis that more complex societies require a differentiated and flexible form of government. Finally, our findings are at odds with the classic claim of both liberal and Marxist theory that democracy is a creation of the bourgeoisie, the dominant class of capital owners.

However, the balance of class power is not the only factor shaping the conditions for formal democracy. The correlation between capitalist development and democracy is far from perfect, and this imperfection is due in large part to the impact of the other two power clusters, the structure of the state and of state-society relations and international structures.

The structure of the state and state-society relations are critically important to the chances for democracy. The state needs to be strong and autonomous enough to ensure the rule of law and avoid being the captive of the interests of dominant groups. However, the power of the state needs to be counterbalanced by the organizational strength of civil society to make democracy viable. The state must not be so strong and autonomous from all social forces as to overpower civil society and rule without accountability. The different parts of the state, in particular the security forces, must be sufficiently under presidential and/or parliamentary control to insure de facto accountability.

International power relations are equally important to the chances for democracy. Aside from the impact of war (typically creating a need for mass support and discrediting ruling groups in case of defeat), power relations grounded in the changing constellations of world politics and the world economy can very strongly affect the structure and capacity of the state, the constraints faced by state policymakers, state-society relations, and even the balance of class power within society.

It was, and is, our hypothesis that these three clusters of power are not only important in the establishment and the maintenance of formal democracy but are also critical in deepening formal democracy toward more fully participatory democracy and advancing toward social and economic equality.

## On the Conditions of Participatory and Social Democracy: Past Research and Theoretical Expectations

Several bodies of literature are relevant for the development of our hypotheses on the determinants of participatory and social democracy. The first deals with the determinants of political participation across countries. We do not limit political participation to voting but include all forms of politically relevant mobilization as well as the effective translation of citizens' demands into the political process via institutional channels such as political parties. The literature on comparative social policy and the interrelated literature on social democracy, including wage bargaining, union organization, and workers' participation and codetermination, are also relevant to our argument. We can draw only selectively on these voluminous bodies of literature here, but our review faithfully reflects the main thrust of past research.

### The Balance of Class Power and Class Coalitions

The interlock between our theory of the social origins of formal democracy and the empirical findings of the bodies of literature bearing on the determinants of participatory and social democracy is very tight in the case of class power relations. Indeed, our arguments on the effects of class power and class coalitions on formal democracy can be seen as the exact counterpart of the "class power resources" approach to explaining cross-national differences in welfare state development and more broadly variations in the social democratic policy agenda as characterized above.[8] The central tenets of this approach have received substantial support in both comparative historical and cross-national quantitative research. On the redistributive impact of welfare provisions, on their "decommodifying" impact, on the provision of public social services, and on their impact on gender equality, rule by social democratic parties or union strength appears as the single most important explanatory variable.[9]

The social democratic policy pattern is not limited to social policy. Indeed, it is not limited to government policy but also includes, most importantly, the outcomes of bargaining between employers and unions. Various studies have shown a close relationship between social democratic governance and/or union strength and workers' rights, codetermination, egalitarian wage policy, and unemployment.[10] Other studies have shown that the egalitarian policy pattern promoted by social democracy has not come at the expense of economic growth.[11] Given its high wage costs and generous social provisions, the social democratic growth model (and, incidentally, the German Christian Democratic model) of economic success has taken the "high road" to international competition, based on capital intensive, high labor quality export production.

Though grounded in a very different theoretical approach, some of the principal findings of the literature on cross-national differences in participation mesh well with this class mobilization view of the welfare state.[12] This research shows that cross-national differences in participation result primarily from differences in the participation of socioeconomic status groups. These differences, in turn, are the product of the institutional setting: countries with strong unions and strong parties, especially working-class parties, are characterized by no socioeconomic differences in voter turnout and relatively small ones in other types of participation.

## State and Civil Society

The empirical work bearing on participatory and social democracy does not address the relationship between the state and civil society in the same fashion as we, along with other scholars, have done in analyzing the social and historical origins of formal democracy. However, a large body of work addresses the effect of state structure and state actors on the welfare state and can be refashioned to fit our way of framing the question.

Before outlining the hypotheses suggested by this literature, it is necessary to comment on the concepts of the "density of civil society," "citizen mobilization and participation," and "power of subordinate classes." These concepts are distinct but refer to closely interrelated phenomena. Given the close links between organization and participation in the political process shown in the empirical literature, the density of civil society and the degree of citizen mobilization and participation must strongly covary across societies. Subordinate class power is primarily a consequence of class organization, so it too must covary with the density of civil society. But they are not the same thing. Bowling leagues and singing associations strengthen civil society without doing much for political participation or class organization. The League of Women Voters and the Sierra Club strengthen civil society and political participation without greatly strengthening class organization. Trade unions and peasant leagues strengthen all three.

It is fundamentally mistaken to view the relation between state action and the self-organization of society as a "tradeoff"—the more of one the less of the other. To the contrary, associations in civil society have tended to grow, both in the United States and in Europe, as the state took on new tasks in society. The self-organization of subordinate classes, too, stands everywhere in a relation of mutual reinforcement with state social policies.

The autonomy as well as the instrumental capacity of the state is critically important for advances toward social democracy. One might be tempted to argue on logical grounds that, in a formally democratic polity, the more autonomous the state is, the less citizens' mobilization and participation in the political process will translate into influence on policy outcomes, other things being equal. In the limiting case, an extremely autonomous state can ignore the demands of citizens no matter how well mobilized they are. However, a distinction between autonomy of the state from dominant socioeconomic interests and overall autonomy complicates the picture usefully: the higher the degree of independence from dominant interests and the greater the responsiveness to broad-based pressures, the greater the chances for advances toward social democracy. Any policy-based advance toward social democracy requires significant instrumental state capacity: the greater the state's capacity to implement policies effectively, the greater the degree to which citizens' mobilization and participation will translate into influences on social outcomes, ceteris paribus.

Some scholars have argued that state autonomy, the policymaking activity of bureaucrats or "political elites," and the insulation of elites from popular pressures (all related but conceptually distinct) lead to social policy innovation.[13] Moreover, while the motivations they attribute to elite innovators vary from benevolence to Bismarckian cooptation, they almost always see innovation as pushing policy in a more generous direction. But the relationship between autonomy and policy development and generosity is a post hoc empirical generalization. Logically, an autonomous state or autonomous political elite could roll back policy just as easily as expand it. What we expect to be decisive is the degree of autonomy from dominant socioeconomic interests and the responsiveness to more broad-based pressures. The latter may include, as in Bismarck's social security legislation, a responsiveness to anticipated pressures and tensions in society.

## Transnational Structures of Power

In the cases of relations of class power and, to a lesser extent, of state power vis-à-vis civil society, our theoretical framework leads us to predict that the same constellation of forces would promote formal as well as participatory and social democracy. In the case of transnational structures of power, however, the effects on formal and social democracy are quite different, and the present conjuncture, though quite favorable for formal democracy, especially for regular elections, freedom of contestation, and universal suffrage, is very unfavorable for participatory and social democracy. We can distinguish two features of transnational structures of power, the international market, on the one hand, and multilateral institutions dominated by core countries and bilateral relations, on the other.

In the recent literature on the welfare state and social democracy in advanced industrial democracies, the impact of the international system on social democratic policy has been a central, probably the central, concern. The main point of departure of recent research has been the contention that recent reversals of social democratic policy in its heartland of northern Europe can be attributed to the increasing internationalization of the economies of advanced capitalist societies in general and the process of European integration in particular, which have constricted—indeed, according to some observers, virtually eliminated—the policy options of these societies' governments.

There are reasons to take the most far-reaching of these claims with a bit of skepticism. As Katzenstein has pointed out, the small democracies of Europe, most of which have been governed frequently by social democracy, had very open economies well before the post-Bretton Woods era of increased internationalization, and their large welfare states can be seen as "domestic compensation" for organized labor's acceptance of wage restraint and other policies to promote international competitiveness.[14] We have argued elsewhere that the modest increases in trade openness of the past two decades have had little effect on the social democratic economic model, and the generous social democratic welfare state has not undermined the competitiveness of the exports of these countries. However, the dramatic internationalization of financial markets has eliminated some of the supply side tools which were central to social democracy's economic model during the golden age of postwar capitalism.[15]

Part of the neoliberal myth contends that the worldwide trend toward liberalization, deregulation, and privatization can be explained entirely by the fact that increased international competition has forced nations to take these measures as steps toward greater efficiency. The role of the U.S. government, the IMF, the World Bank, the Bundesbank, and other international and core country institutions in promoting, at times one should say enforcing, neoliberal policies can not be denied. Thus, the political side of current transnational structures of power, while supporting the expansion of formal democracy, has worked against the promotion of participatory and social democracy because it has closed off consideration of alternative social democratic policy and, by closing off alternatives, has made popular mobilization and participation less meaningful.

## Determinants of Formal Democracy in Contemporary Latin America

Discussion of the trajectory of democracy in Latin America since the late 1970s has to begin with the distinction between the transition phase and the phase after the first democratic elections, generally called the consolidation phase.[16] Conditions that prevailed during the first do not necessarily persist in the second. Moreover, conditions that are favorable for transition may not necessarily be equally favorable for consolidation.

In the dominant conceptualization of consolidation, all relevant actors accept the rules of the democratic game and thus abandon the search for other routes to political power. Consequently, these actors and a larger public believe that democracy will persist for the foreseeable future.[17] Some authors add the elimination of vestiges of authoritarian rule, such as military prerogatives and other restrictions on the authority of elected officials, as a criterion, which is another way of saying that a consolidated formal democracy has to meet fully the requirements in all dimensions, including accountability.[18]

In practice, many democracies have survived without achieving full consolidation in the sense of eliminating these vestiges and ensuring the acceptance and proper functioning of a whole array of democratic rules and institutions.[19] The international community generally regards countries as democracies when they meet the test of regular free and apparently reasonably fair elections with universal suffrage. However, many of these countries are deficient in other criteria that define formal democracy. Most prominently, accountability is often weak because of overpowering presidents and weak legislatures and judiciaries. Second, civil and, to a lesser extent, political rights are very unevenly protected across classes, genders, and territorial units.[20] Third, patrimonialist practices blur lines between the public and the private realms.[21] In a close analysis, many of the new democracies in Latin America conform to our conceptualization of formal democracy only partially.

In terms of our three clusters of power as applied to the new democracies in Latin America, after an upsurge of mobilization during the transition the balance of class power shifted against subordinate classes, and the weakness of subordinate classes is responsible for the deficiencies in formal as well as in participatory and social democracy. As far as the state is concerned, various dimensions of weakness facilitated the transition but then became obstacles both to full realization of formal democracy and to any movement toward social democracy. Finally, the international system has had contradictory influences on formal and social democracy.

## The Balance of Class Power

There is general agreement that the transitions from authoritarian rule began with tensions within the military governments and between them and their bourgeois allies, typically intensified by economic problems.[22] What pushed initial liberalization toward democratization, though, was pressure from a rapidly reemerging civil society. Such pressure came from a whole gamut of associations, ranging from press and bar associations at the top of the social ladder to human rights groups in the middle and unions and neighborhood organizations in poor urban communities at the bottom. For these divisions at the top and pressures from the bottom to result in democratic elections, political parties also had to regroup and furnish the leadership to negotiate the terms of exit with the authoritarian rulers.[23]

The upsurge of mobilization of old and new social movements during the transition was followed by a decline after the first democratic elections. In part, this decline was due to the disappearance of the common target of protest, in part to disenchantment with the failure of democratic rule to bring about significant improvements in the material situation of most citizens, and in part to the difficulties experienced by social movements in attempting to work with and through political parties.[24] In addition, in those countries where economic stabilization and structural adjustment policies were continued and intensified after the transition (for example, Argentina, Brazil, and Peru), civil society, particularly labor, was weakened substantially.

Despite the decline in mobilization and the weakening of organizations of subordinate classes, formal democracies have persisted, albeit in a form meeting principally the criterion of democratic elections and falling short in accountability and protection of civil rights. The deficiencies in formal democracy can easily be explained in our theoretical framework by the lack of strong organizations of subordinate classes. To explain the survival of (often truncated versions of) formal democracy, we need to remind the reader that we have emphasized the delicate balance between pressures from below and threat perception at the top necessary for the installation and survival of democracy.[25] This balance remained favorable for democratic survival, as pressures from below weakened but threat perception declined more radically.[26] This decline in threat perception is in part due to the very weakening of labor, to disarray and lack of a coherent project on the left, and to external pressures reinforcing a neoliberal order favorable to the newly powerful business groups, a topic to which we shall return.

## The Structure of the State

Fragmentation of the state apparatus and disunity among the groups controlling it were conducive to democratic transitions. Divisions opened the space for the upsurge of civil society and for the formation of coalitions among softliners within the state apparatus and members of the democratic opposition.[27] After the transitions, though, continued fragmentation and weakness of state institutions, particularly those that had been suspended or manipulated under authoritarian rule, such as the legislature and judiciary, became an obstacle. They made it difficult to establish the accountability of elected officials as well as universal enforcement of civil and political rights.

In some cases and in some respects developments in the state apparatus have favored the survival of formal democracy. In Argentina the size of the coercive apparatus of the state was reduced, and civilian control over the security forces strengthened. In such countries as Argentina, Brazil, Peru, and Bolivia, state shrinking as a result of structural adjustment policies reduced opportunities for corruption, that is, the blurring between the public and private sphere.

### The International System

The most visible and important impact of the international system on the survival of (albeit deficient forms of) formal democracy has certainly consisted of diplomatic pressures to respect democratic elections.[28] Whereas such pressures from North American and West European countries were crucial in many cases of early transitions, increasingly these pressures have emanated from Latin American countries themselves. Democratically elected governments developed a strong self-interest in ostracizing neighbors deviating from formal democratic election procedures.

Developments in the geopolitical situation, particularly the end of the Cold War, have been conducive to the survival of democracy both directly and indirectly. Directly, they have reduced the tendency of the two superpowers to support nondemocratic but loyal regimes. Indirectly, they have eliminated the perception of a Communist threat among economic elites and thus the fear of potential weaknesses of democratic regimes in the face of such a threat or, even worse from their point of view, of potential complicity of democratic governments with Communist forces.

Developments in the world economy have had a more ambiguous impact on formal democracy. On the one hand, the debt crisis helped the transitions along by intensifying internal tensions in authoritarian regimes and between them and their allies in civil society. Moreover, the insistence of international financial institutions on neoliberal reforms has reduced the perceived threat to private property among economic elites and thus increased their tolerance for formal democracy. On the other hand, continuing debt pressure and the imposition of structural adjustment measures have reinforced a tendency to concentrate power in the executive, insulate economic policymakers, and rule by decree. In other words, they have hampered the institutionalization of democratic consultation and accountability. In addition, they have effected a shift in the balance of power against subordinate classes and thus reduced the potential for a rectification of these deficiencies.

## Determinants of Participatory Democracy in Contemporary Latin America

### The Balance of Class Power

As we pointed out above, comparative research has shown that a high degree of organization among lower classes (or socioeconomic status groups) reduces class differentials (or differentials by socioeconomic status) in political participation.[29] In addition, the literature on the welfare state has demonstrated that among these organizations political parties play a crucial role in articulating lower class demands for redistributive policies and translating them into policy.

The new democracies in Latin America have experienced problems in both areas. In the particular juncture of the transitions, pent-up demands for information about victims of human rights abuses, for economic policy changes and minimal social services, for labor rights, and for democratic elections were strong enough to mobilize citizens into action even in the absence of organizational ties. Yet as the common target of mobilization, the authoritarian regime, was removed, mobilization subsided. Because of their ephemeral organizational structure, most of these movements were not capable of sustaining the intense political involvement of subordinate classes.

Political parties by and large failed to establish ties to subordinate classes and articulate their demands effectively. The clearest case of a party's coming to power on the basis of traditional identification with subordinate class interests and making strong efforts to protect those interests once in office was APRA in Peru in 1985. However, its failure in the area of economic management in the medium and longer run led to popular disaffection and the decimation of its electoral strength. The Peronists under Menem in Argentina and the People's National Party under Manley in Jamaica campaigned on their traditional appeals to subordinate class interests but once in power switched course and implemented neoliberal reforms.[30] In Chile parties traditionally identified with subordinate class interests committed themselves during the transition to continuity in economic policies and stayed the course once in government. Accordingly, they did not make particularly strong attempts to revive their close ties to organizations of subordinate classes that had been broken under military rule. The results in these cases have been greater cynicism among the population toward the political process, lower party loyalty, and lower voter turnout where turnout is not kept high by compulsory voting.

Voter turnout among subordinate classes has been kept high in many cases in a way that does little to effectively translate lower class interests into policy. The political space left empty by weak popular organizations and the failure of political parties to establish organizational ties to subordinate classes has been filled by clientelistic networks. These networks link lower class individuals and informal social groups to individual politicians; they serve at best as transmitters of temporary particularistic favors, not as channels to mobilize citizens into influencing policy formation. This pattern is particularly strong where parties are weak, as in Brazil, Peru, Bolivia, and Ecuador.

## The State and State-Society Relations

To the extent that power has become centralized in the executive and presidents tend to regard legislatures and the judiciary as obstacles rather than legitimate partners in government, there is little room for popular political participation beyond the act of voting, particularly where presidents came to power through loose electoral coalitions and distance themselves from the coalition parties when in office. Pressuring an impotent legislature and working through a presidential party that has little influence on government policy are not promising forms of citizen participation. Repeated failures depress political mobilization among all but the most ideologically committed.

Political decentralization has been high on the agenda of international financial institutions, particularly the World Bank, and several governments

*we need decentralization*

in new democracies. However, decentralization in many cases remained limited to the local administration of centrally determined policies and centrally allocated resources. In some cases it has strengthened the position of local elites and their clientelistic networks. Where control over both resources and policy responsibility have been decentralized, citizen participation at the local level is shaped by previous experiences with mobilization and by the organizations that serve as mobilizing agencies.[31]

### Transnational Structures of Power

In contrast to its positive effect on the survival of formal democracy, the international system has had a depressing effect on citizen participation. External pressures to adopt neoliberal policies have reduced the space for policy debates and greatly constrained citizen participation.

The international system has also contributed powerfully in an indirect way to a decrease in citizen participation. As policies favoring the unrestrained functioning of the market are imposed on and adopted by increasing numbers of countries, the losers in the new economic order lose not only income, job security, and government supports, but often much of their political "voice" as well. Consequently, lower class organization is weakened, further reducing chances for social democratic policies to correct growing socioeconomic inequalities.

Economic problems rooted in the international system, most prominently continuing debt pressures but also growing internationalization of capital, have also weakened a critical part of the infrastructure of participation, political parties, and party systems. The first democratic incumbents confronted exaggerated expectations, and their inability to meet even the most basic economic needs of middle and lower classes caused their parties to be decimated at the polls in the second elections. Chile is the exception that confirms the rule. The government of the *Concertación* under Aylwin inherited an economy with macroeconomic stability, attractive conditions for foreign capital, and a healthy growth rate, which enabled it to make some progress in the area of social spending and real wages and to win reelection under Frei. In Argentina, Peru, and Brazil, in contrast, decimation of the incumbent parties further weakened the capacity of already fragmented party systems to mobilize and process citizen participation.

# Determinants of Social Democracy in Contemporary Latin America

## The Balance of Class Power

Strong organization of labor and electoral strength of prolabor parties are crucial determinants of the effective implementation of distributive policies in advanced industrial democracies. The unfavorable shift in the balance of class power away from labor and toward capital resulting from a combination of labor repression under military rule and neoliberal reforms under both military and democratic rule and the weakness of political parties in the new democracies have been largely responsible for the failure of state policy to address the issue of redistribution in a meaningful way.[32] The neoliberal adjustment policies implemented to different degrees in virtually all the new democracies have made this issue highly salient because they have significantly aggravated previously high socioeconomic inequality. The combination of financial liberalization and privatization of state enterprises has led to a high concentration of economic assets. The combination of trade liberalization and emphasis on market allocation of resources has promoted a new mode of integration into the world economy based on production with low skill/low wage labor. Finally, cuts in government expenditures for subsidies and social services have hit the lowest income groups particularly hard.

Economic concentration, of course, means the concentration not only of wealth but also of power. The power of capital vis-à-vis both labor and governments has been further enhanced by financial liberalization and the internationalization of production chains. These developments have made capital much more mobile, and thus the threat of exit more credible, which constrains governments in their policy options and induces labor to make concessions. This power shift has been felt even in advanced industrial democracies, and it is more pronounced in new democracies.

The beneficiaries of neoliberal reforms, then, have become very powerful constituencies and obstacles to the pursuit of social democratic policies. With very few exceptions, the new democracies have done little to reverse the trend toward increasing poverty and inequality. Even in the economically successful cases, such as Chile and (up to late 1993) Mexico,[33] the real minimum wage has lagged greatly behind productivity increases and has remained well below the levels of the preadjustment period.[34] Among the new democracies in Latin America, Chile is arguably the country where the strongest efforts have been made to combat poverty through social policy. It has reduced the poverty rate from 40 percent in 1990 to roughly 30 percent in 1994.[35] However, very little has been done to strengthen organized labor and other popular organizations that could function as effective mobilizers of redistributive pressures.

## The State and State-Society Relations

Social democratic policies are premised on the fact that the market has inegalitarian consequences that can be corrected only by state intervention. Aside from the political will and power base to undertake redistributive state intervention, a state apparatus must be capable of executing such policies in a consistent, coherent, and effective manner. The lack of such a state is a major problem in the new democracies of Latin America. Most of these new democracies inherited a state apparatus characterized by fragmentation, overlapping responsibilities, nonmeritocratic hiring, and often corruption. Consequently, state intervention, particularly redistributive intervention that goes against vested interests, is difficult to implement. The neoliberal ideology and practice of state shrinking have done little or nothing to correct these problems. In fact, to the extent that they led to an antistate attitude and drastic cuts in salaries for public servants, they caused demoralization and exit among the most qualified incumbents in the bureaucracy.

In contrast to claims that the autonomy of state bureaucrats was the source of generous social policy in advanced industrial democracies, the experience of the new democracies suggests that executive autonomy from broad-based domestic political pressures has been used mainly in the opposite direction, to cut social expenditures. Of course, there is an important difference between advanced and developing societies: the degree of autonomy from external pressures. In the new democracies, international financial institutions and other supporters of the "Washington consensus" have actively enhanced executive autonomy from broad domestic political pressures, precisely in order to put the executives in a better position to implement these "consensus" policies. Once the neoliberal policies took effect and created their own support among the winners, the large financial and export firms, these constituencies became more politically assertive. It is reasonable to hypothesize that their growing power will limit executive autonomy. But it will also reinforce the pattern of state-society relations that is least likely to shift policy in the direction of redistribution and reduction of inequality: the growing dependence of state elites on economically powerful groups and a high degree of autonomy vis-à-vis subordinate classes.

## Transnational Structures of Power

Increasing internationalization of financial operations and production chains has reduced governments' room to maneuver even more in developing than in advanced industrial countries. Moreover, the new democracies in Latin America have also had to increase trade openness greatly, causing dislocations well beyond those caused by changing conditions of international competition in the traditionally much more open economies of European redistributive welfare states. The key here has been the continuing debt pressure in many new democracies and thus their exposure to pressures for rapid and rather indiscriminate trade liberalization. The speed and range of these reforms made it too difficult for many firms to adapt to the new conditions, resulting not in retooling for export production but rather bankruptcies, rising unemployment, and low economic growth.

Financial internationalization reduces, in particular, governments' capacity to influence interest rates in order to stimulate investment. Competition in the world economy on the basis of cheap labor reduces governments' capacity to raise corporate taxes, including payroll taxes for social security contributions. Finally, excessive reliance on the market and abandonment of state interventionism to promote progress toward competition in the world market on the basis of higher skill/higher wage production keep real wages very low even in economies that are successful from the point of view of macroeconomic stability and growth. In other words, the dominant mode of integration of the new Latin American democracies into the world economy deprives governments of some of the crucial traditional policy instruments to increase employment, raise real wages, and finance redistributive social policies.

## Conclusion

The theoretical expectations we derived from our earlier comparative historical analysis of the relationship between capitalist development and democracy and from the historical experience of European welfare states proved themselves powerful in accounting for current developments in Latin America. The apparent contradiction between advances in (modest forms of) formal democracy and mounting obstacles in deepening democracy toward more participation and dealing with socioeconomic inequality finds a consistent explanation if we look at the impact of the three clusters of power—the balance of class power, the structure of the state and of state-society relations, and international power structures—and their interaction. We argued that in the current conjuncture the balance of class power is unfavorable for advancing toward participatory democracy and pursuing social democratic policy but mildly favorable for the survival of formal democracy, albeit of a deficient variety. Neoliberal reforms have increased economic concentration and thus greatly strengthened some sectors of capital, at the same time they have undermined the economic base and organizational power of subordinate classes, particularly labor. This decline in the organizational strength of subordinate classes removed a crucial basis for mobilization into political participation. A weaker power base and lower participation on the part of those who stand to benefit from redistributive reforms, in turn, have left the winners of neoliberalism with no effective political adversaries capable of pushing through social democratic policies.

The balance of class power favors the survival of formal democracy, at least in the present favorable international political context for formal democracy, because the threat perception of elites is low, in part precisely because of the weak organizational power base of subordinate classes and in part because powerful external economic actors firmly support the economic model that has strengthened the most powerful members of the economic elite. However, we have also argued that the weakness of political parties representing interests of subordinate classes has resulted in weak accountability, that is, in deficiencies even in formal democracy.

State structure and state-society relations have not developed in a favorable direction for either complete formal or for participatory and social democracy. With a few exceptions, most notably Chile, bureaucracies persist in far from Weberian practices, and the combination of economic crisis and state shrinking has weakened the judiciary and other agencies in charge of overseeing the executive branch. The shift in power relations in civil society has weakened state autonomy from dominant class interests and increased state autonomy from subordinate class pressures. These developments have had parallel negative effects on accountability, incentives for citizen participation, and social democratic reform.

Finally, in the current conjuncture international power structures have opposite effects on formal democracy and participatory and social democracy. They encourage formal democracy, while virtually blocking a deepening of democratic decisionmaking and policies aimed at a reduction of social and economy inequality. Moreover, we have also identified the incipient forms of a more vicious cycle. Market-oriented economic policies supported by international pressures and by local constituencies gaining from them tend not only to undercut social democratic reform policies, but also to threaten the foundations of even formal democracy.

Can we generalize from Latin America to the less developed world as a whole? Clearly not, as far as specific conditions are concerned. Yet the fundamental forces are similar across the globe. African political economies seem, overall, to be far more vulnerable to international pressures, have weaker internal supports for democratic governance, and have less effective states than Latin America. Countries in the former Soviet bloc are coping with much more radical economic transformations than Latin America, while their states, especially in the former Soviet Union, have yet to gain the coherence and efficiency necessary to shape social and economic developments, quite aside from the constraints imposed by the international system. The chances for formal democracy seem better in East Central Europe and in the long run even in South and East Asia. But the prospects of a deepening of participation and social democratic policies are there, too, subject to the same factors as elsewhere: the balance of power in civil society, the structure of the state and state-society relations, and the impact of world politics and the world economy on the balance of power within countries.

Are there policy alternatives that allow at the same time for economic growth and the development of formal democracy into more participatory and social democratic forms? And do such policy alternatives have a chance to be realized in the context of the international economic and political system? In this article we can hardly give definitive answers to these questions. However, we can offer some observations based on our ongoing research on the chances for social democratic policy alternatives in Europe and Latin America.[36] The past successes, current difficulties, and future prospects of social democratic reform in Europe have a number of lessons for Latin America. First, social democratic reform can be carried through in the context of low tariff barriers, high dependence on trade, and fiscal conservatism. European social democracies actually thrived on such conditions, delivering both growth and equity during the three decades of their greatest achievements following World War II. The left and labor in Latin America have been successful in pursuing their policies of equalization and protection of workers' interests only in protected economies, with fiscal deficit as a frequent tool and, arguably, at the expense of growth.[37] Second, in many Latin American countries unemployment and precarious employment in the informal sector contribute much more to the severity of the problem of inequality than do low wages in the formal sector. Third, though Latin American countries are better situated to compete on the basis of low wage costs in the current international economy than European countries, many countries in the world economy, above all in Asia and Africa, will always be able to undercut Latin American wages. Moreover, the goal of economic development is ultimately to raise people's living standards. Basing an economic model on low wages is the antithesis of this goal. Latin American countries must seek to rebuild state capacity in order to invest in human resources and thus promote employment and higher skill, higher wage production. Higher levels of employment and skill in turn would facilitate the organization of subordinate classes and could set in motion a virtuous cycle of political mobilization in support of reformist political movements, strengthened formal democracy, and social democratic policies that would enable ever larger sectors of the population to make effective use of their political, civil, and social rights.

NOTES

1.  Dietrich Rueschemeyer, Evelyne Huber Stephens. and John D. Stephens, *Capitalist Development and Democracy* (Chicago: University of Chicago Press, 1992), p. 10. The change in the order in which our names appear here is due exclusively to the name change of one of the coauthors; the order remains alphabetical and does not represent any statement about our relative contributions.

2.  The existence of political systems that fall short of full formal democracy has led to the proliferation of what Collier and Mahon call secondary radial categories of democracy. For instance, O'Donnell coined the concept of delegative democracy for systems that are particularly weak in the third dimension but also deficient in the fourth dimension. David Collier and James E. Mahon, "Conceptual 'Stretching' Revisited," *American Political Science Review* 87 (December 1993), pp. 845–55; Guillermo O'Donnell, "Delegative Democracy," *Journal of Democracy* 5 (January 1994), pp. 55–69.

3.  Our view of participatory democracy is instrumentalist, or processual. We claim that it is valuable, not because of its psychological effects on the participating citizenry (though it may be), but rather because it prevents rule by privileged

minorities and promotes equal representation of interests and redistributive economic and social policies. Whereas the level of participation and differences in participation rates across social categories are analytically distinct, they are empirically related; where participation rates are low, differences among social categories tend to be high, with lower socioeconomic groups participating less.

4. In Collier and Mahon's terminology, we are treating participatory and social democracy as secondary classical categories in that we add defining elements to the primary category of formal democracy.

5. "Social democratic" will be used here in this sense, as the designation of policies that effectively advance social and economic equality; the term does not refer specifically to the (European) political movement bearing the same name. For a similar usage, see Luiz Carlos Bresser Pereira, José Maria Maravall, and Adam Przeworski, *Economic Reforms in New Democracies* (New York: Cambridge University Press, 1993).

6. O'Donnell, "Delegative Democracy."

7. Rueschemeyer, Stephens, and Stephens; for a summary, see Evelyne Huber, Dietrich Rueschemeyer, and John D. Stephens, "The Impact of Economic Development on Democracy," *Journal of Economic Perspectives*, 7 (1993), pp. 71–85.

8. John D. Stephens, *The Transition from Capitalism to Socialism* (Urbana: University of Illinois Press, 1979); Evelyne Huber Stephens and John D. Stephens, The Labor Movement, Political Power, and Workers' Participation in Western Europe," *Political Power and Social Theory*, 3 (1982); Walter Korpi, *The Democratic Class Struggle* (London: Routledge and Kegan Paul, 1983); Gøsta Esping-Andersen, *Politics against Markets* (Princeton: Princeton University Press, 1985). Korpi refers to the "power resources" approach. We add "class" to indicate the class analytic base of the theory.

9. Walter Korpi, "Power, Politics, and State Autonomy in the Development of Social Citizenship," *American Sociological Review* 54 (1989), pp. 309–29; Gøsta Esping-Andersen, *The Three Worlds of Welfare Capitalism* (Princeton: Princeton University Press, 1990); Evelyne Huber, Charles Ragin, and John D. Stephens, "Social Democracy, Christian Democracy, Constitutional Structure and the Welfare State," *American Journal of Sociology*, 99 (1993), pp. 711–49; Evelyne Huber and John D. Stephens, "Political Power and Gender in the Making of the Social Democratic Service State," paper prepared for delivery at the meetings of the American Political Science Association, San Francisco, September 1996; Evelyne Huber and John D. Stephens, "Political Parties and Public Pensions," *Acta Sociologica*, 36 (1993), pp. 309–25.

10. For example, see David Cameron, "Social Democracy, Corporatism, Labour Quiescence, and Representation of Economic Interest in Advanced Capitalist

Society," in John Goldthorpe, ed., *Order and Conflict in Contemporary Capitalism* (Oxford: Clarendon Press, 1984), pp. 143–78; Stephens and Stephens. "The Labor Movement"; Douglas A. Hibbs, "Political Parties and Macro-economic Policy," *American Political Science Review* 71 (1978).

11. Peter Lange and Geoffrey Garrett, "The Politics of Growth," *Journal of Politics* 47 (1985), pp. 792–827; Geoffrey Garrett and Peter Lange, "Political Responses to Interdependence," *International Organization* 45 (1991), pp. 539–64.

12. For example. see Harry Eckstein, *A Theory of Stable Democracy* (Princeton: Center of International Studies, Princeton University, 1961); Sidney Verba, Norman Nie, and Jae-on Kim, *Participation and Political Equality* (New York: Cambridge University Press, 1978); Russell J. Dalton, *Citizen Politics* (Chatham: Chatham House, 1996).

13. Hugh Heclo, *Modern Social Politics in Britain and Sweden* (New Haven: Yale University Press, 1974); Ann Orloff, *The Politics of Pensions* (Madison: University of Wisconsin Press, 1993); Theda Skocpol, *Protecting Soldiers and Mothers* (Cambridge: Harvard University Press, 1992); Harold Wilensky, *The "New Corporatism," Centralization. and the Welfare State* (Beverly Hills: Sage, 1976).

14. Peter Katzenstein, *Small States in World Markets* (Ithaca: Cornell University Press, 1985); Dani Rodrik, "International Trade and Big Government," paper to be included in the Festschrift in honor of Peter B. Kenen, edited by Benjamin J. Cohen, shows that the positive relationship between trade openness and government expenditures on education, subsidies, social security and welfare, and public investment holds for a larger sample than the OECD countries.

15. Evelyne Huber and John D. Stephens, "Internationalization and the Social Democratic Model," *Comparative Political Studies* (forthcoming).

16. See, for example, the essays in Scott Mainwaring, Guillermo O'Donnell, and J. Samuel Valenzuela, eds., *Issues in Democratic Consolidation* (Notre Dame: University of Notre Dame Press, 1992).

17. For example, Philippe Schmitter, "Consolidation and Interest Systems," in Larry Diamond and Gary Marks, eds., *Comparative Perspectives on Democracy* 35 (March–June 1992).

18. For example, J. Samuel Valenzuela, "Democratic Consolidation in Post-Transitional Settings," in Mainwaring, O'Donnell, and Valenzuela, eds.

19. Guillermo O'Donnell, "Illusions about Consolidation," *Journal of Democracy* 7 (April 1996), pp. 34–51.

20. O'Donnell, "Delegative Democracy."

21. O'Donnell, "Illusions."

22. Guillermo O'Donnell and Philippe Schmitter, *Transitions from Authoritarian Rule: Tentative Conclusions about Uncertain Democracies* (Baltimore: The Johns Hopkins University Press, 1986); Alfred C. Stepan, *Rethinking Military*

*Politics* (Princeton: Princeton University Press, 1988); Scott Mainwaring, "Transitions to Democracy and Democratic Consolidation," in Mainwaring, O'Donnell, and Valenzuela, eds.; Stephan Haggard and Robert Kaufman, *The Political Economy of Democratic Transitions* (Princeton: Princeton University Press, 1995).

23. The Chilean protests of 1983 demonstrate that, where unity prevailed within the authoritarian regime and political panics failed to provide coherent leadership for regime change, even very intense popular protests remained unsuccessful. Manuel Antonio Garreton, "Popular Mobilization and the Military Regime in Chile, " in Susan Eckstein, ed., *Power and Popular Protest* (Berkeley: University of California Press, 1989). Among the successful transitions, the degree to which authoritarian rulers PR their imprint on the emerging political system varied considerably. See Terry Karl, "Dilemmas of Democratization in Latin America." *Comparative Politics* 23 (October 1990), pp. 1–22; and Terry Karl and Philippe C. Schmitter, "Modes of Transition in Latin America, Southern and Eastern Europe," *International Social Science Journal* 128 (May 1991), pp. 269–84.

24. See, for example, Jane Jaquette, *The Women's Movement in Latin America*, 2nd ed. (Boulder: Westview Press, 1994).

25. Rueschemeyer, Stephens, and Stephens, *Capitalist Development and Democracy*, pp. 62–63, 282–83.

26. Here the difference between the transition and consolidation (or survival) phases is apparent. The balance of low pressure and extremely low threat perception would be conducive, not to regime change, but to democratic survival.

27. O'Donnell and Schmitter, *Transitions*; Adam Przeworski. "The Games of Transition," in Mainwaring, O'Donnell, and Valenzuela, eds.

28. For a comprehensive treatment of international influences on democratization, including economic, imperial, ideological, and domino factors, see Paul W. Drake, "The International Causes of Democratization, 1947–1990," in Paul W. Drake and Matthew McCubbins, eds., *The Origins of Liberty* (forthcoming).

29. Verba, Nye, and Kim, *Participation*.

30. Of course, Jamaica is not a new democracy, but it underwent the same dynamics and consequences as far as this point is concerned.

31. Jonathan Fox, "The Difficult Transition from Clientelism to Citizenship," *World Politics* 46 (January 1994), pp. 151–84.

32. Neoliberal reforms have weakened unions mainly by shrinking employment in traditionally well organized sectors, mainly manufacturing and the public sector.

33. Mexico is not (yet) a new democracy, but the lessons from its economic policies are instructive.

34. Alvaro Diaz, "Restructuring and the New Working Classes in Chile," Discus-

sion Paper 47 (Geneva: United Nations Research Institute for Social Development, 1993); John Sheahan, *Conflict and Change in Mexican Economic Strategy* (La Jolla: University of California, San Diego, Center for U.S.-Mexican Studies, 1991).

35. Diaz, "Restructuring"; ECLAC, *Social Panorama of Latin America 1994* (Santiago: United Nations Economic Commission for Latin America and the Caribbean, 1994).

36. Evelyne Huber, "Options for Social Policy in Latin America," in Gosta Esping-Andersen, ed., *Welfare States in Transition* (London: Sage, 1996); Huber and Stephens, "Internationalization."

37. Cf. Bresser Pereira, Maravall, and Przeworski, *Economic Reforms*.

# 9 Modes of Transition and Democratization: South America and Eastern Europe in Comparative Perspective

*Gerardo L. Munck and Carol Skalnik Leff*

Transitions, defined as periods of regime change, are formative or founding moments. As such, they set a society on a path that shapes its subsequent political development. This thesis, which is at the heart of path dependent analysis of democratization, has recently been articulated by a long list of prominent scholars who have sought to link the mode of transition from authoritarian rule to the problems and prospects of democratic consolidation.[1] Their contributions notwithstanding, their work has suffered from both conceptual imprecision and a dearth of conclusive findings,[2] deficiencies that have bred scholarly skepticism about assessing the impact of modes of transition.[3] A decade after this debate was initiated, it thus remains unclear not only how modes of transition affect political developments but, more fundamentally, if they matter at all.

However, the appeal of a path dependent analysis of democratization persists. Therefore, rather than dismiss the debate on the potential impact of modes of transition, we seek to revisit it. We begin by clarifying the key concept of mode of transition and by spelling out the causal mechanisms whereby the defining attributes of this concept generate consequential political legacies. We define the mode of transition in terms of the identity of the actors who drive the transition process and the strategies they employ; we then argue that these modalities shape the posttransitional regime and politics by affecting the pattern of elite competition, institutional rules crafted during the period of transition, and disposition of key actors to accept or reject the new rules of the game. Through these causal mechanisms the mode of transition helps to explain whether and how democracies emerge and consolidate. To substantiate this argument, we analyze several South American and East Central European countries: Argentina, Brazil, Chile, Bulgaria, Czechoslovakia, Hungary, and Poland.

The mode of transition is not the only factor affecting democratization. Nor are the legacies of modes of transition permanently fixed. However, we wish to stress that an eminently political factor, the process of transition itself, has continuing political relevance. We thus draw upon two of Dankwart A. Rustow's main arguments in his seminal article, "Transitions to Democracy": his critique of theories that stress social and economic prerequisites to the exclusion of political factors, and his development of a process-oriented approach to democratization.[4] In stressing the centrality of transitions from authoritarian rule, however, we put a new twist on Rustow's significant proposition that "the factors that keep a democracy stable may not be the ones that brought it into existence."[5] Building upon the distinction between transition from authoritarianism and transition to democracy, our path dependent argument advances a slightly different proposition: the very process of transition from authoritarian rule, independently of the conditions that generated it, helps determine not only the prospects of democratic consolidation but also the success of the transition to democracy in the first place.


## Modes of Transition and Their Impact

The concept of mode of transition distinguishes the different processes whereby the rules that define political regimes are jettisoned. All too often the literature on modes of transition has failed to distinguish between transitions from established regimes and transitions to new regimes and thus reduced the assessment of modes of transition to their impact on the consolidation of democracy. The mode of transition not only affects the consolidation of new regimes but also helps determine whether the transition is to democracy or some other regime type.

How can we distinguish among transitions from established regimes? Two basic criteria can be extracted from the existing literature. Strongly influenced by the contrast between Portugal and Spain, the early literature emphasized the degree of control that outgoing rulers exerted over the process of transition. In more dynamic terms, these studies targeted the strategies employed by the relevant actors in the transition process.[6] They distinguished transitions that advanced through different degrees of accommodation and confrontation between actors seeking change and defenders of the old order, thus differentiating transitions that broke with the old regime from those that proceeded within a preset legal framework or through agreements with the incumbent elites. It rapidly became clear, however, that this single criterion did not capture important differences in the transition process even in the cases that inspired it, and various scholars thus proposed new criteria.

Probably the most interesting of the alternative formulations was the suggestion that transitions should also be distinguished in terms of the identity of the primary agents of change. This criterion highlights a critical variable: whether a transition is carried out by elites within the established structure of power, by counterelites who challenge incumbent elites, or by some combination of the two.[7] Moreover, when conjoined with the first, strategic criterion, this two-dimensional conceptualization of modes of transition has the virtue of directly capturing a distinctive feature of transitions: they are uniquely fluid processes defined by the identity of regime challengers and their strategies in challenging the old regime. This concept of mode of transition highlights who makes transitions and how they are made.

Two basic questions remain to be confronted. Why do modes of transition matter, and how do they matter? Transitions matter because they generate fairly durable legacies that affect the posttransitional regime and politics. Different modes of transition are likely to have distinct consequences for a country's politics. The primary challenge is to explain how modes of transition matter by specifying the causal mechanisms and significance of these legacies. A number of scholars has tackled this challenge. One productive line of inquiry has sought to link the relative balance of power between rulers and opposition during the transition to the choice of particular institutional rules that both persist beyond the transition period and shape the prospects for regime consolidation.[8] However, our analysis is somewhat broader.

We argue that the mode of transition affects the form of posttransitional regime and politics through its influence on the pattern of elite competition, on the institutional rules crafted during the transition, and on key actors' acceptance or rejection of the new rules of the game. A probabilistic connection between modes of transition and democratization can thus be spelled out. A given mode of transition is likely to increase the odds for the emergence of democracy if it generates a more or less balanced pattern of elite competition. And it is likely to increase the odds for consolidation of newly installed democracies if it facilitates the adoption of institutions suited to the management of elite conflict and the willingness of all major actors to accept the democratic rules of the game.

## The South American and East European Cases

The recent transitions from military rule in South America and from Communism in East Central Europe provide excellent cases to test this argument. We have selected seven countries as examples (see figure 9.1).

This sample not only maximizes the amount of variation in our key explanatory variable, a methodological desideratum, but is also small enough to allow for the use of a "process tracing" methodology uniquely suited to verify that the causal mechanisms we posit are actually at work. Moreover, it includes two pairs of cases that share a mode of transition (Brazil and Poland, Argentina and Czechoslovakia) despite substantial variance in other respects. Thus, in addition to the use of process tracing, this sample allows us to exploit the strengths of a "most different" systems design.[10]

In each case, we date the transition and justify its placement within the possible modes of transition.[11] We then focus on how the mode of transition helps to explain the emerging type of political regime. Finally, we consider posttransitional political dynamics, especially the distinctive challenges of regime consolidation. To facilitate comparison, we start with Chile at one pole and proceed through the cases to Bulgaria at the other pole (see figure 9.1).

### Reform from Below: Chile

In Chile's transition, the impetus for change came from outside the incumbent elite, from groups that were excluded and vehemently resisted by the outgoing military rulers, led by General Augusto Pinochet. Though failing to avert a change in regime, incumbent elites may well have exerted more control over the transition than in any other recent case of regime

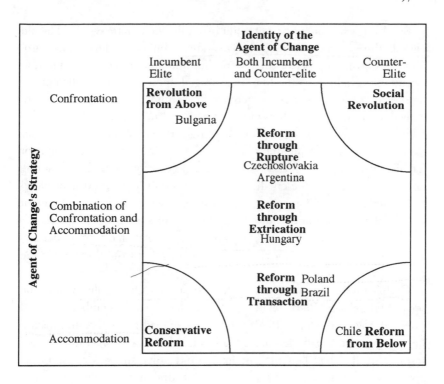

**Identity of the
Agent of Change**

|  | Incumbent Elite | Both Incumbent and Counter-elite | Counter-Elite |
|---|---|---|---|

**Agent of Change's Strategy**

Confrontation — **Revolution from Above** / Bulgaria — **Social Revolution**

**Reform through Rupture** Czechoslovakia Argentina

Combination of Confrontation and Accommodation — **Reform through Extrication** Hungary

**Reform through Transaction** Poland Brazil

Accommodation — **Conservative Reform** — Chile **Reform from Below**

**FIGURE 9.1** Modes of Transition: Some South American and East European Cases

change. Pinochet's opponents were thus forced to advance their agenda within the legal framework of the old regime, through a purely accommodationist strategy. The transition was launched on the basis of a constitutionally mandated plebiscite in October 1988 which the opposition won. Chile's transition was a case of reform from below.

The impact of these basic features of Chile's mode of transition is evident first in the type of regime crafted during the transition. To effectively challenge the incumbent elite from outside, antiregime forces needed to forge a broad-based coalition. The transition then opened the political process to a wide array of social forces. Moreover, because Chile's old elites remained a viable political force, the transition did not simply displace the incumbent elite by counterelites. Rather, Chile's mode of transition generated a system of fairly balanced elite competition, that is, a democracy.

But Chile's transition did not result in a fully democratic system. The old elites both resisted democratic change and exerted a high degree of control over the transition process. They were thus able to enforce a quid pro quo whereby the viability of the transition hinged upon the democratic opposition's acceptance of overtly undemocratic features, many of which were embedded in the constitution Pinochet had designed in 1980. Specifically, Chile's new regime accepted Pinochet's right to remain army commander in chief for eight years after transferring power and thereafter become senator for life, nine appointed senators, a national security council with strong powers and military representation, a packed supreme court, and an electoral law crafted by the military to favor right-wing parties and prevent amendment of the 1980 constitution without the consent of supporters of Pinochet's regime.[12] Chile's transition, in short, produced a restricted form of democracy that did not provide for elections to all key offices and that limited the power of elective offices.

Chile's mode of transition also affected posttransition politics, after the opposition defeated Pinochet in the general election of December 1989 and assumed power in March 1990.[13] Indeed, it shaped the actors and institutional rules: the broad, democratic, anti-Pinochet coalition, counterpoised to the elite that had benefited under the old order and was questionably committed to democracy. This configuration underpins Chile's posttransitional political dynamics. On the one hand, democratic politicians have sought to eliminate the undemocratic restrictions on the scope and authority of elected offices. On the other hand, they have been keenly aware that the right-wing élite would use its legally sanctioned position to block reform of these "authoritarian enclaves" and that obliteration of them could trigger a powerful conservative backlash. The mode of transition left its legacy in a constrained pattern of elite contestation that obstructs democratic consolidation in Chile by making the acceptance of a restricted form of democracy the price for stability.[14]

## Reform through Transaction: Brazil and Poland

Brazil and Poland exemplify reform through transaction. Although the impetus for change did not originate equally within and outside the incumbent elite, because incumbent elites remained ambivalent as counterelites pushed for democratic changes, incumbent elites in Brazil and Poland were sufficiently powerful to force the opposition to advance its agenda through negotiations. The legacies of the transitions likewise displayed important similarities, despite the otherwise vast differences between the two countries.

In analyzing Brazil, the first problematic issue to be resolved concerns the dating of the transition. Although most analysts pinpoint 1974 as the beginning of Brazil's regime change, prior to 1982 Brazil actually underwent a process of liberalization rather than democratization which sought to broaden the social base of the existing authoritarian regime.[15] It is more accurate, then, to date the transition from 1982. In elections held that year the opponents of military rule made such substantial gains that they confronted the incumbent elites with a critical choice: either to adopt increasingly repressive measures to halt liberalization or to allow democratization. The incumbent elites chose not to block democratic change, but rather concentrated their considerable residual power over the transition process to force the counterelites to adopt an accommodationist stance.

The impact of these features of Brazil's transitional politics was manifest, first of all, in the complexity of the transition process. In an exercise of power that displayed their ambivalent attitude toward democracy, the military rulers staunchly rebuffed a massive opposition campaign in early 1984 for direct and popular presidential elections and forced their opponents to accept an indirect method of nomination. Even when the opposition's presidential candidate won in 1985, the military rulers effectively prolonged the transition and retained considerable control over the outlines of the future regime. Contrary to most interpretations, José Sarney's assumption of the presidency in 1985 did not conclude the transition. Sarney actually led an interim government during which the new rules of the game were established. Only as a result of an extended process—constituent assembly elections in 1986, approval of a new constitution in 1988, the first direct presidential election in November 1989, the assumption of power by Collor de Mello in March 1990, and congressional and gubernatorial elections in October 1990—did Brazil's transition come to an end.

The mode of transition, through this extended process, also affected the new form of government. Because elements within the incumbent elite increasingly accepted and embraced the external impetus for change, the transition's political opening not only sanctioned competition among political elites, but also generated a regime that lacked the explicitly undemocratic features found in Chile. However, the absence of an overtly antidemocratic

right-wing elite also had drawbacks. In Chile, the presence of an antidemocratic right encouraged unity in the antiauthoritarian coalition during
and after the transition. In Brazil, in contrast, the willingness of the traditional elites formerly sympathetic to military rule to cooperate with and even
enter the main opposition party, the Party of the Brazilian Democratic Movement (PMDB), in the electoral college vote of 1985 diluted the PMDB's
identity. The momentum of the forces most committed to democracy was
severely weakened.[16]

Loss of identity within the antiauthoritarian coalition, in conjunction
with the outgoing rulers' capacity to control the transition, affected Brazil's
new constitution. Though the PMDB won a sizable majority in the 1986
elections for the constituent assembly, former supporters of the military in-
filtrated it, and conservative clientelist strongholds in the underdeveloped
north and northeast (as a result of biased electoral laws) were overrepresented
in it. Former supporters of the military rulers actually outnumbered the
original PMDB leaders.[17] President Sarney's power to reject demands that
would have made the constituent assembly independent, moreover, weakened its ability to break with the past. Thus, while the new constitution,
ratified in 1988, nullified the authoritarian aspects of the old military constitution and included many progressive provisions, it was shaped in decisive
ways by the military and its allies. Most significantly, the proposal to adopt
a parliamentary system was defeated, and federalism was reinvigorated without introducing changes that would strengthen political parties and prevent
fragmentation of the party system.[18] Though the new regime was clearly
democratic, the most authentic proponents of change lost momentum, and
the outgoing rulers controlled the transition process, thereby ensuring the
adoption of far from optimal institutional rules for democracy.

The mode of transition also affected Brazil's posttransitional politics. Multiple elites competed for power as in Chile, but no actor directly opposed
the new regime. Brazil's posttransitional political dynamics were not driven
by the refusal of some actors to submit to democratic rules. Rather, actors
experienced difficulties in managing conflicts within the democratic rules
adopted during the transition. Specifically, the electoral laws facilitated the
fragmentation of the party system; nineteen parties were represented in the
chamber of deputies in 1990. Moreover, the electoral laws in conjunction
with the presidential system reduced the likelihood of a presidential majority
in congress. A key dysfunctional feature of Brazil's posttransitional politics
has indeed been legislative-executive conflicts. The combination of presi-

dentialism and multipartism, a direct legacy of the mode of transition, has impeded democratic consolidation in Brazil.[19]

In Poland, the impetus for change also came originally from outside the incumbent elite, from the labor-based social movement Solidarity, founded in 1980. However, the transition did not get underway until 1989 when the incumbent elites relaxed earlier repressive measures and initiated roundtable negotiations with Solidarity. While the impetus behind the decision to negotiate was to legitimate the Communist economic program in a time of economic crisis, not to introduce the democratic changes sought by Solidarity, this step represented a departure from the central premise of the old regime: the Communist claim to a monopoly of political power. Incumbent elites nonetheless retained considerable control over the transition process. Indeed, the Polish Communists benefited from being the first country in the Soviet bloc to pursue a political opening; uncertainty about the scope of change Gorbachev was willing to countenance gave them the advantage that attended the lingering threat of Soviet intervention. As in Brazil, then, the Polish transition began when incumbent elites allowed a marginal opening that undermined the basic outlines of the *ancien régime*, while retaining sufficient control over the transition process to force antiincumbent elites to negotiate.

The transition process in Poland experienced some of the same complications witnessed in Brazil. While Solidarity won relegalization of its trade union in the roundtable agreement of April 1989, the Communists restricted opposition participation in elections to a mere 35 percent of the seats in the pivotal lower house (*Sejm*). The incompletely democratized, "contractual" *Sejm* was thus dominated by holdovers from the former regime. Moreover, a constitutional revision established a president, to be selected by the *Sejm*, with potentially substantial but ill-defined independent powers crafted as an additional foothold for Communist Party leader General Wojciech Jaruzelski. As in Brazil in 1985, these restrictions were not foolproof. The opposition exploited the restricted legal opening to deal incumbent elites a setback. Solidarity's shockingly strong electoral showing in June 1989, attributable to the sheer strength of the opposition, its mass base, and the leadership skills of Lech Walesa, showed that the Communist strategy had backfired. After much maneuvering, a mixed Communist-Solidarity government headed by Solidarity activist Tadeusz Mazowiecki was installed in September 1989. But just as important, the constraining influence of the roundtable pact turned the transition into a complex and protracted process that affected the configuration of the new regime. As in Brazil, then, the Polish transition advanced in stepwise fashion. Its main landmarks included a power-sharing arrangement that operated through existing Communist institutions as modified by the roundtable, the popular election of the president in fall 1990, and competitive elections to parliament in October 1991, which ended the transition.

The impact of this protracted transition on the new regime was considerable. Because the Communists acquiesced in the demand of noncommunist elites to liquidate the restrictions on political contestation, overt constraints on elite competition were gradually eliminated. As in Brazil, Poland emerged from its transition with a fully competitive democracy, but the ability of the old elites to shape the initial roundtable breakthrough and their continued engagement in the democratization process impeded a clean break with the past in several important ways. First, the attenuated Communist threat to democratization helped undermine the unity of the anti-authoritarian coalition in a manner that directly affected the design of democratic institutions. When Solidarity leader Walesa, who had stayed aloof from the mixed government of Prime Minister Mazowiecki for strategic reasons, found himself sidelined, he did not hesitate to attack the legitimacy of the very Solidarity-Communist cabinet alliance whose creation he had negotiated. Reentering politics through the institutional opening created by the roundtable agreement, Walesa successfully forced direct elections to the presidency, which he won in December 1990 in a bitter internecine challenge to the democratic credentials of his Solidarity allies.

In turn, the election of Walesa to the roundtable's still ill-defined but potent presidency affected institutional choices in a convoluted manner, setting the stage for legislative-executive conflict. Walesa could draw upon his elective authority to threaten a veto of any constitutional settlement crafted by the tarnished "contractual" *Sejm*, a body widely perceived to lack legitimacy as a constituent assembly. The combination of Walesa's election and the ever-present legacies of the roundtable agreement created a constitutional deadlock. This outcome would have been highly unlikely had a fully legitimate constituent assembly been free to act, without the constraint of the roundtable presidency.

Solidarity's fragmentation also directly affected the electoral law for the first fully competitive elections in October 1991. Increasingly doubtful of their electoral following, the Solidarity factions in the *Sejm* joined with the overrepresented Communists to adopt, against Walesa's wishes, a highly pro-

portional electoral system without thresholds for representation. Institution-
ally, like Brazil, Poland chose a problematic multiparty presidential system.

In the posttransitional phase, it became increasingly clear that the key
actors were committed to a system of elite competition. The protracted process of overcoming the limitations of the initial bargain effectively incorporated the former elites into the new democratic system. As in Brazil, the
key obstacles to democratic consolidation lay instead in the problematic
workings of the democratic institutions. The unrestrictive electoral law produced a fragmented *Sejm* of twenty-nine parties, heralding a prolonged period of government by successive minority coalitions, none of which had
sufficient support or time in office to enact a constitution.[20] The repeated
clashes between president and parliament that characterized the latter part
of the transition persisted, only partially checked by the "little constitution"
of August 1992, a detailed attempt to clarify the legislative-executive balance
of power in response to the jurisdictional clashes. Even the more compact
1993 *Sejm*, elected with a threshold, could not strike a constitutional bargain
as long as Walesa was president. As in Brazil, inadequate mechanisms to
regulate legislative-executive conflict, a direct legacy of the mode of transition, continued to prevent the establishment of a routinized pattern of elite
interaction and impeded the consolidation of Poland's democracy.

*Reform through Extrication: Hungary*

In Hungary, the transition was negotiated by opposition and incumbent
elites who both had a stake in pursuing an opening. The reform wing of the
Communist elite had been building bridges to the more responsive currents
in the political and cultural opposition for several years prior to 1989, in
search of a political liberalization formula for "socialist pluralism" that would
validate effective economic reform. These reformers clearly hoped to preempt an anticommunist backlash by gaining credit for their responsiveness
to political change. When younger, more flexible leaders took over the
party's leadership after a massive housecleaning of the Politburo septuage-
narians in May 1988, they pursued a divide-and-conquer strategy of negotiating separately with opposition groups according to their divergent na-
tionalist-populist and urban-cosmopolitan tendencies. This strategy
ultimately failed. The opposition temporarily succeeded in coordinating

their positions; support for change increased in the course of popular protests; and events in Poland weakened Communists throughout eastern Europe by revealing the Soviet Union's unwillingness to defend the status quo. In June 1989 the Communists initiated talks with the key opposition groups in a Polish-style roundtable format that included all the major nascent parties and social organizations and reached an agreement with the opposition in September 1989. Hungary's "negotiated revolution" is thus a good example of reform through extrication. Both the old rulers and counterelites sought change, and the incumbents, though weaker than in Poland and Brazil, were still sufficiently in control to force the opposition to bargain.[21]

Hungary's transition was relatively uncomplicated. In contrast to Poland, where the penalty of being first to test Soviet tolerance for change was acceptance of undemocratic restrictions and a prolonged process of removing them, Hungary's transition was not constrained. The September 1989 agreement reflected the relatively equitable balance of power between rulers and opposition and the broad consensus for change and led directly to a full political opening in the competitive parliamentary elections of March 1990. While Poland's transition dragged on over two and a half years, Hungary's was complete in less than nine months.

The electoral law was also agreed to consensually. The Communists proposed a majoritarian system that they believed, misguidedly, would favor them as the party with superior organizational resources against a divided opposition. However, the final law resulted from a compromise. The very complex, mixed electoral system reflected the opposition's fear of Communist strength and demand for dilution of the majoritarian principle.

The one complication was related to the Communists' effort to create an institutional base for themselves, in a manner reminiscent of Poland, by instituting a popularly elected presidency prior to the first competitive parliamentary elections. Communist strategists calculated that their better-known and better-organized candidate would win on a crest of popular appreciation of the Communists' willingness to open the system. The opposition Hungarian Democratic Forum (HDF) initially accepted this proposal, but the stratagem was torpedoed when the rest of the opposition took the issue to a popular referendum in fall 1989. The balance of power then shifted from the Communists to their opponents in the course of the negotiations, aborting the Communists' attempt to create a more presidential system. As a result of its mode of transition, Hungary created a new regime with no overtly undemocratic rules, a complex majoritarian electoral law, and a parliamentary system.

After the transition, no major actor remained opposed to democracy.[22] The institutional choices of the transition period also allowed Hungary to avoid the serious legislative-executive clashes that characterized Brazilian and Polish posttransitional politics. The complex majoritarian electoral rules accorded seat bonuses to large parties, turning pluralities into near HDF majorities in 1990 and ex-Communist majorities in 1994. This electoral system not only facilitated the entry of the Communists' successor, the Hungarian Socialist Party, into the political system as a "normal" political actor playing by the new rules, but it also potentially generated the conditions for coherent policymaking. It would be misleading, however, to suggest that Hungary's relatively unrestricted negotiated settlement left no negative legacies. Ironically, despite their otherwise positive effects, Hungary's electoral rules exacted a toll on the legitimacy and responsiveness of the inaugural HDF government. Its disproportionate parliamentary strength after the first elections reinforced its sometimes highhanded tendency to regard itself as the only true arbiter of Hungarian interests, especially in pursuing its own nationalist agenda to the partial neglect of other pressing issues. When viewed comparatively, however, Hungary's reform through extrication generated considerably less troubling legacies for democratic consolidation than other modes if transition.

## Reform through Rupture: Argentina and Czechoslovakia

Both Argentina and Czechoslovakia are cases of reform through rupture. In Argentina, the impetus for change clearly came from groups in society opposed to military rule. The transition itself, however, did not start until the military rulers capitulated to demands for regime change following their defeat by the British in the Falklands/Malvinas war in June 1982. Military defeat also rendered the incumbent elite too weak to control the transition, and the transitional agenda was dictated by the counterelites.

Thus, Argentina's transition was particularly straightforward. In contrast to Chile, the incumbent elite's acquiescence reduced the uncertainty of the transition process. Furthermore, in contrast to Brazil and Poland, the weakness of the old elite ensured that the advance of the opposition would not be complicated or slowed by constraining mechanisms. Finally, in contrast to Hungary, the political vulnerability of the old rulers and their allies prevented them from shaping the future regime through negotiations. Argentina's transition broke cleanly with the past.

The fact that Argentina's transition was overseen by an incumbent care-taker government, an interim form of government in which the old rulers usually set the terms of the transition and force accommodation on coun-terelites, is misleading. The agenda of the transition was actually set by the antiincumbent elites and accepted by the outgoing military rulers. The mili-tary rulers rapidly conceded to the demand of the *Multipartidaria*, the mul-tiparty opposition alliance, for competitive elections, the compromise ar-rangement of the various parties that had united in opposition to military rule. The military rulers were largely powerless to craft institutional rules to protect their interests or improve the chances of their allies. Having failed to introduce a new constitution at the peak of their power and now incapable even of amending the existing one, the military resorted expediently to the wholesale resurrection of the 1853 presidentialist constitution. The new electoral law did not establish a sequence of elections but simply reintrod-uced a system of proportional representation that neither hampered the mili-tary's opponents nor favored its weak allies. Thus, Argentina's transition was rapidly completed. Without competition from the old rulers, the two main parties of the *Multipartidaria* faced off in elections in October 1983, and the newly elected president and congress assumed power in December 1993. Argentina adopted an unconstrained democratic system.[23]

The legacies of Argentina's transition through rupture were partially posi-tive. No undemocratic measures restricted and no major actors opposed the democratic rules of the game. But they also posed a distinctive problem of elite competition. The securely positioned *Multipartidaria*, not needing to unify against an authoritarian opponent or to defend free elections, started to disintegrate in late 1982. In contrast to Brazil and Poland, this disintegra-tion did not complicate or prolong the transition process. Indeed, the pow-erlessness of Argentina's old rulers was so extreme that it was even possible and convenient for the counterelites to defer resolution of key constitutional issues. However, the breakup of the antiauthoritarian coalition rapidly turned former allies into fierce competitors who were unable to forge con-sensus on a new constitution. The administrations of both Alfonsín (1985–89) and Menem (1989–95) sought to present themselves as the embodiment of the nation and to use their temporary majorities to become the hegemonic party by unilaterally resolving constitutional issues. Due to its reform through rupture, Argentina squandered the opportunity to tackle such issues before the consensus generated in the antiauthoritarian struggle dissipated in the heat of electoral competition. Its democracy has thus been threatened

) constitutional issues

by the reluctance of the key political actors to see themselves as parts of a larger system, a defining feature of democracy.

Czechoslovakia's so-called velvet revolution was also a reform through rupture. The transition was triggered by an upsurge of popular mobilization in response to the repression of a student demonstration in November 1989. Thereafter previously isolated dissident leaders received validation in the approbation of the crowds at almost daily rallies, and a brief symbolic general strike ("revolution on the lunch hour") telegraphed the defection of the workers from the Communist leadership. This dramatic revelation of regime weakness, coupled with the already evident refusal of the Soviet Union to intervene coercively, induced the previously inflexible Communist rulers to abandon their resistance to change.

As in Argentina, the transition was brief and fairly uncomplicated. The opposition seized the initiative and imposed its improvised program on the retreating incumbent elite. Negotiations took the form largely of iterative cycles of opposition demands, evasive government action, expanded opposition demands, and eventual and grudging government acceptance, all compressed within a two-week period. Whereas opposition elites accepted conditions imposed by the old rulers in Chile, Brazil, and Poland, they forced the incumbent elites to make massive concessions that amounted to capitulation—in particular, the abandonment of the dogma of the leading role of the party and commitment to competitive elections—in Czechoslovakia. As in Argentina, expediency in the face of the opportunity for a rapid transition dictated the temporary retention of the Communist constitution which, in contrast to the earlier Czechoslovak democratic constitution of 1920, provided for a federal structure of government for the multinational state. The transition was rapidly completed in June 1990 when parliamentary elections inaugurated a fully competitive democratic system.

Despite its ease and the unconstrained institutional arrangement it produced, Czechoslovakia's transition also left a problematic legacy for posttransitional politics. As in Argentina, the mode of transition first encouraged the deferral of fundamental constitutional issues; the posttransition logic of electoral competition then made it virtually impossible to resolve them in a consensual manner. Even though Czechoslovakia's antiauthoritarian coalition was more unified throughout the transition than Argentina's, serious differences among the anticommunist forces, particularly regarding the long-troubled Czech-Slovak relationship, were already visible in the symbolic struggle over the state's postcommunist name and in the division along national lines of both the opposition front and the party system that emerged from the June 1990 elections.

The detrimental consequences of this legacy came fully to the fore at the beginning of the posttransitional phase. First, the two cooperating anticommunist movements, the Czech Civic Forum and the Slovak Public against Violence, dissolved in 1990 and 1991, respectively. More significantly, their successor parties merged into the broader currents of two increasingly hardened, ethnically segmented political subsystems. As the constitutional question of Czech-Slovak relations emerged on the political agenda, no statewide force generated consensus on the basic rules of Czech and Slovak elite interaction within a more decentralized state. Indeed, Slovak elite politics largely opposed Pragocentrism and the Czech leadership. This centrifugal tendency was further reinforced by the retention of the "consociational" Communist constitution, which provided both national groupings in the federal assembly, regardless of size, a veto power over constitutional revision.[24] This provision was a formula for deadlock. As in Argentina, then, reform through rupture contributed to a particularly pernicious political dynamic. Czechoslovakia's particular cleavage structure differed from Argentina's pattern of elite hegemonic pretensions. The politics of ethnonational segmentation led to the dissolution of the Czechoslovak state in January 1993. Even if the breakup was a peaceful, "velvet divorce," it still represented Czechoslovakia's ultimate failure to institutionalize the rules of elite contestation and to consolidate its new democracy.[25]

## Revolution from Above: Bulgaria

In Bulgaria, the ruling elite lacked pressure from a strong opposition and was unreceptive to a political opening until the regional collapse of Communist power. These external events, with their message of Soviet nonintervention, shifted the internal power balance and prompted a preemptive opening from above. Younger, less implicated Communist leaders in the ruling center consulted with Gorbachev in November 1989 before initiating a "palace coup" that displaced the discredited top leadership. This move, which marked the beginning of Bulgaria's transition, can be understood as a preemption of mounting, though weakly organized, resistance to Communist rule assembled under the umbrella Union of Democratic Forces

(UDF). Indeed, the Communist strategy was to open competition so as to forestall a fuller popular mobilization that might attenuate their dominance.

The impact of this revolution from above on the outcome of the transition was quite evident. The Bulgarian Communist party, renamed the Bulgarian Socialist Party, scheduled and won elections to a parliamentary/constituent assembly in June 1990 on the basis of a majoritarian electoral law that favored the better organized and prepared incumbents. From this victory the former Communists had the power to fashion the rules of the new regime in the constitution of 1991, a largely democratic document that lifted all major constraints on competition but nonetheless contained language potentially restrictive of free speech and minority organization. When the transition came to an end with the holding of competitive elections in October 1991, Bulgaria emerged as a democracy, though one that bore the marks of Communist control of the transition.

Unsurprisingly, the most direct impact of the mode of transition on posttransitional political dynamics was the strategic advantage it bestowed upon the former rulers. Superficially, it appeared that the incumbent's strategy backfired when the opposition edged out the ex-Communists in the 1991 elections. But the new government, based on a UDF coalition with the minority Turks, was incapable of governing and collapsed after a year, paving the way for the more cohesive and better organized ex-Communists to return to government and to win the 1994 election handily, as well. As in Chile but unlike the other East European cases, the UDF held together tenuously in the face of continued Communist power; in contrast to Chile, however, the UDF's "premature birth" in the Communist-initiated transition impaired its ability effectively to counterbalance the ex-Communists.[26]

Bulgaria's posttransitional politics have thus been characterized by a lopsided pattern of elite contestation, which has raised the stakes of politics and impeded the normalization of interelite relations through mutual acceptance of the concept of loyal opposition. The deleterious effect of the mode of transition on the process of democratic consolidation is very clear in the questionable commitment to democratic rules by both the ex-Communists and the opposition, each side justifying deviations from democratic norms by referring to the antisystem behavior of the other. Posttransitional politics, indeed, have been marked by sporadic violations of democratic procedures, including canceled or invalidated local elections, frequent reports of electoral manipulation and fraud, and conflict with the mainstream media, engendering government criticism and the jailings of key journalists. Bulgaria's

revolution from above has spawned a pattern of elite interaction that constrains democracy by weakening the commitment of key actors to its basic
rules.

## Conclusion

Our analysis suggests that in reforms from below, exemplified by Chile,
broad opposition movements open up the political system by demanding
their inclusion in the political arena, but simultaneously strong incumbent
elites are able to impose constraints on elite contestation. The regime that
emerges from this mode of transition is a restricted democracy. The challenge of democratic consolidation is to reform the undemocratic aspects,
while avoiding a backlash from the old elites, whose commitment to democracy remains uncertain and who appear unwilling to play the role of
loyal opposition.

Reforms through transaction are associated with more complicated and
protracted transitions and less restricted versions of democracy. As Brazil and
Poland show, because the incumbent elites acquiesce in regime change,
reforms through transaction generate political openings for elite competition
and subsequently create a stake in the new system for both old and new
elites. The problem with cases like Brazil and Poland is not the overtly
undemocratic nature of the transition's legacies or the disloyalty of the old
elites toward the new regime. Rather, the lingering power of the old elites
and the loss of identity of the antiauthoritarian coalition, two factors that
manifest themselves in the stepwise process of transition, lead to the adoption
of institutional rules that are not optimal for democratization. More specifically, the new institutional rules generate repeated clashes between the
executive and legislature and leave a legacy that hinders governability and
democratic consolidation.

Reforms through extrication, like reforms through transaction, result in
unrestricted democracy. Both the incumbent and counter elites accept the
need for elite contestation. However, as Hungary shows, the old rulers are
unable to mold the transition; the agenda of the transition is basically resolved on the terms of the counterelites. The transition process thus marks
a clearer break with the past and avoids the costly complications associated
with reforms through transaction. Nonetheless, the lingering power of the

old elites has a moderating effect and makes the break somewhat smoother than in reforms through rupture. While the Hungarian Communist elites were unable to impose their conditions on the transition, they engaged the opposition in serious bargaining, which forced the counterelites, in contrast to Argentina and Czechoslovakia, to confront issues of constitutional design before competitive elections were held and the divisive struggles of normal politics fully took hold. The balanced strength of old and new elites increases the likelihood that the former rulers will adapt to democratic rules and not threaten the system. Reforms through extrication, in short, make both the process of transition to democracy and steady progress toward democratic consolidation easier.

Reforms through rupture, as exemplified by Argentina and Czechoslovakia, appear to be the most unproblematic type of transition. They break dramatically with the past and allow the opposition to impose its demand for unrestricted elections. On the positive side, the weakness of the old elites allows the establishment of a new institutional framework without the problematic constraints associated with more controlled transitions. But the old rulers and the ease of the transition itself create their own negative legacies. Because counterelites achieve a breakthrough without serious, sustained negotiations with the old rulers, the rapid transition can defer debate on constitutional issues, and the interim institutional framework can be accepted out of expediency. Subsequently, the logic of posttransitional electoral competition pits former allies against each other and impedes consensual resolution of constitutional issues. The old rulers are too weak to pose a common threat that could convince counterelites to compromise. Intense elite competition within an institutional framework that does not ameliorate distrust or facilitate conflict resolution makes it increasingly difficult to contain competition within the existing democratic framework. Ironically, reforms through rupture make the transition to democracy relatively easy but also hamper democratic consolidation by reducing the incentive for counterelites to develop cooperative relationships and consensus on key institutional rules during the critical period of transition.

Finally, revolutions from above resemble reforms through rupture in their relative lack of complexity. However, as Bulgaria shows, the less complicated transition is due, not to the power of opposition elites to set the agenda, but rather to the ability of a segment of the incumbent elites to break with the old order and singlehandedly define a transitional agenda from above. Because their basic aim is to preempt or control more sweeping changes, this mode of transition also generates a political opening. But as in reforms through rupture, the conditions that enable a swift transition to democracy may encumber democratic consolidation. The former rulers are likely to retain a disproportionate influence within the political system vis-à-vis the still incoherent opposition. A lopsided pattern of elite contestation undermines mutual trust among competing elites and tempts the party in power periodically to abridge the democratic rules of the game. The lack of an effective counterbalance to the elite that oversees the transition impedes routinization of competition and acceptance of the concept of loyal opposition. In comparative terms, revolution from above is probably the mode of transition least likely to sustain steady progress toward the consolidation of democracy.

In sum, an essentially political factor, the process of transition itself, is important in determining the likelihood that the outcome of transition will be a democratic form of government, as well as the distinctive challenges new democracies face when they try to consolidate themselves. This focus on the process of transition advances the debate on modes of transition in two fundamental ways. First, it conceptualizes modes of transition as different types of transition from established regimes, rather than conflating the transition from an established regime and the transition to a new regime. We are thus able to demonstrate how the mode of transition helps to account, not only for posttransitional political dynamics, but also for the resulting regime, a key explanatory challenge. Second, much of the confusion in the debate about modes of transition can be dispelled by conceptualizing modes of transition in terms of two dimensions that capture the uniquely fluid nature of the transition process and by specifying the causal mechanisms whereby the legacies of modes of transition are generated.

To be sure, the precise mechanisms whereby a transition's legacies are produced and reproduced need to be clarified, and different modes of transition need to be linked with various subtypes of democracy and their distinctive dynamics. The debate about modes of transition needs to be connected with some of the most systematic attempts to conceptualize institutional variants of democracy. Further research is also needed on possible linkages between the mode of transition, which we have taken as an independent variable, and the character of the prior regime. Finally, a crucial, though daunting, task still to be confronted is to integrate the political determinants of democratization emphasized here with approaches that focus on sociological and economic factors. This article cannot elaborate such a research agenda. It has accomplished its goal if it has made the more modest suggestion that such an agenda is worth developing.

NOTES

1. Juan 1. Linz, "Some Comparative Thoughts on the Transition to Democracy in Portugal and Spain," in Jorge Braga de Macedo and Simon Serfaty, eds., *Portugal since the Revolution: Economic and Political Perspectives* (Boulder: Westview Press, 1981); Guillermo O'Donnell and Philippe Schmitter, *Transitions from Authoritarian Rule: Tentative Conclusions about Uncertain Democracies* (Baltimore: The Johns Hopkins University Press, 1986), pp. 11, 37–39; Terry Lynn Karl, "Dilemmas of Democratization in Latin America," *Comparative Politics* 23 (October 1990), pp. 1–21; Terry Lynn Karl and Philippe Schmitter, "Modes of Transition in Latin America, Southern and Eastern Europe," *International Social Science Journal* 128 (May 1991), pp. 269–84; Giuseppe Di Palma, *To Craft Democracies: An Essay on Democratic Transitions* (Berkeley: University of California Press, 1990), chs. 4, 6; Samuel Huntington, *The Third Wave: Democratization in the Late Twentieth Century* (Norman: University of Oklahoma Press, 1991), ch. 3; Guillermo O'Donnell, "Transitions, Continuities, and Paradoxes," in Scott Mainwaring, Guillermo O'Donnell, and J. Samuel Valenzuela, eds., *Issues in Democratic Consolidation: The New South American Democracies in Comparative Perspective* (South Bend: University of Notre Dame Press, 1992); J. Samuel Valenzuela, "Democratic Consolidation in Post-Transitional Settings: Notion, Process, and Facilitating Conditions," in Mainwaring, O'Donnell, and Valenzuela, eds.; Yossi Shain and Juan J. Linz et al., *Between States: Interim Governments and Democratic Transitions* (Cambridge: Cambridge University Press, 1995); Stephan Haggard and Robert Kaufman, *The Political Economy of Democratic Transitions* (Princeton: Princeton University Press, 1995), pp. 14–15, 163–74, 368–71, ch. 4; P. Nikiforos Diamandouros and Richard Gunther, "Preface," in Richard Gunther, P. Nikiforos Diamandouros, and Hans-Jürgen Puhle, eds., *The Politics of Democratic Consolidation: Southern Europe in Comparative Perspective* (Baltimore: The Johns Hopkins University Press, 1995), pp. xii-xxvii; P. Nikiforos Diamandouros, Hans-Jürgen Puhle, and Richard Gunther, "Conclusion," in Gunther, Diamandouros, and Puhle, eds.. pp. 397–98, 402–7; Juan J. Linz and Alfred Stepan, *Problems of Democratic Transition and Consolidation: Southern Europe, South America and Post-Communist Europe* (Baltimore: The Johns Hopkins University Press, 1996), pp. 71–72.

2. The debate whether pacts are beneficial or dysfunctional for democratization is a case in point. After an initial consensus that pacted transitions were more conducive to democratic consolidation, a position advanced by O'Donnell and

Schmitter in 1986, the negative aspects of pacts were stressed by Karl and Valenzuela. However, Karl's argument, to the effect that pacts usually entail exclusionary elements that impede democratic consolidation, has in turn been criticized by Di Palma and Diamandouros, Puhle, and Gunther. In a further twist, O'Donnell has recently argued for a third position, stressing the negative aspects or tradeoffs associated with both pacted and nonpacted transitions, a position shared by Huntington, O'Donnell, and Schmitter, p. 39; Karl, pp. 9–12, 14; Valenzuela, pp. 76–78; Di Palma, pp. 122–25; Diamandouros, Puhle, and Gunther, pp. 406–7: O'Donnell, pp. 24–37; Huntington, p. 276.

3. See, most forcefully, Adam Przeworski, *Democracy and the Market: Political and Economic Reforms in Eastern Europe and Latin America* (Cambridge: Cambridge University Press. 1991), pp. 94–99.

4. Dankwart A. Rustow, "Transitions to Democracy: Toward a Dynamic Model," *Comparative Politics*, 2 (April 1970), 337–63.

5. Ibid., p. 346.

6. Because actors' strategies of change are conditioned by the relative power of the outgoing rulers, these are really two parallel characterizations. We follow Karl, "Dilemmas of Democratization in Latin America," pp. 8–9, in distinguishing transitions in terms of actors' strategies instead of the more common alternative of highlighting the degree of control exercised by the outgoing rulers. For conceptualizations that emphasize the relative power of the outgoing rulers. see Linz, "Some Comparative Thoughts"; and Scott Mainwaring, "Transitions to Democracy and Democratic Consolidation: Theoretical and Comparative Issues," in Mainwaring, O'Donnell, and Valenzuela, eds., pp. 317–26.

7. Though Karl distinguishes among actors who dominate the transition process, her conceptualization emphasizes the relative prevalence of elite versus mass actors and does not directly target a crucial issue in transitions: the contest between incumbent elites and counterelites. Indeed, her conceptualization would conflate transitions that are initiated by incumbent elites with those that result from the actions of counterelites. Our conceptualization is closer to Valenzuela's emphasis on "the attitude of the last ruling elites of the authoritarian regime toward democratization," by emphasizing whether change comes from within or outside the incumbent elite. Karl, "Dilemmas of Democratization in Latin America," pp. 8–9; Valenzuela, "Democratic Consolidation in Post-Transitional Settings," pp. 73–78.

8. On institutional choices, see Arend Lijphart, "Democratization and Constitutional Choices in Czechoslovakia, Hungary and Poland, 1989–91," *Journal of Theoretical Politics* 4 (1992), pp. 207–23. In the consolidation of specific institutional arrangements, see Juan J. Linz and Arturo Valenzuela, eds., *The Failure of Presidential Democracy, Volume 1: Comparative Perspectives* (Baltimore: The Johns Hopkins University Press, 1994).

9. Here we follow Przeworski, *Democracy and the Market: Political and Economic Reforms in Eastern Europe and Latin America*, p. 10, who argues that in the current era, in which restrictions on mass participation are rare, "the possibility of contestation by conflicting interests is sufficient to explain the dynamics of democracy. Once political rights are sufficiently extensive to admit of conflicting interests, everything else follows."

10. The value of cross-regional comparisons has been hotly debated. The ultimate test of the utility of such comparisons is whether they produce theoretically compelling explanations. See the exchange between Philippe Schmitter and Terry Karl and Valerie Bunce in *Slavic Review* (Spring 1994, Spring 1995, and Winter 1995).

11. Placement of all cases does not coincide in similar coding efforts. This discrepancy is due to differing criteria used to define mode of transition, the coding of cases by causes rather than characteristics of the transition process, and new information about the cases. For other attempts to code transitions, see Karl and Schmitter, p. 276; Huntington, p. 113; Valenzuela, "Democratic Consolidation in Post-Transitional Settings, p. 77; James W. McGuire, "Interim Government and Democratic Consolidation: Argentina in Comparative Perspective," in Shain and Linz et al., pp. 194–95; and Felipe Agüero, *Soldiers, Civilians, and Democracy: Post-Franco Spain in Comparative Perspective* (Baltimore: The Johns Hopkins University Press, 1995), p. 65.

12. Valenzuela, "Democratic Consolidation in Post-Transitional Settings, pp. 62–67.

13. While some authors have correctly stressed that Chile had an "incomplete transition" because important constitutional issues remained on the political agenda, it is still accurate to state that the transition ended in 1990, when the basic features of the new regime were defined.

14. Gerardo L. Munck, "Democratic Stability and Its Limits: An Analysis of Chile's 1993 Elections," *Journal of Interamerican Studies and World Affairs*, 36 (1994), 1–38; Manuel Antonio Garretón, *Hacia una nueva era política: Estudio sobre democratizaciones* (Mexico: Fondo de Culture Ecónomica, 1995), pp. 34–42, 111–29, 216–17.

15. Most analysts of Brazil implicitly take liberalization as the beginning of a transition. But, as Przeworski, *Democracy and the Market: Political and Economic Reforms in Eastern Europe and Latin America*, pp. 54–66, argues, "liberalization does not always lead to transition." It is crucial to distinguish clearly between liberalization and democratization.

16. Frances Hagopian, "The Compromised Consolidation: The Political Class in the Brazilian Transition," in Mainwaring, O'Donnell, and Valenzuela, eds., *Issues in Democratic Consolidation*, pp. 266, 247–48.

17. Thomas Bruneau, "Constitutions and Democratic Consolidation: Brazil in

Comparative Perspective," in Diane Ethier, ed., *Democratic Transition and Consolidation in Southern Europe, Latin America and Southeast Asia* (Basingstoke: Macmillan, 1990), pp. 178–84.

18. Ibid., p. 184–90; Hagopian, "The Compromised Consolidation," pp. 272–77.

19. Scott Mainwaring, "Presidentialism, Multipartism, and Democracy: The Difficult Combination" *Comparative Political Studies* 26 (July 1993), pp. 198–228.

20. Lijphart, "Democratization and Constitutional Choices," pp. 211, 213; Krzysztof Jasiewicz. "From Solidarity to Fragmentation," *Journal of Democracy* 3 (April 1992), pp. 55–69.

21. László Bruszt and David Stark, "Remaking the Political Field in Hungary: From the Politics of Confrontation to the Politics of Competition," *Journal of International Affairs* 45 (1991), pp. 201–45.

22. Adras Bozoki, "Party Formation and Constitutional Change in Hungary," in Terry Cox and Andy Furlong, eds., *Hungary: The Politics of Transition* (London: Frank Cass, 1995).

23. Gerardo L. Munck, *Authoritarianism and Democratization: Soldiers and Workers in Argentina, 1978, in Comparative Perspective* (University Park: Pennsylvania State University Press, forthcoming), ch. 6.

24. Lijphart, "Democratization and Constitutional Choices," pp. 216–17.

25. Carol Skalnik Leff, *The Czech and Slovak Republics: Nation versus State* (Boulder: Westview Press, 1996).

26. Georgi Karasimeonov, "Parliamentary Elections of 1994 and the Development of the Bulgarian Party System," *Party Politics*, 1 (October 1995), pp. 579–88.

# 10 Explaining India's Transition to Democracy

*Šumit Ganguly*

## The Continuing Puzzle of Indian Democracy

The vast majority of states in Asia and Africa that emerged from the detritus of the European colonial empires have failed to make viable transitions to democratic rule. Authoritarianism, whether civilian or military, quickly replaced the colonial state. A handful of other states emergent from British colonial rule did successfully made a transition to democracy. However, most of these states have fallen prey to authoritarian temptations since their genesis. India's democratic experience has been singular. Apart from a period of 20 months between 1975 and 1977, when Prime Minister Indira Gandhi declared a "state of emergency" and suspended civil rights and personal liberties, democracy in India has not only survived, but indeed has thrived. Today, though politically unstable, India is in the process of expanding franchise and consolidating democracy.[1]

The Indian constitution guarantees and the executive and judiciary, in large measure, uphold certain civil and political liberties. (Admittedly, some of these have been sharply curtailed when the state has perceived significant threats to national security.)[2] The country also holds regular elections at local, state, and national levels. Most commentators contend that the vast majority of these elections are free from coercion or malfeasance. When instances of either are unearthed by a remarkably free press, the Election Commission countermands the results and requires fresh polls. Popularly elected governments, after losing their mandate, have peacefully remitted power to successful opponents. Most remarkably, the powerful Indian Army remains strikingly apolitical. It has shown less than scant interest in governing the country.

Of course, Indian democracy has its shortcomings: Rampant political corruption has infected the body politic. Today, a former prime minister Narasimha Rao, still stands in the dock accused of a series of illegal transactions. Laloo Prasad Yadav, a former chief minister of India's most economically backward state, Bihar, is now out on bail after being charged with raiding the exchequer in a state-run animal fodder scheme. Large numbers of elected legislators in India's most populous state, Uttar Pradesh, have criminal backgrounds or have criminal investigations pending against them.

Another dimension of Indian politics is equally unsavory. Since the early 1980s, many of India's politicians have come to rely on *condotierri* to enforce their writ against recalcitrant voters or to intimidate political opponents. In an attempt to draw attention to this growing politician-criminal nexus the Rao government commissioned a study to assess its scope and significance. A former civil servant of unimpeachable qualifications, N. N. Vohra, was entrusted with this task. Though various Indian newsmagazines and newspapers published excerpts from it, the Vohra Commission Report has yet to be made public.

A related issue concerns the loss of probity and neutrality of significant sections of the police force in India. On a number of occasions in recent years, state-level police forces, especially in the states of Uttar Pradesh, Bihar, and Maharashtra, have completely failed to stop sectarian violence. Worse still, in December 1992, the local police proved to be passive spectators when a Hindu mob affiliated with the jingoistic Bharatiya Janata Party (BJP) destroyed the Babri mosque in Uttar Pradesh.[3] Later, as communal riots ensued in a number of Indian cities, especially in Bombay (now Mumbai), the police tacitly collaborated with Hindu rioters attacking Muslim communities.

Nevertheless, these shortcomings are unlikely to fundamentally undermine India's democratic ethos. The Indian polity possesses sufficient self-correcting mechanisms to ensure the continuity of democratic norms and practices amid political malfeasance and chicanery. For example, many political institutions denuded in the 1970s and 1980s are regaining their robustness. India's increasingly activist judiciary is trying to restore some probity and efficacy to a variety of institutions.[4] For example, it is primarily due to the Supreme Court's willingness to entertain public interest litigation that Narasimha Rao is still under investigation on corruption charges. The once-somnolent Election Commission has now emerged as a powerful watchdog. Also, since 1992, faced with considerable international and domestic criticism for the harshness of its response to the insurgency in Kashmir, the government created the National Human Rights Commission (NHRC).[5] Justice Jaganath Mishra, a retired judge of India's Supreme Court, was made the head of the NHRC. Initially, most human rights activists dismissed its creation as merely a symbolic gesture designed to deflect sharp criticism of the government's human rights record. Yet, contrary to these expectations, the NHRC has acquired a degree of organizational autonomy. Though still wary of publicly upbraiding the government on national-security-related issues, it has shown signs of increasing independence.

Simultaneously, civil society in India is becoming increasingly stronger. The Indian press, which has long been feisty, has now become a formidable source of political accountability. A plethora of grassroots nongovernmental organizations routinely contend with the executive on a range of issues. Finally, the forces of economic liberalization, which were unleashed in the wake of a fiscal crisis in 1991, have also narrowed the scope of official graft and corruption. Businessmen no longer have to supplicate and bribe bureaucrats and ministers or to negotiate a Byzantine maze of regulations to enter new industries, expand plant capacity, or locate new factories.[6]

## Searching for Explanations

What factors explain this form of Indian "exceptionalism?" The answers that various social scientists have provided are inadequate at best, and often flawed. An eminent scholar of Indian politics, Myron Weiner, has argued that democracy in India is "tutelary."[7] In his view, democracy was bequeathed to India as part of the British colonial heritage. This argument is not entirely without merit.[8] However, it does not provide an adequate explanation. Pakistan, of course, gained independence at exactly the same time. Yet that nation's transition to democracy is still a work in progress.[9]

A pre-eminent scholar of comparative sociology, Barrington Moore, also attempted to provide an explanation for India's transition to democracy. However, a close reading of Moore's work reveals that the argument he constructs is more about India's failure to modernize than a delineation of India's pathway to democracy. Encapsulated in his argument are many well-documented propositions dealing with the structure of the nationalist movement that facilitated the transition to democracy. For example, Moore explicitly recognizes Mohandas Gandhi's critical role in transforming the organizational structure of the principal nationalist organization, the Indian National Congress. Specifically, Gandhi's contribution lay in transforming a quintessentially moderate, Anglicized and upper-middle-class party into an organization with a mass political base.[10] In pursuit of this end, Gandhi successfully mobilized India's disenfranchised and poor through the adoption of the tactic of mass civil disobedience. One such episode included the Salt March, where he led thousands of poor and illiterate Indians to violate the British colonial government's monopoly on salt making.

Judith M. Brown, a historian of contemporary India, provides a sweeping narrative account of the origins of Indian democracy.[11] From her narrative it is possible to glean certain general propositions that contribute to an explanation of India's transition to democracy. She cites three interrelated sets of factors: the lengthy experience of working under British democratic structures, Nehru's role in fostering debate within the Congress party, and the ideological commitments of a segment of India's politicians to the creation of a democratic state. Her argument is largely accurate and compelling. However, she does not specify which of these various factors proved to be the most significant. Furthermore, all British practice in colonial India could hardly be deemed to be democratic. For example, Congress refused to participate in the war effort due to the British failure to consult its leadership before committing India. In response to Congress's unwillingness to support Britain in the struggle against the Axis powers the colonial authorities incarcerated much of the Congress leadership. Simultaneously, they permitted the Muslim League, an essentially sectarian party under the tutelage of Mohammed Ali Jinnah, to operate at will.[12]

Sunil Khilnani, a political scientist of Indian origin, in a recent work on postindependence Indian politics, provides yet another account of India's successful transition to democracy. He explicitly argues that democracy in India is the result of neither deep-rooted Indian traditions nor the legacy of British colonialism. Instead, he contends that democracy in India arose from distinct elite choices.[13] A critical segment of the Indian nationalist elite adopted democratic norms and practices and infused these into the body of the Indian polity. Subsequently, one of the principal architects of Indian democracy, Prime Minister Nehru, almost didactically built upon the legacy of the nationalist movement. Khilnani's analysis is fundamentally sound. However, he fails to explicate in his slender volume the pre-independence structures, mechanisms, and social forces that predisposed India toward democracy in the postindependence era.

## The Roots of Democratic Practice

To explain the success of India's transition to democracy from quasi-authoritarian British rule it is necessary to carefully examine the ideology, organization, and structure of the Indian nationalist movement. I will test all four of Dankwart Rustow's critical propositions that predispose a state toward a democratic transition: the forging of a sense of national unity, the existence of entrenched conflict, the conscious adoption of democratic rules, and the "habituation" of the electorate and the leadership to democratic norms and practices.[14] All four of these conditions obtained to varying degrees in the Indian nationalist context.

### The Forging of National Unity

The Anglicized upper-middle-class representatives who formed the Indian National Congress in 1885 did not entertain explicit notions of popular sovereignty and extensive democratic franchise. Instead it was a quintessentially reformist organization pursuing ameliorative goals. Its principal objective was to establish some limited prospect of self-governance, not to challenge the legitimacy of British rule in India. The Indian National Congress maintained its reformist agenda into the early 1920s. During this decade, under the stellar influence of Mohandas Gandhi, the organization underwent a fundamental transformation. Gandhi's singular contribution to the development of Indian nationalism lay in the metamorphosis that he brought about in the structure, organization, and membership of the Congress. Under his tutelage Congress adopted the principle of "purna Swaraj," or complete independence.[15] More to the point, Gandhi successfully democratized the Congress Party. Through his adoption of mass-based civil disobedience movements he politicized large segments of India's peasantry and dispossessed. By the early 1930s the Congress had largely shed its elitist orientation and was beginning to strike deep roots in the Indian soil.

Gandhi had successfully democratized the principal organ of India's nationalist movement. However, the task of forging a sense of national unity fell to one of his closest and most able lieutenants, Jawaharal Nehru, whose contribution to forging a vision of national unity simply cannot be overestimated. In many ways, through his copious writings and speeches Nehru successfully developed a usable past for India. The emergence of India as a state, he contended, contrary to British colonial historiography, was not a function of British colonialism. Instead a civilizational entity had long preceded the arrival of British colonialism and had a deep, underlying sense of unity. He wielded this argument with considerable force in bringing together what must be the largest concentration of human diversity within a fixed geographic space. Unless it was possible to demonstrate that India possessed some intrinsic and underlying unity, the postindependence Indian polity could easily divide into ethnic, religious, and linguistic fragments. In this regard, Nehru and other Indian nationalists faced a key challenge. They had to effectively counter much British colonial historiography that sought to portray India as a quintessentially fragmented entity composed of primordial nations.[16] Worse still, British colonial policy reflected such beliefs. For example, thanks to the entreaties of certain leaders of the Muslim communities of India, the British in an initial step toward democratic governance had granted separate electorates to Muslims and Hindus under the aegis of the Minto-Morley Reforms in 1909. The creation of these electorates helped shape a distinctive, nationwide Muslim identity and provided a structural basis for later Muslim separatism.[17]

To combat colonial visions of Indian disunity, Nehru self-consciously attempted to create an alternative perspective on India's precolonial heritage which emphasized unity and continuity. To this end, Nehru wrote copiously and cogently about India's underlying unity despite the existence of widespread ethnoreligious, linguistic, and regional diversity. One sample of his prodigious output will suffice:

> Some kind of dream of unity has occupied the mind of India since the dawn of civilization. That unity was not conceived as something imposed from outside, a standardization of externals or even beliefs. It was something deeper and, within the fold, the widest tolerance of belief and custom was practised and every variety acknowledged and even encouraged.[18]

Yet Nehru was astute enough to realize that the forging of this sense of national unity could not be accomplished through the creation of a mere nationalist myth. Nor could he hope to meld disparate ethnoreligious groups through coercion or personal charisma. He well realized that the only way India could be effectively governed was through some form of a democratic dispensation. Only as long as the disparate regions and groups agreed on some common political framework with neutral rules could the state forge national unity. The mechanism that provided this arena was liberal, parliamentary democracy.

The key instrument in the quest for a democratic order in postindependence India was the development of the Congress party. As independence approached, the party had successfully constructed a mass political base and sought, however imperfectly, to represent all Indians regardless of religious affiliation, regional loyalty, or ethnic background. Admittedly, it was not entirely successful in drawing in significant segments of India's largest minority, the Muslims.[19] Muslim nationalism, under the leadership of Mohammed Ali Jinnah, while opposed to British rule, increasingly took on a separatist orientation. In the last few years prior to the independence of the two states, the prospects of cooperation between the Muslim League and the Congress steadily vanished.

It is also necessary to underscore that one segment of the majority Hindu population, though violently opposed to British rule, nevertheless remained outside the ambit of the Congress. This portion of the population cared little for Congress's secular outlook. Instead a vision of ethnic Hindu nationalism animated Hindu jingoists, who feared the intrusion of British and Western cultural mores and sought to realize a pristine (and largely imaginary) Hindu polity that they claimed once existed. Accordingly, they found refuge in the Hindu Mahasabha Party.[20]

These limitations notwithstanding, the Congress proved quite inclusive on another count; it included members of widely varying political persuasions. One segment of the party was firmly committed to free enterprise while others professed their allegiance to some form of socialism. The upper echelons of the Congress also evinced these diverse ideological propensities. Sardar Vallabhbhai Patel, who would become India's first Home Minister, embodied the pro-business element within Congress. Nehru, on the other hand, represented those who subscribed to a variant of British Fabian socialism.[21] The strength of the Congress lay in its ability to subsume these markedly divergent ideological proclivities of its membership. In effect, the party became an umbrella organization.[22]

The only group that did not actively participate in the nationalist movement were the potentates of the 500-odd "princely states." In fact, many of them feared the departure of the British Crown. Though subservient to the Crown, these rulers had enjoyed wide latitude in the conduct of their affairs. Some of these rulers were benevolent and forward-looking individuals. Others were despotic, cruel, and did little or nothing to ameliorate the lives of their subjects. Indeed the behavior of many resembled Marx's portrait of Oriental despots. Regardless of their proclivities, however, they all realized that under the new political dispensation in New Delhi they would soon lose their powers and perquisites. Their misgivings were hardly ill-founded. Within a few years after independence the new Congress government in New Delhi had stripped them of their powers, changed their state boundaries, and had absorbed their subjects into the larger Indian fold.[23]

## The Existence of Entrenched Conflict

According to Rustow, the second condition that predisposes a regime toward democracy is the existence of entrenched conflict. In the Indian case the entrenched conflict was largely between the forces of British imperial rule and the nationalist movement. Indeed this form of entrenched conflict coupled with the inclusive ideology of the Congress gave considerable force to the creation of a democratic nationalist movement.

The first challenge to foreign and specifically the British presence in India came in 1857 in the twilight of the Mughal empire. The uprising against the East India Company, the forerunner to British imperial control, had briefly united Hindus and Muslims.[24] The British managed to quickly, if brutally, suppress the uprising. This movement, while clearly a reaction against the intrusion of foreign mores, customs, and practices, cannot be fairly characterized as the beginning of the nationalist movement. However, it marked the initial challenge to the entry of foreign customs into Indian society. A more formal movement emphasizing ideas of self-government and political representation emerged toward the end of the nineteenth century.

At the inevitable cost of some oversimplification, three phases of opposition to British imperial rule can be delineated. The initial phase started toward the end of the late nineteenth century. During this phase, nationalist demands were exceedingly limited in scope and were essentially reformist.

They did not seek to overthrow British rule but sought a limited measure of self-government. A second phase emerged during which there were outbursts of terrorist activity alongside demands for constitutional reform.[25] This phase lasted from the early part of the twentieth century to the late 1920s. The third phase emerged in the late 1920s. Under the influence of Mohandas Gandhi, the nationalist movement, despite differences in tactics and strategy, sought nothing less than complete independence.

## The Conscious Adoption of Democratic Rules

Under the aegis of the Congress party a variety of views and positions could contend with one another. In the process, the membership became socialized into the norms of parliamentary debate and discourse. Most importantly, they learnt the significance of political compromise and logrolling. W. H. Morris-Jones, a long-time analyst of Indian politics has trenchantly argued that

Congressmen were accustomed then to holding together in one organization many interests frequently thought of as requiring much reconciliation and mutual adjustment. Congress, that is to say, was used to performing in some degree the work of a national parliament where clashing viewpoints and concerns meet to determine a generally acceptable line of policy.[26]

Many of these developments took place in the wake of the Government of India Act of 1935 which provided for limited representation. Specifically, the act led to creation of provincial legislatures based upon limited suffrage. In the wake of the 1937 elections, held under the terms of the Government of India Act of 1935, the Congress moved from its agitational role to that of a parliamentary party focused on representation and governance. Congress, which won an overwhelming victory in the 1937 elections, did govern until the outbreak of World War Two. The British failure to consult with Congress prior to committing India to the war effort led to the resignation of all Congress governments. Subsequently, at the end of World War Two, and in the wake of the January 1946 elections, Congress came to power in September

1946. Earlier in the year, the British authorities, in a last-ditch attempt to leave behind a unified India, had proposed the Cabinet Mission Plan. This plan envisaged the creation of a three-tier federal system with considerable autonomy for various regions of the country. Only defense, foreign affairs, and communications would be the preserve of the national government in New Delhi. For different reasons, both the Congress and the League, after their initial and conditional acceptances, ultimately chose to reject the Cabinet Mission Plan.[27]

One portion of the Cabinet Mission Plan, however, led to the creation of the Constituent Assembly. The task of this Assembly was to write a constitution for postindependence India. The Muslim League, placing the worst possible construction on a careless remark of Nehru, chose to stay out of the constitution-framing process.[28] Subsequently, Nehru and the Congress did make overtures to convince the League to join the Constituent Assembly but to little avail. The last British efforts to forge some unity between Congress and the League failed.

Eventually, the Congress leaders turned their attention to the task of constitution-making. The principal framers of the constitution, with one exception, came from highly privileged backgrounds. Four of them, Maulana Abul Kalam Azad, Pandit Jawaharlal Nehru, Dr. Rajendra Prasad, and Sardar Vallabhbhai Patel, though representing different temperaments and ideological positions, were all Congress stalwarts. One other individual, Dr. Ambedkar, a Harijan (an untouchable), also played a critical role in shaping the constitution's position on minority rights. It is to their credit that they fashioned a document that set the terms of democratic and representative discourse in India. As Granville Austin, the foremost American authority on the Indian Constitution, has written:

> One might assume, aware of the character of monolithic political systems in other countries, that a mass-party in India would be rigid and narrow in outlook and that its powerful leadership would silence dissent and confine policy and decision-making to the hands of the select few. In India the reverse was the case. The membership of the Congress in the Constituent Assembly and outside held social, economic and political views ranging from the reactionary to the revolutionary, and it did not hesitate to voice them. The leaders of the Assembly, who played the same role in the Congress and in the Union Government, were national heroes and had unlimited power; yet decision-

making in the Assembly was democratic. *The Indian Constitution expresses the will of the many rather than the needs of the few* [emphasis added].

The constitution that they produced and that India adopted in 1950 had a number of salient features that distinguished it from the structures of British colonial rule. Among other matters, it guaranteed certain fundamental rights, including the right to private property, freedom of religion, assembly, movement, and association. Simultaneously, it provided minorities guarantees to protect their language, script, and culture. The constitution also abolished untouchability; discrimination on the basis of religion, race, caste, sex and place of birth; and outlawed forced labor. It also affirmed the sovereignty of parliament and granted the Supreme Court the power of judicial review. In turn, it provided various mechanisms by which citizens would be able to move the Supreme Court and lower courts to enforce fundamental rights. At another level, it created a quasi-federal polity, with significant powers, especially those dealing with fiscal matters, vested in the central government. Perhaps most significantly from the standpoint of democratic participation, it guaranteed universal adult franchise.

In addition to the fundamental rights that it enshrined, the constitution also had an important preamble, the Directive Principles of State Policy. These principles, which are nonjusticiable, exhort the state to ensure that its citizens possess an adequate means of livelihood, that the economic resources of the country are harnessed to promote the common good, that the health of workers is not endangered and that the state will make every effort to improve the standard of living of the citizenry.

## The "Habituation" of Leaders and Electorate to Democratic Norms

Rustow's fourth and final condition, the "habituation" of the leadership and electorate to democratic norms and practices, also played a critical role in ensuring India's transition to democracy. One episode in particular is emblematic. In August 1945, as independence approached, the Congress leadership was faced with an important dilemma. Certain members of the British Indian Army had defected to the Japanese during the war and had

formed the Indian National Army (INA) under the leadership of a disaffected
Congress leader, the Bengali nationalist Subhas Chandra Bose.[29] In the wake
of the Japanese defeat in Southeast Asia, British forces either killed or captured the majority of the INA in the Burmese theater.

The British authorities decided that they would prosecute the captured
senior echelons of the INA. The British decision to try these individuals for
treason generated considerable nationalist sentiment. A number of Congress
stalwarts, including Sir Tej Bahadur Sapru, Aruna Asaf Ali, and Jawaharlal
Nehru, rallied to the defense of these men. Eventually, they were either
acquitted or Viceregal decrees suspended their sentences. The greater significance of the INA trials for the future of India's democracy lay elsewhere.

In defending these individuals, Nehru supported their right to take up
arms against a colonial, oppressive power. He argued that they had acted
with the highest of motives. However, after the conclusion of the trials and
with the onset of independence, he categorically refused to reinstate them
into the Indian Army. Their motivations aside, Nehru held that they had
broken the oath of office and had become politicized. Consequently, they
could sow discord within the army's ranks. By refusing to reinstate the INA
leadership into the Indian Army, Nehru quickly established the supremacy
of civilian authority over the military. Any Bonapartist ambitions harbored
by members of the armed forces were effectively quashed.

The significance of this episode for India's transition to democracy cannot
be overstated. Nehru and his colleagues realized the signal importance of
the establishment of civilian supremacy over the military in any democratic
order.[30] Nehru's instincts proved to be uncannily correct. In neighboring
Pakistan, the civilian authority became increasingly dependent on the military for maintaining public order in the wake of independence. As the military's role in society expanded and civilian institutions proved to be weak,
the armed forces gathered increasing power. In 1958 the Pakistani military
staged a coup. Since then Pakistan has seen long periods of authoritarian
military rule punctuated by brief, fitful steps toward democracy.[31] Much of
the nationalist legacy, especially institutional norms and practices, decayed
in India in the 1970s. But the one norm, of firm civilian control over the
military, despite many challenges, has survived unscathed. Unlike in much
of the developing world the Indian armed forces remain singularly apolitical.
In recent years, even a suggestion of expanding the military's role in governance brought sharp rebukes and stern warnings from the defense minister.

In the early years of the Indian republic, Nehru again played a vital role in socializing India's elected representatives in parliament to internalize democratic norms. The pre-independence history of the Congress party had emphasized debate, discussion, and compromise. Long before independence, thanks to its diverse social and ideological composition, Congress had acted as a microcosm parliament. Consequently, norms of parliamentary conduct were hardly unknown to the vast majority of India's elected representatives. The existence of this tradition made his task considerably easier. Nevertheless, Nehru rarely lost an opportunity to persuade, hector, and cajole his parliamentary colleagues, acting much like a schoolmaster imparting civics lessons to his pupils.[32]

Finally, the constitutional dispensation that India's elite created helped in the "habituation" of the electorate to democratic norms and principles. The constitution drafted by members of the Constituent Assembly squarely upheld the principle of universal adult franchise. The extension of suffrage from the very outset had the effect of, at least notionally, enfranchising all of India's adult electorate. A series of elections at local, regional, and national levels in which growing sections of the eligible electorate participated made Indians, regardless of their station in life, realize the significance of adult suffrage.

## Peril and Promise: Indian Democracy Approaches the Millennium

Where does Indian democracy stand today? It is virtually a commonplace assertion that India's political institutions have decayed since the early 1970s. A number of social scientists have concerns about India's "crisis of governability."[33] The sources of such decay are usually traced to the populist policies of Indira Gandhi. In attempts to consolidate her personal power, the argument goes, she systematically subverted every institution that her father, Jawaharlal Nehru, had so carefully nurtured. She undermined internal democracy in the Congress party by her failure to hold intraparty elections. She undermined judicial independence and politicized the central bureaucracy. She contested the 1971 national election on the slogan of *garibi hatao* (literally, "abolish poverty"). Even national elections under her leadership became largely plebiscitary exercises. She resorted to a series of populist slogans and policies designed to circumvent institutional checks and constraints. In another populist gesture, she nationalized the banking industry. Yet one of the inadvertent byproducts of her populist slogans and policies was a dramatic rise in political mobilization. Tantalized by her promises to change the existing social order, a range of hitherto disenfranchised groups sought to enter the political arena. Furthermore, fitful increases in levels of literacy, mass media exposure, and the practice of participation in a variety of electoral exercises expanded political demands beyond the capacity of India's political institutions.

However, Indira Gandhi alone cannot be held responsible for the decline of India's political institutions. A congeries of other structural factors also contributed to institutional decay. These included the shrinking electoral base of the Congress Party, the concomitant entry of new social groups into Indian politics, and the fragmentation of the electoral base along ethnoreligious, regional, and class lines. Many of the new entrants into the political arena also undermined democratic norms and procedures. Some of these parties, especially the two communist parties, the pro-Soviet Communist Party of India (CPI) and the pro-Chinese Communist Party of India (Marxist) (CPI/M), openly contested parliamentary norms and parliamentary procedures.[34] Worse still, they encouraged work stoppages, organized strikes and politicized police forces in the states that they governed. In the state of West Bengal, in the early 1970s, in addition to the emergence of a Communist-dominated United Front government, a neophyte Maoist guerrilla movement developed in the border district of Naxalbari. This organization—the Communist Party of India Marxist-Leninist, or CPI (M-L), popularly known as the Naxalites—received both material and ideological assistance from the People's Republic of China. The CPI (M-L), unlike the other two communist parties, made no pretense of its contempt for democratic institutions.[35]

Other political parties, such as the ultranationalist Jana Sangh, the predecessor to today's Bharatiya Janata Party (BJP), sought to mobilize along caste and ethnoreligious lines, particularly appealing to the Brahmin and Bania castes. Such mobilization contributed significantly to widespread political instability and communal violence. In later years, the BJP significantly capitalized on the shortcomings of the practice of Indian secularism to stoke the sentiments of communal hatred.[36] For example, in 1986 the Indian Supreme Court had chosen to grant an indigent Muslim woman alimony in contravention of Muslim personal law. The prime minister, Rajiv Gandhi, fearful of losing Muslim votes, chose to legislatively overturn the decision and granted Muslims a separate dispensation. The BJP promptly went on the offensive, attacking the Congress government for practicing "pseudo-secularism" and "pampering" minorities.

What does the future hold for India's democracy? The shortcomings of Indian democracy aside, there is little question that most of India's political leadership and electorate have become "habituated" to democratic norms and practices. As early as 1977, as Indira Gandhi ended the "state of emergency" and declared elections, India's poor and illiterate ousted her from office. Their decision to cast Indira Gandhi and the Congress out resoundingly demonstrated their understanding of the power of the ballot. Today, even though significant numbers of India's politicians are manipulative and venal, they have to comport themselves within the ambit of democratic norms and rules or risk a similar fate. Consequently, though breaches and breakdowns of these norms and principles do occur, the structure of a democratic polity remains above question.

What about India's national unity? Journalistic accounts of secessionist movements in various parts of the country and tales of sanguinary ethnoreligious violence frequently suggest that India is on the verge of collapse. Yet every one of these lugubrious predictions have been proven wrong. The Indian state has simultaneously weathered multiple crises and has not collapsed. It wields enormous coercive power, which it can bring to bear to produce order if not law. Additionally, despite the existence of centrifugal forces in various parts of the country, a high level of economic and social integration has been achieved in India. Above all, India's democratic political structures, though compromised, provide important outlets for venting a variety of grievances. Consequently, comparisons with the fates of other polyethnic states, such as the former Soviet Union and Yugoslavia, are invidious and polemical.

This optimism about the future of democracy notwithstanding there are at least two issues that bode ill for India's democratic future: the decline of political institutions in India and the rise of ethno-religious fervor.[37] Yet there exist a number of countervailing institutional mechanisms and social forces that will place limits on these two corrosive tendencies.

Obviously, some political institutions in India are debile. However, others have successfully been resurrected. Moreover, as argued earlier, new institutions have been created to deal with emergent exigencies. Consequently, the picture of institutional decay can hardly be painted in uniform colors. In parts of India, especially in much of Bihar and Uttar Pradesh, the state cannot perform its most elementary functions. It fails to meet the Weberian standard of possessing a monopoly on the legitimate use of force. Or to put it in Marxian terms, the state has indeed withered away but not quite in the fashion that Marx had intended. Yet significant other parts of India are fairly well administered and are also economically prosperous. As long as the overall institutional balance remains in favor of a moderately neutral state as opposed to perverse social elements and forces, democracy in India will survive.

What about the Hindu revivalistic threat to Indian democracy? The BJP, which has spearheaded this movement, became a formidable force in Indian politics in the 1980s and 1990s after having been at the margins of the polity for four decades. The party will no doubt continue to remain a significant player in the Indian political arena. However, its threat to India's secular landscape may be overstated. India still possesses sufficient countervailing forces to prevent the BJP from implementing its antisecular manifesto. Indeed, following the initial collapse of the United Front coalition government in 1997 the BJP made a concerted bid to form a national government. To its dismay, it failed miserably to co-opt any significant political party to participate in this endeavor. Admittedly, the unwillingness of most political parties to join forces with the BJP may not have stemmed from the most pristine of motives. In all likelihood, their leaders feared the opprobrium of joining an unelected party with a blatantly antisecular outlook. More to the point, once in office, and faced with the task of actually governing the country, the BJP leadership was quickly forced to moderate its stance on a variety of domestic and foreign policy issues. Parties in opposition can frequently wield the wrecking ball.

With the collapse of the Janata Dal led United Front government fresh national elections took place in February 1998. In these elections, the BJP emerged as the largest party in parliament and was asked to form a government. It successfully managed to cobble together a coalition drawing on the support of a host of small and regional parties. The structure of this diverse coalition, which represents varied interests, prevented the BJP from pursuing some of the more extreme goals in its agenda including the passage of a uniform civil code or the building of a temple at Ayodhya.

The existence of larger social forces will also act as important contraints on the BJP's pursuit of some of its ideological goals. In particular, the mobilization of India's minorities as well as its lower castes places important societal limitations on the BJP's upper-caste and anti-secular orientation.[38] Consequently, this form of contestation will force the BJP's ideologues to adopt more pragmatic policies to maintain social peace and garner electoral support. Though the anti-secular challenge to Indian democracy cannot be dismissed it is still too early to write its epitaph.

## NOTES

The author gratefully acknowledges the criticisms and suggestions of Jyotirindra Das Gupta, Robert L. Hardgrave, Jr., Pratap Mehta, Traci Nagle, and Jack Snyder.

1.  For a thoughtful discussion see Pratap Bhanu Mehta, "India's Disordered Democracy," *Pacific Affairs* 64:4 (Winter 1991–92), pp. 536–548.

2.  The disregard for civil liberties and human rights has been particularly noticeable when combating insurgencies in northeastern India, the Punjab, and most recently in Kashmir.

3.  Hindu zealots attacked and destroyed the mosque in the town of Ayodhya, Uttar Pradesh, on the putative grounds that it had been built on the ruins of a Hindu temple consecrating the birthplace of Lord Rama, an important member of the Hindu pantheon. The Hindu zealots claim that the Mughal emperor Babur had destroyed the temple. For a discussion of the issue see S. Gopal, ed., *Anatomy of a Confrontation: The Ram Janmabhoomi-Babri Masjid Issue* (New Delhi: Viking Penguin, 1991).

4.  On the decline of political institutions in India see Paul R. Brass, *The Politics of India Since Independence* (Cambridge: Cambridge University Press, 1994); for a nuanced discussion see Jyotirindra Das Gupta, "Democratic Becoming and Combined Development," in Larry Diamond, Juan J. Linz, and Seymour Martin Lipset, eds. *Democracy in Developing Countries: Asia* (Boulder: Lynne Rienner, 1989)

5.  For a detailed discussion of Indian strategy and tactics in suppressing the Kashmir insurgency see Šumit Ganguly, *The Crisis in Kashmir: Portents of War, Hopes of Peace* (Cambridge and Washington, D.C.: Cambridge University Press and the Woodrow Wilson Center Press, 1997).

6.  Jagdish Bhagwati, *India in Transition: Freeing the Economy* (Oxford: Clarendon Press, 1993).

7.  Myron Weiner and Samuel Huntington, *Understanding Political Development* (Boston: Little, Brown, 1987), p. 33.

8.  See for example the pioneering work of Eric Stokes, *The English Utilitarians and India* (Delhi: Oxford University Press, 1959).

9.  Allen McGrath, *The Destruction of Democracy in Pakistan* (Karachi: Oxford University Press, 1996).

10. Barrington Moore, *The Social Origins of Dictatorship and Democracy: Lord and Peasant in the Making of the Modern World* (Boston: Beacon Press, 1966), p. 372.

11. Judith Brown, *Modern India: The Origins of an Asian Democracy* (Oxford: Oxford University Press, 1994), pp. 378–79.

12. See for example Stanley Wolpert, *Jinnah of Pakistan* (New York: Oxford University Press, 1984).

13. Sunil Khilnani, *The Idea of India* (New York: Farrar, Straus and Giroux, 1997), p. 34.

14. Dankwart A. Rustow, "Transitions to Democracy: Toward a Dynamic Model," *Comparative Politics* 2:3 (April 1970), pp. 337–63.

15. Bipan Chandra, Mridula Mukherjee, Aditya Mukherjee, K.N. Panikkar and Sucheta Mahajan, *India's Struggle for Independence* (New Delhi: Viking Penguin, 1988), pp. 266–69.

16. Sunil Khilnani, "India's Democratic Career," in John Dunn, ed., *Democracy: The Unfinished Journey, 508 BC to AD 1993* (Oxford: Oxford University Press, 1994), p. 193.

17. Peter Hardy, *The Muslims of British India* (Cambridge: Cambridge University Press, 1972).

18. Jawaharlal Nehru, *The Discovery of India* (New Delhi: Jawaharlal Nehru Memorial Fund, 1995), p. 62.

19. Several factors account for Congress's failure to bring significant sections of Muslims under its aegis. Most of the senior leaders of the Congress were firm secularists. However, in its quest for electoral advantage, Congress on many an occasion had to make common cause with local notables. The secular credentials of these local satraps left much to be desired. Consequently, many Muslims feared Hindu domination in the aftermath of British rule. On this point see Hardy, *Muslims of British India*.

20. For the most comprehensive treatment of the origins and evolution of Hindu nationalism see Christophe Jaffrelot, *The Hindu Nationalist Movement in India* (New Delhi: Viking Penguin, 1996). Also see Bruce Graham, *Hindu Nationalism and Indian Politics* (Cambridge: Cambridge University Press, 1990).

21. Claude Markovits, *Indian Business and Nationalist Politics, 1931–1939* (Cambridge: Cambridge University Press, 1985), pp. 102–109.

22. Rajni Kothari, "The Congress 'System' in India," *Asian Survey* 4:2 (December 1964), pp. 1161–73.

23. During the period of British colonial rule there were two classes of states in the British Indian Empire. One class was directly ruled from Whitehall and constituted British India. The other class consisted of the "princely states," nominally independent but whose rulers swore allegiance to the British Crown. As independence approached British policy toward these nominally indepen-

dent states was ambiguous at best. Lord Mountbatten, the last viceroy, was in favor of their amalgamation with either India or Pakistan based upon their religious composition and geographic location. Other British officials, such as Sir Conrad Corfield, Mountbatten's political adviser, encouraged many of the princes to seek independence. Not surprisingly, the Indian nationalists were staunchly opposed to any such plans. In their view, the independence of the princely states would amount to the Balkanization of India. On this point see the excellent work of Ian Copland, *The Princes of India in the Endgame of Empire, 1917–1947* (Cambridge: Cambridge University Press, 1997).

24. For a variety of perspectives on the causes of the uprising see Ainslie T. Embree, ed., *India in 1857: The Revolt against Foreign Rule* (New Delhi: Chanakya Publications, 1987).

25. On the role of political terror, especially in the state of Bengal, see Bipan Chandra et al., *India's Struggle for Independence*, pp. 142–45. For the transformation of the Congress party in the first three decades of the twentieth century see Gopal Krishna, "The Development of the Indian National Congress as a Mass Organization, 1918–1923," *Journal of Asian Studies* 25 (May 1966), pp. 413–30.

26. W. H. Morris-Jones, *The Government and Politics of India* (London: Eothen Press, 1987), p. 35.

27. The League also chose initially to boycott the Interim Government. Its refusal to enter the government stemmed from its dissatisfaction with not being granted an equal number of portfolios in the Interim Government. When it finally joined the government it proved to be a largely obstructionist force intent more on undermining Congress's initiatives than on tackling the strenuous tasks of administration and governance. Faced with the mutual intransigence of the Congress and the League the British chose to transfer power to two separate entities, India and Pakistan. On this point see the discussion in Chandra et al., *India's Struggle for Independence*, pp. 492–95.

28. On this point see the superb discussion in Granville Austin, *The Indian Constitution: The Cornerstone of a Nation* (Oxford: Clarendon Press, 1966), pp. 6–9.

29. Stephen P. Cohen, *The Indian Army* (Berkeley: University of California Press, 1971).

30. Sumit Ganguly, "From the Defense of the Nation to Aid to the Civil," *Journal of Asian and African Affairs* 26:1–2 (1991), pp. 11–25.

31. Hasan Askari Rizvi, *The Military and Politics in Pakistan* (Lahore: Progressive Publishers, 1986). Also see Saeed Shafqat, *Civil Military Relations in Pakistan: From Zulfikar Ali Bhutto to Benazir Bhutto* (Boulder: Westview Press, 1997).

32. Michael Brecher, *Nehru: A Political Biography* (Boston: Beacon Press, 1959).

33. The classic statement on the relationship between political mobilization and

institutional decay is Samuel Huntington, *Political Order in Changing Societies* (New Haven: Yale University Press, 1968). For an application of Huntington's thesis to the Indian context see Atul Kohli, *Democracy and Discontent: India's Crisis of Governability* (New York: Cambridge University Press, 1990).

34. For a discussion of these forces and trends see Francine Frankel, *India's Political Economy, 1947–1977: The Gradual Revolution* (Princeton: Princeton University Press, 1978).

35. Marcus Franda, *Radical Politics in West Bengal* (Cambridge: MIT Press, 1971).

36. For a discussion of these issues see Sumit Ganguly, "Ethno-Religious Conflict in South Asia," *Survival* 35:2 (Summer 1993), pp. 88–109.

37. On the rise of Hindu ethnoreligious fervor see Peter Van der Veer, *Religious Nationalism: Hindus and Muslims in India* (New Delhi: Oxford University Press, 1996). Also see David Ludden, ed., *Making India Hindu: Religion, Community, and the Politics of Democracy in India* (Delhi: Oxford University Press, 1996).

38. Taufiq Subhan, "India's diversity seen as checking BJP's growth," *India Abroad*, July 3, 1998, p. 2.

# 11  Democratization in Africa after 1989: Comparative and Theoretical Perspectives

*Richard Joseph*

The upheavals in much of Africa after the Berlin Wall was opened in November 1989 have been referred to as a second independence. The anticolonial movement of the 1960s, which first won independence, was inspired by the most fundamental of democratic principles: the people should rule themselves through governments of their own choosing. However, a decade after overt forms of external political rule were removed, Africa slid under an authoritarian carapace that hardened as cold war antagonists and their aid agencies bolstered their clients, proxies, and allies.

This essay will examine some of the theoretical issues raised by the dynamics of political change in Africa within the context of the global wave of democratization. More than half the forty-seven states of sub-Saharan Africa undertook reforms leading to more competitive and pluralist political systems after 1989 for largely conjunctural reasons. This essay will explore some of the key external and internal elements of that conjuncture, as well as the nature of the unfolding political changes, whether they involved transitions to more liberalized and democratic systems or retreat to forms of authoritarianism.

## An Infertile Terrain

Democratization was not supposed to happen in Africa. It had too little of what seemed necessary for constitutional democratic polities. African countries were too poor, too culturally fragmented, and insufficiently capitalist; they were not fully penetrated by western Christianity and lacked the requisite civic culture. Middle classes were usually weak and more bureaucratic than entrepreneurial, and they were often coopted into authoritarian political structures. Working classes, except in a few cases such as Zambia and South Africa, were embryonic. Who would be the social agents of democracy?[1] According to the main theories about the prerequisites or favorable conditions for democracy, most African countries constituted infertile terrain.

When Samuel Huntington wrote in 1984 that, "with a few exceptions, the limits of democratic development may well have been reached," he did not include African countries among the likely exceptions. "Most African countries are by reason of their poverty or the violence of their politics unlikely to move in a democratic direction."[2] Similarly, Robert Dahl did not expect "any dramatic changes in the number of polyarchies within a generation or two,"[3] and Giuseppe Di Palma considered the prospects of democracy in "Africa as a whole" to be "bleak."[4] In fact, even close students of Africa, such as Michael Bratton, generally agreed with this prognosis. "It hinges on whether political leaders can be installed and deposed by political will and held accountable while in office. At the moment, this seems too big a question, too remote a prospect."[5] Crawford Young spoke for the academic community, Africanist as well as non-Africanist, when he described as "stunning" the return of competitive party politics to many African countries by the end of 1991, including the electoral defeat of long-entrenched rulers such as Mathieu Kerekou of Benin and Kenneth Kaunda of Zambia.[6]

The political developments in Africa and in other "infertile" areas signal the need for adjustments in the study of democratization. Dankwart A. Rustow anticipated this adjustment when he postulated "many roads to democracy" that may not always involve "the same social classes, the same types of political issues, or even the same methods of solution."[7] Although notable attempts have been made to salvage aspects of the "prerequisites" approach to democracy and democratization, Huntington, who once actively explored conditions that appeared to favor or impede democratization, now contends that "the causes of democratization are . . . varied and their significance over time is likely to vary considerably."[8]

The student of democratization in Africa after 1989 does not have a ready-made explanatory framework or set of defining conditions that can simply be tested in the African context. Developments in Africa oblige us to approach seemingly settled issues anew and to adopt a critical approach regarding such fundamentals as the meaning of democracy and democratization. Students of African transitions must also become more actively engaged in formulating theory, heretofore dominated by students of other areas of the world. To be avoided is the passive application to Africa of externally devised frameworks, as well as the analysis of African politics solely within Africa-derived paradigms.

## Schumpeter's Triumph

The leaders and militants of African independence movements, while assuming control of the institutions erected by departing colonial administrations, believed they could develop political and economic systems based on theories of governance that would be more in accordance with the traditions and norms of their own societies. Although they largely failed, the exercise is not forever forsaken. After 1989 the dominant set of political institutions in western industrial nations and their theoretical justification moved to a position of near global hegemony.

Overshadowed by the struggle between capitalism and western democracy, on the one hand, and communism and socialist democracy, on the other, was the debate among western democrats over the very meaning of democracy. J. Peter Euben captured the crux of the dispute as taking place between the "contemporary consensus view" that "democracy is largely a matter of choosing among elites in periodic elections" and "what it literally meant: the *kratia* (power, rule, mastery) by the *demos*."[9]

Huntington declared that "by the 1970s the debate was over and J. D. Schumpeter had won."[10] He rephrased Schumpeter's formulation, to which the consensus was anchored: "in all democratic regimes the principal offices of government are chosen through competitive elections in which the bulk of the population can participate. Democratic systems thus have a common institutional core that establishes their identity."[11] Yet this victory may not be final. It is possible to accept, according to John Dunn, that "what the *demos* of modern representative democracies in fact does . . . is to choose between relatively organised teams of candidates to govern" without believing that the most fundamental questions about the meaning of democracy, and thus of democratization, have been settled.[12] I argue here that the dominant way of characterizing democracy according to a set of electoralist, institutionalist, and proceduralist criteria must be expanded into a broader conceptualization.[13]

Some authors have returned to the etymology of democracy to build a conceptualization that avoids what Parekh refers to as "democracy defined and structured within the limits set by liberalism"[14] and the attendant danger, according to Euben, that "liberalism will overwhelm democracy."[15] The tension between democracy as an idea, and even as an ideal system, and particular institutional arrangements that communities have chosen or accepted to govern themselves cannot be eliminated just because of the economic or other efficacy of the latter. "The normative and persuasive function" of the democratic idea, in Sartori's view, should not be buried under its "descriptive and denotative function."[16]

My understanding of democracy combines its deliberative and liberal elements. I consider a political system democratic to the extent that it facilitates citizen self-rule, permits the broadest deliberation in determining public policy, and constitutionally guarantees all the freedoms necessary for open political competition. All political systems, including western pluralist democracies, should be subject to analysis and assessment based on values that cannot simply be reduced to how well and frequently elections are conducted among organized groups of political aspirants. This definition is also consistent with well-known conceptualizations such as Robert Dahl's, which identifies the central features of participation and contestation together with a facilitating set of civil liberties. By applying the term polyarchy to modern western pluralist democracies, Dahl retained for democracy its more open-ended and prescriptive meaning.[17] This definition also seeks to capture the arguments advanced by proponents of "deliberative democracy," conceived as "an association whose affairs are governed by the public deliberation of its members."[18]

With regard to Africa, there are important reasons for a less culture-bound definition. African states are, as Parekh says of India, "an association of individuals and a community of communities."[19] Pluralist and competitive democracy in Africa has tended to take the form of competition among communities rather than individuals, parties, and administrative subunits. W. Arthur Lewis argued in 1965 that in African plural societies electoral systems that yield governments based on a simple aggregation of votes and majority rule will not work, and his argument has been largely confirmed.[20] It is no wonder that power-sharing formulas and consociational systems are everywhere being actively encouraged in the post-1989 transitions.

The participatory and communal elements that were central features of Athenian democracy are also constitutive elements of many African societies. The writings of Julius Nyerere, who tried to capture these normative features, are echoed in almost every argument that emphasizes the deliberative aspects of a political system characterized by "a commitment to the resolution of problems of public choice through public reasoning."[21] Nyerere's notion that African democracy rests on individuals "talking until they agree," which he contrasted with the resort to mechanical majority votes to resolve issues, is echoed in the work of contemporary scholars who emphasize the transformative capacity of democratic arenas in which individuals arrive at decisions that are "ethically based judgments about matters of common concern."[22] Tanzania's prolonged retention of disastrous economic policies, however, suggests the need to combine open deliberation of policy issues with the constitutional right to organize politically to challenge prevailing interests and viewpoints.

Peter Ekeh's seminal writings on Africa's two publics, one derived from the colonial superstructure and the other from a "deeper" African communal structure, also resonate in these discussions.[23] The authoritarian leaders who entrenched themselves throughout Africa in the 1970s and 1980s shaped communalism to their advantage, tying the fortunes and even basic security of kin groups to their hold on power. Everywhere, the exploitation of political offices for the personal benefit of their occupants was rationalized along communal lines.[24] Ekeh has recently discussed how the limited commitment to a national civic realm hinders the installation of pluralist democracies. Authoritarian rulers, under challenge to democratize, take advantage of the "fractured response to tyranny" among the different communal publics.[25]

In post-1989 Africa a major challenge is the need to design institutions with procedures and practices that are socially rooted in the task of constructing national democratic systems. This project would take into account Parekh's observation that "societies define and individuate people differently."[26] Societies in which communal solidarity and obligation remain fundamental pose collective action problems different from those in which preferences may be superficially treated as "individual" and subject to aggregation and resolution by majority vote.[27] Relevant to this project is Rustow's contention that democracy involves not just competition but equally conciliation and accommodation. His further argument that democracy is, "above all, a process for resolving conflicts within human groups" is particularly relevant in light of the upsurge in violent conflicts in several African countries.[28]

## Liberal Democracy as Virtual Democracy

Despite the extraordinary volume of writing on democracy and democratization by authors ranging from the social democratic left to liberals of various hues to conservatives, they have remarkably converged in regard to a system that may be called "virtual democracy." Several core elements of virtual democracy can be presented as a series of paradoxes. First, it is formally based on citizen rule, but the making of key decisions, especially in the area of economic reform policies, is insulated from popular involvement. Second, hegemonic economic forces in society, as well as those in control of the state apparatus, must be secure in the protection of their interests and able to minimize threats to them by formerly excluded or dominant groups for a smooth transition from authoritarian rule to occur. Third, central to this variant of democracy is the creation of opportunities for the further development of a capitalist or market economy. While capitalism can exist without democracy, there are no contemporary democracies that are not capitalist or that do not create the institutional framework for the expansion of capitalism. Fourth, external forces are critical to the establishment of democracy in areas formerly under authoritarian rule. Now that global capitalism has no economic rivals, the institutional certainties of democratic systems are usually preferred to the arbitrariness of autocratic rule. Nevertheless, various hegemons have their own perceived interests in particular arenas which may lead them to hinder transitions from authoritarian rule. Fifth, most decisive in democratic transitions are the choices made by those enjoying governmental and social power when faced with challenges to their dominance. Such individuals and groups often realize that democratization can be manipulated to legitimize their continuation in power. Sixth, while the core institutions and practices of contemporary democracy rest on the premise of a free play of ideas and interests, certain substantive policy outcomes are ruled out, and others are assured. Participation may be broad, but policy choices are narrow. Finally, all areas of the world formerly under authoritarian systems—Africa, Asia, eastern Europe, South America, and southern Europe, whatever the prior ideological complexion of the governments—are encouraged to take a particular path when challenged to dismantle authoritarian systems. Recognition that the democratic system may be "virtual" and will not threaten established interests often facilitates this "choice."

Joel Barkan has argued that "today the western concept of democracy is more or less accepted throughout the world." However, he overstates his case when he adds that "western programs to support democratization are welcomed by all save those who would be dislodged by the process."[29] Pluralist constitutional democracy in Africa represented a real challenge to autocratic regimes for no more than three years after 1989. By the end of 1992 most leaders learned "how to control the process of competitive elections so that they can win a grudging stamp of approval from western donors but still hang on to power."[30]

## Democratization and Economic Distress

Between March 1957, when Ghana became independent, and March 1990, when the South African flag was lowered over Southwest Africa (Namibia), the last colony in the continent, changes in African regimes took place primarily through military coups.[31] The concept that African presidents held office only for a designated period or as long as they enjoyed the freely expressed confidence of the citizens was alien. There were few exceptions to this rule. In the 1970s Burkina Faso (then Upper Volta), Ghana, and Nigeria all conducted competitive elections. Although elected governments took power, they were soon pushed aside by the military. Authority was transferred to designated successors after the death of independence leaders in Gabon and Kenya and while the head of state was still alive in Cameroon and Senegal. In none of these countries, however, did the regime change significantly.[32] In Cameroon, the departed ruler, Ahmadu Ahidjo, tried to shoot his way back into power two years after relinquishing it in 1982. His successor, Paul Biya, was saved only by a faction of the military and security forces and subsequently reneged on his promise to liberalize the system.

By 1995 almost all sub-Saharan African countries introduced some measure of political liberalization, and a majority permitted competitive elections.[33] In just under a third (fourteen), entirely new governments were elected, and in nine of these elections incumbents were defeated. In contrast, in the three decades of postcolonial rule before 1989 an elected government peacefully took power from an elected incumbent only in the off-shore island nation of Mauritius.[34] This transformation can be traced to three significant factors: the weakening of most African states by a prolonged fiscal crisis, the increasing control of international financial institutions and the allied bilateral agencies of the industrialized nations in determining eco-nomic policy, and the shift of western powers (especially the United States) after the end of the Cold War from tolerance of and alliance with authori-tarian regimes to liberalization of their systems.

Private African and non-African actors steadily increased their efforts on behalf of human rights, civil liberties, and pluralist democracy during the 1980s. However, they had little impact in hindering the entrenchment of authoritarian regimes. Although the cataclysmic events in eastern Europe emboldened the African people, were it not for these three factors advocates of political reform would have been brushed aside with impunity.

Much effort has been made to relate democratization to economic change. Huntington has revised his earlier views by identifying a "political transition zone," a range of per capita incomes in which opportunities for effecting a transformation of authoritarian systems appear to increase.[35] The most recent wave of democratization, however, has demonstrated little re-spect for such distinctions. It has swept across Asian countries with mounting incomes and robust economies, as well as Latin American, East European, and African ones with declining or collapsed economies. Like the Latin American fiscal crisis in the early 1980s, the economic contraction in Africa at the end of the decade seems to have facilitated political transformations. In Latin America, according to Whitehead, "lending surged and then went into reverse, leaving over-confident authoritarian regimes suddenly respon-sible for unmanageable fiscal crises."[36] Their political vulnerability increased as their options narrowed; "the business interests and foreign investors that had rallied to authoritarian military regimes in the 1960s began to see these overly statist and apparently unaccountable governments as a source of dan-ger rather than of protection, so they withdrew their support."[37]

Many authors have discussed the statist economic systems erected by most African governments under both socialist and state-capitalist auspices. Apart from extractive industries in such sectors as oil and copper, private investors increasingly shunned the African continent. Private foreign banks never reached the level of exposure in Africa that they had in Latin America. "By the late 1980s," according to van de Walle, "more than half the nations in sub-Saharan Africa were effectively bankrupt, and most of the others were propped up by western public capital."[38] Some case studies trace how African regimes stoutly resisted the demands of the Bretton Woods agencies to change their failed economic policies until the growing budgetary deficits, the unwillingness of their bilateral partners to continue to provide relief, and the lack of interest of private banks in the continent eventually obliged them to accept highly conditioned loans from the IMP and World Bank.[39] The self-styled Marxist regime in Benin became one of the first to permit multiparty elections, in which a former World Bank official, Nicephore Soglo ousted the incumbent. Richard Westebbe has shown how Benin became a classic case of fiscal collapse and could no longer resist demands for comprehensive reforms by the external agencies.[40]

Zambia, like Benin, was another early "domino" to fall. In both countries leaders in power more than two decades had mastered a range of survival skills. Despite the great fanfare with which Kaunda, the Zambian leader, twice abandoned agreements with the IMF, he also had nowhere else to go to obtain the resources to maintain his monopolistic political system. Not having to face an organized opposition for seventeen years, he assumed that the people would support his party because of its populist and economic nationalist policies. However, in Zambia and elsewhere the stabilization and structural adjustment programs that African authoritarian governments were forced to implement as conditions for loans from multinational agencies steadily eroded their popular support. They had to sharply devalue the currency, cut back the public sector, remove price controls on basic commodities, impose fees on a range of public services, and liquidate unproductive state enterprises. In October 1991 Kaunda went down to a crushing defeat, sending a message heard around the continent that the single-party system was endangered.

One of the most determined holdouts against the international agencies was Julius Nyerere's government in Tanzania. He eventually had to stand down, first as president, then as party chairman, when his country's long-time generous supporters, especially the Nordic countries, would no longer shield his failed social democracy from the rigors of economic liberalization.[41] As Larry Diamond rightly concludes, the power of external donors to press for both economic and political reforms "was nowhere greater than in Africa." Moreover, the power of these donors "to induce democratic change . . . through aid conditionality is directly proportional to the dependence of the aid recipients (or debtors) upon them and to the unity of the donor community."[42]

## External Involvement in Political Reforms

Transitions to liberalized and democratic systems can range from the slow evolution of structures and mechanisms in Great Britain to their imposition on defeated countries after World War II. At the time of Africa's "first independence," except in a few instances such as Guinea in 1958 where the French pulled out abruptly, departing colonial powers had a strong hand in devising representative structures. Once the decision was made to withdraw, however, they devoted more attention to the retention of desired economic, diplomatic, and security arrangements than to the operation of new governmental institutions in accordance with constitutional and democratic principles.

After 1989, while local citizens invariably decided the details of the transition, they seldom determined the decision to introduce political reforms solely or independently. A complex and dynamic interplay between external and local forces determined particular outcomes along a continuum from renewed authoritarianism to various degrees of liberalization and democratization. Cases in which there was a sustained "push" from outside (Kenya, Malawi, South Africa) can be distinguished from regimes that were able to parry external intervention (Nigeria, Zaire). In others, the external patron rushed to the defense of beleaguered client regimes (Cameroon, Togo), while in a special group led by military economic reformers external agencies alternated between nudging and nursing (Ghana, Uganda).[43]

Whatever the mix of strategies, external forces were often able to narrow the options available to recalcitrant regimes (when they were so inclined) and to encourage and bolster insurgent groups. However, they were also prepared to subordinate democracy to other geostrategic considerations (as in Algeria, where Islamic fundamentalists would have taken power) or, in the absence of any compelling external interest in the outcome, let the contestants fight it out (as in Madagascar, where the most massive demonstrations occurred). In short, they chose to act in a variety of ways, or not to act, and each decision had important implications. In his earlier work, Robert Dahl rather caustically dismissed attempts to promote democracy from abroad. "As a strategy for transforming nonpolyarchies into polyarchies, the American foreign aid program must be adjudged a total failure. As far as I am aware, it has not a single such success to its credit."[44] Laurence Whitehead's comprehensive review in the mid 1980s confirmed this conclusion.

"Despite the rhetoric, Washington's real achievements in the promotion of democracy in Latin America have been relatively meager."[45] Huntington also believed that "the ability of the U.S. to affect the development of democracy elsewhere is limited" and echoed Dahl's contention that the "process of transformation is too complex and too poorly understood to justify" such initiatives.[46]

While students of democratization tend to be skeptical of external efforts to promote political reform, Rueschemeyer, Stephens and Stephens, and Di Palma make it a fundamental component of their theoretical framework. The former identify three "power clusters" as being most significant in determining democratic transitions: an external one, the state, and domestic classes and class coalitions. They contend that a balance of power "beyond a country's borders . . . determines the chances of democracy."[47] Di Palma's focus on the top-down "crafting" of democracy also recognizes the role of external actors in "favoring (or hindering) present and impending democratization."[48] He identifies "a new force," "the direct exportation of democracy by democratic powers with global, regional or colonial clout," that must be taken into account.[49] He points out that "a regional hegemon" such as the USSR could for years exercise a "veto of democracy," a characterization that would also apply to France's policies in most of its former African colonies.[50]

The African experience, when carefully disaggregated, should contribute significantly to our understanding of why, when, and how liberalized and democratic systems have been imposed, facilitated, blocked, or treated with "benign neglect" by external actors and what factors explain their choices. The impact of external forces may also affect specific outcomes. Terry Karl argued that in Latin America in the early 1960s they "encouraged a democratic outcome while simultaneously limiting the degree of democracy in the new system."[51] In Africa, a similar analysis could be conducted on two levels: the general impact of external forces (based on promotion of liberal democracy as virtual democracy) and, within this framework, the specific postcolonial hegemonic relationships.

Dahl remarked that "dictators and oligarchs are not easily beguiled by foreign assistance into destroying their regimes."[52] This observation would apply to the ambivalent external demands confronting Africa through much of its modern history. However, by the late 1980s foreign assistance was no longer a discretionary component of national budgets but was increasingly the lifeline of regimes. With the resurgence of demands for political reform after 1989, external agencies were able to decide, often case by case, if that lifeline should be shortened, cut, or lengthened. African leaders, even with their backs to the wall, gradually learned that they could influence external forces and even manipulate their divisions and rivalries, as they were doing with increasing success with their domestic adversaries.[53] While external forces demonstrated a greater positive impact in the early phase of democratization after 1989 than Laurence Whitehead discerned for earlier periods, the later phase conforms to his general findings. "Policies aimed at 'promoting democracy' . . . are likely to constitute an open invitation for manipulation by local political actors," including such practices as staged elections whose results are predetermined.[54]

## Democracy as a Global Project

David Held posed a challenging question: "Is democratization an essentially western project, or is it something of wider universal significance?"[55] In responding to this question with regard to the Middle East, a region even more resistant to democratization than Africa, Simon Bromley described democracy as "a form of rule in which the state apparatus is formally responsible to elected decision-makers who are chosen by means of a universal and equal franchise."[56] A critical condition for the establishment of democracy is "a significant degree of separation between the institutions of rule and surplus appropriation," which he argues is absent for the most part in Middle East states.[57] He then refers to the "profound uncertainty" of these states as they contend with the failure of state-led economic policies under "pressure from the advanced capitalist world mediated by the World Bank and the IMF."[58] Bromley's discussion is relevant to Africa because he tackles several problems of the contemporary conjuncture that impart a peculiar dynamic to democratization.

Domination of the world economy by market-oriented economies, the geostrategic hegemony of western industrialized nations, and direct or indirect external pressures for democratization are critical aspects of this conjuncture. As Dunn observes, "the modern secular constitutional representative democracy, firmly founded on an essentially market economy, dominates the political life of the modern world." While making "democracy safe for a modern capitalist economy," it can also be seen as a "political framework . . . to ensure the unobstructed workings of the free market across

the globe."[59] Competitive interactions among political elites over two centuries in the former paradigmatic case of Britain laid the basis for a high
degree of mutual security prior to the introduction of universal suffrage and
mass politics.[60] However, contemporary transitions seek to replicate this outcome in a matter of years. While opportunities for political participation and
contestation expand, it is critical that the *demos*, or collective citizenry, subordinate its voice to the political elites. Moreover, economically disadvan-
taged sections of society must be induced to postpone satisfaction of pressing
material needs to an indeterminate future while economic restructuring is
implemented under international tutelage.

Huntington refers to this exchange as "the democratic bargain," a "tradeoff between participation and moderation."[61] Contemporary democratization requires concessions from those who were formerly excluded from participation; they must tolerate many years of material inequities while
agreeing "to work through elections and parliamentary procedures."[62] Studies of the outcome of democratic transitions in southern Europe and South
America provide substantial confirmation of the thesis that deradicalization
and even demobilization of popular forces are intrinsic to late-twentieth-
century democratization. Political participation is also exchanged for substantive inequities prompted or deepened by market-based strategies.[63] There
are currently no major alternatives to this paradigm and certainly none in
Africa. Although the ANC-led South African government is making a bold
attempt to address the massive needs of its black population, the ANC has
abandoned socialist strategies and accepted the minority-dominated capitalist system explicitly or tacitly in order to assume (and share) political power.
Similarly in Namibia, the Southwest Africa People's Organization (SWAPO)
not only allayed concerns that it would uphold the constitutional democracy
devised to transfer power from South Africa in 1989–90, but also became a
strong advocate of the capitalist economy bequeathed by the apartheid
regime.

In addition to political moderation, Di Palma identifies a conservative
socioeconomic imperative: "in the interests of democratization, the corporate demands of business and the state may have to take precedence over
those of labor."[64] Adam Przeworski also advances a striking hypothesis: "only
where the Left lost the first competitive election has the process of democratization not been reversed."[65] The victory of economic conservatives in the
first set of transitional elections may actually improve the prospects of "democratization."[66] "We must lose in order to win" is not a banner under which

democratic insurgents can comfortably fight. In Africa, such defeats are unlikely to be temporary.

Liberal democracy in the late twentieth century, therefore, connects processes of participation and contestation to a particular kind of economy and
a preferred state structure. The genius of liberal democracy in Przeworski's
construction is its ability to generate "the appearance of uncertainty," which
draws the major political forces "into the democratic interplay"; while it
protects key vested interests, others are convinced to postpone fulfillment of
their substantive demands to a later date.[67] Scholars on the left also recognize
the "social defeat" that contemporary democratic transitions entail. Rueschemeyer and Stephens observe that the political dominance of conservatives "serves to defend the interests of the upper classes within the system
and keep the substantive demands of the lower classes off the immediate
political agenda." They even describe this phenomenon as "the positive
contribution of the existence of a strong party of the right to the survival of
democracy."[68]

In Africa, ideological distinctions have featured minimally in the competition among political parties. Electoral campaigns since 1989 have seldom revolved around alternatives to economic liberalization but rather focus
on political renewal, corruption, ascriptive group interests, and the efficient
and fair implementation of market reforms. Due to the economic weakness
of African states and the hegemony of multilateral and bilateral agencies the
"unobstructed workings of the market economy" will accompany whatever
political reforms are introduced. In short, African democratization is highly
consistent with the imperatives of political moderation and conservative socioeconomic policies that have been identified in late-twentieth-century
transitions. A key question is what these imperatives imply for the "quality"
of African democratization.[69]


## Democratization and Ruler Conversion

In a brief but insightful essay, Robert Bates reflected on the nature of the
"end-game bargaining" between authoritarian rulers and insurgent democrats that is particularly relevant to Africa's personalist systems.[70] While the
appearance of "uncertainty" draws insurgents into the process, the prospect
of institution-based security convinces autocrats to yield. As democrats "stand
on the brink of political victory . . . tyrants convert. They seek the protection

of the law and the courts; they demand due process . . . they propound the inviolability of persons and property. Formerly the most dangerous enemies of liberal government, they now become among its most important champions."[71]

Bates's schema is also relevant to the market-expanding reforms that underlie and often prompt African transitions. In historical terms, the political struggle to curb monarchical power narrows to one between "revenue-seeking" leaders and "asset-owning citizens."[72] In the late twentieth century liberal democracy offers a retreating autocrat the opportunity to benefit from the protections of life and property guaranteed by institutions. When rulers' options become losing all by further resistance or preserving much of what they possess except hegemonic power, "tyrants convert." Using similar language, Crawford Young commented that "aspirant life presidents such as Omar Bongo [of Gabon] appear converted to multiparty politics only as a stratagem in an old game."[73] A preliminary classification would differentiate among apparent conversion (De Klerk, South Africa; Pereira, Cape Verde; Kerekou, Benin; Kaunda, Zambia; Saibou, Niger), feigned conversion (Compaore, Burkina Faso; Metes, Ethiopia; Eyadema, Togo; Mobutu, Zaire; Conte, Guinea; Babangida, Nigeria), concession without conversion (Rawlings, Ghana; Biha, Cameroon; Houphouet-Boigny, Ivory Coast; Moi, Kenya; Museveni, Uganda; Mugabe, Zimbabwe), and deposing before conversion (Traore, Mali).

Most of these "conversions" were made reluctantly as tactical moves to retain power. The five "apparent conversions" agreed before 1992 to a political opening. Three were defeated in honest elections; Frederick de Klerk convinced the ANC to accept a power-sharing arrangement; and Ali Saibou retired from politics. After the pivotal Zambian election of October 1991, in which senior and respected head of state Kenneth Kaunda was humbled, "African leaders began to advise each other on how to hold democratic elections without being voted out of office."[74] The most effective instrument in dislodging rulers in French-speaking Africa after 1989 was the sovereign national conference. Following its initial successes in Benin, Congo, and Niger, it was vigorously rejected in Cameroon, physically intimidated in Togo, and rendered chaotic and impotent through a Byzantine combination of concession and retractions in Zaire. Those who feigned conversion maintained highly repressive systems after promising liberalization, while those who made concessions without converting dismissed demands for change until they could control and dominate the forces unleashed by liberalization.

Moussa Traore was the only African leader to be overthrown prior to the restoration of competitive party politics. Popular mobilization against his misrule was high, and the prevailing faction in the armed forces decided to depose him and permit a transition to proceed relatively freely. Consequently, Mali has installed one of the most open and competitive constitutional systems in Africa. Had Traore held on longer, he might have learned, like his neighbors Compaore, Conte, and Eyadema, how to survive while apparently conceding.

## Impediments to Change: Rulers, Regimes, Systems

Gerardo Munck has argued that within the literature on democratization there has been a "shift from 'prerequisites' to 'process' or from structural determinants to strategic choices."[75] This observation is highly relevant to African transitions because of the conjunctural forces that brought them into being. Because the normal underpinnings of pluralist democracy were absent or weak, political liberalization in Africa became overwhelmingly a "strategic choice" adopted with great reluctance by "regimes in distress."[76] The new emphasis on transitions as "moments of plasticity" in which strategic actors craft democracy recalls Rustow's emphasis on the "decision phase." He regarded democratization as a "process of conscious decision . . . a genuine choice" to which "a large variety of mixed motives" contribute.[77]

The triangular forces involved in African transitions—regime, domestic opponents, external agencies—are also relevant to this issue. While the 1990–91 period could be described as "stunning" because of the way long-entrenched regimes were swept away, since 1992 the struggle has become more evenly matched as African leaders constantly devise new ways to submit without succumbing. They gradually discovered the limits to which external agencies were prepared to go to support internal democratic movements and the leverage they still had, especially when they were willing to unleash their military and other security forces. Moreover, after being thrown on the defensive by the sudden collapse of external sources of support and upsurge in political mobilization by once quiescent forces, African leaders soon discovered ways of dividing their opponents at home and abroad. Even opposition political parties, which had long been viewed as threats to public order and hence proscribed, were now regarded as instruments that could be manipulated to serve the incumbent regime (especially since they could be induced to proliferate). As the transition process became more prolonged, opposition forces fragmented into ethnic and personalist groupings, while external powers were often obliged to reduce their pressure for change because of their own rivalries, as well as concerns about the upsurge of armed conflicts, collapsed states, and humanitarian emergencies.

The overwhelmingly autocratic nature of pre-1989 African political systems explains why the "strategic choices" of regimes in responding to pressure from internal and external prodemocratic forces are often discussed in personalist terms. However, another set of factors poses a more profound obstacle to the establishment of democratic systems. A particular system of rule has become consolidated in much of Africa, with differences largely of degree rather than kind among specific countries. As postcolonial governments banned opposition parties, arrested or drove into exile anyone who protested, and established de facto or de jure single-party rule, they simultaneously made their regimes the gatekeeper to economic resources of all kinds and the manager of publicly owned enterprises.[78]

Although these statist systems, capitalist or socialist, civilian or military, were economically inefficient, politically they were quite effective in maintaining regimes. The prolonged economic crisis from the mid 1970s gradually undermined these systems and, according to van de Walle, contributed "to a breakdown of the accommodation process that leaders had fashioned to reward clients to maintain political stability."[79] "The disruption of rent seeking networks" unsettled the state elite before the upsurge of popular protests in 1989.[80] Structural adjustment programs heightened tensions by reducing such normal sources of state patronage as public employment, procurement contracts, access to foreign currency, and import licenses. In Benin and Togo, Kathryn Nwajiaku shows the relationship between the weakening or replenishment of these resources and the capability of authoritarian leaders to resist demands for pluralist democracy.[81]

In virtually none of the countries of sub-Saharan Africa has it been possible within telescoped time-frames to restore full political contestation, implement draconian economic reforms, conduct fair multiparty elections, and shift to forms of governance in which the state no longer monopolizes access to wealth-making activities. Moreover, the multiplicity of factors in play in most African countries is redounding to the benefit of incumbent regimes, which have been able to ride out the initial upheavals and provoke caution among external powers regarding how much instability they are prepared to risk for the sake of rapid democratization.

## Conclusion: Africa's Uncertain Prospects

Processes of economic and political liberalization in Africa are not just concurrent events in the late twentieth century: they are part of a broader dynamic of global transformation. While substantive changes have occurred, many of these "transitions" also exhibit an illusory quality. Whitehead has referred to one outcome of the dynamic in Latin America as "democracy by default," characterized by "a lowering of popular expectations of what can be achieved through political action."[82] The concerns expressed by political theorists that democracy will be "overwhelmed by liberalism" has become a reality. "The only path to democratic 'consolidation,' " according to Whitehead, "is through sustained implementation of drastic 'neo-liberal' market reforms," which implies the exclusion of "many of the features commonly associated with full liberal democracy (high participation, authentic political choice, extensive citizen rights)."[83]

In Africa, the pronounced role of external forces in promoting transitions has been a mixed blessing. The international financial agencies, which dominate economic policy and resource mobilization in Africa, are ill-equipped to play political midwife, while the diplomatic services of western industrialized countries are seldom able to counter the strategies of incumbent regimes to adopt variations of the "Chinese model," market reforms accompanied by limited or deferred political liberalization. Mobutu Sese Seko of Zaire, whose regime seemed doomed after 1991 when his opponents appeared to be taking control of all governmental institutions, demonstrated once again how it is possible to ride out waves of intense external financial and diplomatic pressure. Similar regimes in Cameroon, Nigeria, Togo, and Kenya have done the same. In these and other countries, domestic adversaries became fragmented, brutalized, discouraged, and financially depleted.

Two further suggestions by Rustow appear particularly pertinent to the theoretical work that is currently assessing democratization in Africa. Instead of assuming that "to promote democracy you must first foster democrats," Rustow suggested that "we should allow for the possibility that circumstances may force, trick, lure, or cajole non-democrats into democratic behavior."[84]

This argument is consistent with the emphasis on conjunctural developments in African transitions after 1989 and the important role of external actors in encouraging the "conversion" of leaders. Rustow's recognition that the factors "that keep a democracy stable may not be the ones that brought it into existence" is also relevant.[85] While weak economies, states, and civil societies may make Africa an infertile terrain for building sustainable democracies, these factors do not explain which countries have installed such systems and which have not.

Most African countries are likely to settle into "some sort of halfway house." A minority will continue liberalization and democratization; some will revert to repressive autocracies.[86] In the majority of cases, however, the paradoxes of "liberal democracy as virtual democracy" will reflect political life. This prognosis should not be taken as pessimistic. Pre-1989 Africa had become politically and economically calcified. After the first upheavals in 1990, the calcification began to dissolve, fully in some places, partially in others. The forces unleashed domestically and internationally were eventually wrestled to an uneasy stalemate. Despite this mixed outcome, political freedom was reborn all over Africa, extensively in several countries and dispersed in others.[87] In comparison with the nearly complete collapse of democratic systems after the end of colonial rule and the sharp swings experienced by the other areas of the world, this position is not so disadvantageous.

As the novelty of multiparty elections diminishes in Africa and the new authoritarianism in a liberal guise is widely recognized, analysis and advocacy based on a broader conception of democracy are likely to follow. Africa's post-1989 experiences are intimately connected with global trends. It should therefore not be surprising if novel experiments in Africa to transcend the global project of Schumpeterian democracy inspire other continents.

NOTES

The author thanks several colleagues, especially Crawford Young, for their helpful comments on an earlier draft and the Ford Foundation and Carnegie Corporation of New York for research support.

1. Barrington Moore, *The Social Origins of Dictatorship and Democracy: Lord and Peasant in the Making of the Modern World* (Boston: Beacon Press, 1966).

2. Samuel Huntington, "Will More Countries Become Democratic?," *Political Science Quarterly* 3 (Summer 1994), pp. 216, 218.

3. Robert Dahl, *Polyarchy: Participation and Opposition* (New Haven: Yale University Press, 1971), p. 208.

4.  Giuseppe Di Palma, *To Craft Democracies: An Essay on Democratic Transitions* (Berkeley: University of California Press, 1990), p. 2.

5.  Michael A. Bratton, "Beyond the State: Civil Society and Associational Life in Africa," *World Politics* 51 (1989), 430.

6.  Crawford Young, "Democratization in Africa: The Contradictions of a Political Imperative," in Jennifer A. Widner, ed., *Economic Change and Political Liberalization in Sub-Saharan Africa* (Baltimore: The Johns Hopkins University Press, 1994), p. 235.

7.  Dankwart A. Rustow, "Transitions to Democracy: Toward a Dynamic Model," *Comparative Politics* 2 (April 1970), p. 345.

8.  Samuel P. Huntington, *The Third Wave: Democratization in the Late Twentieth Century* (Norman: University of Oklahoma Press, 1991), p. 39. See also Myron Weiner, "Empirical Democratic Theory and the Transition from Authoritarianism to Democracy," *PS: Political Science & Politics* 20 (Fall 1987), pp. 862–63.

9.  J. Peter Euben, "Democracy Ancient and Modern," *PS* 26 (September 1993), p. 478. Cf. Giovanni Sartori, *The Theory of Democracy Revisited, Part One* (New Jersey: Chatham House, 1987), p. 22.

10.  Huntington, *he Third Wave*, p. 109.

11.  Ibid., p. 7.

12.  John Dunn, ed., *Democracy: The Unfinished Journey, 508 BC to AD 1993* (Oxford: Oxford University Press, 1992), p. 260.

13.  Cf. Nancy Bermeo, "Rethinking Regime Change," *Comparative Politics*, 22 (April 1990), p. 374, note 1. This minimalist definition significantly lowers the threshold for authoritarian regimes to democratize.

14.  Bhikhu Parekh, "The Cultural Particularity of Liberal Democracy," in David Held, ed., *Prospects for Democracy: North, South, East, West* (Stanford: Stanford University Press, 1993), p. 157.

15.  Ibid., p. 178.

16.  Sartori, p. 8.

17.  See Robert Dahl, *Democracy and its Critics* (New Haven: Yale University Press, 1989).

18.  Joshua Cohen, "Deliberation and Democratic Legitimacy," in Alan Hamlin and Philip Pettit, eds., *The Good Polity: Normative Analysis of the State* (Oxford: Basil Blackwell, 1989), p. 17. Also, David Miller, "Deliberative Democracy and Social Choice," in David Held, ed.. pp. 74–91.

19.  Parekh, "The Cultural Particularity of Liberal Democracy," p. 157.

20.  W. Arthur Lewis, *Politics in West Africa* (New York: Oxford University Press, 1965).

21.  Cohen, p. 21. Philippe Schmitter and Terry Lynn Karl, "What Democracy Is

. . . and Is Not," *Journal of Democracy* 2 (Summer 1991), pp. 78–9, add co-operation to Schumpeter's model.

22. Miller, "Deliberative Democracy and Social Choice," p. 88; Julius Nyerere, *Ujamaa: Essays on Socialism* (London: Oxford University Press, 1968), and *Freedom and Unity: Uhuru na Umaja* (London: Oxford University Press, 1966).

23. Peter Ekeh, "Colonialism and the Two Publics in Africa: A Theoretical Statement," *Comparative Studies in Society and History*, 17 (1975). Also, Richard Sklar, "The African Frontier for Political Science," in Robert H. Bates, V. Y. Mudimbe, and Ken O'Barr, eds., *Africa and the Disciplines: The Contributions of Research in Africa to the Social Sciences and Humanities* (Chicago: University of Chicago Press, 1993), pp. 83–110.

24. See Richard Joseph, *Democracy and Prebendal Politics in Nigeria: The Rise and Fall of the Second Republic* (Cambridge: Cambridge University Press, 1987).

25. Peter Ekeh, "The Concept of Second Liberation and the Prospects of Democracy in Africa: A Nigerian Context," paper given at the Conference on Dilemmas of Democracy in Nigeria, University of Wisconsin, November 10–12, 1995, p. 25.

26. Parekh, "The Cultural Particularity of Liberal Democracy," p. 169.

27. See Harvey Glickman, ed., *Ethnic Conflict and Democratization in Africa* (Atlanta: African Studies Association Press, 1995).

28. Rustow, p. 358.

29. Joel Barkan, "Can Established Democracies Nurture Democracy Abroad? Lessons from Africa," paper presented at the Nobel Symposium, Uppsala University, Sweden, August 1994, p. 3.

30. Michael Bratton, "International versus Domestic Pressures for Democratization in Africa," MSU Working Papers on Political Reform in Africa No. 12 (November 15, 1994), p. 10.

31. See Samuel Decalo, *Coups and Army Rule in Africa* (New Haven: Yale University Press, 1976); Henry Bienen, *Armies and Parties in Africa* (New York: Holmes & Meier, 1978); and John W. Harbeson, ed., *The Military in African Politics* (New York: Praeger, 1987).

32. See Linda Beck, "Advancing Beyond Semi-Democracy in Senegal," in Richard Joseph, ed., *The Democratic Challenge in Africa* (Atlanta: The Carter Center, 1994); and Christian Coulon, "Senegal: The Development and Fragility of Semidemocracy," in Larry Diamond, Juan J. Linz, and Seymour Martin Lipset, eds., *Politics in Developing Countries: Comparing Experiences with Democracy* (Boulder: Lynne Rienner, 1995).

33. See *Africa Demos* (Atlanta: The Carter Center, 1990–96); Richard Joseph, "Africa: The Rebirth of Political Freedom," *Journal of Democracy*, 2 (Fall 1991),

pp. 11–24; and Ernest Nwokedi, *Politics of Democratization: Changing Authoritarian Regimes in Sub-Saharan Africa* (Hamburg: Lit Verlag, 1995).

34. Although an elected government came to power in Sierra Leone after defeating the incumbent, a coup and countercoup intervened between the elections in 1967 and the restoration of civilian rule in 1968. See Fred M. Hayward, "Sierra Leone: State Consolidation, Fragmentation and Decay," in Conor Cruise O'Brien et al., eds., *Contemporary West African States* (Cambridge: Cambridge University Press, 1989) p. 166.

35. Samuel Huntington, "Democracy's Third Wave," *Journal of Democracy* 2 (Spring 1991), pp. 30–31.

36. Laurence Whitehead, "The Alternatives to 'Liberal Democracy': A Latin American Perspective," in Held, ed., p. 314.

37. Ibid.

38. Nicolas van de Walle, "Neopatrimonalism and Democracy in Africa, with an Illustration from Cameroon" in Widner, ed., p. 135.

39. See Thomas M. Callaghy and John Ravenhill, eds., *Hemmed In: Responses to Africa's Economic Decline* (New York: Columbia University Press, 1993).

40. Richard Westebbe, "Structural Adjustment, Rent-Seeking, and Liberalization in Benin," in Widner, ed., pp. 80–100. Also, Kathryn Nwajiaku, "The National Conferences in Benin and Togo Revisited," *Journal of Modern African Studies*, 32 (1994).

41. Mwesiga Baregu, "The Rise and Fall of the One-Party State in Tanzania," in Widner, ed., pp. 158–81.

42. Larry Diamond, "Promoting Democracy in the 1990s: Actors and Instruments, Issues and Imperatives," Report to the Carnegie Commission on Preventing Deadly Conflict (December 1995), pp. 56–57.

43. See Nwokedi, *Politics of Democratization*, pp. 179–213.

44. Dahl, *Polyarchy*, pp. 212–13.

45. Laurence Whitehead, "International Aspects of Democratization," in Guillermo O'Donnell, Philippe C. Schmitter, and Laurence Whitehead, *Transitions from Authoritarian Rule: Comparative Perspectives* (Baltimore: The Johns Hopkins University Press, 1986), p. 37.

46. Huntington. "Will More Countries Become Democratic?," p. 218; and Dahl, *Polyarchy*, p. 214. Despite these demurrals, Huntington provided detailed advice to authorities in South Africa and Ethiopia on political reform strategies.

47. Dietrich Rueschemeyer, Evelyne Huber Stephens, and John D. Stephens, *Capitalist Development and Democracy* (Chicago: University of Chicago Press, 1992), p. 7.

48. Di Palma, *To Craft Democracies*, p. 12.

49. Ibid. p. 18.

50. Leaders of French-speaking countries welcomed and democratic activists con-

demned Jacques Chirac's statement in February 1990 that multiparty politics were not appropriate for Africa. See Pearl Robinson, "The National Conference Phenomenon in Francophone Africa," *Comparative Studies in Society and History* 36 (July 1994), pp. 585.

51. Terry Lynn Karl, "Petroleum and Political Pacts: The Transition to Democracy in Venezuela," in Guillermo O'Donnell and Philippe C. Schmitter, eds., *Transitions from Authoritarian Rule: Prospects for Democracy* (Baltimore: The Johns Hopkins University Press, 1986). p. 216. Also, Whitehead, "International Aspects," pp. 17–18.

52. Dahl, *Polyarchy*, p. 12.

53. See Nwokedi, *Politics of Democratization*; Bratton, "International versus Domestic Pressures."

54. Whitehead,"International Aspects," p. 45.

55. Held, *Prospects for Democracy*, p. 4.

56. Simon Bromley, "The Prospects for Democracy in the Middle East," in Held, ed., p. 380.

57. Ibid., p. 402.

58. Ibid., p. 403.

59. Dunn, *Democracy*, pp. 250, 253.

60. Dahl, *Polyarchy*, p. 39.

61. Huntington, *The Third Wave*, p. 169.

62. Ibid., p. 170.

63. See Adam Przeworski, "Democracy as a Contingent Outcome of Conflicts," in Jon Elster and Rune Slagstad, eds., *Constitutionalism and Democracy* (New York: Cambridge University Press and Norwegian University Press, 1988), p. 63; *Human Development Report 1996* (Oxford University Press, 1996)

64. Di Palma, *To Craft Democracies*, p. 97.

65. Przeworski, "Democracy as a Contingent Outcome," p. 72.

66. But see Frances Hagopian, "Democracy by Undemocratic Means: Elites, Political Pacts, and Regime Transition in Brazil," *Comparative Political Studies* 23 (July 1990), pp. 147–70.

67. Adam Przeworski, *Democracy and the Market: Political and Economic Reforms in Eastern Europe and Latin America* (Cambridge: Cambridge University Press, 1991), pp. 12–13.

68. Rueschemeyer, Stephens, and Stephens, *Capitalist Development nd Democracy*, p. 274. Weiner, "Empirical Democratic Theory and the Transition from Authoritarianism to Democracy," p. 865, also contends that "transition to democratic rule is made possible by the presence of a centrist or conservative party to which power could be transferred."

69. For the similar debate on "delegative democracy," see Guillermo O'Donnell, "On The State, Democratization and Some Conceptual Problems: A Latin

American View with Glances at Some Postcommunist Countries." *World Development* 21 (1993), 1355–69, and "Delegative Democracy," *Journal of Democracy* 5 (January 1994), pp. 55–69.

70. Robert Bates, "The Economics of Transitions to Democracy," *PS* (March 1991), pp. 24–27.
71. Ibid., p. 25.
72. Ibid.
73. Young, "Democratization in Africa," p. 243.
74. Nwokedi, *Politics of Democratization*, citing Joel Barkan, p. 202.
75. Gerardo Munck, "Democratic Transitions in Comparative Perspective," *Comparative Politics* 26 (April 1994), pp. 370.
76. Jeffrey Herbst, "The Dilemmas of Explaining Political Upheaval: Ghana in Comparative Perspective," in Widner, ed., pp. 182–98.
77. See Munck, "Democratic Transitions in Comparative Perspective," p. 370; and Rustow, pp. 355–57.
78. See Michael Bratton and Nicolas van de Walle, "Neopatrimonial Regimes and Political Transitions in Africa," *World Politics*, 46 (July 1994).
79. Van de Walle, "Neopatrimonialism and Democracy in Africa," p. 139.
80. Ibid., p. 131.
81. Nwajiaku, "The National Conferences in Benin and Togo Revisited," pp. 434–38, 446.
82. Whitehead, "Alternatives to 'Liberal Democracy,' " p. 325.
83. Ibid., p. 321.
84. Rustow, p. 345.
85. Ibid., p. 346.
86. Munck, "Democratic Transitions in Comparative Perspective," p. 362.
87. See Richard L. Sklar, "Towards a Theory of Developmental Democracy," in Adrian Leftwich, ed., *Democracy and Development: Theory and Practice* (Cambridge, Mass.: Blackwell Publishers, 1996), pp. 25–44.

# 12 Fortuitous Byproducts

*John Waterbury*

> Democracy . . . was sought as a means to some other end or it came
> as a fortuitous by-product of the struggle.
>
> —Dankwart A. Rustow[1]

At a moment when the institutions of competitive, electoral
democracy appeared irrelevant in the developing world, Dankwart A. Rustow, in near splendid isolation, laid out what gives rise to and sustains the
democratic process. His genetic theory provided for historical contingencies,
accidents, and inadvertent decisions as the precursors to democratic transitions. He saw no necessary or sufficient socioeconomic or cultural preconditions of democracy. He stressed political stalemate and the acceptance of
second-best solutions by bitterly opposed sides. Once underway, the transition required sustaining mechanisms quite different from what launched it.
He was quite aware of the possibility of reversals, as his Turkish case exemplified. He posed as a background condition the need for national identity,
with which I disagree and which I think weakened his argument. Nevertheless, his article stands as a prescient and well-specified rejection of the proposition of entrenched autocrats and ethnocentric social scientists: "This
country ain't ready for democracy."

Rustow staked out a well-defined position in what might be called the
contingency school in explaining the initiation and institutionalization of
democracy. The opposing, structuralist school emphasizes socioeconomic
and occasionally cultural preconditions for democracy. These schools are
not warring camps, nor are their positions mutually exclusive. One emphasizes a combination of social structural variables—broad-based middle
classes, private entrepreneurial groups, widespread literacy, and sustaining

civic values—while the other stresses a kind of compromise between contending groups that have repeatedly failed to impose their will upon one
another. Rustow first defined the latter position, and I propose to treat it here.

I will examine five paths toward democratic transition: jump-starting the
process in systems with no cultural predispositions and socioeconomic prerequisites for or historical experiences with democracy; extrication from
stalemated winner-take-all struggles; bargaining and accountability between
taxpayers and governments; bargaining for legal space in authoritarian systems; and inducing transitions by powerful third parties. In each, the transition is the byproduct of some other process. It is therefore unintended and
fortuitous. It must be stressed that not every path will automatically lead to
a transition or that, once started, the transition will continue.

Rustow's enquiry did not concern how democracies came into existence
as much as what conditions might sustain them. He made the crucial point
that what brings them about may have little to do with what sustains or
undoes them. Rustow distanced himself from the socioeconomic function-
alism of Seymour Martin Lipset and Philips Cutright and offered instead a
"genetic" explanation that separates cause from correlate. Both structure and
the highly contingent nature of political competition must be interwoven.

> Many of the current theories about democracy seem to imply that to
> promote democracy you must first foster democrats—perhaps by
> preachment, propaganda, education, or perhaps as an automatic by-
> product of growing prosperity. Instead we should allow for the possi-
> bility that circumstances may force, trick, lure, or cajole nondemocrats
> into democratic behavior and that their beliefs may adjust in due
> course by some process of rationalization or adaptation.[2]

If Rustow is right, democratic processes may be initiated in many social
and political contexts. It does not follow that all contexts are equally hospi-
table to democratic transitions or that the values cherished by the protagonists are irrelevant. However, most analyses that stress prerequisites are potentially misleading.

Rustow excluded from his analysis democracies "where a major impetus
came from abroad," such as occupied Germany or Japan. He posited a *sine
qua non*, what he calls a "background condition," that "the vast majority of
citizens in a democracy-to-be must have no doubt or mental reservations as
to which political community they belong to."[3] Neither the exclusionary
principle nor the background condition, it seems to me, is theoretically

grounded. In fact, if we disregard them, as I will argue we should, the overall logic of Rustow's argument is strengthened.

Applying his own rules of thumb, Rustow came up with twenty-three democracies in 1969, thirteen of them in Europe.[4] Among the less developed countries he cited Chile, Ceylon, Colombia, Costa Rica, India, Lebanon, the Philippines, Turkey, Uruguay, and Venezuela.[5] This latter subset for the most part strayed from the democratic path within a few years of the appearance of his article. Few scholars at the time saw any indications of imminent democratization.

My own research has focused primarily on the Middle East. Since the mid 1950s there have been only four democracies in the region. Turkey, one of the cases examined in Rustow's article, began a transition in 1950, stumbled back into military authoritarianism in 1960, then relaunched its transition in 1965. But in the year Rustow's article appeared, the military intervened again. Lebanon was a second democracy. Its civil war in 1958 brought General Chehab to power, and it seemed that Lebanon might pursue a Nasserist path. It did not; beginning in 1975, it entered into sixteen years of civil war. The Sudan, in sociostructural terms the least likely venue for a democratic transition, oscillated between elected civilian governments and military rule until, in 1969, Ja'afar Nimeiri ushered in a military regime that lasted until 1985. Finally, Israel established a democracy that functioned mainly for its Jewish citizens.

None of these experiments was emulated by its neighbors. For the Arab regimes Turkey, as the successor state to the old Ottoman masters, could not provide a palatable model. (In fact, some of the Turkish officers who engineered the takeover of 1960, like Alparslan Türkeş, accepted the label of Nasserist.) The archenemy, Israel, could not safely be emulated. And Lebanon was always regarded by its own citizens, by its national charter, and by its neighbors as *sui generis*. The Sudanese experiment was peripheral to the Arab heartland and basically ignored.

Even prowestern monarchs disowned their own tepid liberal experiments. The Jordanian and Kuwaiti parliaments were periodically dissolved in the late 1950s and 1960s; the Moroccan parliament was suspended in 1965; and the Libyan monarchy, which had undertaken no liberalization, was overthrown by praetorians in 1969. In the mid 1970s the shah of Iran substituted a one-party regime for a wholly contrived two-party system that had been in place since 1957.

Democracy, or its more frequent absence, did not preoccupy analysts at the time. Rather, authoritarianism, even in its most benign form of "guided democracy" (a term first coined by General Ayub Khan of Pakistan), was taken as given. The questions that were addressed concerned the origins, nature, and goals of various authoritarian experiments. The compelling explanations of what was going on were to be found in the somewhat admiring theses of Manfred Halpern on the new middle class and its military vanguard and in the ambivalent if not tortured commentaries of Marxists such as Samir Amin (Hassad Riad) and Anouar Abdel-Malek. Like Rustow, they too were concerned with transitions, but of a different variety, to revolutionary or guided democracy and socialist modernization.[6] A more conservative observer, Samuel P. Huntington, stated flatly that "the problem is not to hold elections but to create organizations."[7] Thus, Rustow's analysis flew in the face of a scholarly consensus that coincided with the authoritarian agendas of the very leaders under scrutiny.

Rustow stressed that democracy primarily concerns procedure rather than substance.[8] The same analysts referred to above, and many others as well, stood this proposition on its head or at least on its side. They contended that democracy can be achieved only if the masses are lifted out of poverty, the bureaucracy made rational, the exploiters driven from politics and the economy, and all territories liberated. They thoroughly subordinated procedure to substantive goals. This consensus led many of us to belittle the role of codified political procedures and institutions, because constitutions, charters, and plebiscitary elections were such patent charades. More important, we tended to view the protagonists of conflict within Middle Eastern societies (ethnic groups, sects, class actors) as obstacles to the substantive goals of populist authoritarian regimes (whether or not we approved of them), not as potential catalysts of democratic transitions.

The Middle East did not appear unique in these respects. Argentina, Brazil, Chile, and Peru fell to military authoritarians by the mid 1970s. Marcos put the Philippines under emergency rule; Pakistan moved from the civilian authoritarianism of Zulfikar Bhutto to the military authoritarianism of Zia al-Haq; newly liberated Bangladesh followed the same path; and even India, the bastion against all odds of democratic procedure, succumbed to the Emergency of 1975–77. The Turkish military ended the decade by once again deposing an elected, civilian government.

The accentuation of authoritarianism in the 1970s, especially in countries that had experienced considerable growth, demanded an explanation. With some overlap in their approaches, Guillermo O'Donnell in his work on bureaucratic authoritarianism and Cardoso and Faletto in their work on dependency shaped the research of the 1970s.[9] Once again, Rustow's article was regarded at best as an interesting curiosity.

Twenty years later I took up some of the same issues. I began to study how the post-1983 civilian, elected governments of Turkey could sustain formal democracy and implement painful structural adjustment reforms.[10] Then I addressed what had become known as Middle Eastern "exceptionalism." Many countries initiated democratic transitions by the end of the 1980s.[11] But the Middle East hardly changed. Turkey reestablished democratic civilian rule in 1983; Lebanon did so after the Taif Accords of 1990 under the watchful eye of authoritarian Syria; the Sudan briefly experienced elected civilian government between 1986 and 1989; and Israel maintained its democratic procedures without interruption. Jordan held elections in 1989; Algeria held and then aborted them in 1991; and the two Yemens groped toward unification and national elections that led to civil war and the reestablishment of military rule. Kuwait, after Operation Desert Storm, restored its parliament, responsible to the 40,000 males of proven Kuwaiti ancestry who constitute the electorate. No democratic wave swept the twenty-three states in the region.

Against this backdrop I tried to discern how democracy might be nurtured in an unfriendly environment. The theses I advanced are in large measure inspired by Rustow's article and Adam Przeworski's book, *Democracy and the Market*.[12] I focused on a region that had never known democracy, had descended from empire, nurtures militarism, and is steeped in the "authoritarian" values of Islam. How could it ever welcome democratic transitions? The answer is "easily," not just for the reasons advanced by Rustow, but also for several others.

Rustow posited, once his background condition of national identity was satisfied, a three-phased transition, lasting probably a generation or more. The "preparatory" phase arises from a long inconclusive struggle among nondemocratic factions (often, as in Sweden, class actors). Stalemate leads to acceptance of second-best solutions within a grudging "democratic" compromise. In the "decision" phase nondemocratic leaders decide to continue to play the game. Finally, in the "habituation" phase citizens themselves begin to absorb and respect the rules of the second best solution. Rustow's model makes no reference to levels of development, middle classes, or culture as necessary factors in the transition.

In his study of political and economic liberalization in Latin America and eastern Europe, Adam Przeworski followed an analogous line of reasoning. He treated democracy as a series of negotiated equilibria.[13] He said virtually nothing about socioeconomic preconditions and enabling political cultures. Rather, Przeworski stresses the rational pursuit of strategic advantage by diverse interests. "When is it rational for the conflicting interests voluntarily to constrain their future ability to exploit political advantage by devolving some of their power to institutions?"[14]

Przeworski outlines two crucial phases in transitions with, in some instances, important disjunctures between them. In the "extrication" phase forces opposed to the authoritarian status quo ally, and in the "constitution" phase they seek those institutional equilibria that will keep everyone voluntarily in the game. In the latter phase the initial alliance tends to break down as different interests among the winners maneuver for strategic advantage. As in Rustow's analysis, there is no linear progression from extrication to constitution; indeed, there is the strong possibility that the transition will be aborted. In sum, successful transitions occur when bargained equilibria lead to the establishment of institutional arrangements from which no significant actors have any incentive to defect. This process is highly contingent.

## Jump-Starting

Can civic-democratic values be nurtured in the bosom of autocracy? Rustow states that "consensus on fundamentals is an implausible precondition" of democracy.[15] Walter Murphy captured the dilemma eloquently.

> To survive and prosper, constitutional democracy needs, perhaps more than any other kind of political system, leaders who have both patience and wisdom, virtues that have never been in great supply. Constitutional democracy also needs a political culture that simultaneously encourages citizens to respect the rights of fellow citizens even as they push their own interests and hold their representatives accountable for advancing those interests-a culture whose force cannot diminish when private citizens become public officials. That such a political culture will pre-exist constitutional democracy is unlikely, making it necessary for the polity to pull itself up by its own boot straps by helping to create the very milieu in which it can flourish. Turning that paradox into a fait accompli is likely to require generations.[16]

One must entertain the possibility that a civic culture can be nurtured in the bosom of autocracy. Was that not the English pattern, which Rustow rejects because the transition was too prolonged? Democratic values, one might hypothesize, are most intensely and explicitly held where they are most denied. Conversely, they may be taken for granted or even debased where the democratic game is sustained purely in terms of the differential rewards it bestows on citizens.[17]

Outside of Europe, democratic experiments are recent, somewhat at odds with local cultures, frequently elite-driven, and increasingly reactive to external threats and inducements. Without judging the nature or the outcome of its transition, I want to outline the process of jump-starting in Uganda since 1986.

Uganda has not enjoyed a competitive democracy since it achieved independence. It has exhibited a number of features that might qualify it for a Rustowian stalemate: marked class differences, especially in the control of rural resources, a strong north-south cleavage, a deep Catholic-Protestant split, and rivalries among the remnants of older ethnolingual kingdoms.[18] All of these cleavages manifest themselves in a predominantly rural society with high rates of adult illiteracy.

The north lies above the Kyoga Nile that cuts Uganda virtually in two. Uganda's two most notorious dictators, Milton Obote and Idi Amin, were both northerners. The bone they could never quite swallow was the old southern kingdom of the Baganda. It could be subjugated, but it would not disappear. Neither the plebiscitary authoritarianism of Obote nor the erratic military dictatorship of Amin could produce a winner-takes-all solution.

In his second coming, Obote was carried to power by the Tanzanian armed forces which overthrew Amin. In 1980 he held widely boycotted elections. A young radical southerner, Yoweri Museveni, participated, lost in his own home district, then "went to bush" to combat Obote's regime. Most of the guerrilla warfare took place in the Luwero triangle, a Baganda region proximate to Kampala. The Baganda supported Museveni against their archenemy, Obote, and their region was laid waste in the course of the fighting.

In 1986 Museveni triumphed and took power. It is said that if he had any external model in mind for a new political system, it was Libya's *jamahirria* (loosely, "republic of the masses"). But Museveni reads *rapports de force* accurately and well. Tanzania, where he had lived and studied for years, was already in its post-Nyerere phase of structural adjustment and timid political liberalization. Its brand of single-party African socialism was no longer viable. The Ugandan economy was likewise in shambles, and only access to western capital could revive it. Museveni undid Idi Amin's most popular move, the 1972 expulsion of the "Asians" (Indians). They were allowed to return to Uganda and reclaim their properties and businesses.

Museveni's moves toward political liberalization were much more cautious. External donors, especially the United States, and the experiences of other African states brought pressure upon him to democratize. He faced the dilemma of transforming his National Resistance Army into a well-organized political movement. The only rivals to what became the National Resistance Movement (NRM) were the older established parties, the United Peoples Congress of Obote (now in exile in Zambia) and the Democrat Party.

Museveni needed time to build his organization. A new constitution was drafted and vetted from late 1988 to 1995. His opponents claimed that the lengthy process was rigged, that the drafting was carefully manipulated by the NRM, and that the constitutional commission that took the draft out to the hustings consisted mainly of people loyal to the NRM.[19] A constituent assembly was elected in March 1994 and approved and adopted the draft constitution, which came into effect on September 22, 1995. Presidential and parliamentary elections followed in spring 1996.

The constitution stipulated in its controversial articles 269–271 that for four years after the election of the parliament the country would be governed by a "movement" regime and that candidates in elections could not run under party banners. Indeed, the elections to the constituent assembly were held under the same rule. Nevertheless, 68 of the 284 delegates had thinly veiled party affiliations. The debate over Articles 269–71 effectively divided the country into "movementists" and "multipartyists." The U.S. ambassador and others warned that, once a movementist legislature and presidency came into place, the democratic game would be over. Museveni won an overwhelming victory in the May 1996 presidential elections. In contrast to Ambassador Southwick's forebodings, Museveni has gone on record that multipartyism will descend rapidly into tribalism and parties must wait until there is a large middle class.[20]

So far the story is fairly simple: an unwilling democrat buys time and fends off foreign donors in order to set up a "single-movement" regime. However, Museveni made an important concession and an inadvertent error.

The concession was made to the Baganda, many of whom thought that their support of the NRA during the guerrilla war would earn them federal status in post-Obote Uganda. Museveni and the NRM have rejected formal federalism but recognized the old Buganda kingdom, and a new king has been enthroned. The kingdoms of Bunyoro, Toro, and Ankole followed suit.[21] Although the so-called "federos" were left thirsting for more, Museveni conceded a new legal space for and quasi-legitimation of an important set of political actors. Political parties, which the constitution recognizes with severe strictures, enjoy a similar position.

The error lay in the long vetting process of the constitution. The constitutional commission, through subgroups of its members, toured the country to educate citizens on the merits of the draft text. Sessions were intended to be and initially were top-down, didactic affairs in which silent audiences were marched through the arcana of constitutional law. They were organized by the local national resistance committees which were viewed as extensions of the NRM. This lengthy process allowed Museveni to consolidate the NRM, and the subgroups revisited many locales. The top-down preachings turned into real town meetings. Exchange of views, often heated, replaced quiescence. The ostensible purpose of the exercise was actually achieved: average citizens learned a lot about constitutional issues.

Some Ugandans feel that in the space of four years political culture, at least in some regions and for some strata, was fundamentally transformed. Deference toward the representatives of political power gave way to skepticism and criticism. In the constituent assembly elections of March 1994 half the candidates of the National Resistance Committees were defeated, with two-thirds losing in the north.[22] Citizens became concerned with understanding their rights.

Thus, a country without the socioeconomic, class, or cultural prerequisites of democracy may be an example of jump-starting a transition. Its leadership does not consist of enlightened democrats; it has little social capital; and a significant part of the bourgeoisie is not even regarded as fully Ugandan. Nevertheless, strategic maneuvering by incumbents and challengers has yielded Rustowian byproducts.


## Stalemate

Unresolved social conflict and stalemate is crucial to Rustow's genetic model of transition. However, he does little to operationalize stalemate. We must, at a minimum, identify three variables: the nature of the protagonists (classes, interest groups, *ethnies*, and the military) and the issues, the duration of the stalemate (the fatigue factor), and the intensity of the struggle. If the stalemate is violent and prolonged, an authoritarian solution might be more likely than a democratic transition. Museveni is right when he suggests that struggles over interests are more susceptible to peaceful resolution than those over religious values or blood. Yet South Africa has begun a democratic transition after decades of bloody, unresolved struggle involving race, religion, and class. Neither of the main actors, the ANC and De Klerk's National Party, entered into their initial bargain steeped in democratic habits.

In the Middle East two well-defined stalemate situations, one partially resolved and the other unresolved, exist in Lebanon and Algeria. Lebanon's informal national pact of 1946 led to the establishment of a parliamentary democracy founded on a paper-thin balance between Christians and Muslims. Christians were to be represented in a ratio of 6:5 over Muslims (on the basis of the proportions identified in the 1932 census). There were further de facto representational subdivisions within the two major confessions. This pact was rooted in distrust, not accommodation; the two main protagonists held guns at each other's temples.

Nonetheless, a bumpy habituation phase began. But before more benign interconfessional feelings could take root, Christian president Camille Chamoun sought to prolong his mandate unconstitutionally, thereby provoking a civil war. Christian general Fouad Chehab took over the presidency, with the support of the Eisenhower administration. A decade of strong economic growth followed and papered over the underlying cracks in the political and social edifice.[23]

The trigger was pulled in 1975, after an abrupt influx of Palestinian refugees and armed PLO fighters from Jordan, most of whom were Muslim, at the beginning of the decade. They were embraced by the local Sunni Muslim community, Palestinians who had been in the country since 1948, and local Arab nationalists and communists. Maronite Christians felt their survival was at stake and fired the first rounds in what was to become a sixteen-year civil war. It is estimated that over 150,000 of the country's three million inhabitants were killed.

In 1990 a truce and new pact were brokered by Saudi Arabia, Syria, and representatives of the Arab League in Taif, Saudi Arabia. The only changes made in the 1946 pact evened the Muslim/Christian ratio to 50:50 and reduced the powers of the presidency while strengthening those of the confessionally apportioned cabinet. All significant political decisions had to be vetted with the Syrians, who maintained their military occupation of the eastern Beka'a valley. They will surely not leave before Israel closes down its security zone in southern Lebanon, and maybe not even then. In 1995 the Syrian dictator, Hafiz al-'Assad, decided to renew the mandate of Christian president Elias Hrawi in violation of the constitution. The assembly dutifully voted the necessary constitutional change.

It would be heroically optimistic to claim that Lebanon is on the brink of the decision phase, no less reentering the habituation phase. But it is not impossible, despite the fact that Rustow's background condition has always been missing. Until recently Lebanon has had no firm sense of national identity. The national pact of 1946 explicitly recognized this fact and outlined a confessional truce in which Christians would foreswear help from their traditional Christian allies in Europe, mainly France, if the Muslims would not seek to integrate Lebanon into the greater Arab, Muslim nation. If Lebanese national identity is stronger now than it was in 1946, it is because of the combined occupations of Syria and Israel. In particular, many Lebanese prior to the occupation had seen themselves as Syrian.

In Algeria the situation is similar to Poland prior to the collapse of the Communist regime, when Solidarity was pitted against General Jaruzelski. In Algeria the stalemated protagonists are the Front for Islamic Salvation (FIS) and President Lamine Zeroual and the remnants of the Front for National Liberation (FLN), Algeria's single legal party prior to 1989.

Algeria's aborted democratic transition began in 1989, before a stalemate but after years of economic austerity and the bloody riots of October 1988. The president, Chedli Benjedid, was a product of the revolutionary war against France (1954–62) and a stalwart of the FLN who had been in office since 1979. He decided to liberalize the single-party system out of expediency.[24] The riots laid bare the regime's lack of legitimacy, but economic austerity could not be avoided. A political opening offered Benjedid a way to dissociate himself from the FLN and present himself as president of all the people. No one predicted that within a year a legalized Islamic party, the FIS, would sweep municipal and regional elections and stand poised in January 1992 to take control of the national legislative assembly. Before the second round of the parliamentary elections could be held, the Algerian military intervened, called off the elections, deposed Benjedid, dissolved the FIS, and clapped its leadership in jail.

Since 1991 a near civil war has raged in Algeria between the FIS and successive presidents put up by the military. Twenty-five to fifty thousand may have died in the last five years. In fall 1995 President Zeroual, who had initially been appointed by the military junta, ran for president against four others, including a moderate Islamic leader. The FIS and the even more militant Armed Islamic Group (GIA) called for a boycott of the elections. Nevertheless, an estimated 70 percent of the electorate voted, uncoerced, and gave a major mandate to Zeroual.

Once again, we find an arena bereft of leaders or movements with any democratic credentials. The major challenger is driven by religious zealotry, while incumbents stubbornly cling to power because to give it up appears too dangerous. Can a democratic transition be cobbled out of this stalemate? The elections of 1995 give cause for hope. They appear to have registered the fatigue of the electorate with the violence but, more significantly, a substantial distancing from the FIS. The leadership of the FIS has received the message and, in good second best fashion, is seeking a compromise with Zeroual. It is hard to imagine any compromise that would not entail new legislative elections in which the FIS would be allowed to participate so long as it pledged to honor the constitution.

As a final note, it can be argued that the military intervention of 1992 sent a message, as yet not revoked, that the FIS would not be allowed to win an election outright. Incumbents have delivered similar messages to Islamic challengers in Egypt, Jordan, Tunisia, the Palestinian entity, and, more ambiguously, Turkey.[25]

In terms of Przeworski's argument, Muslim organizations should not voluntarily adhere to the rules of the game if they have no prospect of benefiting from them. However, this factor should not preclude Muslim organizations from playing the democratic game. Participation may earn them some shreds of power, a local power base in specific districts, and some access to patronage. Nonparticipation will be read, rightly or wrongly, as hostility to the regime and to the legal political process and will trigger official repression and violence. Moreover, much like the "Eurocommunists" after 1956, playing the game may appear the lesser of evils. In the absence of revolution, proletarian or Islamic, terminal marginalization may be the only alternative to playing the game.

Stalemate remains empirically and theoretically ill-defined. Violent stalemates without accommodative or democratic outcomes have been common, and peaceful, proto-democratic resolution may be extremely fragile, as the civil war between north and south Yemen, after democratic elections, illustrates. Dahl posited that "polyarchy" cannot accommodate two or more relatively large factions who view the victory of the other as a fundamental threat to "highly ranked values" and cited the U.S. civil war as the result of such a situation.[26] It would seem impossible for the current stalemate in Rwanda to yield a democratic outcome. After the near-genocide of the Tutsi and

Hutu fears of a commensurate Tutsi reprisal, a regime based on one person, one vote would yield an overwhelming Hutu victory (85 percent of the population is Hutu and would vote as Hutus) with which no Tutsi could abide.

## Extraction Contracts and Democratic Public Goods

The consequences of economic mismanagement and changes in the international economy fall as heavily on nondemocrats as on democrats.[27] Since the early 1980s the majority of less developed countries have had to implement structural adjustment programs and reorganize their public finances. To contain or reduce public deficits, expenditures have been slashed and taxes raised. Consumer and producer subsidies have been cut. Some countries unwilling to cut public outlays, such as Turkey, have resorted to the inflation tax to transfer resources from citizens to the government.

The manner in which and the level at which governments tax their citizenries significantly affect the kind and level of governmental accountability. We may hypothesize that institutional forms of accountability and representation emerge from tacit or explicit bargaining between the government and various interests it seeks to tax. This hypothesis is venerable but very difficult to confirm parsimoniously.[28] The hypothesized process may also be initiated in a nondemocratic setting in which the protagonists are oblivious to the democratic implications of their bargaining.

Taxed populations can hold the taxing authority to account in many ways. Only a few involve explicit or formal political action. Goran Hyden documented how Tanzanian peasants, gouged by government marketing boards that sought to maximize production of commercial and export crops, fled into subsistence agriculture or smuggling. Over time, as commercial production declined along with export earnings, the Tanzanian government had to make price concessions (that is, reverse the agricultural terms of trade) to lure the peasantry back into market crops.[29] This sort of accountability involved no formal political expression of peasant grievances or change in the single-party political system.

In highly regulated, quasi-planned economies with administered prices many economic actors exited the formal economy and entered the informal sector. There frustrated entrepreneurs could make real profits, civil servants could supplement their low wages, and goods could be found at a price without queuing. As more and more economic activity escaped the direct controls of the government, less and less national product was subject to taxation. Repression of informal activities seldom worked, so with time governments began to deregulate and legalize activities that had heretofore been proscribed or strangled. Like Tanzanian peasants, those in the informal sector also sent a message to the government that brought about policy change. But it did not, at least initially, bring about institutional or political change.

A third example is capital flight. Individual, somewhat anonymous economic actors decide that their money is not safe in their home country. They may, of course, simply follow the lead of nonnational, institutional investors. The stock of flight capital held by Middle Easterners outside the Middle East may be on the order of $600 billion.[30] It will take policy and institutional reform to lure it back. Capital flight involves no formal political expression of collective interest and no institutionalized bargaining.[31] If greater accountability ensues, it comes as a by-produced public good.

The level of accountability should be lowest where taxes are light and indirect. Several observers of Middle Eastern politics, myself included, have partially attributed the viability of authoritarianism to the region's access to unusually high levels of external rents.[32] The major stream of rents has been generated by petroleum exports, which have in turn generated rents in the form of remittances to labor—exporting countries in the region. Throughout the Cold War a number of states received substantial strategic rents from one or the other of the great powers or from militarily vulnerable oil exporters in the region. Rents allowed governments to lessen the tax burden on their citizens and to maintain extensive welfare and subsidy programs to neutralize economic discontent. Formal mechanisms of accountability atrophied or, as in Iraq, disappeared altogether.

Political analysts, therefore, welcomed the era of adjustment and austerity because, it was hoped, authoritarian leaders would finally have to forge organic, even if adversarial, relations with the citizenry. Cost-of-living riots in fact prompted some political liberalization in the Sudan (1985–86), Jordan (1989), and Algeria (1988). Several governments had to experiment with new taxes to increase public revenues and reduce deficits. Ironically, as political scientists looked hopefully for signs of greater reliance on direct taxes on incomes and profits—because the bite is felt individually or by firms— economists backed by the donors advocated increased indirect taxes, especially the VAT, because their bite is felt less directly and is therefore easier to collect.[33] The economists' logic of maximizing public revenues ran and runs counter to the political scientists' logic of increasing accountability.

Perhaps the distinction between direct and indirect taxes is not all that crucial. Tanzanian peasants were acutely aware of the indirect tax on their produce brought about by the administered pricing system, and it is likely that consumers and wage earners will not be oblivious to consumption or inflation taxes. They have certainly reacted strongly to reductions in consumer subsidies. However, the prevailing economic orthodoxy makes it virtually certain that the economic transition will be accompanied by worsening income distribution and inequality. Income will no longer be redistributed through taxation.[34] Poor administration and powerful upper-income groups will defeat any attempts at redistributive taxation; the costs of collection will probably outweigh the yield.[35] Greater inequality could preclude democratic transition. As Zehra Arat argues, a democratic system cannot be maintained without affirming socioeconomic rights and reducing inequality.[36]

Business groups and investors may have a particularly important role to play in the preparatory phase. Business interests are not innately democratic. However, in many less developed countries they were denied political legitimacy and frequently smothered by an expanding state sector. Out of self-interest they sought ways to relax state controls. In the era of austerity and curtailed public expenditures they have become crucial to the investment programs that alone can bring about growth. They have acquired new bargaining power vis-à-vis the government, and, as with the *Partido de Acción Nacional* (PAN) in Mexico, have become independent political actors as well.[37]

In most instances they bargain to protect or advance their business activities. In the past bargaining often involved individual deal-cutting and opportunities for rent-seeking negotiated with the public authorities. Those habits will die hard for both parties; once business interests have won some concessions they may seek to freeze the process and collect their rents. Moreover, Przeworski and Limongi assert that business has no rational, interest-based preference for democracy.[38] The autocrat's commitment to protect private property is no less credible than the democrat's.[39]

The Turkish Businessmen's and Industrialists' Association ( *Tüsiad*) is paradigmatic. It has existed since 1971 but has been politically docile. During Turkey's major structural crisis of 1979, it issued a stinging critique of the government's economic policies, which was published in the major newspapers. It also supported the military intervention of 1980. It preferred an end to the killing and insecurity even if Turkey's democracy had to be suspended. But it set a precedent of corporately criticizing the government and established the practice of regular appearances by government officials before *Tüsiad's* membership to explain policy and seek advice.

A kind of public good—the obligation of the government to deal directly with significant economic interests in society—has thus been created. Further, it will be difficult to deny similar rights to other interests except on a purely arbitrary basis. In many ways this move sounds like what Schmitter called "social corporatism," which some have seen as the backbone of some of Europe's most successful democracies.[40]

Taxation and representation have been linked in western democratic theory since its inception. The linkages, or lines of causality, are murky. Many cultures and civilizations have exhibited high levels of extraction and high levels of autocracy for centuries, if not millennia. The most common response of the taxed has been to find some form of exit from the system. The twentieth century affords similar opportunities, but mainly for the privileged. These interests may be the inadvertent vanguard of broader citizen engagement with revenue-hungry governments.

## Legal Space

As part of the preparatory phase, or even of a prepreparatory phase, various groups in society must carve out for themselves legally recognized space, that is, they must become juridical entities. In Europe these spaces were first occupied by the church, municipalities, universities, estates, and eventually the press. Autocrats conceded and legalized the space.

In less developed countries the groups seeking legal recognition are likely to be more heterogeneous and, to the liberal mind, more troubling. In this context I challenge Rustow's background condition. An intuitive sense of belonging to a specific community may help initiate the preparatory phase, but the converse need not and should not hold. For example, Lebanon's fragile democracy has been rooted in and dependent on confused identities and national disunity. This argument can be extended to Ethiopia.

The forging of an Ethiopian nation has in many ways been similar to the historical process of "nation-building" in France, Spain, Iran, and many other countries. A dominant culture and language, embedded in a religious establishment and residing in a geographic core, was imposed, sometimes violently, on a heterogeneous periphery, whose elites over time bought into the hegemonic project.[41] In the last 130 years, the Amhara of the central

Ethiopian highlands slowly built modern, geographic Ethiopia and through the church and the imperial administration spread its language and political control throughout a land the size of France and Spain combined. The history of recent conquest and partial cultural assimilation is well-known.[42] The process is anything but complete and since 1991 has been brought to a halt.

Meles Zenawi, the Prime Minister of Ethiopia in 1995–96, led the Tigrean Peoples Liberation Front to power in 1991, in alliance with the Eritrean Peoples Liberation Front and the Oromo Liberation Front. Meles had been a member of the radical Ethiopian Students' Movement that initially supported the military, Marxist dictatorship of Mengistu Haile Meriam in 1974. A common slogan of both the students and Mengistu and his junta (the Derg) was self-determination for the peoples of Ethiopia. The Derg and the students soon parted company, and the military cracked down brutally on their erstwhile allies. The regime thenceforward dealt ruthlessly, albeit ineffectively, with ethnic challenges. The two main theaters were Eritrea and Tigray. Eventually the radical insurrectionary fronts in these two areas, with the help of neighboring Sudan, tilted the military balance against Mengistu.[43] In 1991 the TPLF and its allies seized Addis Ababa.

From 1991 until the adoption of a new constitution in 1995 the new regime, known as the Ethiopian Peoples Revolutionary Democratic Front, declared that the right of self-determination must be enshrined in the constitution and that the constitution must establish Ethiopia as a federal state based on ethnic regions. In 1993 the "province" of Eritrea opted for independence by referendum. By acquiescing in Eritrean independence the EPRDF moved beyond mere slogans. The 1995 constitution lays out the procedures if a region wants to secede.

Underlying this bold experiment is the belief that Ethiopia will hold together only if its parts have the legal right to leave. To the dismay of Amhara elites, the new regime has declared 130 years of nation-building a form of cultural imperialism that has failed and cannot be revived in its former hegemonic framework. In May 1995 Ethiopia held legislative elections under international supervision, based on the new ethnolingual regions of the country. A number of parties boycotted the elections, especially the Oromo Liberation Front and the All Amhara Peoples Organization. Turnout was nonetheless high, and the voting peaceful. However, international observers refrained from describing the process as free and fair.

For many Ethiopians the process now underway is not democratization but rather the consolidation of a new Tigrean autocracy. This assessment is not unreasonable, given Meles's background as radical student and guerrilla fighter. However, the EPRDF has set up a legal order that could make autocracy extremely difficult. The federal system grants certain taxing powers and the right to undertake certain economic activities to the regions without approval from the center. There is not yet much wealth to tax in Ethiopia, but we should not prejudge the future.

It therefore behooves "transitologists" to pay close attention to those forces that challenge national unity and identity and thereby extract legal recognition from the central authorities. India's federal system and democracy have followed this pattern since 1947, and the existence of "fissiparous tendencies" has made the democratic process imperative (except, unfortunately, in Kashmir). Between 1972 and 1983 the southern Sudan employed legal regional autonomy to keep its black, non-Arab, non-Muslim populations within the union. In 1970–75 the Ba'athi dictatorship in Iraq granted regional autonomy to the northern Kurdish region. Creative stalemates may thus result from the absence of a sense of national identity. The prime actors in this case will almost always be defined by sect, language, or blood, rather than by class or interest.


## Induced Transitions

Rustow explicitly excluded from his universe of democracies those countries made democratic by military occupiers (Japan and Germany) and those made democratic by immigrants from preexisting democracies (the U.S., Australia, New Zealand, Israel). We are now in an era in which powerful democracies seek to leverage democracy out of economically weak societies. I suspect that Rustow in 1969–70 would have been uncomfortable with this phenomenon (he generally dismissed "impulses from abroad") but it existed even then. Franco's Spain had been excluded from membership in both NATO and the Common Market because of its political system.

The OECD countries and some multilateral organizations have practiced several forms of conditionality in the last decade or so. Positive inducements offer accession to trading blocks or most favored nation status if countries improve their human rights record or expand the political rights of their citizens. Negative pressure threatens to suspend assistance or apply sanctions if a country aborts a democratic process or systematically abuses human rights. Bratton and van de Walle found such negative inducements in sub-Saharan Africa to be negatively correlated with political liberalization.[44]

Positive inducements may aid and abet, if not initiate, a transition. In Cambodia the United Nations tried to act as godfather to a democratic transition at the cost of $2.6 billion. The experiment has been anything but successful.[45] It remains to be seen if U.N. inducements will work in Angola.

Perhaps the best example of the power of positive, external inducements can be found in Turkey, a country that figured prominently in Rustow's analysis. Since the 1960s Turkey has been a candidate for membership in the European Union. It thus opened itself up to close scrutiny by its potential European partners. The Turkish military was aware that its repeated interventions into civilian politics did not enhance Turkey's application. After civilian government was restored in 1983, European countries pressured Turkey to revise its constitution to allow broader freedoms of political organization (the constitution forbade the formation of parties on the basis of religion, language, or region), to introduce stricter legal guarantees of human rights, and to rectify the denial of Kurdish rights.

The pressures have been inexorable. Turkish leaders have been on the defensive for years. Sixteen articles of the constitution have been amended by the grand national assembly, and to gain accession to an EU customs union article 8 of the antiterror law was likewise amended.

This kind of arm-twisting could lead to a backlash in Turkey, perhaps orchestrated by the Islamic Welfare party. Turkey could abandon its quest for full membership in the EU, reverse its democratic experiment, and turn to the Arab and Central Asian countries for trading partners. However, Turkey may have already entered Rustow's habituation phase. Moreover, its trade with Europe is on the order of $20 billion and cannot be easily reoriented. The EU's inducements will keep the debate over democratic institutions, tolerated forms of representation, and minority rights very much alive and center stage.

## Conclusion

Social structural, historical, and cultural factors may all be important in initiating and continuing democratic transitions. However, as Rustow first argued, they are not necessary and therefore not sufficient. Whatever the environment and preexisting conditions, nondemocratic actors, with nowhere else to turn, may seek negotiated, second-best solutions to contingent dilemmas that thrust them unwittingly on the path to democratic practice.

## NOTES

1. Dankwart A. Rustow, "Transitions to Democracy: Toward a Dynamic Model," *Comparative Politics*, 2 (April 1970), 351.
2. Ibid., pp. 344–45.
3. Ibid., p. 350
4. Rustow excluded Japan and Germany for reasons already mentioned (but included Italy), as well as the United States, Australia, New Zealand, and Israel because their democracies came in the baggage of immigrants. Great Britain was excluded because Rustow was interested in relatively rapid transitions.
5. He excluded Greece, which fell under military dictatorship in 1967, and Mexico, because it had not enjoyed three or more consecutive, popular, contested elections. Presumably, Peru was excluded because of the 1969 military takeover, but Rustow does not mention it.
6. Anouar Abdel-Malek, *Egypt: Military Society* (New York: Vintage Books, 1968); Manfred Halpern, *The Politics of Social Change in the Middle East and North Africa* (Princeton: Princeton University Press, 1963); Hassan Riad, *L'Egypte Nasserienne* (Paris: Editions de Minuit, 1964).
7. Samuel P. Huntington, *Political Order in Changing Societies* (New Haven: Yale University Press, 1968), p. 7.
8. Rustow, p. 345.
9. Fernando Henrique Cardoso and Enzo Faletto, *Dependency and Development in Latin America* (Berkeley: University of California Press, 1979); Guillermo O'Donnell, *Modernization and Bureaucratic Authoritarianism* (Berkeley: Institute of International Studies, 1973). In fairness to O'Donnell, by the late 1970s he was already writing about the internal contradictions in the bureaucratic-authoritarian state. See Guillermo O'Donnell, "Tensions in the Bureaucratic-Authoritarian State and the Question of Democracy," in David Collier, ed., *The New Authoritarianism in Latin America* (Princeton: Princeton University Press, 1979), pp. 285–318.
10. John Waterbury, "Export-Led Growth and the Center-Right Coalition in Turkey," *Comparative Politics* 24 (January 1992), pp. 127–46.
11. Michael Bratton and Nicholas van de Walle, *Will Africa Democratize?* (New York: Cambridge University Press, 1997), record that in 1989 there were forty-two unambiguously authoritarian regimes in sub-Saharan Africa; by 1992 forty had taken measures to restore political rights. Only Liberia and the Sudan failed to do so. Granting political rights is not tantamount to democratization, but there was far more liberalization in sub-Saharan Africa than in the Middle East.
12. Adam Przeworski, *Democracy and the Market: Political and Economic Reforms in Eastern Europe and Latin America* (New York: Cambridge University Press, 1991); John Waterbury, "Democracy without Democrats? The Potential for

Political Liberalization in the Middle East," in Ghassan Salame, ed., *Democracy without Democrats?* (London: I. B. Taurus, 1994), pp. 23–47.

13. Przeworski, p. 73. Also, Adam Przeworski, "Democracy as a Contingent Outcome of Conflicts," in Jon Elster and Rune Slagstad, eds., *Constitutionalism and Democracy* (New York: Cambridge University Press, 1988), p. 69.

14. Ibid., pp. 37–38.

15. Philippe Schmitter, "Transitology and Consolidology: Proto-Sciences of Democratization?," unpublished ms., Stanford University, September 1994; Rustow, p. 362.

16. Walter Murphy, "Civil Law, Common Law, and Constitutional Democracy," *Louisiana Law Review* 91 (1991), pp. 100–14, as cited in Stephen Marks, "The New Cambodian Constitution: From Civil War to a Fragile Democracy," *Columbia Human Rights Law Review* 26 (1994), p. 109.

17. Or as Dahl pithily put it: "In a rough sense, the essence of competitive politics is bribery of the electorate by politicians." Robert Dahl, *A Preface to Democratic Theory* (Chicago: University of Chicago Press, 1956), pp. 68.

18. See Phares Mutibwa, *Uganda since Independence* (Kampala: Fountain Publishers, 1992); Mahmoud Mamdani, *Critical Reflections on the NRM* (Kampala: Monitor Publications, 1995).

19. Akiiki Mujaju, "Towards an NRM Constitution in Uganda," Political Science Seminar, Maketere University, Kampala, November 7, 1995.

20. Ibid., p. 31; and John Balzar, "Profile of Yoweri Museveni," *Los Angeles Times*, June 27, 1995, p. 5. Unlike earlier populist cum corporatist leaders, Museveni is willing to live with conflict. In the *Los Angeles Times* he is quoted as follows: "We need to reach the point where there is competition between interests, not identities. Today you have Buganda against Acholi. That is very unhealthy. But once you have employees struggling against employers, ah! There is no way an employer will want to massacre all his employees. There will be struggle, yes, but neither side wants to get rid of the other."

21. Apolo Nsibambi, "The Restoration of Traditional Rulers," in Holger B. Hansen and Michael Twaddle, eds., *From Chaos to Order: The Politics of Constitution-Making in Uganda* (Kampala: Fountain Publishers, 1995?), pp. 11–60.

22. Judy Geist, "Political Significance of the Constituent Assembly Elections," in Hansen and Twaddle, eds., pp. 90, 113, notes the high level of registration and voter turnout.

23. See Michael Hudson, *Lebanon: Precarious Republic* (New Haven: Yale University Press, 1968).

24. See Severine Labat, *Les islamistes algériens* (Paris: Seuil, 1995), p. 98.

25. At the time of writing, Turkey's Islamic Welfare (Refah) Party formed a coalition government with the True Path Party of Tansu Ciller. It is not clear whether this coalition can survive, but the Welfare Party cannot, and will not be allowed by the Turkish military, to govern alone.

26. Dahl, *A Preface*, p. 98.
27. See Adam Przeworski and Fernando Limongi, "Political Regimes and Economic Growth," *Journal of Economic Perspectives* 7 (Summer 1993), p. 63.
28. See John Waterbury, "The Political Economy of Authoritarianism and Democracy: From Social Contracts to Extraction Contracts," in John Entelis, ed., *Islam, Democracy, and the State in North Africa* (Bloomington: Indiana University Press, 1997).
29. Goran Hyden, *Beyond Ujamaa in Tanzania* (Berkeley: University of California Press, 1980).
30. See Alan Richards and John Waterbury, *A Political Economy of the Middle East* (Boulder: Westview, 1996), p. 224. The estimate originates with the IMF.
31. On the relative bargaining strenghts of "liquid" and fixed capital, see Robert Bates and Da-Hsiang Lien, "A Note on Taxation, Development and Representative Government," *Politics and Society*, 1 (1985); and Robert Bates, "A Political Scientist Looks at Tax Reform," in Malcolm Gillis, eds., *Tax Reform in Developing Countries* (Durham: Duke University Press, 1989), pp. 473–91.
32. See Hazem Beblawi and Giacomo Luciani, eds., *The Rentier State* (London: Croom Helm, 1987).
33. Waterbury, "The Political Economy of Authoritarianism and Democracy."
34. John F. Due, *Indirect Taxation in Developing Economies* (Baltimore: The Johns Hopkins University Press, 1988); and Richard Goode, "Tax Advice to Developing Countries: An Historical Survey," *World Development* 21 (1993), pp. 37–53.
35. Roy Bahl, "The Political Economy of Jamaican Tax Reform," in Gillis, ed., pp. 115–76.
36. Zehra Arat, *Democracy and Human Rights in Developing Countries* (Boulder: Lynne Rienner, 1991), p. 103.
37. Bratton and van de Walle, *Will Africa Democratize?*, found in their multivariate analysis of political protest and liberalization in sub-Saharan Africa that the number of business associations in a country was positively associated with levels of protest. See also Nancy Bermeo with Jose Garcia-Duran, "Spain: Dual Transition Implemented by Two Parties," in Stephan Haggard and Steven Webb, eds., *Voting for Reform: Democracy, Political Liberalization, and Economic Adjustment* (New York: World Bank/Oxford University Press, 1994), pp. 88–127.
38. Przeworski and Limongi "Political Regimes and Economic Growth."
39. It could be argued that it is easier to bribe a single autocrat than an entire legislature. Also, democratization is usually accompanied by a strengthening of the judiciary, the right of appeal, and responsibility of elected officials to the electorate and thus offers greater protections. One of Uganda's leading Asian businessmen, Mayur Madhvani, stated that, while he considered himself apo-

litical, he advocated multiparty democracy. "You see, if there are no checks and balances, things can go wrong, so it is important that other parties also function and prove through their manifestos that they have something to offer." Interview, *The Monitor* (Kampala), Feb. 23–26, 1996. See Andrei Shleifer, "Establishing Property Rights," *Proceedings of the World Bank Annual Conference on Development Economics* (Washington, D.C.: World Bank, 1994), p. 97.

40. John Freeman, *Democracy and the Markets: The Politics of Mixed Economics* (Ithaca: Cornell University Press, 1989).

41. See David Laitin, "The National Uprisings in the Soviet Union," *World Politics* 44 (October 1991), pp. 139–77.

42. See Bahru Zewde, *A History of Modern Ethiopia* (Addis Ababa: Addis Ababa University Press, 1994); and Richard Pankhurst, *A Social History of Ethiopia* (Addis Ababa: Institute of Ethiopian Studies, 1990).

43. Mengistu supported the Southern People's Liberation Army in the Sudan, which since 1983 waged war against the government in Khartoum. Under Colonel Omar al-Bashir and the National Islamic Front of Hassan Turabi in 1989, the Sudanese government helped Ethiopians opposed to the Derg.

44. Bratton and van de Walle, *Will Africa Democratize?*

45. Marks, *The Economist*, Nov. 25, 1995, p. 35.

# Bibliographical Essay:
# The Genealogy of Democratization

*Elke K. Zuern*

The development of the literature on democratization has, with a few important exceptions, closely followed the lessons of these historical processes around the globe. Before the most recent wave of democratization began, in 1974, most writers on the subject spoke of democracy rather than the process of democratization; they focused their analysis on identifying the basic attributes of existing democracies, often comparing them to nondemocratic countries. After a number of countries in Southern Europe and Latin America underwent transitions to democracy, whether for the first time or for a repeat performance, the discussion moved to one of a process of democratization instead of democracy itself. Writers who addressed these regions stood in the forefront of a new and growing literature which sought to explain and also often encourage this process. By 1990, another dramatic historical change was evident. Growing numbers of states outside of the earlier transition regions were now experimenting with democracy. In Eastern Europe, Asia, and Africa, authoritarian rulers fell or were pushed and not only new rulers but also new regimes were established in their place. By and large, the short-term results of these changes would not be fully functioning democracies but rather very imperfect attempts at such systems. At the same time, practitioners and analysts in those countries that went through the democratization process in the prior decades were now more acutely aware of the difficulties of consolidation. These events account for the extremely guarded optimism in the current literature on the prospects for democracy across the globe.

The following bibliography is organized to reflect these monumental changes both in the real world and in the literature which strives to unravel and explain complex democratization processes. It encompasses key theoretical arguments, incorporating a variety of different methodologies and perspectives, and draws examples from around the world. The list begins with some of the best-known works available to Dankwart Rustow when he made his path-breaking argument in 1970 and follows the development of the English language, largely American, literature, roughly decade by decade, from that point. It does not include any but the briefest mentions of democratic theory, nor does it include discussions of the workings of well-established democracies or the vast literature concerning the relationship between democracy and various forms of capitalism or socialism. It does not include arguments concerning corporatism and its affects upon democracy, nor does it address the important issues of human rights and transitional justice which are closely associated with democratization. These are all important topics, but remain beyond the scope of this book and this list. Also, while the following list does include discussions of the experiences of countries across the globe, it is not meant to cover all democratizing countries or all aspects of each of these processes. This task must be left to regional or country specialists. What this list does provide, however, is an overview of the changing state of the literature as represented by some of its most prominent works.

The first section of the bibliography includes articles and books published prior to Rustow's (1970): "Transitions to Democracy" and the virtually simultaneous publication of Robert Dahl's very influential *Polyarchy* (1971). Rustow's article stands in stark contrast to the other works on this list; as its title indicates, it is the only work that addresses the question of a transition to democracy. While questions of modernization and development clearly preoccupied political scientists at this time, discussions of democracy tended to focus on defining democracy and its variants or identifying the requisites of such a system. Prominent scholars such as Seymour Martin Lipset (1959) and Philips Cutright (1963) employed statistical correlations to compare democratic societies with their less democratic counterparts in order to isolate these requisites. Rustow challenged these approaches. First, he distinguished questions regarding the functioning of a democratic system from those of its genesis; second, he defined only one background condition—national unity—and attributed far greater causal importance than his predecessors to the choices made by political leaders. Rustow also paved the way for future analyses of democratization by defining the various (though not necessarily sequential) stages of democratization.

While the value of Rustow's early work is clearly recognized today, it did not immediately give rise to a new body of scholarship; most political scientists writing in the 1970s did not focus on issues of democracy or democraticization. Instead, Latin American scholars such as Guillermo O'Donnell (1973) pointed to the structural connection between modernization and what he called "bureaucratic authoritarianism," arguing that the experiences of a number of Latin American states directly challenged earlier predictions of the parallel processes of modernization: economic development and the spread of democracy. Other prominent academics such as Juan Linz and Alfred Stepan (1978) challenged the determinacy of these structural models and instead applied elite-actor models to explain the great uncertainty surrounding democratic breakdowns. Scholars of other regions underlined the continuing and powerful role of the military in politics, and Samuel P. Huntington's slightly earlier but highly influential *Political Order in Changing Societies* (1968) stressed the central importance of political institutionalization in developing countries and deemphasized democracy and political freedoms.

The next decade brought renewed interest in questions of democracy and democratization as the process that started in Southern Europe began to spread to Latin America. Scholars of these regions blazed new trails in working to understand varying processes of democratization and to draw lessons from them. Numerous publications provided important, in-depth experiences of one or a few countries. In contrast, the five-volume series edited by Guillermo O'Donnell, Phillippe Schmitter, and Lawrence Whitehead (1986) attempted to bring together the lessons of a dozen countries spanning the two regions. In the fifth volume of the series *Tentative Conclusions About Uncertain Democracies* (1986), O'Donnell and Schmitter laid out what they saw to be the patterns evident in many of the recent transitions. In contrast to their earlier work, these authors now turned away from structural conditions and followed Rustow in articulating the central importance of elites in bringing about transitions. This new literature developed in contrast to an earlier literature on revolutions which specified rapid and fundamental changes in both the state and society. In the case of democratization, the change was expected to be significantly more gradual: negotiations between opposing parties take time; the pacts that bring about the transition are signed between power holders and opposition groups, so that neither side gains all its demands while both make significant concessions. There need be almost no bloodshed as the masses take a back seat to government and opposition leaders, and those departing from power are more likely to be given a golden parachute than be forced to the guillotine.

While predictions for the success of these transitions in Latin American and Southern Europe were generally guardedly optimistic, the 1990s brought a new decade of greater trepidation concerning the consolidation of new democracies. These newer works addressed the difficulties of consolidation, or "habituation" in Rustow's terminology, as well as new political and economic perspectives on democratization. Scholars interested in issues of consolidation underlined the fact that the mere continued existence of a newly democratized regime did not in any way imply the consolidation of democracy; the consolidation of democracy requires the building of a broad-based commitment to democracy, a delicate process which is threatened by the legacy of authoritarianism and, as Frances Hagopian (1990) points out, the political pacts made during transition processes. In volumes such as those edited by: Richard Gunther, P. Nikiforos Diamandouros, and Hans-Jürgen Puhle (1995), Juan Linz and Alfred Stepan (1996), and Mainwaring, O'Donnell and Valenzuela (1992), analysts pointed to the challenges to democratic consolidation: the continued political decisionmaking power of nonelected elites, including the military, biased electoral processes which skew the vote in favor of powerful constituencies, economic crises which threaten the stability of the democratically elected governments, the threat of military coups, partial judicial systems, and the lack of an institutionalized party system. Once again, structural conditions assumed greater causal importance in assessing the fate of regimes. The imperfect nature of these new democracies has led writers such as O'Donnell (1994) to call for more nuanced definitions and descriptions of regime types which would transcend the simple dichotomy of authoritarianism versus democracy.

The late 1980s and early 1990s also brought a large number of countries outside of Latin America and Southern Europe into the club of aspiring democracies. The lessons from regions beyond Latin American and Southern Europe came principally from states in Eastern and Central Europe as well as some states in Africa, Asia, and the Middle East; the experiences of these countries challenged many of the conclusions that had been drawn from the earlier processes of democratization. The former communist countries, led by Poland, pointed to the importance of the masses in bringing about democracy; in stark contrast to the general experiences of the earlier transitions, here, protest preceded transition. Transitions here were further complicated by the need to simultaneously transform both the political and the economic systems; authors such as Claus Offe (1991) demonstrated the contradictions inherent in such simultaneous transitions. The African experience also emphasized that elites would not always be the prime movers in the transition. Authors such as Michael Bratton and Nicholas van de Walle, in their comparative work: *Democratic Experiments in Africa* (1997), point out that almost all African transitions occurred only after sustained popular protest; the experiences of these states also challenge the notion that democratization will be the result of elite pacts. A number of Asian countries provided evidence that leaders could elect to transform a regime without a significant economic crisis; the experiences of both new democratic regimes and potential democratizers as discussed in James Morley's (1993) edited volume and Minxin Pei's article (1995) suggest, once again, that economic growth can and does contribute to the chances of and pressures for democratization; the verdict, however, on cases such as China is still out. Cross-national studies such as: Stephan Haggard and Robert Kaufman's *The Political Economy of Democratic Transitions* (1995) as well as Adam Przeworski's *Democracy and the Market* (1991), have provided analyses of the political and economic dynamics of transition across regions.

The empirical lessons of the 1990s greatly enhanced scholarly understanding of the dynamics of transition and consolidation, and contributed to interest in two additional, broad bodies of scholarship. First, actors in civil society, absent from much of the analysis of transitions in Latin American and Southern Europe, have now assumed a much greater role. The contributions of civil society actors in Eastern Europe, such as Solidarity in Poland, as well as the clear importance of civil society in the consolidation processes in Latin America have brought about a widespread resurgence of scholarship on civil society. Earlier works such as the edited volume by John Keane (1988) and the detailed work of Jean Cohen and Andrew Arato (1992) provided the basis for many important later works such as those by Marcia Weigle and Jim Butterfield (1992), Michael Foley and Bob Edwards (1996), and Stephen Ndegwa (1996). Robert Putnam's influential: *Making Democracy Work* (1993) also promoted much greater attention to this level of analysis. Questions of constitutional choice and institutional design have also gained attention. As the transitioning regimes write their new, democratic constitutions, they offer models of what an ideal society of the future might look like and present challenges to future lawmakers and politicians to uphold their principles. Edited volumes such as those by Jon Elster and Rune Slagstad (1988) as well as Douglas Greenberg et. al. (1993) illustrate this trend. Institutional debates over the merits of presidentialism and parliamentarism have also drawn attention; interestingly, while many scholars of Latin America, such as Juan Linz (1990), stress the dangers of presidentialism for democracy, the leaders of the countries within these regions have almost universally elected presidentialism. Such discrepancies between academic theory and historical choices present a challenge to future scholars and politicians. Finally, the sharp distinction drawn by Rustow and his followers between theories of democracy and theories of democratic transitions should not discourage students of democratization from studying questions regarding the nature of democracy itself. A few discussions of democratic theory are included here; these works push readers to consider what is understood by democracy in light of the experiences of democracy and democratization across the globe.

# Bibliography

## A. Democracy, Its Requisites, and Rustow's Response

Almond, Gabriel A. and Sidney Verba. *The Civic Culture: Political Attitudes and Democracy in Five Nations*. Princeton: Princeton University Press, 1963.

Barker, Ernest. *Reflections on Government*. London: Oxford University Press, 1942.

Bentley, Arthur Fisher. *The Process of Government: A Study of Social Pressures*. Chicago: Chicago University Press, 1908.

Bryce, James. *Modern Democracies*. New York: The Macmillan Company, 1921.

Crick, Bernard. *In Defense of Politics*. Chicago: University of Chicago Press, 1962.

Cutright, Philips. "National Political Development: Measurement and Analysis." *American Sociological Review* XXVIII (April 1963).

Dahl, Robert A. *A Preface to Democratic Theory*. Chicago: University of Chicago Press, 1956.

Dahl, Robert A. *Who Governs? Democracy and Power in an American City*. New Haven: Yale University Press, 1961.

Dahl, Robert A., ed. *Political Oppositions in Western Democracies*. New Haven: Yale University Press, 1966.

Dahl, Robert A. *Pluralist Democracy in the United States: Conflict and Consent*. Chicago: Rand McNally, 1967.

Dahl, Robert A. *Polyarchy: Participation and Opposition*. New Haven: Yale University Press, 1971.

Dahrendorf, Ralf. *Class and Class Conflict in Industrial Society*. Stanford: Stanford University Press, 1959.

Eckstein, Harry. *A Theory of Stable Democracy*. Princeton: Center of International Studies, Princeton University, 1961.

Eckstein, Harry. *Division and Cohesion in a Democracy: A Study of Norway*. Princeton: Princeton University Press, 1965.

Hartz, Louis et al. *The Founding of New Societies: Studies in the History of the United States, Latin America, South Africa, Canada, and Australia*. New York: Harcourt, Brace and World, 1964.

Jennings, W. Ivor. *The Approach to Self-Government*. Cambridge: Cambridge University Press, 1956.

Lijphart, Arend. *The Politics of Accommodation: Pluralism and Democracy in the Netherlands*. Berkeley: University of California Press, 1968.

Lijphart, Arend. "Typologies of Democratic Systems." *Comparative Political Studies* 1 (April 1968).

Lijphart, Arend. "Consociational Democracy." *World Politics 21* (January 1970).

Lipset, Seymour Martin. "Some Social Requisites of Democracy: Economic Development and Political Legitimacy." *American Political Science Review* LIII (March 1959).

Lipset, Seymour Martin. *Political Man: The Social Bases of Politics*. New York: Doubleday, 1960.

McClosky, Herbert. "Consensus and Ideology in American Politics." *American Political Science Review* LVIII (June 1964).

Moore, Barrington. *The Social Origins of Dictatorship and Democracy: Lord and Peasant in the Making of the Modern World*. Boston: Beacon Press, 1966.

Neubauer, Deane. "Some Conditions of Democracy." *American Political Science Review* LXI (December 1967).

Palmer, R. R. *The Age of the Democratic Revolution: A Political History of Europe and America, 1760–1880*. 2 vols. Princeton: Princeton University Press, 1959–64.

Prothro, James W. and Charles M. Grigg. "Fundamental Principles of Democracy: Bases of Agreement and Disagreement." *Journal of Politics* XXII (May 1960).

Rejai, M. *Democracy: The Contemporary Theories*. New York: Atherton Press, 1967.

Rustow, Dankwart A. *The Politics of Compromise: A Study of Parties and Cabinet Government in Sweden*. Princeton: Princeton University Press, 1955.

Rustow, Dankwart A. "Turkey: The Tradition of Modernity," in Lucian W. Pye and Verba, eds. *Political Culture and Political Development*. Princeton: Princeton University Press, 1965.

Rustow, Dankwart A. "The Development of Parties in Turkey," in Joseph LaPalombara and Myron Weiner, eds. *Political Parties and Political Development*. Princeton: Princeton University Press, 1966.

Rustow, Dankwart A. *A World of Nations: Problems of Political Modernization*. Washington: Brookings Institution, 1967.

Schattschneider, E. E. *The Semi-Sovereign People: A Realist View of Democracy in America*. New York: Holt, Rinehart and Winston, 1960.

Truman, David B. *The Governmental Process: Political Interests and Public Opinion*. New York: Knopf, 1951.

## B. 1970s—Retreat from Democracy: Bureaucratic Authoritarianism and Military Rule

Bienen, Henry. *Armies and Parties in Africa*. New York: Africana Publishing Company, 1978.

Collier, David, ed. *The New Authoritarianism in Latin America*. Princeton: Princeton University Press, 1979.

Finer, Samuel. *The Man on Horseback: The Role of the Military in Politics*, 2nd ed. Harmondsworth, Middlesex: Penguin, 1975.

Huntington, Samuel P. *Political Order in Changing Societies*. New Haven: Yale University Press, 1968.

Janowitz, Morris. *Military Institutions and Coercion in the Developing Nations*. Chicago: University of Chicago Press, 1977.

Kennedy, Gavin. *The Military in the Third World*. New York: Charles Scribner's Sons, 1974.

Linz, Juan J. *The Breakdown of Democratic Regimes: Crisis, Breakdown, Reequilibration*. Baltimore: The Johns Hopkins University Press, 1978.

Linz, Juan J. and Alfred Stepan, eds. *The Breakdown of Democratic Regimes: Latin America*. Baltimore: The Johns Hopkins University Press, 1978.

Linz, Juan J. and Alfred Stepan, eds. *The Breakdown of Democratic Regimes: Europe*. Baltimore: The Johns Hopkins University Press, 1978.

Nordlinger, Eric. *Soldiers in Politics: Military Coups and Governments*. Englewood Cliffs, N.J.: Prentice Hall, 1977.

O'Donnell, Guillermo. *Modernization and Bureaucratic-Authoritarianism*. Berkeley: Institute for International Studies, 1973.

O'Donnell, Guillermo. "Reflections on the Pattern of Change in the Bureaucratic-Authoritarian Regimes in Latin America." *Latin American Research Review* 13 (1978).

O'Donnell, Guillermo. "Tensions in the Bureaucratic-Authoritarian State and the Question of Democracy," in David Collier, ed., *The New Authoritarianism in Latin America*. Princeton: Princeton University Press, 1979.

Stepan, Alfred C. *The Military in Politics: Changing Patterns in Brazil*. Princeton: Princeton University Press, 1971.

Valenzuela, Arturo. *The Breakdown of Democratic Regimes: Chile*. Baltimore: The Johns Hopkins University Press, 1978.

## C. 1980s—Lessons from Latin America and Southern Europe

Baloyra, Enrique, ed. *Comparing New Democracies: Transition and Consolidation in Mediterranean Europe and the Southern Cone*. Boulder: Westview, 1987.

Bermeo, Nancy. *The Revolution within the Revolution*. Princeton: Princeton University Press, 1986.

Bermeo, Nancy. "Rethinking Regime Change." *Comparative Politics* 22 (April 1990).

Burton, Michael G. and John Higley. "Elite Settlements." *American Sociological Review* 52 (June 1987).

Carr, Raymond and Juan Pablo Fusi Aizpurua. *Spain: Dictatorship to Democracy.* London: George Allen & Unwin, 1979.

Clark, Robert and Michael Haltzel, eds., *Spain in the 1980s: The Democratic Transition and a New International Role.* Cambridge: Ballinger, 1987.

Diamond, Larry, Juan Linz, and Seymour M. Lipset, eds., *Democracy in Developing Countries: Latin America.* Boulder: Lynne Rienner, 1989.

Fishman, Robert. "Rethinking State and Regime: Southern Europe's Transition to Democracy." *World Politics* 42 (April 1990).

Fishman, Robert. *Working-Class Organization and the Return of Democracy in Spain.* Ithaca: Cornell University Press, 1990.

Huntington, Samuel. "Will More Countries Become Democratic?" *Political Science Quarterly* 99 (Summer 1984).

Karl, Terry Lynn. "Dilemmas of Democratization in Latin America." *Comparative Politics* 23 (October 1990).

Keck, Margaret. *The Workers' Party and Democratization in Brazil.* New Haven: Yale University Press, 1989.

Linz, Juan. "Some Comparative Thoughts on the Transition to Democracy in Portugal and Spain," in Jorge Braga de Macedo and Simon Serfaty, eds., *Portugal since the Revolution: Economic and Political Perspectives.* Boulder: Westview, 1981.

Levine, Daniel. "Paradigm Lost: Dependence to Democracy." *World Politics* 40 (April 1988).

Malloy, James and Mitchell Seligson, eds. *Authoritarians and Democrats: Regime Transition in Latin America.* Pittsburgh: University of Pittsburgh Press, 1987.

Maravall, José. *The Transition to Democracy in Spain.* London: Croom Helm, 1982.

McDonald, Ronald H. and J. Mark Ruhl. *Party Politics and Elections in Latin America.* Boulder: Westview Press, 1989.

O'Donnell, Guillermo, Philippe C. Schmitter, and Laurence Whitehead, eds., *Transitions from Authoritarian Rule: Comparative Perspectives.* Baltimore: The Johns Hopkins University Press, 1986.

O'Donnell, Guillermo, Philippe C. Schmitter, and Laurence Whitehead, eds., *Transitions from Authoritarian Rule: Southern Europe.* Baltimore: The Johns Hopkins University Press, 1986.

O'Donnell, Guillermo, Philippe C. Schmitter, and Laurence Whitehead, eds., *Transitions from Authoritarian Rule: Latin America.* Baltimore: The Johns Hopkins University Press, 1986.

O'Donnell, Guillermo, Philippe C. Schmitter, and Laurence Whitehead, eds., *Tran-*

*sitions from Authoritarian Rule: Prospects for Democracy.* Baltimore: The Johns Hopkins University Press, 1986.

O'Donnell, Guillermo, Philippe C. Schmitter, and Laurence Whitehead, eds., *Transitions from Authoritarian Rule: Tentative Conclusions About Uncertain Democracies.* Baltimore: The Johns Hopkins University Press, 1986.

Pastor, Robert. ed. *Democracy in the Americas: Stopping the Pendulum.* New York: Holmes and Meier Publishers, 1989.

Preston, Paul. *The Triumph of Democracy in Spain.* London: Methuen, 1986.

Pridham, Geoffrey. ed., *New Mediterranean Democracies: Regime Transition in Spain, Greece, and Portugal.* Totowa: Frank Cass, 1984.

Remmer, Karen. "Redemocratization and the Impact of Authoritarian Rule in Latin America." *Comparative Politics* 17 (April 1985).

Share, Donald. *The Making of Spanish Democracy.* New York: Praeger, 1986.

Share, Donald and Scott Mainwaring. "Transitions through Transaction: Democratization in Brazil and Spain," in Wayne Selcher. ed., *Political Liberalization in Brazil: Dynamics, Dilemmas and Future Prospects.* Boulder: Westview Press, 1986.

Stepan, Alfred. *Rethinking Military Politics: Brazil and the Southern Cone.* Princeton: Princeton University Press, 1988.

Valenzuela, J. Samuel. "Labor Movements in Transitions to Democracy: A Framework for Analysis." *Comparative Politics* 21 (July 1989).

## D. 1990s—The Difficulties of Consolidation: New Political and Economic Perspectives on Democratization in Latin America and Southern Europe

Agüero, Felipe. *Soldiers, Civilians, and Democracy: Post-Franco Spain in Comparative Perspective.* Baltimore: The Johns Hopkins University Press, 1995.

Alvarez, Sonia E. *Engendering Democracy in Brazil: Women's Movements in Transition Politics.* Princeton: Princeton University Press, 1990.

Bartell, Ernest and Leigh A. Payne, eds. *Business and Democracy in Latin America.* Pittsburgh: University of Pittsburgh Press, 1995.

Bermeo, Nancy. "Democracy and the Lessons of Dictatorship." *Comparative Politics* 24 (April 1992).

Bermeo, Nancy. "Sacrifice, Sequence, and Strength in Successful Dual Transitions: Lessons from Spain." *Journal of Politics* 56 (August 1994).

Collier, Ruth Berins and David Collier. *Shaping the Political Arena: Critical Junctures, the Labor Movement, and Regime Dynamics in Latin America.* Princeton: Princeton University Press, 1991.

Fox, Jonathan. "The Difficult Transition from Clientelism to Citizenship: Lessons from Mexico." *World Politics* 46 (January 1994).

Frieden, Jeffery. *Debt, Development and Democracy: Modern Political Economy and Latin America*. Princeton: Princeton University Press, 1991.

Gillespie, Charles. *Negotiating Democracy: Politicians and Generals in Uruguay*. Cambridge: Cambridge University Press, 1991.

Gonzalez, Luis. *Political Structures and Democracy in Uruguay*. Notre Dame: University of Notre Dame Press, 1991.

Gunther, Richard, P. Nikiforos Diamandouros, and Hans-Jürgen Puhle. eds. *The Politics of Democratic Consolidation: Southern Europe in Comparative Perspective*. Baltimore: The Johns Hopkins University Press, 1995.

Gunther, Richard, P. Nikiforos Diamandouros, and Hans-Jürgen Puhle. "Debate: Democratic Consolidation—'O'Donnell's Illusions:' A Rejoinder." *Journal of Democracy* 7 (October 1996).

Hagopian, Frances. "Democracy by Undemocratic Means: Elites, Political Pacts, and Regime Transition in Brazil." *Comparative Political Studies* 23 (July 1990).

Hagopian, Frances. "After Regime Change: Authoritarian Legacies, Political Representation, and the Democratic Future of South America." *World Politics* 45 (April 1993).

Higley, John and Richard Gunther. eds. *Elites and Democratic Consolidation in Latin America and Southern Europe*. Cambridge: Cambridge University Press, 1992.

Huber, Evelyne, Dietrich Rueschemeyer, and John D. Stephens. "The Impact of Economic Development on Democracy." *Journal of Economic Perspectives* 7 (Summer 1993).

Linz, Juan and Alfred Stepan. "Toward Consolidated Democracies." *Journal of Democracy* 7 (April 1996).

Linz, Juan and Alfred Stepan. *Problems of Democratic Transition and Consolidation: Southern Europe, South America and Post-Communist Europe*. Baltimore: The Johns Hopkins University Press, 1996.

Lowenthal, Abraham F. ed. *Exporting Democracy: The United States and Latin America*. Baltimore: Johns Hopkins University Press, 1991.

Mainwaring, Scott, Guillermo O'Donnell, and J. Samuel Valenzuela, eds. *Issues in Democratic Consolidation: The New South American Democracies in Comparative Perspective*. Notre Dame: University of Notre Dame Press, 1992.

Mainwaring, Scott. "Presidentialism, Multipartism, and Democracy: The Difficult Combination." *Comparative Political Studies* 26 (July 1993).

Mainwaring, Scott and Timothy Scully, eds., *Building Democratic Institutions: Party Systems in Latin America*. Stanford: Stanford University Press, 1995.

McSherry, J. Patrice. *Incomplete Transition: Military Power and Democracy in Argentina*. New York: St. Martin's Press, 1997.

Munck, Gerardo L. "Democratic Stability and Its Limits: An Analysis of Chile's 1993 Elections." *Journal of Interamerican Studies and World Affairs* 36 (Summer 1994).

Munck, Gerardo L. *Authoritarianism and Democratization: Soldiers and Workers in Argentina, 1976–1983.* University Park: Pennsylvania State University Press, 1998.

O'Donnell, Guillermo. "Delegative Democracy." *Journal of Democracy* 5 (January 1994).

O'Donnell, Guillermo. "Illusions about Consolidation." *Journal of Democracy* 7 (April 1996).

O'Donnell, Guillermo. "Debate: Democratic Consolidation—Illusions and Conceptual Flaws." *Journal of Democracy* 7 (October 1996).

Remmer, Karen L. "Democracy and Economic Crisis: The Latin American Experience." *World Politics* 42 (April 1990).

Remmer, Karen L. "New Wine or Old Bottlenecks? The Study of Latin American Democracy." *Comparative Politics* 23 (July 1991).

Rueschmeyer, Dietrich, Evelyne Huber Stephens, and John D. Stephens. *Capitalist Development and Democracy.* Chicago: University of Chicago Press, 1992.

Schedler, Andreas. "What is Democratic Consolidation?" *Journal of Demcracy* 9 (April 1998).

Schmitter, Philippe. "Consolidation and Interest Systems," in Larry Diamond and Gary Marks, eds., *Comparative Perspectives on Democracy* 35 (March-June 1992).

Schmitter, Philippe. "Dangers and Dilemmas of Democratization." *Journal of Democracy* 5 (April 1994).

Skidmore, Thomas. ed. *Television, Politics and the Transition to Democracy in Latin America.* Washington, D.C.: Woodrow Wilson Center Press, 1993.

Tulchin, Joseph S. with Bernice Romero. *The Consolidation of Democracy in Latin America.* Boulder: Lynne Rienner, 1995.

## E. 1990s—Lessons from Regions Beyond Latin America and Southern Europe

### a. Eastern Europe, Central Europe and the former Soviet Union

Balcerowicz, Leszek. "Understanding Postcommunist Transitions." *Journal of Democracy* 5 (October 1994).

Bermeo, Nancy. ed. *Liberalization and Democratization: Change in the Soviet Union and Eastern Europe.* Baltimore: Johns Hopkins University Press, 1992.

Bova, Russell "Political Dynamics of the Post-Communist Transition: A Comparative Perspective." *World Politics* 44 (October 1991).

Bruce, Valerie. "Should Transitologists be Grounded?" *Slavic Review* 54 (Spring 1995).

Bruszt, Laszlo and David Stark, "Remaking the Political Field in Hungary: From the Politics of Confrontation to the Politics of Competition." *Journal of International Affairs* 45 (Summer 1991).

Cox, Terry and Andy Furlong. eds. *Hungary: The Politics of Transition.* London: Frank Cass, 1995.

Dawisha, Karen and Bruce Parrott, eds. *The Consolidation of Democracy in East-Central Europe.* New York: Cambridge University Press, 1997.

Derlien, Hans-Ulrich and George J. Szablowski. "Eastern European Transitions: Elite, Bureaucracies, and the European Community." *Governance* 6 (July 1993).

Holmes, Stephen. "What Russia Teaches Us Now: How Weak States Threaten Freedom." *The American Prospect* (July-August 1997).

Jasiewicz, Krzysztof. "From Solidarity to Fragmentation." *Journal of Democracy* 3 (April 1992).

Karasimeonov, Georgi. "Parliamentary Elections of 1994 and the Development of the Bulgarian Party System." *Party Politics* I (October 1995).

Karl, Terry Lynn and Philippe C. Schmitter. "From an Iron Curtain to a Paper Curtain: Grounding Transitologists or Students of Post-Communism? *Slavic Review* 54 (Winter 1995).

Koing, Klaus. "Bureaucratic Integration by Elite Transfer: The Case of the Former GDR." *Governance* 6 (July 1993).

Laitin, David. "The National Uprisings in the Soviet Union." *World Politics* 44 (October 1991).

Lijphart, Arend. "Democratization and Constitutional Choices in Czechoslovakia, Hungary and Poland, 1989–91." *Journal of Theoretical Politics* 4 (1992).

Michnik, Adam. "Gray is Beautiful: Thoughts on Democracy in Central Europe." *Dissent,* New York (Spring 1997).

Nodia, Ghia. "How Different are Postcommunist Transitions?" *Journal of Democracy* 7 (October 1996).

Offe, Claus. "Capitalism by Democratic Design? Democratic Theory Facing the Triple Transition in East Central Europe." *Social Research* 58 (Winter 1991).

Offe, Claus. *Varieties of Transition: The East European and East German Experience.* Cambridge, MA: MIT Press, 1997.

Quigley, Kevin F. F. *For Democracy's Sake: Foundations and Democracy Assistance in Central Europe.* Washington, D.C.: Woodrow Wilson Center Press, 1997.

Remington, Thomas F. ed. *Parliaments in Transition: The New Legislative Politics in the Former USSR and Eastern Europe.* Boulder, CO: Westview Press, 1994.

Schmitter, Philippe and Terry Lynn Karl. "The Conceptual Travels of Transitologists and Consolidologists: How Far to the East Should they Attempt to Go?" *Slavic Review* 53 (Spring 1994).

Simon, Janos. "Post-Paternalist Political Culture in Hungary: Relationship between Citizens and Politics during and after the Melancholic Revolution (1989–1991)." *Communist and Post-Communist Studies* 26 (June 1993).

Stark, David. "The Great Transformation? Social Change in Eastern Europe—From System Identity to Organizational Diversity: Analyzing Social Change in Eastern Europe." *Contemporary Sociology* 21 (1993).

Stepan, Alfred. "Democratic Opposition and Democratization Theory." *Government and Opposition* 32 (Autumn 1997).

Sztompka, Piotr. "The Intangibles and Imponderables of the Transition to Democracy." *Studies in Comparative Communism* 24 (September 1991).

Treisman, Daniel. "Dollars and Democratization: The Role of Power and Money in Russia's Transitional Elections." *Comparative Politics* 31 (October 1998).

von Beyme, Klaus. "Regime Transition and Recruitment in Eastern Europe." *Governance* 6 (July 1993).

### b. Africa

Adler, Glenn and Eddie Webster. "Challenging Transition Theory: The Labor Movement, Radical Reform and Transition to Democracy in South Africa." *Politics and Society* 23 (March 1995).

Ake, Claude. "Rethinking African Democracy." *Journal of Democracy* 2 (1991).

Ake, Claude. *Democracy and Development in Africa*. Washington, D.C.: Brookings Institution, 1996.

Bratton, Michael and Nicolas van de Walle. "Neopatrimonial Regimes and Political Transitions in Africa." *World Politics* 46 (July 1994).

Bratton, Michael and Nicholas van de Walle. *Democratic Experiments in Africa: Regime Transitions in Comparative Perspective*. New York: Cambridge University Press, 1997.

Callaghy, Thomas M. and John Ravenhill, eds. *Hemmed In: Responses to Africa's Economic Decline*. New York: Columbia University Press, 1993.

Glickman, Harvey. ed. *Ethnic Conflict and Democratization in Africa*. Atlanta: African Studies Association Press, 1995.

Joseph, Richard. "Africa: The Rebirth of Political Freedom." *Journal of Democracy* 2 (October 1991).

Joseph, Richard. ed. *The Democratic Challenge in Africa*. Atlanta: The Carter Center, 1994.

Jung, Courtney and Ian Shapiro. "South Africa's Negotiated Transition: Democracy, Opposition, and the New Constitutional Order." *Politics and Society* 23 (September 1995).

Nwajiaku, Kathryn. "The National Conferences in Benin and Togo Revisited." *Journal of Modern African Studies* 32 (1994).

Nwokedi, Ernest. *Politics of Democratization: Changing Authoritarian Regimes in Sub-Saharan Africa*. Hamburg: Lit Verlag, 1995.

Nzomo, Maria. "The Gender Dimension of Democratization of Kenya: Some International Linkages." *Alternatives: Social Transformation and Humane Governance* 18 (Winter 1993).

Robinson, Pearl. "The National Conference Phenomenon in Francophone Africa," *Comparative Studies in Society and History* 36 (July 1994).

Sisk, Timothy D. *Democratization in South Africa: The Elusive Social Contract*. Princeton: Princeton University Press, 1995.

Young, Crawford. "Democratization in Africa: The Contradictions of a Political Imperative," in Jennifer A. Widner, ed., *Economic Change and Political Liberalization in Sub-Saharan Africa*. Baltimore: The Johns Hopkins University Press, 1994.

### c. Asia

Bertrand, Jacques. "Growth and Democracy in Southeast Asia." *Comparative Politics* 30 (April 1998).

Bourchier, David and John Legge. eds. *Democracy in Indonesia 1950s and 1990s*. Australia: Monash University, 1994.

Chou, Yangsun and Andrew J. Nathan. "Democratizing Transition in Taiwan." *Asian Survey* 27 (March 1987).

Eldridge, Philip J. *Non-government Organizations and Democratic Participation in Indonesia*. Kuala Lumpur: Oxford University Press, 1995.

Kohli, Atul. *Democracy and Discontent: India's Crisis of Governability*. New York: Cambridge University Press, 1990.

Lo, Shiu Hing. "Political Participation in Hong Kong, South Korea, and Taiwan." *Journal of Contemporary Asia* 20 (1990).

McGrath, Allen. *The Destruction of Democracy in Pakistan*. Karachi: Oxford University Press, 1996.

Morley, James, ed. *Driven by Growth: Political Change in the Asia-Pacific Region*. Armonk: M. E. Sharpe, 1993.

Ng, Margaret. "Hongkong, Singapore, and 'Asian Values:' Why Asia Needs Democracy." *Journal of Democracy* 8 (April 1997).

Pei, Minxin. " 'Creeping Democratization' in China." *Journal of Democracy* 6 (October 1995).

Uhlin, Anders. *Indonesia and the 'Third Wave of Democratization': The Indonesian Pro-Democracy Movement in a Changing World*. New York: St. Martin's Press, 1997.

Villegas, B. M. "The Philippines in 1986: Democratic Reconstruction in the Post-Marcos Era." *Asian Survey* 27 (Fall 1987).

### d. Middle East

Anderson, Lisa. "Peace and Democracy in the Middle East: The Constraints of Soft Budgets." *Journal of International Affairs* 49:1 (Summer 1995).

Bahgat, Gawdat. "Democracy in the Middle East: the American Connection." *Studies in Conflict and Terrorism* 17 (January/March 1994).

Barkey, Henri. "Can the Middle East Compete?" *Journal of Democracy* 6 (April 1995).

Entelis, John. ed. *Islam, Democracy, and the State in North Africa*. Bloomington: Indiana University Press, 1997.

Rutherford, Bruce K. "Can an Islamic Group Aid Democratization?" in Chapman, John W. and Ian Shapiro, eds. *Democratic Community*. New York: New York University Press, 1993.

Salame, Ghassan. ed. *Democracy without Democrats?* London: I.B. Taurus, 1994.

Sullivan, Antony T. "Democracy, Dragons and Delusions: the Middle East Today and Tomorrow." *The Middle East Journal* 51 (Summer 1997).

### e. Crossnational Studies and New Perspectives

Arat, Zehra. *Democracy and Human Rights in Developing Countries*. Boulder: Lynne Rienner, 1991.

Armijo, Leslie Elliott, Thomas J. Biersteker, and Abraham F. Lowenthal. "The Problems of Simultaneous Transitions." *Journal of Democracy* 5 (October 1994).

Bates, Robert. "The Economics of Transitions to Democracy." *PS: Political Science & Politics* XXIV (March 1991).

Diamond, Larry. "Promoting Democracy." *Foreign Policy* 87 (Summer 1992).

Diamond, Larry, Juan J. Linz, and Seymour Martin Lipset, eds. *Politics in Developing Countries: Comparing Experiences with Democracy*. Boulder: Lynne Rienner, 1995.

Di Palma, Giuseppe. *To Craft Democracies: An Essay on Democratic Transitions*. Berkeley: University of California Press. 1990.

Dix, Robert H. "History and Democracy Revisited." *Comparative Politics* 27 (October 1994).

Drake, Paul W. "The International Causes of Democratization, 1947–1990," in Paul W. Drake and Matthew McCubbins, eds., *The Origins of Liberty: Political and Economic Liberalization in the Modern World*. Princeton: Princeton University Press, 1998.

Dunn, John. ed. *Democracy: The Unfinished Journey, 508 BC to AD 1993*. Oxford: Oxford University Press, 1994.

Ethier, Diane. ed., *Democratic Transition and Consolidation in Southern Europe, Latin America and Southeast Asia*. Basingstoke: Macmillan, 1990.

Haggard, Stephan and Steven B. Webb. eds. *Voting for Reform: The Politics of Adjustment in New Democracies*. New York: Oxford University Press, 1994.

Haggard, Stephan and Robert Kaufman. *The Political Economy of Democratic Transitions*. Princeton: Princeton University Press, 1995.

Held, David ed., *Prospects for Democracy: North, South, East, West*. Stanford: Stanford University Press, 1993.

Horowitz, Donald. "Democracy in Divided Societies." *Journal of Democracy* 4 (October 1993).

Huntington, Samuel P. *The Third Wave: Democratization in the Late Twentieth Century*. Norman: University of Oklahoma Press, 1991.

Jaquette, Jane S. and Sharon L. Wolchik. eds. *Women and Democracy: Latin American and Central and Eastern Europe.* Baltimore: John Hopkins University Press, 1998.

Karl, Terry Lynn and Philippe Schmitter. "Modes of Transition in Latin America, Southern and Eastern Europe." *International Social Science Journal* 128 (May 1991).

Kitschelt, Herbert. "Comparative Historical Research and Rational Choice Theory: The Case of Transitions to Democracy." *Theory and Society* 22 (June 1993).

Lipset, Seymour Martin. "The Social Requisites of Democracy Revisited: 1993 Presidential Address." *American Sociological Review* 59 (February 1994).

Mansfield, Edward and Jack Snyder. "Democratization and War." *Foreign Affairs* 74 (May/June 1995).

Munck, Gerardo L. "Democratic Transitions in Comparative Perspective." *Comparative Politics* 26 (April 1994).

Nelson, Joan. ed. *Intricate Links: Democratization and Market Reforms in Latin America and Eastern Europe.* New Brunswick, N.J.: Transaction Publishers, 1994.

O'Donnell, Guillermo. "On the State, Democratization and Some Conceptual Problems: A Latin American View with Glances at Some Postcommunist Countries." *World Development* 21 (1993)

O'Donnell, Guillermo. "Delegative Democracy." *Journal of Democracy* 5 (January 1994).

Pereira, Luiz Carlos Bresser, José Maria Maravall, and Adam Przeworski. *Economic Reforms in New Democracies.* New York: Cambridge University Press, 1993.

Przeworski, Adam. *Democracy and the Market: Political and Economic Reforms in Eastern Europe and Latin America.* New York: Cambridge University Press, 1991.

Przeworski, Adam and Fernando Limongi. "Political Regimes and Economic Growth." *Journal of Economic Perspectives* 7 (Summer 1993).

Przeworski, Adam, et al. "What Makes Democracies Endure?" *Journal of Democracy* 7 (January 1996).

Pye, Lucian W. "Political Science and the Crisis of Authoritarianism." *American Political Science Review* 84 (March 1990).

Remmer, Karen. "New Theoretical Perspectives on Democratization." *Comparative Politics* 28 (October 1995).

Rustow, Dankwart. "Democracy: A Global Revolution?" *Foreign Affairs* (Fall 1990).

Shain, Yossi and Juan J. Linz et al. *Between States: Interim Governments and Democratic Transitions.* Cambridge: Cambridge University Press, 1995.

Shin, Doh Chull. "On the Third Wave of Democratization: A Synthesis and Evaluation of Recent Theory of Research." *Word Politics* 47 (October 1994).

## F. The Resurrection of Civil Society

Bratton, "Michael A. "Beyond the State: Civil Society and Associational Life in Africa." *World Politics* 51 (April 1989).

Cohen, Jean L. and Andrew Arato. *Civil Society and Political Theory*. Cambridge: MIT Press, 1992.

Diamond, Larry. "Rethinking Civil Society: Towards Democratic Consolidation." *Journal of Democracy* 5 (July 1994).

Di Palma, Giuseppe. "Legitimation from the Top to Civil Society." *World Politics* 44 (October 1991).

Fatton, Jr. R. *The State and Civil Society in Africa*. Boulder: Lynne Rienner Publishers, 1992.

Foley, Michael and Bob Edwards. "The Paradox of Civil Society." *Journal of Democracy* 7 (July 1996).

Geremek, Bronislaw. "Problems of Post-Communism: Civil Society Then and Now." *Journal of Democracy* 3 (April 1992).

Glaser, Daryl. "South Africa and the Limits of Civil Society." *Journal of Southern African Studies* 23 (1997).

Harbeson, John W., Donald Rothchild, and Naomi Chazan. *Civil Society and the State in Africa*. Boulder: Lynne Reiner Publishers, 1994.

Jones, David Martin. "Democratization, Civil Society, and Illiberal Middle Class Culture in Pacific Asia." *Comparative Politics* 30 (January 1998).

Keane, John, ed. *Civil Society and the State: New European Perspectives*. London: Verso, 1988.

Lewis, Peter M. "Political Transition and the Dilemma of Civil Society in Africa." *Journal of International Affairs* 46 (Summer 1992).

Miller, Robert. *The Development of Civil Society in Communist Systems*. Sydney: Allen and Unwin, 1992.

Ndegwa, Stephen N. *The Two Faces of Civil Society: NGOs and Politics in Africa*. Connecticut: Kumarian Press, 1996.

Norton, Augustus Richard, ed. *Civil Society in the Middle East*. (2 volumes) Leiden: E.J. Brill, 1996.

Perez-Diaz, Victor. *The Return of Civil Society: The Emergence of Democratic Spain*. Cambridge, Mass: Harvard University Press, 1993.

Putnam, Robert D. *Making Democracy Work: Civic Traditions in Modern Italy*. Princeton: Princeton University Press, 1993.

Robinson, Pearl. "Democratization: Understanding the Relationship between Regime Change and the Culture of Politics." *African Studies Review* 37 (April 1994).

Shils, Edward. "The Virtue of Civil Society." *Government and Opposition* 26 (Winter 1991).

Weigle, Marcia and Jim Butterfield. "Civil Society in Reforming Communist Regimes: The Logic of Emergence." *Comparative Politics* 25 (October 1992).

Wilmot, James and Daria Caliguire. "The New South Africa: Renewing Civil Society." *Journal of Democracy* 7 (January 1996).

Wood, Ellen Meikins. "The Uses and Abuses of 'Civil Society,' " in Ralph Milband, ed. *The Socialist Register, 1990*. New York: Monthly Review Press, 1991.


## G. Constitutional Choices and Institutional Design

Austin, Granville. *The Indian Constitution: The Cornerstone of a Nation*. Oxford: Clarendon Press, 1996.

Baaklini, Abdo I. and Helen Desfosses, eds. *Designs for Democratic Stability: Studies in Viable Constitutionalism*. Armonk, N.Y.: M.E. Sharpe, 1997.

Elster, Jon and Rune Slagstad, eds., *Constitutionalism and Democracy*. New York: Cambridge University Press, 1988.

Fischer, Mary Ellen, ed. *Establishing Democracies*. Boulder: Westview Press, 1996.

Greenberg, Douglas. et al. *Constitutionalism and Democracy: Transitions in the Contemporary World*. New York: Oxford University Press, 1993.

Hansen, Holger B. and Michael Twaddle. eds. *From Chaos to Order: The Politics of Constitution-Making in Uganda*. Kampala: Fountain Publishers, 1995.

Horowitz, Donald L. "Comparing Democratic Systems." *Journal of Democracy* 1 (Winter 1990).

Lijphart, Arend. "Constitutional Choice for New Democracies." *Journal of Democracy* 2 (1991).

Lijphart, Arend. "Democratization and Constitutional Choices in Czechoslovakia, Hungary and Poland, 1989–91. *Journal of Theoretical Politics* 4 (1992).

Lijphart, Arend and Carlos H. Waisman, eds. *Institutional Design in New Democracies*. Boulder: Westview Press, 1996.

Linz, Juan J. "The Perils of Presidentialism." *Journal of Democracy* 1 (Winter 1990).

Linz, Juan J. and Arturo Valenzuela, eds. *The Failure of Presidential Democracy, Volume 1: Comparative Perspectives*. Baltimore: The Johns Hopkins University Press, 1994.

Linz, Juan J. and Arturo Valenzuela, eds. *The Failure of Presidential Democracy, Volume 2: The Case of Latin America*. Baltimore: The Johns Hopkins University Press, 1994.

Marks, Stephen. "The New Cambodian Constitution: From Civil War to a Fragile Democracy." *Columbia Human Rights Law Review* 26 (1994).

Soltan, Karol Edward and Stephen L. Elkin, eds. *The Constitution of Good Societies*. University Park: Pennsylvania State University Press, 1996.

Stepan, Alfred C. and Skach, Cindy. "Constitutional Frameworks and Democratic

Consolidation: Parliamentarism versus Presidentialism." *World Politics* 46 (October 1993).


## H. A Few Relevant Discussions of Democratic Theory

Benhabib, Seyla. *Democracy and Difference: Contesting Boundaries of the Political*. Princeton: Princeton University Press, 1996.

Cohen, Joshua. "Deliberation and Democratic Legitimacy," in Alan Hamlin and Philip Pettit, eds., *The Good Polity Normative Analysis of the State*. Oxford: Basil Blackwell, 1989.

Collier, David and Steven Levitsky, "Democracy with Adjectives: Conceptual Innovation in Comparative Research," *World Politics* 49 (1997).

Dahl, Robert. *Democracy and Its Critics*. New Haven: Yale University Press, 1989.

Elster, Jon. ed. *Deliberative Democracy*. New York: Cambridge University Press, 1998.

Euben, Peter. "Democracy Ancient and Modern." *PS: Political Science & Politics* XXVI (September 1993).

Grey, Robert D. ed. *Democratic Theory and Post-Communist Change*. Upper Saddle River, NJ : Prentice Hall, 1997.

Gutman, Amy and Dennis Thompson. *Democracy and Disagreement*. Cambridge, MA: Belknap Press, 1996.

Held, David. *Models of Democracy*. Stanford, Calif. : Stanford University Press, 1987.

Held, David. *Political Theory and the Modern State: Essays on State, Power and Democracy*. Cambridge, UK : Polity Press, 1989.

Lakoff, Sanford A. *Democracy: History, Theory, Practice*. Boulder, Colo. : Westview Press, 1996.

Manin, Bernard. *The Principles of Representative Government*. New York: Cambridge University Press, 1997.

Monga, Celestin. *Measuring Democracy: A Comparative Theory of Political Well-being*. Boston, MA : African Studies Center, Boston University, 1996.

Sartori, Giovanni. *The Theory of Democracy Revisited, Part One*. New Jersey: Chatham House, 1987.

Schmitter, Philippe and Terry Lynn Karl. "What Democracy Is . . . and Is Not." *Journal of Democracy* 2 (Summer 1991).

Sklar, Richard L. "Towards a Theory of Developmental Democracy," in Adrian Leftwich, ed., *Democracy and Development: Theory and Practice*. Cambridge, Mass.: 1996.

Weiner, Myron. "Empirical Democratic Theory and the Transition from Authoritarianism to Democracy." *PS: Political Science & Politics* 20 (Fall 1987).

# Index

---

Index Compiled by Kim L. Callihan

www . locaflat . com
www . parisnet . net